ENTER PLATO

ALVIN W. GOULDNER

Enter
Plato

Classical Greece and the Origins of Social Theory

BASIC BOOKS, INC., PUBLISHERS   NEW YORK   LONDON

For Robert K. Merton

PREFACE

Writing, says Kafka, is a form of prayer. Until this book, I was never sure that he intended to include the writing of social scientists, and, in any event, I never quite knew what he meant.

I think I now know: a man begins to work with something vague and formless within himself. He reaches for it at first with his practiced professional skills and familiar techniques and well-worn work habits and by relying on that settled knowledge of himself that has so far served him well enough. But this thing is so formless and big that he comes in time to see that his standard routines can never weave the net that will trap it and that, if it is to be landed at all, he must go down after it with his whole being. So the issue is at last joined and the contest finally pursued to the point at which he has to take reluctant leave of the secure, manageable routines and swim down into the inky waters of the self; he comes at length to that unsettling knowledge that the quality of his work—if it is to be more than a routine performance—depends, not only on what he knows and certainly not on any mere tricks of his craft, but on what he *is*.

It is bad enough when a man has to put his skills up for inspection, but writing becomes a form of prayer when what he places on the line is himself. Yet not all prayers can be granted, and perhaps some are never heard. There is no avoiding this hazard, and, at any rate, this is the only way that I have learned: I have never believed that anything is worth working on unless I seriously risk compromising myself in doing it.

My friends certainly did what they could. I am particularly grateful to my colleagues at Washington University and elsewhere for criticism that penetrated deeply, but never stung because it was offered in friendship. I can only thank them and mention their names: Howard S. Becker, Helen P. Gouldner, Jules Henry, Irving L. Horowitz, Lee Rainwater, William Sale. I am indebted also to Miriam Gallaher and Marilyn Harrington for very helpful editorial service, to Adeline Sneider for devoted secretarial assistance, and to Elly Dubinsky for checking my use of Greek terms. I am also grateful for the opportunity to have been a Fellow at the Center for Advanced Study in the Behavioral Sciences at Palo Alto, where the first draft of this manuscript was completed, and for the stimulation and encouragement of the Fellowship. My debt and gratitude to Helen P. Gouldner are of a very special order.

ALVIN W. GOULDNER

Cortivallo, Switzerland
November 1965

CONTENTS

Preface   *vii*

Part One   THE HELLENIC WORLD

1. Civil War in the *Polis*   *3*

2. The Greek Contest System: Patterns of Culture   *41*

3. Self and Society in Greece   *78*

4. The War between the Cities   *133*

Part Two   ENTER PLATO

5. An Alternative to Politics   *165*

6. Social Diagnosis: Plato's Analysis of Social Disunity   *197*

7. Social Diagnosis: Lacunae and Assumptions in Plato's Diagnosis   *234*

8. Therapeutics: Planned Social Change in Plato's Theory   *259*

9. Therapeutics: Law and Universalism   *297*

10. The Fatigue of Reason and the Metaphysics of Authoritarianism   *326*

11. Death and the Tragic Outlook   *361*

Glossary of Greek Terms   *389*

Major Dates in Greek History   *393*

Index   *397*

I come to give you something, and the gift
Is my own beaten self: no feast for the eyes;
Yet in me is a more lasting grace than beauty.

—Sophocles, *Oedipus at Colonus*

ENTER PLATO

PART ONE

The Hellenic World

1

Civil War in the Polis

There is an oracle of Necessity, a decree of the
Gods from of old, everlasting, with broad oaths
fast sealed, that, whensoever one of the daemons,
whose portion is length of days, has sinfully stained
his hands with blood, or followed Strife and sworn
a false oath, he must wander thrice ten thousand
seasons away from the Blessed, being born throughout the time in all manner of mortal forms, passing
from one to another of the painful paths of life.

For the power of the Air drives him seaward;
and the Sea spews him out on the dry land; Earth
hurls him into the rays of the blazing Sun, and Sun
into the eddies of Air. One from another receives
him, and he is loathed of all.

Of these now am I also one, an exile from God
and a wanderer, having put my trust in raging
Strife. —Empedocles [1]

SOCRATES, it has been said, was the crafty serpent who tempted Western
man with the apple of wisdom, luring him into the arid exile of modern
rational civilization. It might also be said, however, that Socrates was the
Owl of Athena whose flight signaled the impending midnight of Hellenic
society.[2] There is no question, in any event, that Socrates marks the end of
an old and the beginning of a new wisdom. He is the watershed, the boundary and dividing line, the long-gathered energy of a great instant or, as he
preferred, the midwife:

Dire are the pangs which my art is able to arouse and to allay in those
who consort with me, just like the pangs of women in childbirth; night
and day they are full of perplexity and travail which is even worse than
that of women. . . . Come then to me, who am a midwife's son and
myself a midwife, and do your best to answer the questions which I
will ask you.[3]

3

It was this Socrates who delivered the new and characteristically Western forms of thought from their convulsive parturition in the Greek *polis* and who, with an irony alternately malicious and gentle, gave them the breath of a new vision. Serpent or owl, after Socrates the standards, interests, and ambitions of Western thought are unmistakably transfigured.

Socrates' mission in Athens crystallized a new turn in the intellectual development of the West. It did so because Socrates had worthy enemies and was fortunate in his students; because he had seen the best and known the worst, the Periclean culmination and the Peloponnesian exhaustion; because he had lived in close tension with the things he spoke about; and because he had a sense of his tradition and a belief in his rebel premonition. Like every midwife, he knew that the story did not begin with him and that the future did not belong to him; yet he had reason to hope that it would remember him.

In this and the next three chapters, I attempt to describe as concisely as I can some of the salient features of Athenian social structure and culture and, where it seems helpful, of Hellenic society. The aim is not to reveal new facts [4] about this much-studied civilization; it is rather to apply such perspectives as are common to sociologists to help understand how this civilization gave rise to and shaped Plato's *social* theory. In one part, then, this is a study in the sociology of knowledge—of the Platonic origins of Western social theory, of some of the earliest secular diagnoses of and proposed remedies for the human condition, and of the growth of critical reflection on human relationships as it emerged in ancient Greece.

I shall assume throughout that no service is done to the understanding of ancient civilizations by divorcing classical studies from modern social science. The Greek achievement is not blurred but is etched the more clearly by comparing it to historically inconsequential societies. Still less is it believed that justice is done to contemporary social science itself by ignoring the massive body of data concerning ancient civilizations; by separating sociological from historical studies; or by pretending that these Greeks were just another people, essentially no different from, say, the Comanche or Ifaluk. Only a juvenile romanticism parading as scientific objectivity could imagine that, since all societies are unique and worthy of study, ancient Greece has no special meaning and significance for Western man. If at times I mention events and processes in Greek antiquity well known to many broadly educated persons, let alone to classicists, I do so in the expectation that I am not the only student of the social sciences who was taught more about the Trobrianders, Nuer, and Hopi than about the Athenians.

PEOPLE AND ECOLOGY

Some time around 2000 B.C., an Indo-European–speaking people present themselves in the Hellenic Peninsula.[5] In Homer they are called Achaeans; some are also called Ionians, and in time they came to call themselves Hellenes; with a victor's prerogative, the Romans were later to call them *Graeci*, or Greeks. In successive waves of migration these groups of semi-nomadic shepherds wrested the peninsula from its native inhabitants and penetrated an area where Minoan culture, from which they borrowed certain elements, had preceded them by at least a thousand years. In the course of another thousand years, they will create "Greek" culture in the familiar sense and will transform themselves into a new people.

The invaders first came as a tribal people; Aristotelian tradition has it that there were four tribes (or *phylai*), each chanting its own war cry and each with its own god.[6] The nuclear unit of the tribe was the *genos*, composed according to this tradition of thirty members (*gennētai*), whereas thirty of the *genē* (plural of *genos*) comprised one of the three phratries into which each tribe was organized. The phratry consisted of these *genē* and of other groupings, the *thiasoi*, which were religious units like the *genē* but were not based on an imputed common kinship. The *genos* was a patriarchal group whose members shared a common fictional ancestor or god and whose chief came into his powers by patrilineal succession. Belonging as a group to the same phratry, the *gennētai* shared a religious cult administered by the chief, who interpreted and expounded the *themistes*, the sacred family code, knowledge of which he received from his father.

Out of these traditional units the Hellenic tribes began a development into urban individualism, moving with remarkable agility from a sacred or folk society toward the secularized and sophisticated city-state, or *polis*. But even at the height of their urban achievement in the classical period, the Greeks never completely surrendered tribal forms, which continued to find expression in their civic and military life. They are in a way the first "modern" people, and they may yet embody a lesson for those concerned with understanding the emergence of the new nations today among contemporary "underdeveloped" peoples. In any event, the full measure of the Greek achievement can be taken only if it is remembered that it was made by a people who had not yet fully clambered out of the trenches of tribalism.

In the peninsula, the Hellenes found themselves in a land of many small, secluded valleys. Since the Greeks were never great road builders, the mountainous rims of these valleys established natural boundaries for distinct communities. At the same time, the land, which fingered irregularly into the sea, was endowed with many harbors. These facilitated communication and trade with distant and diverse people and provided staging areas for efforts at colonization.

As distinct from the forced migration of the Mycenaean families to the east—occasioned by the invasions of the Dorian Greeks around 1000–900 B.C.—true Greek colonization began about 750 B.C.[7] By about the fifth century B.C. the Greeks had fanned out east and west across the Mediterranean, dropping colonies in what we now call Turkey, in southern Italy and Sicily, on the coast of North Africa, and along parts of the coastline of southern France.[8] Each of the Greek cities differed from the others in many respects—indeed, until about 300 B.C. they commonly spoke different dialects—and each aspired to and was fiercely jealous of its independence. Although they came increasingly to use a common literary language and to share a common Hellenic culture, marking them off from surrounding peoples whom they collectively termed "barbarians" (i.e., non-Hellenic), these cities were never to be unified into anything like a single state of their own.

By modern urban standards, the cities were small. At its greatest, Athens was about 1,000 square miles, Argos about 550, Corinth some 330, and Sparta, which held the southern two fifths of the Peloponnese, was a comparative giant of some 3,300 square miles.[9] In her Periclean prime (circa 460 B.C.), Athens' population surpassed all others, ranging, according to various estimates, from 25,000 to 40,000 citizens, apart from her slaves and *metoikoi*. In this regard, Sparta, with an estimated 8,000 male citizens in 481 B.C.[10] (or, with their families, perhaps about 12,000–15,000 [11]), was far nearer the average, Greek cities of more than 10,000 citizens being infrequent.[12]

The valleys of the Hellenic peninsula were conducive to intensive communication [13] and interaction within each of the small enclaved populations which shared a common ethnic heritage and common ecological problems. The valleys were, in effect, natural incubators of communities. They fostered the differentiation of customs and institutions within, while sea boundaries allowed a stimulating contact with alien cultures and conveyed the profits of piracy and trade. In this and other ways, their new terrain and natural ecology presented the settlers with distinctive problems and opportunities of abiding influence on their cultural development.

By reason of their similar climate and terrain, the communities on the peninsula produced the same things, and thus each could offer the other little that they did not already have. This stimulated the push toward the sea, a push also intensified by population pressure and by the poor quality of the soil, which was dry and rocky and scarcely ever produced enough subsistence as urban concentrations gathered. The Greeks were fortunate, for the Aegean was a hospitable school for seafarers. It was dotted with almost five hundred islands, and small boats could make long voyages by easy stages, remaining near sheltering coasts that provided ready refuge in the event of sudden turns in the weather. Ultimately, many of the Greek communities and particularly Athens, of which we know most, will find their futures on the seas in trade and in naval empire.

Two other features of the peninsula's ecology are worth mentioning, even in this scant account. One involves the military consequences of the terrain as they affected the Athenian system of class stratification. Though this will be considered more fully later, it may be noted here that the Athenian aristocracy had difficulty in maintaining its social position as naval forces, rather than land forces, came to be the fulcrum of military power—especially insofar as social position was then regarded as dependent on military contribution. The opportunity for naval ventures to supplant land operations was clearly based in large part on the accessibility of the sea.

Not only did this naval growth weaken the position of the landed gentry in Greece, but so, too, did the topology of the land, for the small valleys often did not provide ground areas large enough for the complex maneuver of large bodies of cavalry. Like other land forces, the cavalry was financed primarily by individuals, rather than by the state, and it could, therefore, have become the military center of power for the rich. As Aristotle remarks: "Where the nature of the country can admit a great number of horse, there a powerful oligarchy may be easily established . . . those who can support the expense of horsemen must be persons of some considerable fortune." [14] As it was, however, the terrain favored the foot soldier, whose less costly equipment could be purchased more readily by the average citizen. It was therefore difficult for the landed aristocracy to monopolize military power and honor which were, correspondingly, distributed more widely among the citizenry, legitimating as well as empowering their political claims.

The use of cavalry was inhibited not only by the nature of the terrain but also by the climate, which, being relatively dry, often did not provide water in the amounts needed to maintain many horses. The role of a military elite based on cavalry was also limited since horseshoes had not yet been invented, increasing the hazard that horses would be lamed in the rocky country.[15] Finally, the Greek saddle was not a solid one and had no stirrups to provide a firm platform from which a solid blow could be struck.

Partly as a result of this combination of ecology and technology, the city's basic land forces came in time to be *hoplitai* (named after their shields), heavily armored foot soldiers, traditionally fighting at close quarters in a solid phalanx eight ranks deep. This highly disciplined form of fighting "was not the place for single-handed exploits, for the epic *aristeia* of champions," [16] and did not lend itself well to the heroic aspirations of a landed elite reared in Homeric traditions.

The second notable ecological characteristic bears on the local water supply and its sources. Greece is a land of winter rains and summer droughts, Attica averaging only about sixteen inches of rain annually. It is also a land lacking rivers that could have been used for large-scale irrigation. Where used in Greece, irrigation seems to have been employed only on a local, small-scale basis for watering orchards and gardens. This, it has been suggested, meant that the kind of centralized bureaucratic social organization required for administering such large-scale irrigation projects as those on the Nile or Euphrates was unsuitable and unnecessary in Greece.[17] Such early bureaucracies of the irrigation economies were often administered by a priesthood, in part because it was relatively well educated and could maintain the necessary records. In the absence of an irrigation economy, the position of religious functionaries in the Greek state could be restricted. The role of a specialized priesthood in Greek society was probably also circumscribed by the increasing power of the military chieftains, which was enhanced by wars against the native inhabitants of the peninsula or among the Greek tribes themselves.

Possibly the lack of a centralized, priest-administered bureaucracy also facilitated the use of slaves in productive activities, making them more readily available for work in mines, industries, households, and on the land, rather than in constructing sacred buildings. Certainly a centralized bureaucratic state apparatus administered by a priestly caste would have been radically at variance with those characteristics of Greek society and culture that were subsequently idealized: the close involvement of the citizen in the affairs of the state and the rational or skeptical bent of, at least, its intellectuals.

After the disorganization induced by the Doric invasions, Greece experienced a remarkable efflorescence of civilization: somewhere between 1000 and 750 B.C., the Greeks borrowed and adapted the Phoenician alphabet to their own language; [18] the Homeric literature was composed somewhere between the tenth and eighth century B.C.; [19] writing and its use in literature spread, and there was the beginning of lyric poetry and of historical literature. It was an age in which the use of money developed and the mortgage, both on property and men, was invented. Profoundly important developments occurred in technology and subsistence-getting techniques; iron increasingly supplanted bronze in making weapons and tools; [20] farming methods gradually improved, and there was a general increase in the importance of agriculture relative to the earlier predominance of pastoralism.

By the time of the *Odyssey* there were established markets, frequent trading trips, and a subsequent growth in the number of merchants engaged in trade with Asia Minor and Egypt. The Greeks sold their excess oil, wine, and pottery; they purchased timber, which they needed for their ships, silphium, and barley and wheat, of which they were almost always short; and they also bought slaves.

From about the ninth to the sixth century, several major related social developments may be discerned: the increasingly rapid breakdown of the older tribal social order, the emergence of urban communities centered in the city-state, or *polis*, and increasing social stratification with the growth of class conflict.

DEVELOPMENT OF THE CLASS STRUCTURE

To unravel the tensions permeating the *polis*, the knowledge of which forms an indispensable background for understanding the emergence of Socrates and Plato, we could do far worse than to begin with an examination of the class structure of ancient society. In "Homeric" society, the salient social distinction was between the great lords, or *aristoi*, and those beneath them in power and wealth, the small, independent farmers.[21] The master–slave division was not yet foremost in the minds of men, even though it was a vital part of the society of which Homer writes. Differences between the *aristoi* and the other freemen, who formed the majority of the community—small freeholders, herders, and craftsmen—were in part related to the size of property holdings. Differences among the *aristoi* themselves were also related to the size of their holdings, as well as to the number of retainers they could support as a permanent part of their household, or *oīkos*.

Correspondingly, differences among the free classes depended in part on whether they were retainers, or *therapontes*. Attached to and under the protection of *aristoi* heading a powerful *oīkos*, the *therapontes* were commonly recruited from noble households and might serve their lord as charioteers, cupbearers, carvers, masters of horse, or as friendly confidants, as Patroclus did for Achilles. Membership in an *oīkos* was important in determining social position in Homeric society. In many ways, even the slave who was part of an *oīkos* might be more advantaged than property-less workers (or *thētes*) who hired themselves out and who were unattached. It is in some part because membership in or exclusion from an *oīkos* was of such importance that it mitigated the significance of slavery as such, diminishing the distinction between the propertyless free and the slaves, so that the word *drēstēr*, meaning one who works or serves, was applied to both.

Most slaves of this period appear to have been women,[22] and this, along with their membership in an *ōīkos,* was probably conducive to closer personal relationships between them and the heads of the household than between the latter and unattached propertyless workers. Homeric literature suggests further that during this period slavery was still conducted on a relatively small-scale, paternalistic basis, the slaves being integrated into the household structure and the families' work activities.[23] They might work alongside their masters in the fields and wash linen together with the mistress of the household; they were sometimes buried in family grounds and might even eat at the table of their masters. Although references to slavery increase during the period from the *Iliad* to the *Odyssey,* the latter still employs the term *drēstēr* to refer to both slaves and propertyless free workers. Later, as slaves come to be used in growing mercantile and manufacturing activities or were let out for hire as day workers and come increasingly from "barbarian" countries, they were less likely to be domiciled in the master's home; the paternalistic and personalized relations between themselves and their masters then waned.

During the Homeric period, the *ōīkos* was the nuclear establishment of the society; it consisted of members of the lord's family, including his sons (who remained until their father's death), his slaves, free hirelings, retainers, and his landed property and personal goods. It is likely that, at least during certain periods, the ties of common membership in an *ōīkos* transcended even communal commitments.[24] Productive work in the *ōīkos* or on the land on which it was based was aimed at establishing the self-sufficiency of the household, at least as far as this could be achieved. Goods and food produced for household consumption were centrally stored in the *ōīkos* and distributed by its head to household members in accordance with their status.

The wealth of the Homeric *ōīkos* derived largely from two sources: from the routine conduct of household crafts or working the land and from booty acquired during warfare. At this time land was used primarily for pasturage, rather than tillage. As indicated previously, Greek soil was relatively dry and rocky, and only some 20 to 25 per cent of the peninsula could be cultivated. Tillage was done with ox-drawn plows or, more often, with hoe and mattock, and the small-scale holdings were intensively worked. Without war, new lands could not be readily obtained except by moving to unsettled frontiers; little or no productive land remained available in settled communities.

The land problem was further intensified by the kinship system. This required that a father's land be divided equally among his sons, with the result that there was, particularly among smaller holders, a constant tendency for the average size of individual holdings to decline.[25] By the end of the fourth century B.C., the average farm in Attica will become only about ten acres.[26] There was, in consequence, continuing pressure on the land supply and continual land hunger.

The tendency of farmholdings to decline in size also meant that slaves could neither be afforded so easily nor used so economically in agriculture, though they were doubtless of more significance on larger holdings. In some part because of these relatively small average landholdings, Hellenic civilization was still primarily agricultural in its economic activities even in the classical periods. Indeed, as late as the end of the fifth century B.C., after the great growth of mercantile and manufacturing enterprises, about three quarters of the Athenian citizenry were still peasants living on the land.[27]

The Homeric *aristoi* derived their wealth and maintained their households not only from pasturage and agriculture but also from piracy and plunder; relatively little of it as yet came from commerce or trade or from investment in these. The *aristoi* were particularly dependent on war to satisfy or replenish their metal requirements, since the main supply of these was in Western Asia and Central Europe. Metals were, of course, needed for weapons and tools, and they were also significant parts of the *ōikos* stored-away "treasure," or *keimēlion,* that was important symbolically and useful as gifts.

Gift-exchange was then probably the most important mechanism of exchange, though there was some outright trade. Gifts were given on all manner of occasions and for many arrangements that we would call fees, rewards, prizes, and even taxes; in Homer there is much frank talk about gift-giving and its appropriateness, lavishness, or adequacy.

Gift-exchange—conducted in ceremonial ways—was an important mechanism for establishing peaceful social relationships among those living in different places and households. Along with intermarriage, it bound together men of different communities. So, too, did the institution of "guest-friendship," householders being under a strict obligation of hospitality which was viewed as supernaturally sanctioned. On departing, the guest-friend would be given gifts in proportion to his status and to the wealth of his host, and, in due time, the recipient was expected to reciprocate: ". . . and there are gifts to match the gifts you brought." [28] Guest-friendship and gift-giving served to provide the head of the household with friendly refuge and with allies in foreign lands and were, in effect, a substitute for kin ties. "For what is there more kindly than the feeling between host and guest?" [29]

Ceremonialized gift-exchange was also a way of making authority relations compatible with the great emphasis placed on personal independence, a notion nuclear to the Greek value system in Homeric as well as in later classical times. Transactions taking place within the framework of a gift-exchange imply, even if they are in effect in the nature of taxes given to an overlord, that they are offered freely and not under coercion or constraint. They are thus expressive of and consonant with the self-image of a "free-man"—so important to the Greek in a slave-owning society.

CLASS STRUCTURE AND THE ACHIEVEMENT SYSTEM

Not only was some part of the wealth of the Homeric ōikos derived from warfare but so too was much of its head's prestige or honor, for the honor of the aristos rested on his military exploits and success. The military morality of this group of warrior-shepherds is vividly portrayed in Hector's prayer: "O Zeus and all ye gods," he asks, "Vouchsafe ye that this my son may likewise prove even as I, pre-eminent amid the Trojans, and as valiant in might and be a great king in Ilios. Then may men say of him, 'Far greater is he than his father,' as he returneth home from battle; and he may bring with him bloodstained spoils from the foeman he hath slain, and may his mother's heart be glad." [30] This speech comes from a god-doomed man whose city is under siege, whose patrimony is imperiled, and whose family faces imminent enslavement by enemies animated by precisely the same warrior values.

The central and most powerful terms of commendation [31] in Greek, both in Homeric and later times, are aretē and agathos (respectively, noun and adjective), as A. W. Adkins brilliantly demonstrates.[32] These are terms that above all commend military prowess and skills useful in war, along with the success they win.[33] In this connection, it bears remembering that the Homeric poems are the Greek's "bible," that they are at the center of Greek education, and that the Greek youths memorize and are drilled in them. It bears remembering that "war is the basic reality of the Iliad." [34] To be agathos is above all to be brave, skillful, and successful in war and, in consequence, to possess the wealth and leisure to enjoy peace and to be prominent during it. It is to be in all circumstances free and independent of the constraint of another, for to be so constrained is viewed as intrinsically insulting to one's manhood and, indeed, to one's very humanity.[35]

There is a drift away from the strictly military implications of these terms, yet they were not to be entirely lost even in late classical times. There is always a lingering echo that to be agathos is to be superior in matters of war or in the defense of the state. Agathos and aretē continued to commend courage in Herodotus, Sophocles, Thucydides, Euripides, and later writers. We may still find Isocrates (436–338 B.C.) remarking that the "men who are responsible for our greatest blessing and deserve our highest praise are, I conceive, those who risked their bodies in defence of Hellas. . . ." [36]

Even when these terms are used in the sense of a generalized superiority or excellence, they entail either overt or implicit association with a military contribution, so that contributing to the costs of warfare by provisioning a ship or purchasing armor would allow a man to claim preferment.

The later, more philosophical or literary usages, in which these terms undergo a kind of sublimation, contain implications of a superiority or virtue that is won, if not in direct military combat, in some kind of interpersonal contest against the resistance of others, as manifested perhaps in a political struggle or in athletic competitions at the Olympics. It is in part because the Greeks were so achievement-oriented and because they conceived of achievement as a competitive struggle that there is considerable justification in Nietzsche's conception of Greek civilization as a "contest" society [37] in which the objective was not simply to improve on one's own past performance but to put the other man down. The "glory that was Greece" was, in some important measure, born of this violent competitiveness.

To be *agathos* gave a man claim to preferential treatment: to honor in the state, to acquittal if he should be a defendant in a court of law, and to deference in normal social relationships. It carried with it, however, the reciprocal obligation to be first in war. This was one of the main ways by which the authority of the Homeric *aristoi* was legitimated and was viewed as entitling a man to the privileges of his rank. Thus Sarpedon says to Glaucus that, since they are so honored in Lycia and advantaged with full cups, meat, and abundant orchards, "Therefore now it behoveth us to take our stand in the first rank of the Lykians and encounter fiery battle, that certain of the well-corseleted Lykians may say, 'Verily our kings that rule in Lykia be no inglorious men, they that eat fat sheep and drink the choice wine honey-sweet; nay, but they are also of excellent might, for they war in the foremost ranks of the Lykians.' " [38]

This, as well as their gift-exchange institutions, plainly indicates that the Greeks believed, and quite explicitly, that benefits received must be reciprocated in some manner. They no less insistently believed in retribution, that injuries must be repaid; [39] the common morality of the time enjoined men not only to help their friends but also to harm their enemies. As Solon's elegy declaims: "Make me sweet to my friends and sour to my foes. To these a man reverend to behold, to those a man terrible." [40]

ACHIEVEMENT VALUES AND GROUP TENSIONS

The value of competitive achievement, stressed by the Homeric *aristoi* and expressed in their belief that bravery and skill in battle justify eminence, often contributed to social discord among the *agathoi*. This was especially likely when the distribution of military skills was at variance with the established distribution of rank, wealth, and power. In a group holding this value, tensions arise when leadership derives from birth and when those who are rich or powerful are not judged commensurately eminent in war. The established system of socially standardized rankings that has derived from previous competition induces those who hold leading positions to lay claim to honor that may be in excess of their actual performance in current competitive situations or in battle. Conversely, some may complain that those with high rank and concomitant wealth are being given greater honor than their current competitive achievements warrant. Thus in the race in the *Iliad,* even though Eumelus comes in last, Achilles wishes to give him the second prize, justifying his reversal of the outcome by pointing out that "the man who is *aristos* has finished last"; needless to say, Antilochus, who had in fact come in second, resents this and a quarrel flares.

Perhaps the best-known example of this tension is illustrated in the *Iliad* by the relationship between Achilles and Agamemnon. There is no indication that Agamemnon's leadership of the Greek host was based on his personal prowess in battle; it rested largely on the fact that he had provided the most ships and fighting men to the combined invading force.[41] Achilles' position, however, rested on the common recognition of his prowess in battle. The conflict between Agamemnon and Achilles arises when the former asserts his rank as head of the host and requires Achilles to relinquish the prize (or *geras*) he had won with his own spear.

It may be suggested that this conflict between Agamemnon and Achilles, so central to the *Iliad,* dramatically exemplifies the tensions that occur between those of established social rank and those who seek honor through competitive military achievement in conformance with the warrior code. It suggests that the older military values were not conducive to the stability of even Homeric society once standardized social rankings emerged; for, at some point, incumbents were open to challenge by ambitious lower-ranked men who believed that those who are first in battle should also be first in rank and in honor-symbolizing rewards. "My hands bear the brunt of furious war," complains Achilles to Agamemnon. "But when the apportioning cometh then is thy meed far ampler." [42] (This tension between war lord and king, between the man pre-eminent in battle and the one foremost in rank, is not peculiar to the Homeric literature, appearing also, for example, in the tensions between Lancelot and King Arthur.)

Stressing individual autonomy and competitive achievement, the Homeric code generated constant tension among the heads of households; ties among the *aristoi* were fragile, and their conflicts were not easily subject to effective social control. Blood feuds were common, and many kings died violently. The "justice" to which the *aristoi* submitted, the various ways by which their conflicts were resolved—such as battle, arbitration, and oath—were essentially solutions applicable only among equals; the *aristoi* did not easily acknowledge the authority of larger communal arrangements, especially if a point of honor was involved. The murder of a clansman commonly required the surviving members of the *genos* to seek vengeance. Euripides' sociological insight into the way in which this code generated a vicious cycle of blood feuds is brilliantly expressed in his *Orestes:* [43] "Where, I want to know, can this chain of murder end? Can it ever end, in fact, since the last to kill is doomed to stand under permanent sentence of death by revenge?"

The stress of the *aristoi* on their personal independence and the autonomy of their *ōikos* suggests that effective communal structures were relatively weak in Homeric times; doubtless, this stress also served to inhibit the emergence of such public structures. When complex forms of community organization developed with the later emergence of the *polis,* the requirements for the maintenance of the new urban social order and the old Homeric military values were dissonant, and the two can hardly be said to have ever attained a stable, mutual accommodation. The aggressive competition for status or honor and the stress on personal autonomy were never adequately controlled by the *polis*. They continually heightened the bitterness of political struggle and encouraged violent remedies to offset political defeat. In extremity, the politically disappointed party or group might take refuge with the enemy and—despite the classical stress on the citizen's love for and indebtedness to his city—take up arms against his own city. The embittered political exile was not uncommon during certain periods in the history of the *polis*.

All this is not to suggest that the older military virtues were impervious to change under pressure of the new requirements of urban living. The "quiet" virtues, as Adkins terms them, stressing cooperativeness or making cooperation feasible—such as temperance, civic service, justice, and wisdom —in time become more salient. The *polis* needed peace and stability within, if for no other reason than to pursue its perennial wars abroad. Yet the newer virtues never entirely displaced the older implications of *agathos* and *aretē* that, as generalized terms of commendation, were encysted with the older military traits. These traits formed a concrete paradigm of propriety underlying the more abstract usage, and they exerted silent inducements to charge military or competitive achievement with a special emotive force.

The viability of the older military virtues in the late classical period were not, however, an anachronism; they must not be regarded as a vestigial "survival" which continues simply through inertia. The military paradigm of virtue persists because it is actively reinforced by the continuing military character and ongoing warlike activities of the city-states.[44] There was, it seems, a fatal contradiction—one among all too many—in the situation. If constant warfare among the city-states required them to emphasize their internal stability and if this, in turn, contributed to the growing importance of the quiet, cooperative values, nonetheless the very continuance of the wars themselves, indeed their lengthening duration and growing ferocity, also called for fighting men with the old military virtues. Since the citizenry were both the major fighting force and, particularly during the periods of democracy, the ultimate decision-makers of the state, they were *situationally* constrained to maintain *both* sets of values and could thus never give full rein to either. It would have been fatal to the state, as then constituted in war-ridden Greece, had the citizenry lost all zest for the military virtues.

The participation of the *dēmos* in the state, with its claim to full participation in decision-making, could be and was in part legitimated in terms of its military contribution. The *dēmos* did not reject but rather emulated the military values of the *aristoi* and insisted that these be universally employed. It said, in effect: the *hoplitēs* fights; therefore he should vote. Aristocratic values were therefore conducive to the development of democracy and the extension of the franchise. Since all who fought could claim to embody the very highest of values, all who fought had a lien on political rights and, when these were extended during the growth of democracy, they did not undermine but rather broadened the support of the military virtues. Conversely, since this tendency could be anticipated, oligarchs seeking to restrict the extension of political rights would be constrained to a restricted military use of available manpower to prevent disfranchised groups from legitimating their claim to new political rights.

The drift of the older military virtues toward more cooperative values was not constant among all groups in the *polis* nor, for that matter, did it occur at random. It seems probable that the older military virtues and the self-images consistent with them would more likely persist, or at least would diminish more slowly, among the landed gentry than among the rising mercantile groups to whom wealth more readily became a salient symbol of success. Even during the Peloponnesian War, when the Athenian landed aristocracy's property had been pillaged and burned by the invaders, disposing them to become something of a "peace party," their spokesmen— among whom we may count Aristophanes—nonetheless continued incongruously to praise the military virtues.[45]

The Homeric *agathoi* had been relatively rich; but they had attained their wealth in a manner befitting a warrior group. They had never been merely rich but were in addition possessed of honor, and justifiably so by their values. By the time of the Theognid literature (circa 550–500 B.C.), however, with the growing use of coined money and the rise of a merchant class in the cities, there is a rising complaint that "wealth has thrown lineage into confusion." Many who under the older warrior code had been denigrated as *kakoi,* or lowly, were then rich. There was a growing *status incongruence,*[46] for one could now have wealth without honor (in the older sense). There is a mounting strain in the system of stratification as well as increasing discord in the value system. The Theognid literature now came to decry the fact that "Many *kakoi* are rich and many *agathoi* are poor," and to maintain belligerently that "we will not take wealth in exchange for our *aretē.* . . ."[47]

CLASS CONFLICTS

From about the ninth to the sixth century B.C., class tensions also proliferate in other ways. Hesiod's work toward the latter half of the eighth century clearly manifests the growing strains between the small landholding peasants and the larger holders, or gentry, in Boeotia. The end of the eighth and the beginning of the seventh century saw a growing land shortage and land hunger and the emergence of a landed aristocracy in Athens, the *eupatridai,* or well-born.[48] Reminiscent of the plaints in the Theognid literature, these aristocrats were subjected to pressure by the newly rising mercantile interests while, at the same time, their conflicts with the small peasants in Attica intensified.

A well-formulated theoretical model has been advanced by A. French,[49] who seeks, among other things, to account for this intensification of class conflict in the countryside: on quitting their nomadic style of life and settling down in the peninsula, the Greek tribes increased in population, says French, expanding "above the carrying capacity of the land by the eighth to the seventh century B.C."[50] Agricultural lands being limited, they were led to cultivate pastoral lands and to work marginal soils. Cattle and horse breeding consequently declines—although oxen remain as plow animals—and the Homeric meat eaters become in time the cereal eaters of the classical period. Moreover, grain crops deplete land rapidly, especially in the absence of crop rotation; the yield declines because the land becomes worked out, because part of it is left fallow to recover, and because marginal land on the hills is brought under cultivation.

The decreasing yield at first raises the price of cereals and, with this, the value of land. This tempts the larger and more powerful landholders to enclose common grazing lands, and it also creates pressure among urban dwellers to import grains from abroad. The declining supply of local grains makes grain importation more necessary, while the increasing price makes it more profitable. With the increased importation of grain, however, its price declines and the small farmer is no longer compensated for his declining yield by high prices. He is, therefore, constrained to secure advances from the large holders in order to meet his needs in a situation in which it is difficult for him to repay them.

Some become "sharecroppers," or *hektēmoroi*, on their own land, which is now marked out by their creditors with "ward stones," or *horoi*, that subject them to a publicly visible status degradation. These social stigmata combine with their economic deprivation to intensify hostilities: "In Attica at the beginning of the VIth century the condition of the tenant appears in the darkest colours. He is called the *hektēmoros* . . . or 'sixth-partner.' The sixth part of the returns, from which he takes his name, is not what he owes the landlord, but what he keeps." [51]

Others, unable to repay their advances, forfeit the personal security they had pledged and, along with their wives and children, were made slaves. This transformation of a once proudly independent group of freeholders into slaves or sharecroppers on their own land generated the bitterest of class conflicts in Attica.

As Athens verged on civil war, in 594 B.C. Solon became archon, or chief magistrate with special powers, when, as he wrote in an elegy, "The oldest land of Ionia is burning in a fever." [52] It was a period when, as Aristotle will later describe it, "The many were the slaves of the few and the commons rose against the men of note. The struggle was bitter; and mutual opposition long, but finally all agreed upon an arbitrator and ruler in the person of Solon, and the reins of government were put in his hands." [53]

Solon sought to compromise the class conflicts of his period and to mitigate the worst of the deprivations to which the poorer classes were subject. Among his better known reforms was the cancellation of debt slavery and the forbidding of loans on personal security, although it is questionable whether he canceled the unpaid balances that debtors still owed. Curtailing privileges of the *eupatridai*, Solon also established a system of four classes based on income; the minimum requirements for these were five hundred drachmae for the highest, three hundred for the next, two hundred for the third, and the last composed of citizens having less than this; this lowest class was excluded from public office, though it was admitted to the assembly and the courts. The highest class (or two classes) [54] could alone supply members for the archonship and was correspondingly responsible for certain special expenditures on behalf of the city.

By providing that income alone, rather than birth, be the legal basis for political participation, Solon's reforms made it possible for the normal processes of commercial development in Athens to increase the number of citizens having access to office. They bore impressive fruit in Athenian upward social mobility between 480 and 431 B.C.: the first three classes came to be 50 per cent of the citizenry instead of the 40 per cent they had formerly been, while at the same time the total number of citizens increased from thirty to forty thousand.[55] The effect of Solon's reforms then was to bridge the status incongruences that had developed by providing a system that enabled men whose income and class positions were improving to have a correspondingly larger share in political powers and honors. This, in turn, strengthened their loyalties to the community and made their energies and resources more willingly available to it. The Solonic reforms laid the groundwork for a new conception of the community, permitting larger numbers to participate ever more fully in its affairs and to think of it as being "their" community. In short, these reforms laid the basis of Athenian democracy.

Solon's reforms also aimed at bringing the citizen into closer contact with the state by weakening the older tribal involvements in which he was still enmeshed. The individual was recognized for the first time as the legal unit. He was given a measure of testamentary freedom so that in the absence of direct heirs he might bequeath property as he wished; he was empowered to initiate legal action himself, rather than retaining this as the exclusive privilege of the family or the clansmen of those who had been wronged. The state released the individual from the confines of the kinship system and, at the same time, bound him to itself through the new privileges it conferred.

This same strategy of mitigating the sources of class conflict and of positively strengthening the bases of civic unity was continued by Pisistratus. About the middle of the sixth century, he divided the estates of the *eupatridai* among the small peasants, reducing revolutionary discontent in the rural areas. At the same time, it appears, the ritual recitation of the Homeric literature was standardized under him, making Athens a center from which Homeric influence spread throughout the mainland.[56] In effect, the effort was to make Olympianism the official religion of the *polis*. While this may have failed ultimately because the Olympian gods were intrinsically too international in character to win purely localistic loyalties, nonetheless they do seem to have transcended the older, more narrowly tribalistic loyalties.

Later in the sixth century, after continued class conflict, Cleisthenes pursued much the same course of strengthening the specifically *civic* character of the new polity by breaking up the old tribal units, by reassigning citizens to parishlike territorial units (*dēmoi*), and by grouping them into ten tribes that were no longer the traditional kinship structures yet still maintained a semblance of continuity with the familiar forms. Although the tribes remained as administrative agencies of the *polis,* they were now composed of units whose members might be neighbors rather than kin. Each new tribe was also composed of *dēmoi* located in each of three different regions of Attica; since one of these was always in the urban area itself, within which all political meetings were held, this meant that the urban sector of the tribe would have increased influence in its affairs. The reapportionment of each tribe among the different regions also meant that it would develop less social solidarity as a tribe, for it would less likely have a single regional, economic, or class interest to which all could rally.

Through these remarkably clear-sighted reforms, the *polis* continued to grow in strength and to increase its dominance over other group ties. Yet these did not alone undermine the foundations of the older tribal structure. With the transition from the collectively held property of Homeric times to private property,[57] there was a decline in the influence of tribal leaders and in the system of extended kinship; the smaller patriarchal family grew in importance. Loyalties to lineage gradually came to be overlaid with or displaced by commitments to the *polis* or the deme.

These societal changes were accompanied by important shifts in the nature of individual personality and in men's self-images. Men came to think of themselves as being not only of a given family or lineage but from a specific city or deme. Indeed, "family names were ignored, and every Athenian without distinction coupled with his own name the name of his deme. At most people of high birth might indulge in the luxury of perpetuating the name of their father, but they never record that of their *genos,* and the most illustrious of the Alcmaeonidae went under the name of Pericles, son of Xanthippus, of the *deme* of Cholargus." [58] By the fifth century B.C., civic and deme identification had become a salient part of the individual's self-image.

Not only does self-identification come to be made in terms of membership in cities, but reference to the civic membership of others or to their lack of it becomes extremely important. The person without a city, or cityless cosmopolitan, is a term of reference often of clearly derogatory import. It is only after the defeat of Athens at the end of the Peloponnesian War (404 B.C.) that one finds a thinker, such as the Cynic Diogenes referring to himself as *kosmopolitēs* in a eulogistic sense. Until this time most of the major thinkers were to regard the *polis* as the highest form of social organization; membership in the *polis* was vauntingly prized and, in large part, quite realistically so, for the city did provide all manner of advantages, and to be cityless was truly to be handicapped.

With the deterioration of the old tribal order in Greece and the concomitant growth of class stratification came a mounting concern with the problem of "justice": there is a growing fear of "gift-devouring kings" who give "crooked" judgments. As older patterns of authority waned, group conflicts proliferated: between the landed aristocracy and the rising mercantile groups, between the rich and the poor, between the landed gentry and the land-hungry, debt-involved small farmers, and between the political factions of the "oligarchs" and the "democrats." "From the seventh century to the time of the Roman conquest, Greek history is full of revolutions and counter-revolutions, of massacres, banishment and confiscations. Party hatred was never experienced with more ferocity than in the small city-states where intestine struggles assumed the forms of veritable vendettas." [59]

Almost all aspects of Greek culture were sucked into this vortex of civil conflict, and class differences found a hundred masks. Political strife between the oligarchic and democratic factions, for instance, obviously reflects the tension between the landed aristocrats, the "few," and the rising mercantile and urban masses, the "many." The various departments of the military forces became disposed toward different social strata and political factions; the *hoplitai* (with whom Socrates did his tours of military service) tending more than the navy toward the landed aristocracy, whereas the naval units, based as they were in harbors and manned by the poorer classes, became somewhat more oriented toward urban mercantile groups and democratic views.

Religious orientations were also shaped by the strife within the city. The democrats and mercantiles tended to become attached to the crafty Hermes, the god of serendipity and of buying, selling, and thieving; and the smashing of the *Hermāi* before the Sicilian expedition was widely interpreted in Athens as an expression of the oligarchical malice of Alcibiades' aristocratic cohorts. In contrast to Hermes, "Apollo moved only in the best society, from the days when he was Hector's patron to the days when he canonised aristocratic athletes while Dionysus was at all periods [*demotikos*], a god of the people." [60]

ECONOMIC OPPORTUNITY AND CLASS STRUCTURE

With the increasing tendency to esteem men because of their wealth, and as the occasions to acquire wealth by trade grew, the older nobility began to venture into the newly developing opportunity structures. They began to produce for the market and for a profit rather than solely for the consumption of their *ōikos,* and they began to finance trade and industrial activities. As they had previously loaned money to peasants, they now loaned it at interest to merchants and traders. The traders, who were a distinctly specialized group by the fourth century B.C., usually had little or no capital of their own, which meant that a high interest rate could be exacted from them; and, since there were no limits on what might be charged, the rate could be as high as 200 to 300 per cent.[61] That the professional traders had little capital of their own was in some part due to the fact that those who did succeed in acquiring it were likely to retire from active trade; commerce was not a high-ranking occupation by conventional Greek values, and active involvement in it did not coincide with the preferred style of life as many citizens saw it. As a result, those who owned and supplied the capital often did not take direct part in commerce but preferred to live as *rentiers*.

Much, though scarcely all, foreign trade and business was left to resident aliens, or *metoikoi*, the lowest class of freemen, rather than to the free citizenry. By the last quarter of the fifth century B.C., there were about a third as many *metoikoi* as citizens; a century later, there were perhaps half as many as citizens. The traditional stress of Greek values on personal autonomy discouraged citizens from entering the employ of others; it is likely that as a result only a minority of citizens committed themselves to careers as industrial workers or employees.

Like the *metoikoi*, the proportion of those who were slaves was also increasing, and, by the end of the fifth century B.C., they composed perhaps about half the total population.[62] In Homer and Hesiod, physical work as such was not regarded as degrading, and even the lord of an *ōīkos* might work in his field without disgrace. The crucial thing was whether he worked for himself and under his own direction and not whether the work was manual.[63] Manual work, however, tended increasingly to be associated with low status groups, such as slaves, whom citizens commonly regarded as living under a despicable constraint, or with *metoikoi*, who, being excluded from citizenship, lived under severe civic handicaps and at the pleasure of the citizenry. Citizens seem to have been clearly dominant only in those crafts entailing ownership of land, such as hog breeding or lime transport. The well-known accounts of the construction of the Erechtheum in 409–408 B.C. indicate that of 71 contractors and laborers only 20 were citizens, whereas the building accounts of Eleusis, in 329–328 B.C., show only 21 citizens among 94 craftsmen.[64]

Metoikoi were legally prohibited from owning land, possession being the exclusive prerogative of the citizens. Among their other disabilities, *metoikoi* could not claim state relief in times of distress; they could not bring lawsuits in their own name; they were excluded from public offices and priesthoods; they had neither voice nor vote in government affairs; and, after Pericles' time, they could not legally marry a citizen.[65] Access to the status and prerogatives of citizens was increasingly protected; for example, in 445 B.C. some five thousand *metoikoi* who had posed as citizens were struck from the city's rolls and sold into slavery. Despite their civic liabilities, *metoikoi* were, however, required to do military service, although their duty was restricted to Attica. Furthermore, during certain periods they also paid a poll tax of twelve *drachmai* a year and were liable for payment of the *eisphorā,* a special capital levy in time of need; indeed, in one of Demosthenes' speeches against Androtion, there is an indication that *metoikoi* paid about one sixth of the total sum thus raised.

From the foregoing, it appears that several basic dimensions would have to be examined for a systematic analysis of social stratification in classical Greece:

(1) It must be considered whether the persons involved derived their income from ownership, operation, or investment in landed properties or from mercantile or manufacturing properties. There are evident tensions between these two groups, particularly insofar as they tended to have different values and insofar as the latter challenged the former for honor and influence in the state. Yet their differences were mitigated to the extent that the landed group derived income from its investments in trade or industry and to the extent that intermarriage could occur. There was also auxiliary stratification within each group depending on the size of holdings or investments, so that one section, particularly in the landed group, would have surplus capital that it could lend to smaller holders. There was further differentiation within each group, again particularly in the landed group, depending on the honorific standing of its lineage.

(2) There were significant differences between citizens and foreigners, the latter being subject to serious civil disabilities and, in particular, excluded from ownership of land. As will be discussed later, the citizen was particularly privileged in his access to opportunities for unearned income. Of course, the landed-mercantile/industrial dimension is not independent of the citizen-foreigner dimension, and the two are, rather, positively correlated; more specifically, all landholders were citizens, although not all citizens were landholders.

(3) Whether a man's residence and productive holdings were located in rural or urban areas also affected his position in the total stratification system. On the whole, physical propinquity to the city's decision-making assembly, particularly during democratic periods, favored urban holders. Insofar as influence was exerted through personal participation and voting in the assembly, those, such as the small peasant, who during spring and summer could not readily and regularly attend, would be systematically disadvantaged in comparison with citizens whose work and homes were in the city itself. Another disadvantage of rural location was its vulnerability to damage through burning and pillaging by enemy armies, while the city itself was protected from direct damage by its walls. Over the long run, those groups whose homes or properties were rurally located would have their

economic positions impaired by warfare and might therefore have their political positions indirectly impaired. Political power would tend to drift increasingly into the hands of those whose homes and investments were situated within the city itself, and would be reinforced by their financial ability to outfit and provision military forces.

(4) Finally, there is the profound distinction between those who were free and those who were slave.

FUNCTIONS AND DYSFUNCTIONS OF SLAVERY

Slavery was commonly regarded in antiquity as a natural phenomenon. In Greek society the poorest peasant, the most underprivileged *metoikos,* and the deepest philosopher were for the most part at one in being unable to conceive a world without slaves. Even during the fifth century enlightenment and the sophistic criticism of almost all institutions, there was relatively little criticism of slavery itself. Whatever questions and objections were raised about slavery involved nothing of the vehemence of nineteenth-century American abolitionism. Slavery was so entrenched in the institutions and culture of the ancient world that even believers in the brotherhood of man, such as the Cynics, Stoics, and early Christians, did not oppose it.[66]

There has been considerable controversy among classicists as to just how "basic" slavery was to Greek society; here, as on some other questions concerning this civilization, the most unlikely positions are taken with a straight face. Indeed, Kitto's remarks about criticism of Greek tragedy, that "there is no position so untenable that some intrepid spirit will not be found occupying it," [67] apply with special force to studies of Greek economics and slavery.

Slavery was consequential for almost every aspect of Greek society. It had reverberating effects on the economy and was obviously intrinsic to the entire system of stratification: to ask whether slavery was "basic" to Greek society is like asking whether serfdom was basic to Feudalism. Slavery affected and was affected by the kinship system.[68] It was implicated in the relations between the city-states and, if only for this reason, was involved in the domestic politics of each. And as we shall also see, it deeply affected the morality and philosophy of the time. Certainly it did not occur to Plato or Aristotle to doubt that slavery was necessary to the good life in the *polis.* As Plato remarks in the *Laws,* "What will be the manner of life among men who may be supposed to have their food and clothing provided for them in moderation, and who have entrusted the practice of the arts to others, and whose husbandry, committed to slaves paying a part of the produce, brings them a return sufficient for men living temperately." [69]

Slave Population

It is in part because of this question—whether slavery was basic—that so much attention has been devoted to estimating the size of the slave population, on the supposition that the importance of slavery must be directly proportionate to the number of slaves. Moses I. Finley has effectively disproved this assumption by pointing out that, in the United States of 1860, the official census statistics reveal that slightly less than a third of the total population in the slave states were slaves and that "nearly three-fourths of all free Southerners had no connection with slavery through either family ties or direct ownership. The 'typical' Southerner was not only a small farmer but also a non-slaveholder." [70] It should seem clear that the importance of an institution is not to be appraised primarily in terms of the numbers of people involved in it. I shall add, and only in passing, that a conservative estimate is that in the fifth and fourth centuries there were approximately three or four slaves for each Athenian household, including those of both citizens and *metoikoi*.

There is another, and it would seem very obvious, reason why the significance of slavery for Hellenic civilization cannot be estimated by computing the number of slaves at any one time. However small a minority this group may have been, and according to most responsible estimates it is not a small minority at all during the classical period,[71] nonetheless it remained a potential status for everyone—even a Plato. Says Aeschylus: "none, neither great nor young, might outleap the gigantic toils of enslavement and final disaster." [72] It is the consensus of modern authorities that "the condition of servitude was one which no man, woman, or child, regardless of status or wealth, could be sure to escape in case of war or some other unpredictable and uncontrollable emergency." [73] As another scholar states, "[O]ver everyone from the highest to the lowest hung that horror of possible enslavement." [74] Because of this fear, if for no other reason, it is necessary to assume that the psychological impact of slavery and potential slavery must have been profound. To attempt, therefore, to appraise the significance of slavery for Greek society by counting the number of slaves is like attempting to appraise the significance of human mortality by counting the number of people who die in any one year.[75]

Psychic Costs of Slavery

The psychological impact of slavery ramified because it was a potential status for every man; it was intensified, however, precisely because the danger loomed not only for himself but also for his loved ones, for parents, wife, and children. In *The Women of Trachis,* Sophocles has Deianira implore: "O Zeus . . . grant that I may never see you come like this against my children. . . ." [76] And preparing for the contest in which he will die, Hector says to his wife: ". . . some mail-clad Achaian shall lead thee weeping. . . . So shalt thou abide in Argos, and ply the loom at another woman's bidding, and bear water . . . and sore constraint shall be laid upon thee." [77] It might be added that she would also very possibly be taken to bed by her new master, as Agamemnon did to Cassandra. It seemed horrible but not unusual to Aeschylus that this should be the fate of captive women: "The girls, new servants, new to misery, must endure a war captives' bed, bed of a man successful." [78]

The ramifications of this emotionally charged potentiality inherent in ancient slavery, its implications for husband–wife relationships, and its possibly adverse effects on the capacity of the male to make a deep psychic investment in his wife are, I believe, yet to be explored seriously. Here I will simply recall certain elementary observations from the Homeric literature on the suspicion that they may be more than casually connected: (1) In Homer, and indeed throughout classical Greek literature, there were no ordinary words that specifically meant "husband" and "wife." Linguistically, a man was called many things: a man, father, warrior, nobleman, king, and hero: he was practically never a husband.[79] Although monogamy prevailed from Homeric times onward, husband–wife ties were not usually deeply emotional; at any rate, they seem less effectively laden than husband–son and man–man relationships. Men seemed to have their most meaningful and intimate ties, even apart from overt homosexual relationships, with other men. (2) The conflict between Achilles and Agamemnon was precipitated by a quarrel over the booty taken by Agamemnon from Achilles; it may be noteworthy that this booty is not simply "treasure" but happens to involve a female captive, Briseis. (3) Most slaves during the Homeric period, as previously mentioned, seem to have been female. (4) Finally, the precipitating incident of the whole Homeric adventure devolves on what might be termed a fantasy of female loss and—even though it here concerns a seduction rather than a forcible abduction—seems in this respect similar to Achilles' loss of Briseis.

The loss, or threatened loss, of women would not seem to be emotionally the same as the loss of other kinds of valuable. Rather, the dramatists make a special point that when a city is sacked, its *women* will be "hailed away, captives, young and old, dragged by the hair, as horses by the mane, and their raiment torn about them." [80] This would seem particularly disturbing to men with a warrior code stressing their manly virtues and who, like Sophocles' dying Hercules, so resent the thought of a stranger having sexual access to their former consort, they might enjoin their son to marry the woman: "You must take this girl as your wife. . . . No other man but you must ever have her who has lain with me. . . ." [81]

Slavery would seem to have had further psychic consequences for at least two other reasons. One is its unpredictable character that would only heighten the anxiety concerning it and, in particular, would tend to disrupt the connection between what a man did and what happened to him. The reassuring feeling that social reality is intrinsically orderly would surely be undermined by the apparent unpredictability of what could occur.

A second reason for suspecting the psychic importance of slavery is that it could happen even to the highest of men, to the wealthiest, the most powerful, and the most honorable. Greek culture insisted that to be successful is not to be immune to the worst disaster. Even the highest were vulnerable, not simply to the ordinary setbacks of life, but to what Greek values define as the very worst thing that could befall a man; for, indeed, by Solon's time slavery was commonly felt to be even worse than death, and, to understate it for the moment, the Greeks had a particular dislike of death.[82] Unlike both the Christian and the democratic fantasy (and I use this term in a technical, nonpejorative sense) that the bottom rail would become the top, the uniquely Hellenic fantasy was that the top rail could become the bottom.

The Jealousy of the Gods and Attitudes toward Authority

The unpredictable dangers of slavery, even to those in the highest reaches of the society, would seem to undermine men's identification with authority; the mystique of authority is drained of emotional need. Certainly the strategy of reliving personal anxieties by identifying with powerful men is a common one. Yet if men on top are vulnerable to slavery, there will be a problem of whether those beneath them can find security by identifying themselves with superiors or, in general, with symbols or persons of authority.

If, as was the case, these powerful men are themselves felt to be subject not only to ordinary earthly disaster but to special supernatural liabilities, they will be even less likely to become objects of an admiring identification through which those beneath them will derive emotional security. The pervasive and frequently powerful envy that the Greeks felt for the attainments of the successful would not then be counterbalanced by sentiments of attachment, and aggression toward them would have freer rein.

This at any rate is consistent with the distinctly Greek belief that excess in any direction—but peculiarly an excess of *success*—will provoke the gods to envy and that they will first strike down those who are highest; [83] "any greatness in human life brings doom." [84] The imminent threat of slavery to all would be most problematic with respect to the vulnerability of those who are the highest. It is not too difficult for men to understand why the poor, the lowly, the unattached, or those without "honor" are vulnerable. The real problem for a culture is to make meaningful the vulnerability of the good and the powerful; in Greece this was done by the belief in the envy of the gods. This is not to say, however, that this belief had as its sole or even main psychic function the accounting for the vulnerability of those at the top of the social system; but it would seem among other things to do this.

The belief in the envy of the gods has other implications for the Hellenic social system. As part of a larger set of elements in the Olympian religion, it accounts for the disorderliness and unpredictability inherent in the system of slavery, the prevalence of warfare, and the ferocity of competition in Greek life. If the belief in the capricious, unpredictable intervention of the gods in human affairs projectively mirrors important parts of the social structure, it bounces back and infuses the disordered social situation with meaning and value. In making social disorder the handiwork of the gods, it generates motives to accept it.

The belief in the envy of the gods is an order-inducing element in still another way; it encourages men at the top of the system to restraint in their relations with those beneath them, limiting the resentment they will provoke. While reality alone might be expected to induce prudence and restraint among those at the bottom of the system, the belief in the envy of the gods provides supernaturally sanctioned motives for restraint and moderation among those at the top who would otherwise be less controllable; controlling deviance at the top was always a major problem of Greek society.

In one vital way, however, the belief in the envy of the gods was unsettling to the class system. By clearly indicating the unusual danger of those in the highest positions, far from making them the special darlings of the gods, it makes them their special victims. If men strike down those in authority or those of eminence, they are acting against a supernaturally vulnerable group, and they might hope to be regarded as agents of the gods in punishing *hybris,* or insolence. Thus in the very process of providing a meaningful account of the vulnerability of those highly stationed, the belief in the envy of the gods heightens their vulnerability. Far from being a quiescence-inducing "opiate of the people," Olympian religion may have been an inhibition-releasing stimulant that fostered rebellion.

Recruitment of Slaves

Greek uneasiness about slavery probably arose not only because all were potential victims but also from the manner in which slaves were "recruited." While slaves were often "barbarians," that is, non-Greeks, coming perhaps especially from Thrace, the lands around the Black Sea, Asia Minor, and the Levant, nonetheless, Greeks also enslaved Greeks, particularly so with the increasing bitterness of their intercity wars during the late fifth and fourth centuries.

Slaves were in large measure won in war. Even if this was not the main source of slaves, it was undoubtedly one of the most important; [85] the slave dealers followed the armies. G. Glotz asserts unequivocally that "the vast majority of slaves came from war. After a pitched battle those prisoners who could not buy their freedom were sold; after the assault of a city the men were put to the sword and the women and children divided among the victors by lot." [86]

Kidnaping was also one of the common sources of slave supply, and there were organized kidnaping rings run on a commercial basis. Kidnaping, however, was not confined to the barbarian countries and "children were stolen in every city in Greece. . . ." [87] That this was not unheard of even in Athens is indicated by the fact that the city made it a capital offense to seize and sell a freeman into slavery.[88] (It would appear, however, that this law would be extremely difficult to enforce since the wrongly enslaved person could not, as a slave, institute proceedings for legal redress on his own behalf and since, further, there was no way of preventing his owner from removing him elsewhere before the trial.) Even after Solon's prohibition of debt slavery, Athenians were still enslaved for other offenses—the *metoikoi,* for instance, because of fraudulent enrollment on the citizen-rolls and because of failure to pay the *metoikia* taxes. Moreover, Solon ended debt slavery only in Athens, but it was permitted in other city-states.[89]

Although the breeding of slaves was uneconomical and not an important source of slave supply in Greece, nonetheless, during the classical period, children born to a slave concubine who had been impregnated by her master —or for that matter by any freeman—would assume the status of their mother.[90] This was in contrast to the situation in Homeric times, when children commonly took their father's status and were freemen if he was free.[91] It may be noted finally that even free parents in Attica occasionally sold their children into slavery.

The point of these remarks is that, as it came to develop, slavery was not simply threatening to the Greeks because it might victimize them but, also, because it was they themselves who were doing the victimizing. The institution of slavery was psychically disturbing not merely because of what it might lead others to do to them but because of what it led or permitted them to do to others whom they recognized as being of their own kind. The Greeks felt that to be made a slave was a terrible fate. To enslave others and especially Greeks, with whom they felt a certain community of culture, very likely induced many to feel that they themselves were doing—not simply suffering—a terrible thing. Plato was by no means alone in believing that the enslavement of Greek by Greek deserved condemnation. Whether what Greeks felt about their enslavement of Greeks was "shame" or "guilt" is difficult to say; but they did seem to feel that they were in this manner transgressing dangerous boundaries and tempting the fates.

More than any other people with whom I, at least, am familiar, the Greeks were aware that they were capable of unspeakable atrocities and lived in dread of retribution: "Let me attain no envied wealth, let me not plunder cities, neither be taken in turn, and face life in the power of another." [92]

Xenophon relates that on a summer night in 405 B.C., when the news of the final disaster at Kynoskephalai reached the waterfront of Athens, it spread to the central town, its passage marked by a trailing cry of lamentation, a wailing *oimōgē:*

> From Piraeus, following the line of the long walls up to the heart of the city, it swept and swelled, as each man to his neighbour passed on the news. On that night no man slept. There was mourning and sorrow for those that were lost, but the lamentation for the dead was merged in even deeper sorrow for themselves, as they pictured the evils they were about to suffer, the like of which they had themselves inflicted upon the men of Melos [and] on the men of Histiaea; on Skione and Torone; on the Aeginetans, and many another Hellenic city.[93]

The city felt that it had at last come to retribution.

In saying that the Greeks were uneasy about slavery, I am not suggesting that they commonly rejected, insistently explored, or even talked a great deal about it as an institution. That they did not do so, however, is an ambiguous datum; it does not speak for itself but needs, instead, to be cross-examined. The Greek silence about slavery is not perforce evidence that they had no ambivalence or anxiety about the institution. On the contrary, their clearly expressed sentiments concerning the status of slaves, the existence of kidnaping, and the Athenian law against wrongly enslaving a freeman suggest otherwise. The developing practice of enslaving defeated Greeks combined with the pessimistic general mood that all men are vulnerable to radical overturns in fortune could only have heightened their sense of vulnerability to slavery and their anxiety about it. Moreover, the fear of slave reprisals grew with increases in the slave population. Sparta, of course, is the classic case in point, while Plato takes it for granted that some slaves hate their masters enough to kill them if only given the chance to do so with impunity.

The Functions of Slavery

There remains the question of why so little seems to have been said about or against slavery if it was, in fact, as tension-inducing as I have suggested. The objections to slavery (and these are only occasional) raised by Plato are directed primarily against one particular form of it, the enslavement of Greeks by Greeks; otherwise he regards slavery as necessary to the good life. Even the free poor, who might be thought to have felt that slave competition was depressing their wage levels,[94] never openly protested slavery.[95] One finds some voices among Plato's arch foes, the Sophists, protesting, as did Antiphon, that "by nature we are all alike," [96] but this never found a popular echo in Hellenic civilization. Yet the reason for this silence concerning slavery, despite its postulated tension-inducing character, does not seem very mysterious. Rather than searching for something obscure, it is the obvious that needs to be said: those who were free benefited directly and substantially from having slaves.

Slaves, after all, did do work. In particular, they did the "dirty work" of Greek society: they were domestic servants, cooks, housekeepers, stewards; they did the shopping, opened the doors, brought the water, cleaned, waited on meals, ground the grain, kneaded the dough, wove cloth, carried luggage on trips, worked in the factories and mines and to some extent in the fields; they were body servants to soldiers in the field and, by being rented out for hire, produced cash incomes for their owners. Last but hardly least, they were convenient bedmates who required no wooing. In general and perhaps best of all, they could be made to take orders and to work under the direct supervision or "constraint" of another. They could thus be made to fill a large variety of positions—some even of a managerial character—that a freeman might resist because they required him to take orders from another.

There are various distinguishable liabilities to which the slave was subject—among them being unable to represent himself in a lawsuit, being subject to seizure as property, being unable to live or go where he pleased. Perhaps the greatest of these, from the Greek standpoint, was the slave's inability to do as he pleased: "They led us here, to take the lot of slaves, and mine is to wrench my will, and consent to their commands, right or wrong. . . ." [97] The slave was one who had to do as he was told, regardless of whether he wished to or not; his ends, will, or volition did not have to be taken into account, for his objections could always be overridden. He was, from one side of the ambivalent Greek viewpoint toward slaves, a "nonperson." [98] He was an *andrapodon,* an unfree body or human-footed stock, a kind of cattle. Indeed, a man owning two *hetairai* might refer to them as a "yoke" or pair of cattle, and the chief market day for slaves was the same as that for cattle.[99] As Aristotle will later term him, the slave was an "animate tool" that rendered services; he was not a person but an instrument that, like other tools, could be used primarily in terms of its economic value and effectiveness for the purposes intended.

The economic advantage of slaves derives from their usability in a predominantly instrumental manner. This means that the number and kinds of employment to which they may be put is less limited by purely moral restrictions. Men are versatile performers and can do many different things but, insofar as they are defined as "persons," they cannot be made to do all of these. To the extent they are defined as "nonpersons," however, their actual utilization can be more fully diversified and unrestricted. They then approximate an economical all-purpose tool, the costs of which can be spread among a greater variety of jobs.

Slavery as such would, also, seem more economical than the Spartan institution of helotism for two reasons: first, the Spartan Helot was permitted to retain everything he produced above a certain quota which he had to deliver to his master; second, the amount he was permitted to retain had to suffice not only for himself as a male adult but also for his family, which might include young, unproductive children or the women taking care of them. In this last respect, helotism had the same uneconomical character as the breeding of slaves.

There was, however, a more potent disability connected with helotism, which, if affecting the Spartan economy only indirectly, was an even more serious sociological liability: the Helots were a perpetual source of rebellion. They were an endemic threat that changed the whole character and history of Sparta, as the citizens sought to adapt to it. This threat derived in part from the numerical superiority of the Helot to the free Spartan; it has been estimated that Helots outnumbered Spartan citizens by about twenty to one, being numerically far more powerful than the Athenian slaves. Indeed it may be that helotism was at the time the only feasible way of administering a subjected group of such relatively great size.

It was not their numbers alone, however, that made the Helots such a threat. It was also the fact that having ties of kinship with one another, having a common ethnic background, and being a native people subjected to "foreigners" in their own land, the Helots had a much greater capacity to feel hostility and to express it effectively in more solidary forms of social organization than did slaves in urban Athens; for the latter had no bonds of kinship, came from diverse cultures, and spoke different native languages and dialects. In comparison with helotism, which was the sociologically feasible and familiar alternative of the time, slavery then seems to have been a more economical and a less socially disruptive mode of controlling labor *within a fluid urban environment.*

The point, then, is that the slave system did provide substantial gratifications for freemen that surely motivated them to maintain it. These help explain why, despite the tensions slavery produced, abolitionist sentiments were never strongly voiced in classical Greece.

Mitigations of Slavery

It has been mentioned that the Athenian's slaves were, in comparison with the Spartan's Helots, a relatively nonrebellious group. At least they were not actively rebellious, and there were few slave uprisings in the classical period. This is due not only to the difficulties in establishing cohesive relations among urban slaves—who in this case lack common ethnic or kinship ties—but is partly attributable to certain mitigating characteristics of the Athenian slave system. The Athenians were simply not as viciously repressive of slaves as the Spartans. Although from a freeman's traditional standpoint, the difference between the slave and freeman is often simplified and dichotomous—Aristotle says that the "free man . . . does not live under the constraint of another"—the legal situation itself is much more complex, allowing for differentiations in types and degrees of bondage, for changes in these, and even for some hope of freedom. While there were few manumissions until the fifth century,[100] there were, however, clubs, or *eranoi,* from which a slave might borrow (but only indirectly, since he was not legally recognized) to buy his freedom and to which he would repay his loan. Such slaves, however, were often freed only conditionally and were, in effect, a kind of urban serf who had to provide his former master, or someone he designated, with payments in kind or coin during the latter's lifetime.[101]

Despite these limitations, the lot of the Athenian slave was better than that of his Spartan counterpart who, as the property of the state, could not be privately emancipated. Indeed, in some respects the slave's liabilities—such as being unable to act for himself before a court of law—were not much different from those of the *metoikos.* The urban class structure was more differentiated than might seem at first and was not polarized between slaves and freemen.

There were other mitigations of the slave's lot. Among these were the laws against *hybris,* or outrageous insult to a slave; the custom of a slave's right to asylum in the Theseum or at the altar of the Eumenides; [102] legal protection for a slave against deliberate murder by his master; a slave's acceptance into the religious—as distinct from the political—community, as evidenced by his admission to certain religious gatherings and public sacrifices; and his partial incorporation into the household of his owner, which might induce the owner to feel called on to avenge his murder [103] by others. It also appears that slaves could wear much the same dress as (at least) lower-class freemen.

The Athenian slave, then, occupied a culturally established *social* status. This entailed traditional privileges more generous than his strictly legal rights, and, while these were vulnerable for that reason, they provided him with certain protections on which he could within limits rely. As Westerman puts it, "In any slave society the slave group has its definite rights—not legal, but actual, and sanctioned by custom," [104] including customary food and clothing allotments. The viability of these traditional status prerogatives was buttressed by the Greek capacity for empathy and pity; [105] but it was also undermined by and basically at variance with the pervasive feeling of contempt for the slave's weakness and with the instrumental view of him as an object. Although the slave may have only in rare instances been treated totally as a "nonperson," he also rarely became more than a rudimentary person.

The point is simply that there were certain mitigating circumstances in the slave's situation, not that this lot was an easy one with which he was contented. There are indications that slaves were sometimes badly beaten and poorly fed. They could usually give testimony in courts of law only under torture, apparently on the assumption that only under physical duress were they trustworthy witnesses. The killing of a slave was not a civic crime but a religious offense entailing a pollution that could be cleansed ritually. Furthermore, the slaves' treatment in the silver mines, which employed large numbers, was particularly harsh: they were branded [106] and chained to their work. Those and other slaves were scarcely content with their lot. They did flee when they could, and it appears that the first form of insurance known in the Western world was insurance against slave runaways.[107] Thucydides relates that some twenty thousand Athenian slaves deserted during the occupation of Decelea. That slaves did not desert more often is doubtless due in part to the fact that they often had no place to which they could run. Wherever they might flee in Hellas, slavery was practiced, and, if "barbarians," their different body types, language, or branding would give them away as escapees—not that privateers, pirates, or kidnapers needed the justification of prior servitude to enslave their captives. Given the circumstances mitigating slavery in the different city-states, it is likely that many slaves felt that the conditions they knew were better than those untried.

NOTES

[1] From the translation by F. M. Cornford, *From Religion to Philosophy* (New York: Harper, 1957), p. 228.

[2] The image in the previous sentence is Nietzschean in origin; the present sentence, though Hegelian in image, also has a parallel in Nietzsche, although one that is somewhat macabre: "Could it be that wisdom appears on earth as a raven, inspired by a little whiff of carrion?" W. Kauffman, ed., *The Portable Nietzsche* (New York: Viking Press, 1954), p. 473. I am perplexed by the fact that frequently where I agree with Nietzsche's intuitions and ideas about things Hellenic, I reject the mood in which they are presented; and where I resonate to his mood, I reject the intellectual kernel. Yet he often provides the yeast for the intellectual substance I gathered elsewhere.

[3] Plato *Theaetetus*. 151AB; Benjamin Jowett, trans. and ed., *The Dialogues of Plato* (New York: Random House, 1937). All subsequent quotations from Plato will be from this edition, which was the third and last of Jowett's translations (1892) and which is probably most readily available to readers. Despite Jowett's tendency to make some dialogues sound like Victorian tea conversation, I have found this version consistently useful. It does, however, require checking against other translations done with special philological interests in mind. For the benefit of my sociological colleagues, I should mention that references to this volume will follow the classicists' convention of referring to the pages in Stephens' text which are given in the margin of Jowett's translation; thus the 151 referred to above is Stephens' page number and is actually on Jowett's page 152 of Volume II. Similarly, the letters A, B, C, D, and E refer to that fifth of Stephens' page on which the quoted material may be found. A further word about my own footnoting practices: aside from following the usual conventions of scholarly footnoting— which when looked at closely often seem more idiosyncratic than conventional—I shall occasionally use footnotes to acquaint social scientists with some of the sociologically significant if elemenary classical literature and classicists with some of the relevant if elementary social-science literature. The emphasis will therefore be on the standard materials in each of the fields, rather than on the technical or esoteric, with the benign if presumptuous aim of increasing the mutual familiarity of social scientists and classicists.

[4] Zimmern remarks rather bleakly of certain classical studies, ". . . the same evidence is marshalled; the same references and footnotes are transferred, like stale tea leaves, from one learned receptacle to another." A. Zimmern, *Solon and Croesus* (London: Oxford University Press, 1928), p. 106. Though overstated, this comment does cast a judicious doubt on the wisdom of relying solely on the emergence of new data to produce substantial developments in our understanding of the classical period in Greece. What is needed is an alliance of some of the newer social-science perspectives with the more traditional tools of classical scholarship. The vital contributions now seem to be made by those whose scholarship has been sharpened by an informed use of Durkheim, Freud, Weber, or Marx. F. M. Cornford, E. R. Dodds, J. Hasebroek, and M. I. Finley or G. Thomson are among the obvious cases in point. Perhaps because of the nature of the English university system, the English classicists today seem to manifest particular flexibility and skill in adapting systematic theoretical perspectives that were developed originally in disciplines other than their own. Yet it is also amply clear, from the outstanding work of some men with more traditionally philological outlooks, such as A. W. Adkins, that there remains no substitute for individual creativity.

[5] Archaeological findings and interpretations of the prehistory of Greece, especially those bearing on the early and middle Helladic periods from 2600 to 1600 B.C., have been emerging so rapidly of recent that conclusions about many major points are still far from definitive. For example, where the people of the early

Helladic came from remains disputed; there is also no unanimity that they were Indo-Europeans. Among much that may be consulted with profit, see: Sir Arthur J. Evans, *The Palace of Minos* (4 vols., London: Macmillan, 1921–1935); S. Casson, ed., *Essays in Aegean Archaeology Presented to Sir Arthur Evans in Honour of his 75th Birthday* (Oxford: Clarendon Press, 1927); A. R. Burn, *Minoans, Philistines, and Greeks*, B.C. *1400–900* (London: K. Paul Trench, Trubner, 1930); G. E. Mylonas, *Ancient Mycenae, the Capital City of Agamemnon* (Princeton: Princeton University Press, 1957); Sir John L. Myres, *Who Were the Greeks?* (Berkeley: University of California Press, 1930). For an able digest of some recent archaeological findings, see W. E. Caldwell, "New Discoveries in Greek History," *South Atlantic Quarterly,* 61 (Winter 1962), 86–96.

6 In this paragraph, I follow H. T. Wade-Gery, "Eupatridai, Archons, and Areopagus," *The Classical Quarterly,* 25, No. 1 (January 1931), 1–11, 77–89. Cf. the important volume by G. Thomson, *Aeschylus and Athens* (London: Lawrence & Wishart, 1941), p. 46, where it is argued that Wade-Gery's definition of the *genos,* as a group whose claimed common ancestor is fictional, is a *non sequitur.* Although I find Thomson's work in many respects excellent, I find his objection here lacking in cogency, for it is clear that the common ancestors claimed by *gennētai* were in fact fictional. If the mythical character of the *genos'* first ancestor does not disprove its claim to common descent, neither does it support this contention. The claim concerning common descent from a mythical ancestor is, first of all, a *social* fact, not a biological one, and it has social *consequences* that the genetic ties as such do not.

7 See M. E. White, "Greek Colonization," *The Journal of Economic History,* 21, No. 4 (December 1961), 443–454.

8 On this and on many points of general orientation to the social organization of the heroic period I have found the anthropologically informed outlook of Finley of great aid and have used it in various connections. See M. I. Finley, *The World of Odysseus* (New York: Meridian Books, 1959).

9 A. R. Burn, *Pericles and Athens* (New York: Collier Books, 1962), 16; G. Glotz, *The Greek City* (London: Routledge & Kegan Paul, 1950), p. 24.

10 *Ibid.,* p. 300.

11 Glenn R. Morrow, *Plato's Law of Slavery and Its Relation to Greek Laws* (Urbana: University of Illinois Press, 1939), p. 23, n. 20, referring to the estimate of Victor Ehrenberg.

12 Glotz, op. cit., p. 27.

13 One need not be a climatological determinist to take serious note of A. J. White's similar comments about the benign effect of the Athenian climate upon that city's patterns of social interaction: "[T]he Athenian climate . . . unlike the rain of Thessaly and the fog of Boeotia, permitted an outdoor life of street-corner discussion and doorstep repartee." "Class Distinctions in Fifth-Century Athens," *Greece and Rome,* 13, No. 37 (January 1944), 17.

14 W. Ellis, tr., *A Treatise on Government* (New York: J. P. Dutton, n.d.), p. 195.

15 F. E. Adcock, *The Greek and Macedonian Art of War* (Berkeley and Los Angeles: University of California Press, 1962), pp. 48–49.

16 *Ibid.,* p. 4.

17 A. D. Winspear, *The Genesis of Plato's Thought* (New York: S. A. Russell, 1956), 14 ff. In this connection, Winspear follows suggestions made by Karl Marx, which are also developed earlier by V. Gordon Childe, *Man Makes Himself* (London: Watts, 1937); see also K. A. Wittfogel, *Oriental Despotism* (New Haven: Yale University Press, 1954). Winspear's remains one of the most stimulating if orthodox applications of Marxism to the classical period and to Plato's work.

18 Cf. M. E. White, *op. cit.,* pp. 451–452.

19 For an argument for the latter date as the latest possible so far as the *Odyssey* is concerned, see A. A. Trever, "The Age of Hesiod: A Study in Economic History," *Classical Philology,* 19 (January–October 1924), 166.

[20] Winspear notes that iron is mentioned slightly more often in the *Odyssey* than the *Iliad; op. cit.*, p. 20. The sociologist Howard Becker corrects him on this in a quantitative content analysis that will surprise some of his colleagues who often thought of him as a prosy if not poetic scholar:

> This is correct enough, but what Winspear fails to take account of is the proportional mention; on this basis iron is mentioned four times as often in the *Odyssey.* . . . In the *Iliad* and *Odyssey* combined, iron accounts for almost 5 per cent of the references; in the *Iliad* alone, slightly more than 5 per cent; in the *Odyssey* alone, a trifle more than 20 per cent.

"Church and State in the Cosmos of Crete," *International Review of Social History*, 1, Pt. 2 (Fall 1956), 2.

[21] G. Nussbaum, "Labour and Status in the Works and Days," *Classical Quarterly*, n. s., 10, No. 2 (1960), 218.

[22] Nussbaum argues against the conventional assumption that Homeric slaves were predominantly female; though interesting, I find his reasoning tenuous and prefer to hew to the direct Homeric evidence where, as Nussbaum acknowledges, "We hear much more of female servants." *Ibid.*, 219. This testimony creates difficulties, but these seem no worse than those created by Nussbaum's long-linked chain of inferences.

[23] *Ibid.*, pp. 216–217.

[24] Finley, *op. cit.*, p. 111.

[25] M. E. White, *op. cit.*, pp. 444–445.

[26] H. Michell, *The Economics of Ancient Greece* (Cambridge: Cambridge University Press, 1940), p. 40.

[27] J. Hasebroek, trans. L. M. Fraser and D. C. Macgregor, *Trade and Politics in Ancient Greece* (London: G. Bell, 1933), p. 96.

[28] Sophocles *The Women of Trachis* ii. 296. 494. References to the tragedies of Aeschylus, Sophocles, and Euripides will be to the translations in D. Grene and R. Lattimore, eds., *The Complete Greek Tragedies* (4 vols., Chicago: University of Chicago Press, 1959). The Roman numeral is the volume number, followed by the page in that volume and the line numbers indicated on the margin.

[29] Aeschylus *The Libation Bearers* i. 117. 702–703.

[30] *Iliad* vi. 125. Translation by A. Lang and W. Leaf (London: Macmillan, 1897).

[31] A. W. Adkins, *Merit and Responsibility: A Study in Greek Values* (Oxford: Clarendon Press, 1960).

[32] A methodological aside here to sociological colleagues: Although Adkins makes no point of it, nonetheless his work implicitly makes a strong case for the *general* utility of analyzing the uses of terms of commendation and derogation—common to a culture or subgroups within it—as a tool for the analysis of value systems and, in particular, of changes in them. There is clearly no reason for believing that Adkins' methodology is valuable only for the study of ancient societies, and it should, in principle, be just as applicable to modern value systems. It would seem, then, that social scientists' familiarity with classical studies may yield more than a substantive understanding of ancient cultures, but can also produce methodological windfalls.

[33] Cf. G. M. Calhoun, "Classes and Masses in Homer, II," *Classical Philology*, 29 (October 1934), 304.

[34] F. E. Harrison, "Homer and the Poetry of War," *Greece and Rome*, second series, 7, No. 1 (March 1960), 9.

[35] Note that to be constrained, although inevitable for man, is in the dramatist's view to make him more of an animal and less of a human being. This is suggested by the frequent use of the "net" image, especially by Aeschylus. To be entrapped is to be caught like a beast. See, for example, *Agamemnon* i. 70. 1115; i. 80. 1375, 1382; i. 86. 1581; *Prometheus Bound*. i. 350. 1079; *Eumenides* i. 140. 147; the "web" imagery in *Agamemnon* i. 83. 1492; note the likening of men to animals in *Libation Bearers* i. 110. 492–493; also Sophocles' use of the "net" image in *The Women of Trachis* ii. 316. 1050 and Euripides' comparison of men with animals in *The Heracleidae* ii. 132. 449.

[36] Isocrates i. 165. Trans. G. Norlin, 3 vols. (London: Heinemann, 1928).

[37] See the posthumously published fragment, "From Homer's Contest," in W. Kaufmann, ed., *op. cit.* I will have more to say about the Greek contest system in a subsequent chapter, in which I use the Nietzschean fragment as a point of departure.

[38] *Iliad* xii. 239.

[39] For the development of this theme compare: Aeschylus *Libation Bearers* i. 97. 121–123; i. 98. 142–144; i. 104. 310–313; i. 107. 400 ff.; Sophocles *Oedipus at Colonus* ii. 90. 229–230; ii. 133. 1189; *Ajax* ii. 245. 840 ff.; Euripides *Hippolytus* iii. 204. 995 ff.; *Heracles* iii. 309. 732; *Helen* iii. 464. 1234; *Orestes* iv. 229. 650; *Hecuba* iv, 506. 271 ff.; iv. 526. 755; *The Suppliant Women* iv. 1832. 1178 ff.

[40] Translation by Georg Misch, *A History of Autobiography* (Cambridge: Harvard University Press, 1951), 81.

[41] Cf. Thucydides, trans. R. Crawley, *The Peloponnesian War* (Garden City: Doubleday, n.d.), p. 17.

[42] *Iliad* i. 6.

[43] iii. 222–223. 510 ff.

[44] The underlying, general model of functional analysis used here is best stated in R. K. Merton, *Social Theory and Social Structure* (Glencoe: Free Press, 1957), especially the introduction on manifest and latent functions.

[45] "There is an unresolved discrepancy in Aristophanes' attitude. At one and the same time he deplores the decline of soldierly virtues and fights the war-mongers." Victor Ehrenberg, *The People of Aristophanes*, "A Sociology of Old Attic Comedy" (New York: Schocken Books, 1962), p. 305.

[46] The point here is, of course, one of general theoretical significance familiar to a sociologist: if we recognize that systems of social stratification are not necessarily unidimensional but, rather, that they consist of several different elements —power, wealth, and prestige or honor— it is obvious that an individual's or group's position on one of these does not always correspond to his position on the others. Such status incongruences or disparities have been shown to be consequential, commonly generating tension for those experiencing them and disposing them to improve the relatively lower status by seeking some modification in social arrangements. For an introductory discussion of the concept of status disparity or incongruence, and of the relevant literature, see A. W. Gouldner and H. P. Gouldner, with J. R. Gusfield, *Modern Sociology* (New York: Harcourt, Brace & World, 1963), pp. 227 ff.

[47] Quoted in Adkins, *op. cit.,* p. 77. For a sampling of the Theognid literature, see R. Lattimore, trans., *Greek Lyrics* (Chicago: University of Chicago Press, 1955), pp. 26–31.

[48] For the argument that the evidence in the Homeric literature for a nobility is "slight and precarious," see Calhoun, *op. cit.,* p. 308. For the argument that the *eupatridai* were not just another *genos* but an honorific group cutting across various *genē* and having special prerogatives with respect to exercise of religious authority, to the exegesis of the laws and sacred traditions, and to control over the early archonship, see H. T. Wade-Gery, *op. cit.*

[49] A. French, "The Economic Background to Solon's Reforms," *The Classical Quarterly,* n. s., 6, nos. 1, 2 (1956), 11–25. French's argument can be seen as dealing with two distinct questions: first, the sources of the rural depression in Attica and, second, the reasons why the larger Attican landholders accepted Solon's reforms. I find both arguments interesting, but the former more cogent. It seems possible to me that the large landholders might have remained self-defeatingly intransigent. They might have rejected Solon's compromise, even if it did protect certain of their basic interests, had they been less rationalistically oriented. In other words, their values and not only their economic interests influenced their reactions to the Solonic reforms; their values affected the way in which they interpreted their interests. I also believe that French unwisely neglects the significance of the rules of inheritance, which required the land to be divided into ever smaller parcels.

[50] *Ibid.,* p. 12.

51 G. Glotz, *Ancient Greece at Work* (New York: Knopf, 1926), p. 81. This interpretation of the *hektēmoroi* is supported by W. J. Woodhouse, *Solon the Liberator*, "A Study of the Agrarian Problem in Attika in the Seventh Century" (London: Oxford University Press, 1938). Yet it is directly at variance with Plutarch's statement, "All the people were indebted to the rich, . . . paying them a sixth part of the increase. . . ."—trans. J. Dryden, *Twelve Lives* (Cleveland: Fine Editions Press, 1950), 90. Here, neither for the first nor last time, do we find radical disagreement concerning some of the most elemental questions. (For others, see footnote 62 below.) Nonetheless, I find Woodhouse's arguments, especially those on linguistic grounds, the more convincing; for these, see his ch. VI.

52 Misch, *op. cit.*, p. 78.

53 From the trans. by Misch, *loc. cit.*

54 Wade-Gery, *op. cit.*, p. 78.

55 Glotz, *Ancient Greece at Work, op. cit.*, 169.

56 G. Murray, *Five Stages of Greek Religion* (Garden City: Doubleday, n.d.), p. 41.

57 A. A. Trever, *op. cit.*, p. 157.

58 Glotz, *The Greek City, op. cit.*, p. 129.

59 *Ibid.*, p. 104.

60 E. R. Dodds, *The Greeks and the Irrational* (Berkeley: University of California Press, 1951), p. 76. Cf. Thomson, *op. cit.*, p. 151.

61 Hasebroek, *op. cit.*, p. 89.

62 Population estimates, particularly those of slaves and *metoikoi* in relation to free citizens, have long been one of the most violently disputed issues among classicists. Their other disputes, concerning the status of women and the prevalence of homosexuality in Greece, also make it obvious that the issues involved are not pursued solely because of academic interests. Among the *extra*-scholarly concerns underlying these polemics is the classicists' commitment to a benign image of Greek culture. Many feel impelled to defend it primarily at those points—slavery, the seclusion of women, and homosexuality—where it offends modern Western, and particularly liberal, values. Classicists often feel toward the Greeks as anthropologists do toward the people they study: they become "my people." A systematic examination of the polemics concerning these issues would provide an excellent point of entry for a study of the classicists as a profession, from the standpoint of the sociology of knowledge.

63 Nussbaum, *op. cit.*, pp. 216–217.

64 Michell, *op. cit.*, p. 126.

65 Ibid., p. 146.

66 M. I. Finley, ed., *Slavery in Classical Antiquity*, "Views and Controversies" (Cambridge: Heffner, 1960), p. 61. This is the definitive anthology on its subject.

67 H. D. F. Kitto, *Greek Tragedy*, (Garden City: Doubleday, n.d.), p. 16.

68 For some indications that the husband's sexual access to female slaves excited jealousy and family tensions we might recall Aeschylus' *Agamemnon* or Euripides' *Andromache*. In the latter see iii. 577. 465 ff. Cf. Sophocles *The Women of Trachis* ii. 298. 539: "So now the two of us lie under the one sheet waiting for his embrace."

69 *Laws* 806E.

70 Quoted from K. Stampp, "The Peculiar Institution," in Finley, *Slavery in Classical Antiquity, op. cit.*, p. 59.

71 Sargent, for example, held that there were from 67,000–103,000 slaves and from 120,000–208,000 *metoikoi* and citizens; Tod estimated 80,000–120,000 slaves, 35,000–40,000 *metoikoi*, and 150,-000–170,000 citizens; Ehrenberg, 80,000–100,000 slaves, 25,000–40,000 *metoikoi*, and 110,000–125,000 citizens; Gomme, 115,000 slaves, 28,500 *metoikoi*, and 172,000 citizens. See Morrow, *op. cit.*, 23, for a bibliographical summary. Glotz, *The Greek City, op. cit.*, p. 127, in fact held that, "The citizens of Attica were a minority. Side by side with them lived at least an equal number of slaves and hardly less than half their number of metics."

72 *Agamemnon* i. 46. 357–360.

73 Finley, *Slavery in Classical Antiquity, op. cit.*, p. 69.

[74] Michell, *op. cit.*, p. 150.

[75] i. 271. 243.

[76] ii. 289. 303.

[77] *Iliad* vi. 125.

[78] *Seven against Thebes* i. 275. 361.

[79] Finley, *The World of Odysseus, op. cit.*, p. 136.

[80] Aeschylus *Seven against Thebes* i. 274. 326–329.

[81] *The Women of Trachis* ii. 323. 1224 ff.

[82] Cf. Robert Schlaifer, "Greek Theories of Slavery from Homer to Aristotle," *Harvard Studies in Classical Philology*, 47 (1936), 185; in Finley, *Slavery in Classical Antiquity*, op. cit., 113

[83] For fuller discussion of this belief and for documentation, see S. Ranulf, *The Jealousy of the Gods and Criminal Law at Athens* (London: Williams & Norgate, 1933), pp. 63–84.

[84] Sophocles *Antigone* ii. 180. 161 ff.

[85] Michell, *op. cit.*, p. 152.

[86] Glotz, *Ancient Greece at Work, op. cit.*, p. 192.

[87] Michell, *op. cit.*

[88] Schlaifer, *op. cit.*, p. 177; Morrow, *op. cit.*, p. 63.

[89] Morrow, *op. cit.*, p. 23.

[90] *Ibid.*, p. 91.

[91] Finley, *The World of Odysseus, op. cit.*, 56.

[92] Aeschylus *Agamemnon* i. 49. 471–474.

[93] Xenophon *Hellenica*, F. R. B. Godolphin, ed., *The Greek Historians*, v. i. 2 (New York: Random House, 1942), 34.

[94] The fact that there is some evidence that slaves and citizens received the same wage rates for the same tasks does not prove that slave competition did not generally depress the wage rate for all; it may simply indicate that free labor was constrained to work at the same low rate as slaves. I am inclined toward Glotz's view that slave labor did depress the general wage level. See Glotz, *The Greek City, op. cit.*, 104, 113, 313.

[95] Finley, *Slavery in Classical Antiquity, op. cit.*, 63.

[96] Quoted from Winspear, *op. cit.*, 146.

[97] Aeschylus *The Libation Bearers* i. 95. 77 ff.

[98] For a generalized theoretical analysis of this concept see E. Goffman, *The Presentation of Self in Everyday Life* (Edinburgh: University of Edinburgh Press, 1958).

[99] Ehrenberg, *op. cit.*, pp. 165, 168.

[100] Cf. Morrow, *op. cit.*, p. 97, and Michell, *op. cit.*, 159, 155.

[101] Westerman, *op. cit.*, p. 3.

[102] Morrow, *op. cit.*, p. 32.

[103] *Ibid.*, p. 51.

[104] Westerman, *op. cit.*, p. 8.

[105] For seeming expressions of such see Aeschylus, *Agamemnon* i. 68. 1069 ff; Sophocles *The Women of Trachis* ii. 289. 296. In some measure, empathy and pity for slaves (such as it was) are connected: Greeks could feel pity because they could imagine themselves enslaved. Needless to add, that pity has this or any other cause does not devalue it; we must be grateful to anything that makes men more human.

[106] On branding see Michell, *op. cit.*, 159. Yet cf. Westerman, *op. cit.*, p. 8.

[107] Michell, *op. cit.*, p. 165.

2

The Greek Contest System: Patterns of Culture

Hero, control that grasping violence.
—Bacchylides of Ceos [1]

GENEALOGIES need not be traced only in noble tragedy, serene sculpture, and exalted sentiment: for all its Christian professions, the daily life of modern Westerners has a kinship with the ancient Greek's disposition to punish enemies and to reward friends.[2] The Judaeo-Christian tradition has tempered, but not eliminated, the elemental rules of reciprocity and retaliation to which the Greeks subscribed unswervingly as a point of manly honor. Yet these potent norms are only a primitive heritage that the Greeks share with practically all other societies,[3] especially those that are tribal or only newly detribalized. The norms of reciprocity and retaliation do not distinguish Greek civilization but show its communality with others.[4]

Some of the more distinguishing values of Greek culture may be found in the popular drinking songs of Attica, and from our understanding of their sentiments we may know that our kinship with them has a somewhat special connection. One such song [5] reveals that they held as first and best a man's health; second, the song says, is to be born beautiful; third is wealth honestly won; finally, is the delight of youth spent with friends. The song suggests much that is important about the Greeks' value system, signaling the extent to which the goods they prized had a *body* locus: youth, health, beauty.

Yet this tells us only about a small part of the Greek value system, a part that somehow needed expression in songs men sang while drinking. It reveals some things that gave them enjoyment even though these things are not thought to be "high," estimable, noble, or involved with propriety, honor, or duty. They deal with what Greeks were readier to express privately to drinking companions than with what was compatible with the standards they lauded in the arena of public life. They manifest more clearly the standards of gratification than the moral standards by which they felt men should properly be judged.[6] In short, while Greeks would enjoy health they could not claim that mere possession of it made a man *better*

41

than others. The man possessing youth, beauty, health, and wealth was felt to be fortunate indeed but not, for that reason, truly superior as a man. The claim to superiority lay elsewhere. It is on these other aspects of the Greek value system and on certain accompanying sentiments that attention will be focused here. The elements to be explored will at first be presented separately, and then an effort will be made to see them as interconnected parts.

That the Greeks sought and developed standards other than those of health, wealth, youth, and beauty and that they invested these others with the highest value is related to what they felt to be the impermanence of body values. It was, in some part, the evident instability of body values that exposed them to critical inspection and spurred a quest for something more enduring. The Greeks had a tenacious hold on reality and would not blink at what they saw. They saw that men grew old, infirm, became worn and haggard, and that all inevitably died; they saw that fortunes could change radically, leaving rich men poor and free men enslaved.

While the Greeks knew what they wanted, they also knew that the things they wanted were riddled with worms. These things would not and could not last. While the Greeks delighted in the juices of life, they had an aftertaste of ashes. Their very capacity for enjoyment heightened their resentment and sense of loss at its passing. The Greeks wanted a good that would last; and some of them came to define that which was most lasting as being the most good. But what could a man do or be that would, in truth, last? For a long while they thought to transcend the most tragic impermanence of all, life itself, by a quest for fame and repute. They came to believe that best of all was to be remembered well.

SOME THEMES IN GREEK CULTURE

(1) A central, culturally approved value of Greek life, embedded in and influencing its system of stratification, is an emphasis on individual fame and honor. The ultimate hope is for a "fame undying." Heraclitus, for example, insists, "The best men choose one thing rather than all else: everlasting fame." Wealth, of course, is commonly associated with the attainment of fame and came, especially with the rise of urban mercantilism, to be seen as a distinct and creditable aim rather than as an enjoyable byproduct of fame-bringing deeds. Thus Solon's elegy beseeches, "Grant me prosperity at the hands of the blessed gods, and good fame ever at the hands of men." [7] Wealth itself, however, is often felt to contain an inherent taint. If the pursuit of fame brought an ennobling danger, especially the "envy of the gods," the pursuit of wealth was distinctly fraught with the threat of a cheapening but no less dangerous dishonor. In this vein Solon's elegy continues:

"Wealth, I desire to possess, but would not have it unrighteously; retribution comes afterwards always." Honor is often counterposed to wealth: In his funeral oration, Pericles makes plain that it is "not riches, as some say, but honor that is the delight of men when they are old and useless." [8]

(2) The fame which is best is that which is earned through one's own active efforts. It is not simply that derived through the inheritance of a good name or wealth. These are by all means pleasant and to be enjoyed to the fullest, as much as a beautiful and a healthy body; but the fame that makes a man memorable is that won by his own achievements. "It is the most experienced and the most capable," says Isocrates, "who in any field of action deserve to be honoured." [9]

Above all, a man is made legendary by his readiness to risk what is precious in continuing strife or competition against others. "Who acts, shall endure," said Aeschylus.[10] A man must continue to strive against the odds; for even when he is fated to failure by the gods his *efforts*—all the more ennobled because they are foredoomed—may yet bring immortal fame. "You will die when the *moirai* spin death for you," says Callinus, "but a man should march straight forward brandishing his spear." [11] A man must never withdraw from the contest.

(3) It is a commonplace to Greeks that fame won in contest brings envy, and vigorous in so many ways, they are also lusty in their envy. Of all the sentiments that moderns may discern in the Greeks, perhaps the most seemingly alien is their unabashed envy; an envy all the more notable to us because it betrays our expectations of a people of a "noble" character, and because envy in our own culture tends to be repressed. To the Greeks, however, envy is a sentiment natural to men; if they have reservations about it, it is not on moral grounds but simply because envy made a man unhappy. Envy, however, signified that a man is successful. Epicharmus says, "It is obvious that a man who is not envied is of no account." Envy is the expected portion of the famous and, indeed, so pervasive is envy felt to be that the gods themselves are given to it and might envy a mortal's earthly successes.

(4) Discrepant though it may seem for so earthy and active a people, Greek lustiness is never far removed from an underlying pessimism; the Greeks, says W. C. Grene, were "constantly visited by melancholy." [12] They seem to feel that the best has already been and that the future will bring only pain. Their proverb says: Count no man fortunate until he is dead. Indeed, one of their greatest and most distinctive cultural innovations, the tragic drama, is characterized by its ending, which is commonly, though not always, an "unhappy" one. While a feeling for the "tragic" is by no means synonymous with pessimism, a sense of the tragic is a way of binding the

fears underlying pessimism, of coming to terms with and controlling them; it is a defense against the paralysis of action—the apathy or panic—that can result from pessimism.[13]

The Greeks believe that the human lot is vulnerable to sudden and smashing disaster, and that the more successful a man, the more certain his destruction. The very gods are seen as thwarting men's hopes. Zeus is said in the *Iliad* to resent men's belief that the gods cause their misery, and well he might; for in the *Odyssey* Penelope laments, "It is the gods who give us sorrow. . . ." The Greeks often feel the very universe is inimical to men and, like the King in Aeschylus' *The Suppliant Maidens* who sees his sudden entrapment by circumstances, they sometimes groan, "I see and shudder."

(5) Counterbalancing an activistic, Promethean striving and the zest for contest is their equally insistent taboo against excess.[14] Man, the Greeks feel, should control and limit both his hopes and his ambitions, neither expecting nor attempting too much, lest the gods regard him as guilty of *hybris*—of arrogance or insolence—and exact retribution. This, of course, is implicated in Olympian religion, one of whose central tenets holds that there is an impassable chasm between men and the gods, between mortals and immortals, which men must not seek to surmount. If in their pride they forget this difference, men are doomed. They must think, therefore, *only* human thoughts; they must remember that they are *only* human and, as Zeus remarks in the *Iliad,* of all things living, "there is nothing more piteous than a man."

(6) Still another pattern that arouses curiosity in examining Greek culture is that which, for want of a better term, I will characterize provisionally as its "rationalism." Certainly it would be naïve to assume that the intellectualism of the philosophers is shared by the peasant in the countryside, or even by the average urbanite. Yet certain aspects of Greek history dispose us to doubt that the growth of philosophical rationalism in the fifth century was completely unheralded or discontinuous with the main drift of Greek culture.

Look, for instance, at the bold pragmatic manner in which constitutions are sometimes established for new colonies, or at the calculating way the older tribal structures are deliberately manipulated with a view to strengthening the unity of the *polis*. Similarly, there is the masterful manner in which Solon went about mending the rift in the Athenian class system; he clearly knows what he is about. In Hesiod, one finds a commendation of the man who practices foresight and takes good advice. In Homer there is the fascinating figure of the wily Odysseus, the man who is never at a loss. The Greeks seem to have a curious ability to turn their back upon their own past and, within surprisingly broad limits, to do what they think their new situation requires, even if this disposes them to behave in a manner at variance with tradition.

There is a long intellectual tradition in Greece, as E. R. Dodds indicates, in which a man's character is habitually discussed in terms of what he *knows*. Achilles' ferocious bravery, for example, is spoken of as a kind of knowing; he "knows wild things, like a lion." [15] There is a linguistic tendency to subsume a man's character under what he knows. Just as terms of commendation reveal a group's values, so too does the vocabulary of derogation, and "the derogatory epithets employed by Athenian writers often imply intellectual rather than moral failing." [16] That the deviant Greek is frequently reproached as in some manner ignorant, as knowing no better, or as lacking in insight, indicates the strong value placed upon effective cognition. Also implicit in the basic injunction of the Delphic oracle is the intimate fusion of knowing and of doing right: Man, know thyself. And it is surely related to the Socratic paradox that no one does evil voluntarily. It is also clear from Greek tragedy that a change from ignorance to knowledge, especially knowledge of the *identity* of the protagonists—the *anagnorisis,* or recognition [17]—is viewed as a major dramatic hinge, consequential for all that follows. "When you know me, rebuke me," says Oedipus.[18]

(7) Finally, I must take note of another pattern long associated with Greek antiquity, male homosexuality or, more strictly speaking, bisexuality. Greek homosexuality is not, as it is in most industrialized societies, a deviant and surreptitious pattern nor is it by any means viewed by the Greeks as unmanly. Although its origins in Greek society are obscure, it seems to be of long standing (deriving in one tradition from the Cretans) and is rather widely accepted, if not equally practiced, throughout Greek society. To an unfortunate extent this pattern has been systematically neglected by many classical scholars, some of whom seem to take the attitude that if the reader is interested "in that sort of thing" he must look elsewhere.[19] Yet it is difficult to escape the suspicion that so distinctive and common a pattern of intimate behavior is linked to or expressive of other basic elements in the culture. Common decency may dispose us to a tactful silence on the question; but common scholarly scrupulousness, not to mention perplexity, will not let us off so easily.

THE CONTEST SYSTEM

In exploring the relations among these several patterns, it will be useful to begin with the first three, the active quest for fame through competitive achievement. Together these comprise what may be called the contest system, essentially a mechanism of social mobility or a method for distributing prestige or public status among the citizen group: it is a "game," if you will, in which aliens or slaves do not play.

The zest for competitive struggle that pervades Greek culture finds all manner of expression, particularly on the occasion of the numerous civic and Panhellenic festivals. The greatest of the latter is, of course, the Olympics. The two main parts of this festival are, first, the offerings to Zeus and to other gods and heroes and, secondly, the contests, which include not only athletic competitions such as foot races, horse races, the pentathlon and others, but also heraldic, rhapsodic, poetic, and painting contests.

Perhaps because they lack precise time-keeping instruments, but clearly for other reasons as well, contestants do not concern themselves with establishing a new "all-time" record in some event, or with beating their own past performance; they are rather bent on determining which of those present is the best man. Competitors in a specific event are divided into groupings or pairs chosen by lot, and the winners among these are paired off until one man emerges as victor.

The importance attributed to these contests may be judged by the "brilliant distinctions [that] awaited the victor on his return home. . . . He made his entry, clad in purple, upon a chariot drawn by four white horses, . . . then rode amid an exultant escort to the temple of the highest god, and there deposited his wreath as a votive offering. . . . [T]he song of victory, often composed by the most celebrated poets, was chanted by choral bands. . . . [A]t Athens the Olympian victor received 500 *drachmae,* the right to a place of honour at all public games, and board in the *Prytaneum* for the rest of his life." [20] Perhaps an even better indication of the profound importance of these contests for Greek culture is that the Hellenic system for reckoning time came to be the four-year unit between Olympics.

It is not simply athletics but almost all other efforts at achievement that are set into the framework of a ritually governed and institutionalized contest. Isocrates remarks of Athens that "it is possible to find with us . . . contests not alone of speed and strength, but of eloquence and wisdom and of all the other arts—and for these the greatest prizes. . . ." [21]

The most notable are, of course, the dramatic contests for both tragedy and comedy. The plays comprise a central part of the religious celebration of Dionysus in Athens, and the festival is open to the Hellenic world. Prisoners are released on bail so that they might attend, along with the rest of the citizenry who came en masse and who will, in time, be paid to do so. The contending entries are initially screened by the chief magistrate, or *archōn;* the three tragedians then admitted to the competition each present tetralogies and the five comic poets selected offer one play each. Wealthier citizens are selected as *chorēgoi*, or producers, who pay the costs for one play. At the end of the presentations, a committee selects the winners, awarding prizes to the victorious poets, actors, and *chorēgoi*.

The Greek competitive drive is also expressed in the dramatic structure of the comedies themselves, each of them having in their first half a standardized part, an *agōn*, which involves a debate between the hero and an accuser. Indeed, the plays of Aristophanes have been said as a whole to be "a dramatised debate, an *agōn*, in which the persons represent opposing principles, for in form the piece is always combative, though the fight may be but a mock fight." [22] The comedies also often contain attacks upon other writers of comedy. "The spirit of competition indeed permeated the work of all the comic poets. . . . The *agōn* within the comedy and that between certain poets are sometimes welded into one," [23] as in *The Frogs*, where Aeschylus and Euripides are portrayed in competition before Dionysus.

This powerful competitive or agonistic spirit of Greek culture is indeed still found by anthropologists today studying contemporary Greek villages. For example, in her study of Vasilika, a village ninety miles from Athens, Ernestine Friedl observes that

> if it were necessary to describe the nature of the villagers' feelings with respect to each other and the world in one word, that word would be "tension," . . . tension created by some kind of struggle. John Peristiany [also] speaks of the agonistic quality of relationships among the Cypriot villagers he knows. . . . [In] Vasilika, when one walks through the field and asks how the work is going, the common response is . . . "We are wrestling." . . . The villagers can amplify with further comments on their perpetual contest with soil, weather, and machinery. . . . But an appeal to fate or to God is never an excuse for neglecting actions which are humanly possible. . . . [The] sense of contest, of struggle, of agony, of a kind of pushing and pulling . . . is also a feature of a large number of encounters with other human beings.[24]

One almost hears in this an echo of Euripides' Theseus: "Be instructed in the ills of man. Struggles make up our life."[25]

The Contest as a Game

Here I wish to set out certain of the more essential characteristics of the contest system, developing a simplified model that may aid in exploring some of its more significant consequences for the equilibrium of the *polis*.

First, as to the objective of the contest: The aim of participants is to achieve as much individual recognition as possible, primarily among the peer group of citizens who are also contestants. The aim is to make their individual persons as well known, and their names as well regarded, as possible. What is being sought, then, is not a limited recognition among a small group of knowledgeable peers, or a small number of experts or specialists similar to oneself but, rather, a *communal* recognition and fame among all members of the public comprised by the citizen group. One does not simply want to be known to aficionados as a great sculptor, poet, or dramatist; he wants to be known as a prominent Athenian, as *agathos* or *agathos politēs,* as a leading citizen, respected throughout the citizenry. Aeschylus' well-known epitaph, very possibly written by himself, thus does not laud his dramatic genius, but reminds its viewer only that he had fought at Marathon.

In subsequently attempting to relate the contest system to the various other patterns mentioned above, I do not intend to suggest that these are all fully, or even predominantly, explainable in terms of the contest system. Doubtless each of the patterns is influenced by other forces, including one another. I have utilized the contest system as a wedge into these interrelated patterns because it does seem to point up their interrelationships, providing a way of identifying connections that might otherwise be obscured and, also, because it appears to be one of the major factors, if by no means the only one, underlying the total configuration: pull this strand out, it seems, and much of importance comes in its train.

The contest system may be thought of as a game governed by a set of tacit instructions. Stated otherwise, we might think of group members as if they were oriented toward a set of unspoken rules. The foremost rules in this game can be stated in something of the following manner:

(1) The object of the game is to win more public prestige or "fame" than all other players. Each citizen is playing against all others.

(2) Fame is won in the following ways: (2.1) "Wars"—forcibly overcoming the resistance of others and taking valuable objects (e.g., their life, treasure, land, people) from them without their consent; (2.2) "Threats"— making others relinquish valuable objects under the threat of force so that they concede defeat without doing battle; (2.3) "Competitions"—inducing others to enter into some publicly visible effort, which is to be compared with your own performance according to certain rules by third parties (judges) who declare to the larger public which of you is victor, through awarding prizes, offices, or deference. The "competition" seems to be a substitute for, if not a sublimation of, the first two modes of obtaining fame; it is a way of obtaining judgments of the relative prowess and superiority of

persons without the loser having to bow in defeat and without the victor having to destroy the loser. (2.3.1) A special case of competition is "honorific expenditures"—expending valuables in ways that the public deems desirable (e.g., through supporting choruses).

(3) The amount of fame that is won depends upon the following: (3.1) The value attributed to the objects which the victor takes from the loser, or the value of the prizes which are awarded him; (3.2) The value of the stakes that the contestant risks and the extent of the risk to which these are subjected. (The concept of "heroism," for example, premises that a man has risked his most precious possession, his life, and it is only the mortality of man that enables him to be a "hero"; the gods therefore cannot be heroes.) (3.3) The higher the ranking of the loser in the established fame hierarchy, the greater the value of a victory over him. (3.4) The greater the fame of those deferring to or acknowledging one as "famed," the greater is one's own fame. (3.5) In a contest between teams or groups, the amount of fame won by the individual is also a function of whether his team has won or lost to others, and further of (3.6) the importance of the individual's position in the leadership hierarchy of his own team. (3.7) The more one's honorific expenditures and the more that activities on which they are spent are judged to excel those of others, the greater the fame won by the spender.

The Contest as a Zero-Sum Game

Certain peculiarities of the contest system deserve to be stressed. For one, it approximates a zero-sum game in that someone can win only if someone else loses. This, of course, is manifest in the case of victory won by "wars" and "threats"; but it also seems to be the case in "competitions," especially by the standards of a "shame culture," [26] which defines any kind of defeat as shameful regardless of circumstances; here a loser does not leave the contest with as much fame as he entered. Losing in such a competition, therefore, does not simply mean a prize foregone but a loss suffered: someone is the loser.

The significance of the zero-sum game can be clarified by contrasting it with others. In other, non-zero-sum games, *all* players can gain relative to their own starting points; one is winner only because he has gained more than the other. This, however, is possible only insofar as the stakes derive from some source other than the contestants who are playing one another. In the non-zero-sum game, therefore, the prizes must be posted by a noncontestant. They must come from the resources of a group outside, or from an over-all increase in the total resources of all players through their productive exploitation of nature. In both these cases, however, there is an increase in the total payoffs available to contestants, while in the zero-sum game there has simply been a redistribution of assets without any increase in their total.

It may be expected, therefore, that defeat will be more difficult to accept the more that social interaction approximates a zero-sum game, operating with inelastic assets, and with the gains of one player tending to equal the losses of another. The zero-sum game will engender more bitterness and a greater inclination to win at any cost, even if this requires violation of the rules. This would be consistent with, and partly explain, the remarked-upon tendency of a "shame culture" such as the Greeks' to disregard the circumstances and intentions of the contestants, and to make success or failure itself the primary basis for commendation or derogation. In a zero-sum game played in a shame culture, the loser is less likely to concede defeat gracefully; he is more likely to break the rules when defeat is imminent or to attempt to conceal or to deny his defeat. A relevant if trivial example of this is the story attributed to Pericles' wrestling companion who complained that even when he threw Pericles he could not get the latter to concede; after Pericles would get up he would use his oratorical skill to persuade the viewers that he had not lost. A similar story has it that Alcibiades once bit another wrestler who was beating him.

Under what conditions will contestants play their game in a zero-sum manner? Here we inquire not into the consequences of playing such a game, but, rather, into the conditions leading such zero-sum rules to be adopted, so that contestants are constrained to gain valuables for themselves by taking them from someone else. One of the most basic of these conditions seems to be whether the contestants can acquire more of what they want in some other manner. Do they, in short, have an alternative?

There are several ways in which contestants can get things they desire without taking them from others. Not the least of these is that they can manufacture them for themselves, or they can trade what they want less for what they want more. In other words, they can expend energies and other resources in the conduct of economic activities, in production and exchange, and can thereby increase the total assets in the game.

Secondly, they can get valuables they desire without taking them from others if the valuables are not already exclusively possessed by others and/or if the means of achieving or producing them is available to those who want them. One way of doing this—which also entails an increase in total assets—is through changing the value system, that is, the way of reckoning assets, so that the kinds of things that they value are not of the sort that are pre-empted by others and are of the sort that they do have means of achieving. For example, if land is valued and if all the land is already allocated, men will, under these assumptions, be more likely to seek land by taking it from others. But if they value wisdom or temperance, there is no reason to believe that the supply of these is inelastic or that all wisdom or temperance is already allocated. The achievement of these values may therefore be within reach of the means men already control. Indeed, these values are intrinsically such that they cannot be *wrested* from anyone else.

Whether men can get what they want without taking it from others depends, first of all, on what they want and hence on the nature of their values. For example, a particularistic commitment to specific objects permits no substitutions to be made and therefore conduces to conflict if the desired object is pre-empted. Universalistic commitment to classes of objects, however, does allow a choice of substitutes and thereby reduces the chance of conflict. If men want *particular* objects that others already possess they can get them only from their owners.

Further, if men lack the means to produce the objects they want, or lack things to exchange for them, they will be more disposed to take what they want from others. Again, if their other beliefs and values induce them to feel that it is not entirely honorable to obtain things through manufacture or exchange—and it would seem that upper-class Greeks more nearly approximate this than, say, Europeans since the Middle Ages—then they will also be more disposed to get what they want by taking it from others.

There is, of course, one basic condition on which all of this depends: Men must want something. Conversely, the less they want the valuables in the game the less will they be disposed to play the game according to zero-sum rules; hence one way in which the intensity of a zero-sum or any other game may be reduced is to limit the players' wants and, in general, to make them want less. Here, to anticipate, is one of the implications of the Greek stress on "nothing in excess."

The Contest and the Class System

Fame could be won by honorific expenditures. Since fame is sought from a larger public rather than a small group of expert peers, such expenditures must be sufficient to be widely visible. Consequently, for those intent upon achieving prominence in the contest system, honorific expenditures could be extremely costly. According to Plutarch, Solon's father "had ruined his estate in doing benefits and kindnesses to other men. . . ." [27] Honorific expenditures could indeed so strain the contestant's resources that he might come to need the booty of war to restore his fortunes. Thucydides, for example, observes of Alcibiades—who might have become Athens' Alexander—that "the position he held among the citizens led him to indulge his tastes beyond which his real means could bear, both in keeping horses and in the rest of his expenditure; and this later on had not a little to do with the ruin of the Athenian state." [28] The implication here is that Alcibiades is in part motivated to press for the disastrous Sicilian expedition because of his hope that it will relieve his straitened circumstances.

That honorific expenditures facilitate one's rise in the contest system means, of course, that those with more money—whether inherited or acquired through their own efforts—are advantaged in the competition. Thus Victor Ehrenberg remarks:

> We know that many noble or at least wealthy men were among the *stratēgoi,* and that fairly often there was a certain heritage in office from father to son. A sort of military aristocracy still held the *stratēgia* and other higher military posts throughout the fourth century. But there were many "new" families, and, moreover, ever since Kleon had been *strategos* in the years 425–422, there had been signs of a gradual invasion by the middle and lower classes. . . . The aristocracy became poorer and in other classes wealth had increased so as to reach upper-class standards. Some rich men were accepted by the aristocrats among their own ranks, and Nikias even became to some extent their political leader. . . . It has been proved from the inscriptions that most of the speakers in the assembly, and the movers of public decrees also, belonged to wealthy families.[29]

And just as money could be transformed into power and fame, so too could power be used to secure money which might then be transformed into popularity and fame: Pericles, "finding himself come short of his competitor in wealth and money . . . ," says Plutarch, "turned to the distribution of the public moneys. . . ." [30]

Dysfunctions of the Contest System

The objective of the Greek contest system is to win more prestige than the other contestants; contestants, therefore, do not simply seek fame increments but seek to increase the difference between their own fame rankings and those of all others. Since they seek to increase their superiority vis-à-vis all others, they cannot, in consequence, always be wholeheartedly committed to a victory of their own team when it enters into a contest with others. For such a victory, even if it increases the fame of all team members by some amount, does not enhance the fame of all equally.

The relative position of certain players might, even under victorious circumstances, be affected adversely. A team victory brings fame in different degrees to the team members, depending on the individual's degree of leadership or eminence relative to others on his team. As Euripides notes,[31] the general wins more fame than the *hoplitēs*. Consequently, it is not merely defeat of one's team that one needs to avoid, but also victories that could impair one's relative position in the fame hierarchy. When the victory of one's own team can impair one's relative standing in the fame hierarchy of the team, then one has a vested interest in the team's defeat.

Under such circumstances, the following disruptive tendencies would seem likely to emerge:

(1) In interteam contests where the expectation of team victory is greatest, there will be an intensification of contests for leadership, and where the prospects of defeat seem greatest, a corresponding reluctance to seek leadership. In other words, the more one's team is winning, the more violent will be the internal contest for the rewards of leadership; and the more it is losing, the more difficult will it be to find people to assume positions of responsibility, and there will be a retreat from public life. In the first instance, the group will suffer from disruptive contests for leadership; in the second, from leadership apathy.

(2) Since successful leadership of a team increases one's fame relative to others, players will resist awarding leadership to those with whom they are most intensively competing. Consequently, they will tend not to award leadership solely in terms of the skill and probability of success of the candidate. For the candidate having greatest probability of success may be the very one with whom they are most intensely competing and who, in the event of a victory led by him, would outdistance them. Selection by merit, therefore, tends to be seriously undermined when leadership is awarded by a group of competitors to one of *their* fellow competitors: "[M]en who live in oligarchies or democracies are led by their mutual rivalries to injure the commonwealth. . . . [They are] ill disposed toward each other and would rather have their predecessors and their successors in office administer the state as badly as possible, in order that they may win for themselves as much credit as possible." [32]

(3) Since the more a man succeeds in his public enterprises the higher will be his fame relative to others, the very men who have a claim to public honor will be most resented. Furthermore, since the more famous the opponent, the more glorious the victory over him, then the more a man has acquired fame by his contribution to the group, the more will he become a target of the less famous, all seeking to pull him down for their own glory. This would seem to be the more likely insofar as envy of the famous can be rationalized as a fear of their *hybris*. Consequently, the more successful a man is on behalf of his team, the less secure with and the more endangered by his teammates is he.

(4) Finally, it is noteworthy that the contestant most wants the plaudits

of those with whom he is in most intense competition. He is in the painful position of seeking validation from his enemies. Esteem, however, is likely to come most readily from those farthest beneath one, from whom it is least appreciated and valued. It is thus difficult to feel worthy and successful; for the validations one does receive are distrusted as the self-seeking flattery of sycophants, while validations are withheld by those from whom they would be meaningful. Consequently, one needs to seek out continued tests in which one's continuing victories are manifest: the victor can never withdraw from the contest; he must always hurl himself back into the fray.

The conditions described above go far, I believe, in showing how the contest system contributes to the instability of the *polis,* undermining the bases of social order within it, for the maintenance of any social order depends on the degree to which a group's collective interests coincide with those of its individual members. Social order depends on the extent to which the individual will simultaneously contribute to the group's needs in pursuing his own ends. The contest system, to the contrary, disposes individuals to make decisions that are often at variance with the needs and interests of their group. Not only is it possible for the individual to realize his own ambitions without contributing to the welfare of the group, but, and much more fatally, the success and welfare of his group might produce changes in the fame hierarchy disadvantageous to him. There is thus induced a destructive conflict between private interests and those of the collectivity.

Achilles' behavior at Troy epitomizes this disjunction between the individual and the group and the manner in which the contest system drives a wedge between them. Having been slighted by Agamemnon, Achilles retires to his tent while his comrades-in-arms are being mauled by the enemy's forces. He returns to battle only after his friend Patroclus has been killed while wearing Achilles' armor and when, in consequence, Achilles' own personal honor and deepest sentiments have been affronted. This, of course, is not history but epic literature. The point is that the Greeks were raised on this literature and, for the most part, found the behavior of its protagonists meaningful and admirable.

In the classical period the best instance of the conflict between individual interests and group needs fostered by the contest system may be found in Thucydides' discussion of Alcibiades, the leading advocate of the Sicilian expedition. By reason of his manifest ambition and ostentatious display, Alcibiades had alienated the *dēmos;* "although publicly his conduct of war was as good as could be desired individually, his habits gave offense to everyone, and caused them to commit affairs to other hands, and thus before long to ruin the city." [33]

In defending himself and his policy against popular criticism, Alcibiades voices with classic purity the sentiments of a protagonist in the contest system. As for his ostentation, he says:

> Custom regards such displays as honorable and they cannot be made without leaving behind them an impression of power. Again, any splendor that I may have exhibited at home in providing choruses or otherwise, is naturally envied by my fellow-citizens. . . . [N]or is it unfair that he who prides himself on his position should refuse to be upon an equality with the rest. . . . [W]e do not see men courted in adversity, [and] on the like principle a man ought to accept the insolence of prosperity. . . . [P]ersons of this kind and all others that have attained to any distinction, although they may be unpopular in their lifetime in their relations with their fellow-men and, especially, with their equals, leave to posterity the desire of claiming connection with them even without any ground.

Alcibiades then makes the decisive point, with respect to the compatibility of individual interests and group needs, that, "Such are my aspirations, and however I am abused for them in private, the question is whether anyone manages public affairs better than I do." [34]

Shortly before the expedition to Sicily is to get under way the mutilation of the *Hermai* occurs, and there is widespread suspicion that Alcibiades is implicated in it. The charge "was taken hold of by those who could least endure him, because he stood in the way of their obtaining the undisturbed direction of the people, and who thought that if he were once removed the first place would be theirs." [35] Alcibiades offers to stand trial before leaving as one of the three generals in charge of the Sicilian expedition, but thinking the moment not right his enemies refuse and propose instead that he be tried after his return from the campaign, "their plan being to have him sent for and brought home for trial upon some graver charge, which they could the more easily get up in his absence." [36] While Alcibiades is embroiled in the war in Sicily, he is ordered back with a view to placing him on trial and executing him, but he escapes and goes over to the Spartans. (Some time later the Syracusan generals encounter a similar treatment.) Few instances reveal more clearly the manner in which the contest system induces behavior disruptive of the group's needs and interests.

CULTURAL PATTERNS: ENVY

The characteristic patterns of Greek culture outlined earlier are related in various ways to the dilemmas of the contest system. The prevalence of envy in Greek society, for example, would appear to be very closely connected with its intense and personalized competition. There are at least two basic ways in which men can appraise their rewards and position in society,[37] one of which is in terms of their own previous experiences or of some set of general standards deriving from experiences which they have internalized. They can feel that relative to their own past rewards they are doing well or poorly; or they may believe that in terms of their notions of propriety, they are getting what they deserve, or more or less. Here it makes no difference what happens to others. Their own satisfaction or dissastisfaction depends solely on what they themselves did or on what has happened to them. In the second way, however, as in the contest system, men's satisfaction depends upon what happens to others in comparison with themselves; it depends upon their ranking relative to that of others.

Within the contest system men can get ahead in either of two ways, and there are two ways in which they can lose out. They can rise relative to others by (1) raising themselves absolutely and leaving the other man behind or by (2) maintaining their own absolute position and cutting the other man down. Conversely, they can fall (1) by moving down while the man above has not changed his absolute position; or they can fall (2) *relative to him,* even when their own absolute position remains the same or improves if his happens to improve still more. Consequently, in the contest system, men's satisfaction with their own position decreases to the extent that others' positions are improved. The good things that happen to others are therefore hurtful to them. This is precisely the nature of envy, which is a feeling of dissatisfaction that arises from the success of others. Envy is particularly apt to occur in a contest system because every success experienced by others—whether or not it means an absolute decline in one's own status—does mean a decline in status relative to theirs; it means a diminution of one's own relative superiority, and it is this relative advantage that is most prized.

Envy is prone to occur in a social system where a man's own situation is appraised and experienced as satisfying or dissatisfying by comparing it with another's. In such a system one is more likely to find, as Aeschylus remarks, that a man "winces again to the vision of a neighbor's bliss," [38] all the more so as competitive animus disposes him to deny that the superior reward is justified by a superior merit. By the same token, it is likely that the contestant will savor the envy of those he outdistances, for it is the one compliment that can be believed: the cry of pain cannot be feigned. The bitter competitiveness of the contest system induces men to relish openly the defeat of their foes—thereby making subsequent reconciliation all but impossible—and to feel, as Euripides remarks, that "there is nothing like the sight of an old enemy down on his luck." [39]

The danger of envy that makes Aeschylus say, "Let me attain no envied wealth, let me not plunder cities," [40] clearly does not come from the gods alone. Euripides pointedly indicates that attempts to do too much are as keenly resented by the citizens as they are by the gods.[41] The Greeks did not wait patiently for divine retribution to be inflicted on the great, but energetically took justice into their own hands. They instituted one of the most remarkable laws known anywhere, ostracism, which permits them during the period it is in effect to exile certain men—usually the most famous among them—who have committed no crime and are charged with none, but whose sheer presence is thought to threaten the stability of the polis.

In one manner or another, Greece usually finds occasion to punish its greatest men—Aristides, Alcibiades, Anaxagoras, Cimon, Demosthenes, Phidias, Pericles, Themistocles, Xenophon—while Aeschylus and Euripides die in self-imposed exile. However novel Socrates' life in other respects, his fate at the hands of the Athenians is scarcely unique. G. C. Field remarks that by the fourth century B.C., "one thing that strikes anyone . . . is the extraordinary sense of insecurity which all public men, orators and generals alike, must have felt. Hardly anyone of prominence escaped trial at some period of his career, and few avoided condemnation either to payment of a heavy fine, to exile, or even to death." [42]

Like any other institution, ostracism performs many functions and expresses diverse motives which shift over time.[43] In its earliest phase, during the Cleisthenic period, ostracism served to prevent the restoration of the tyranny; it was used primarily by democrats against the pro-Persian aristocratic faction which sought a return of the Pisistratan tyrants. Indeed, given the nature of the mass vote it required, ostracism must always have been a mechanism of social control more amenable to the uses of the "many," or the democrats, than to those of oligarchical persuasion.

The possibility of ostracism requires oligarchical leaders to remember that restraint and discretion are the better part of intrigue. Ostracism is a less terrible punishment than loss of possessions and life and exacts no penalty on a man's family. It allows defeated leaders the hope that they might return and fight another day and that they need not seek to cope with defeat by plunging the city into civil war. Ostracism also serves to prevent political stalemates that might arise when competing factions are more or less equal in strength. The vote to ostracize not only indicates which faction and policy has public support, but, in removing the leader of the losing faction, it makes it difficult for the faction to continue its resistance effectively.

To show ostracism as a barrier to the restoration of tyranny is not to deny that it is also expressive of a pervasive envy. The former has to do with its consequences, the latter with some of its underlying motives. Plutarch tells the ironic story of a peasant asking a stranger to mark his *ostrakon* with Aristides' name. The stranger, needless to say none other than Aristides himself, asks the rustic for his reasons. "Although I do not know him," he replies, "it annoys me to hear him cried up everywhere for his righteousness."

CULTURAL PATTERNS: PESSIMISM

Envy—and fear of envy—also links the contest system to the viscous under-current of pessimism in Greek culture, for it is envy that helps, in some part, to generate pessimism. Because of envy, the association of success with great peril and imminent doom is a realistic one: the more one wins, the greater one's danger. "I thought that if I could acquire a greater competence and attain a higher position than others, . . . I should be acclaimed both for the superiority of my teaching and for the excellence of my conduct," says Isocrates with mock ingenuousness. "But the result has been the very opposite; for if I had turned out to be worthless and had excelled in nothing, no one would have made trouble for me. . . . But now, instead of the acclaim which I expected, I have been rewarded with trials and perils and envy and calumny." [44]

One of the moods commonly viewed as an expression of Greek pessimism is the sense of transiency and instability in human affairs; men are recur-rently called "things of a day, a dream of shadows," and are likened to "phantoms." [45] What seems to be most disturbing, however, is the vulner-ability of those who have climbed highest. As Pindar holds, "prosperity must sustain an envy equalling itself; but concerning the man of low estate the rumor is obscure." Thucydides similarly remarks that the rich man is always liable to a change for the worse. Sophocles notes in *Antigone,* "There is no kind of state in human life which I would now dare to envy or to blame." [46] And, again, in *Ajax,* he comments, "One short day inclines the balance of all human things to sink or rise again." [47] This sense of the unpredictable in human life would inevitably be conducive to pessimism, to a haunting prescience of the sudden humbling of the famed and powerful, a potentiality intrinsic to the contest system.

CULTURAL PATTERNS: NO EXCESS

The contest system is also associated with another major theme of Greek culture, that calling for restraint, temperance, and "nothing too much." In some part "nothing too much" is one more expression of the pessimism in

Greek thought, suggesting as it does that men must not hope for too much in this world. The stress on limitation, however, also means that men should not be ceaselessly ambitious and should not strive greedily for success after success. It is in opposition to such an anomic insatiability that Pindar warns of the "madness that springeth from inappeasable desires." In one part, then, the commandment "nothing too much" functions to restrain competitive ambitions which, especially when they are successful, incite the envy of gods and men.

While there are indeed limits in the world, these by themselves would hardly explain why the Greeks are so sensitive to them, for there are limits in all men's worlds. It is not merely realism about the world outside that leads them to be concerned with "limits" but also a fear of their own inner limitlessness; the Greek concern with "limits" would appear to stem from the sense of their own "inappeasable desires." One source of this inner limitlessness is the intense competitive striving generated by the contest system which, more than other systems of status distribution, fosters pressures to win at any cost, gives no security to the victor, and forces him to seek victory after victory.

In the contest system, a man is threatened by the envy and ambition of those lower, and he is envious of those higher. He cannot stand still, for so long as he is alive he may be challenged and overtaken by younger, rising contenders. He may fear that when he is dead the luster of his fame will be so dimmed by the surpassing achievements of those coming later that he will not be remembered and that it will be as if he never was. In this bitter mood Archilochus laments that "no man is respected, no man spoken of when he is dead by his townsmen. All of us, when still alive, will cultivate the live man, and thus the dead will always have the worst of it." [48]

The Greek, with his potent sense of individuality, searches for a realm of posthumous existence, and he hopes that through his achievements his memory will forever be emblazoned in the minds of men. This passion for fame undying, conjoined with the competitive instigations of the contest system, produces contestants to whom "nothing is enough." It is precisely because they are often unwilling to set any limit upon their own ambitions that they sense the danger in their strivings and understand the need for limits.

Surely if one searches for an understanding of the magnificence of the Greek achievement, one must attribute it, at least in part, to the contest system. Indeed, this is no modern hindsight but seems in fact to have been understood by the Greeks themselves. Hesiod, for example, notes expressly that certain kinds of *eris,* or strife, spur men on to achieve, "for a man grows eager to work when he considers his neighbor. . . . This *eris* is wholesome for men." Yet it is this same contest system that also rends the *polis* and so lacerates its social order that at times it appears that, of all the Greek talents, by far their greatest is mutual destruction.

INTERPERSONAL STRAINS AND HOMOSEXUALITY

We might begin an effort, such as that following, to relate the contest system to Greek homosexuality by remembering Hector's soliloquy at the beginning of the twenty-second book of the *Iliad,* where he debates with himself the advisability of accepting Priam's plea to withdraw and fight behind the walls of Troy. He considers the shame of such a retreat, counterbalancing to it the glory of an open fight with Achilles; then vacillating further, he entertains the possibility of stripping himself of his armor and entreating Achilles to accept terms in which Troy would return Helen and give the Achaeans half the city's treasure.

Hector decides against this course, however, for Achilles might "take no pity upon me nor respect my position, but kill me naked so, as if I were a woman. . . . There is no way any more from a tree or a rock to talk to him gently whispering like a young man and a young girl, in the way a young man and a young maiden whisper together." [49] In effect, Hector's momentary fantasy is to approach Achilles as if he were a girl. While it would be too long a leap to allow this to suggest that Greek homosexuality may, in general, be motivated by an underlying fear of aggression and express a quest for security by sexual surrender to the aggressive competitor, it is noteworthy that the contest between Achilles and Hector, the very paradigm of contest for Greek culture, did elicit this incipiently homosexual response.

Such a linking of the contest system with homosexuality may have something to recommend it, but it would lead into some of the more dubious depths of Freudian psychodynamics. I propose to bypass this here, linking homosexuality and the contest system through their interconnections with the friendship system.

The competitive striving and envious sentiments fostered by the contest system could not help but profoundly affect the quality of interpersonal relations. In particular, friendships would seem of necessity to have been strained; as Aeschylus observes, "In few men is it part of nature to respect a friend's prosperity without begrudging him. . . ." [50] Aristotle reports it was "commonly said" that successful and happy men "have no need of friends," and he quotes Euripides' *Orestes* to that effect: "When Fortune smiles on us, what need of Friends?"

In what I think to be one of the most discerning analyses of the dilemmas of friendship ever written, Aristotle notes that men "cease to be friends" when they "drift apart in respect of virtue or vice or wealth or anything else. . . ." [51] If this is true, he asks, then how is it possible for friends truly to wish each other the greatest good? If they get their wish, "they will no longer have them for friends." [52] It would seem then that, if differential success impairs friendship, men must be somewhat ambivalent about wishing their friends well; they therefore cannot wholeheartedly feel the very sentiments deemed appropriate to friends. Because it induces men to seek relative superiority and fosters envy, the contest system inhibits men from feeling the sentiments incumbent upon friends and thereby undermines their relationship.

While friendly sociability is being thus impaired, the need for friends is, however, being heightened: there develops an endemic crisis of intimacy. As the extended kinship system continues to decline it became proverbial that "a man needs friends as well as relatives." There is a growing need for relationships in which a mutual revelation of selves might be made safely and in which feelings of lonely isolation could be overcome; there is, as well, a need for friends with whom one might enter into coalitions even if only temporarily in the contest for fame. Yet the competitiveness, envy, and distrust intrinsic to the contest system make this difficult. Indeed, so deep is mutual distrust that there is for a period an almost pathological fear of being poisoned.[53] As a result of these mutually contradictory forces the orientation toward friendship becomes profoundly ambivalent; on the one hand it is extolled and idealized as the most ennobling and gratifying of relationships, while on the other a pervasive and continual distrust of friendship is expressed. Friendship, like all else, is seen as evanescent and unreliable.

Although there are many forces that doubtless contribute to the development of homosexuality in Greece, homosexuality is probably also reinforced by this crisis of intimacy. Specifically, homosexuality may be seen as enabling Greek men to resolve their ambivalent orientation to men and to establish close relationships with some of them. The homosexual relation provides a basis for trust and security which, by allying interpersonal social needs with sensual or sublimated sexuality, can overcome the avoidance side of the ambivalence toward friends.

The use of homosexuality as a way of coping with the crisis of intimacy is also probably heightened by the decline of alternative forms of personal involvement. One of these, the dissolution of the extended kinship system, means a loosening of the individual's bonds with the family of orientation into which he was born. At the same time, however, these weakened involvements are not counterbalanced by deep attachment to the family of procreation. The low regard in which women are held in the classical period, as well as the seclusion of wives in segregated household quarters, reduces their contact with men; it makes them ignorant of the public affairs in which their husbands are often deeply involved and, to that degree, a less interesting and attractive companion than men.

In short, both the family of orientation and the family of procreation provide men with few opportunities for gratifying and secure personal friendships. These alternatives curtailed, the Greek male—who can, unlike his wife, move freely outside the home—is constrained to seek close personal relations with nonkinsmen, whether male or female. In this connection, the emergence of the *hetairai,* or courtesans, is no less relevant than the spread of pederasty; relationships with *hetairai* serve a similar function of relieving the crisis of intimacy, for men can, and do, talk to them.

The ability of the *hetairai* to function in this manner is, however, limited precisely because they are women. Although obvious, it must be stressed that the crisis of intimacy is most intense in relations among males, for it is the males who are competing most aggressively with one another. And it is only from other men that a man can obtain full validation of his public performance.

If, as we suggest, Greek pederasty is in part a response to the crisis of intimacy occasioned by distrust and envy, then pederasty must be most common among the males most deeply involved in the contest system, and thus most common among the upper classes or aristocracy. This, in fact, appears to be the case. In particular, the section of the aristocracy that affects the Spartan manner, the *Lakōnizontes* (or Spartan sympathizers), view pederasty as a Spartan and hence noble tradition.

Homosexuality, like other forms of sexuality, provides an apt occasion for the development of intimate communication, permitting mutual revelation and validation of the selves involved. The suggestion, then, is that Greek pederasty serves to satisfy a desire for personal closeness in a situation in which self-validation and intimate communication in the context of heterosexual relations is restricted and where friendship among males is undermined by distrust and envy.

If the need for a confidant who could provide validation of a man's public performance and self is one of the underlying motives for Greek pederasty, then we would expect that male slaves would not be preferred as lovers, and this, too, seems to have been the case. It is more difficult to communicate intimately about the self to another who is much lower in status; it is, also, more difficult for the very low to provide those higher with convincing validations of the self.

The same status considerations that inhibit the male slave from serving as an intimate also blocks Greek women from performing a similar role. Women's low status impairs the use of heterosexual relations for intimate and validating self-revelation, reinforcing the pattern of peer homosexuality among males. It is notable that while Greek homosexuality excludes the male slave, Greek heterosexuality includes the female slave. Inasmuch as intimate communication is not conventionally defined as important to heterosexual relations—except perhaps with *hetairai*—low or slave status need not disqualify a woman as a bedmate.

The ideal conception of homosexual relations held by the Greek upper classes stresses that they should occur between a somewhat older and a younger man, the former presumably serving as a model for the latter who, in turn, is supposed to admire, emulate, and learn from the elder with a view to earning his approval. (Doubtless this ideal of homosexuality is fulfilled in reality about as often as our own romantic conceptions of heterosexuality, if that much.) Even in its ideal form, however, the preferred homosexual relation is not seen as one between equals but stresses a well-defined system of superiority and dependence. This establishes an interpersonal context from which all hint of mutual competition has been eradicated, walling the relationship off from the usual stresses of the contest system. It thus provides a context in which the older male could receive a trustworthy validation of his superiority—one all the more valuable to the extent that the younger is attractive and sought by others—while the younger man is able to be closer to men of higher rank and eminence who might sponsor his career, achieving public visibility greater than his youth might otherwise allow.

In one way, the prevalence of homosexuality is a cementing force in the male community, diminishing—as does the isolation of women from public life—the likelihood that their already tense relations will be further imperiled by competition for women. Yet there seems little doubt that homosexuality also heightens other tensions among males and exacerbates the strains of public life. First, there is bound to be competition among the older males for "fair and noble" youths. This would be difficult to isolate from their other forms of competition, which would now be intensified by feelings of sexual jealousy. Secondly, since public fame is a factor in making an older man attractive as a lover, the desire for sexual success would further motivate and exacerbate competitive efforts in the public arena. Third and finally, it is not socially inconsequential that pederasty at its worst could also be expensive; the eel-smooth, bright-cloaked, gold-ringleted boys sometimes require costly presents. If the relationship between an older and younger man lends itself to exploitation, it is not always easy to say who is exploiting whom.

Even under conditions where homosexuality is endorsed by the upper classes and institutionalized, the homosexual relation seems to have been precarious and strained, lacking as it does a stabilizing involvement in the kinship system and the binding constraints of children, marriage, and dowry. In *Phaedrus,* Plato remarks that the lover is "always fancying that everyone is leagued against him. Wherefore also he debars his beloved from society; he will not have you intimate with the wealthy, lest they should exceed him in wealth, or with men of education, lest they should be his superiors in understanding; and he is equally afraid of anybody's influence who has any other advantage over himself. If he can persuade you to break with them, you are left without a friend in the world. . . ." [54] Socrates sums it up, quoting the verse, "As wolves love lambs so lovers love their loves." [55]

Homosexuality often exerts a disruptive effect upon the public life of the *polis* because of these strains, particularly its proneness to sexual jealousies, and because it is especially common among the upper classes most implicated in the contest system. An example of this is the assassination of Hipparchus, the brother of Hippias, who, according to Thucydides, succeeded his father Pisistratus as tyrant of Athens. Their government, says Thucydides, "was not grievous to the multitude, or in any way odious in practice; and these tyrants cultivated wisdom and virtue as much as any. . . ." [56] Yet Hipparchus was assassinated by two lovers, Aristogiton and Harmodius: "Harmodius was then in the flower of youthful beauty, and Aristogiton, a citizen in the middle rank of life, was his lover and possessed him." [57] Harmodius was solicited, without success, by Hipparchus, who, being rejected, insulted him publicly in return, thus exasperating Aristogiton on two counts. In revenge the lovers slew Hipparchus, thereby inducing his brother to take alarm for his own safety and to make his regime more fearful and oppressive. Rather than stressing the manner in which their homosexual love strengthened Harmodius and Aristogiton in a patriotic resolve to strike a blow against tyranny, as do Plato and the *Lakōnizontes,* Thucydides is quite clear that the affair was motivated by personal jealousy and the strains involved in homosexual love: "[O]ffended love first led Harmodius and Aristogiton to conspire . . ."; [58] their daring action "was undertaken in consequence of a love affair." [59]

CULTURAL PATTERNS: RATIONALISM

There are several ways in which the character of Greek rationalism is related to and enhanced by the contest system. For one thing, the contest system leads men to seek to excel over one another, and this in turn is disruptive of traditional styles of craftsmanship. Zealous contestants chafe against time-honored ways and seek to improve on them so that they may produce what is, according to some standard, a superior product. In the Greek theater, for instance, during a relatively short span of time, the number of actors, the kinds of masks and scenery, and the modes of production of the plays, as well as the ways they are written, are by no means frozen by a set of received rules but are continually developed, experimented with, and changed.

If rationalism means, at least in part, a readiness to depart from traditionally received forms and to find better ways of realizing certain objectives, then it would seem the contest system is a spur to rationality. The contest system is also conducive to the development of rationalism to the extent that it undermines the traditional proprieties of interpersonal relations. By instigating men to win under any conditions, it leads them to evaluate methods and strategies primarily with an eye to their efficiency, ignoring the claims of established morality.

The development of sophistic rationalism is, in itself, spurred on by the competitive interpersonal context in which it is displayed, a fact which led Socrates to call it *eristic*. Sophistic disputation is not simply a way in which the truth is impersonally sifted but is still another way in which the Greek zest for contest and repute is pursued passionately and through which the other man could be "put down" to one's own credit. Indeed, the Platonic dialogues themselves are not confined to serene, mutually helpful explorations of an intellectual puzzle but are often enough deeply involving contests.

To talk about Greek rationality is to attempt to identify one of the most distinctive and manifestly important characteristics of Greek culture. Yet to characterize this culture simply as "rational," without further qualification and without attempting to elucidate some of the special attributes of this rationality, is clearly not enough. There is a distinctive character to Greek, and particularly Athenian, rationality which, while difficult to specify, sets it off from the kinds of rationality dominant in the modern world. To clarify this it may be helpful to begin with a specific case.

During the second war with the Persians, when Xerxes' forces threatened Athens in 480 B.C., the Athenians, though having only three hundred ships under their direction to Xerxes' thousand, nonetheless decided to join the issue at sea.[60] "Unable to cope with him by land we went on board our ships with all our people, and joined in the action at Salamis." [61] There, under the direction of Themistocles, they outmaneuvered the Persians and beat them decisively, forcing Xerxes—who had by then captured and sacked Athens—to retreat with his army. However cliché, it must be said that this is surely one of the fulcrum events of world and especially of Western history.

The perplexing thing about this episode is that the Athenians, as some of them put it, "seeing everything in front of us already subjugated, . . . had the spirit, after abandoning our property, . . . to throw ourselves into our ships to meet the danger. . . ." [62] Leaving their wives and children at Troezen across the Saronic Gulf and the older men on the island of Salamis, the Athenians surrender the seats of their ancestral gods and the graves of their forefathers. Leaving behind the treasurers and priestesses at the Acropolis and ignoring the generally defeatist oracles from Delphi, they go out in their boats to fight for everything.

The striking thing about the venture is in part, but only in part, the Athenians' rationality, that is, their ability in the face of impending disaster to size up the situation with cool calculation, to reckon their own weaknesses and strengths, and then to decide that their strong suit was the fleet of triremes with their highly trained and brilliantly captained crews. To say that they clearly and correctly appraised what they needed to do somehow falls short of the mark. It does not quite portray the full character and significance of this bold stroke. We must add that they proceeded to *do* what they thought necessary, and that they did it with a will. But even this is not enough; something important has still been left out.

Total-Commitment Rationality and Low Object Attachment

There are many ways we might attempt to capture this elusive omission. We might, for instance, focus on the enormously daring quality of the Athenians' strategy: daring in the sense that they were willing to risk so much on the correctness of their estimate of the situation, daring in that they seemed in no way to hedge their bets. It is this aspect of Athenian character and strategy, the feeling that it was so "enterprising and revolutionary," that made the Spartans so distrustfully apprehensive of them.[63] It is also the kind of daring that the Athenians were to lose increasingly, especially after their defeat in the Peloponnesian War, but which helps us understand how they staved off this defeat for as long as they did.

During the fight against Persia and indeed up to and throughout the Peloponnesian War—as epitomized by the Sicilian expedition—the Athenians were not "security-minded"; they pursued a strategy of calculated risks which did not keep much in reserve. They risked much to win much. Stated another way, the Athenians seemed to pursue a strategy of "burning their bridges"; the men under Themistocles could recognize that all was lost unless they won, and they could have no second thoughts about turning back or compromising once the issue had been joined. Their policy, therefore, seems better described not simply as "rational" but as a policy of "total-commitment rationality."

Athenian policy at the beginning of the Peloponnesian War manifests a similar, though not identical, expression of total-commitment rationality. At this time, Pericles counsels the Athenians to view themselves as an island and to rely primarily on their naval superiority. "Consider for a moment," he says. "Suppose we were islanders: can you conceive a more impregnable position? Well, this in future should, so far as possible, be our conception of our position. Dismissing all thought of our land and houses, we must vigilantly guard the sea and the city." [64] Abandoning their farms in the countryside, the Atticans move behind the walls of Athens, knowing that they leave their homes and fields to the ravages of the invaders.

There is, however, still another layer in the Athenian orientation suggested by this case, especially when it is placed alongside the earlier response made to Xerxes' invasion; there is a communality in the two cases that deserves to be made explicit. In both, the Athenians seem relatively free of sentimental attachment to their property, homes, furnishings, even land. Another people might have done anything to prevent such injury to their belongings.

The kind of strategy the Athenians pursue, their policy of total-commitment rationality, tells us about their scheme of values or utilities, throwing light on what they were attached to and to what they were not and on the nature of these attachments. The policy of total-commitment rationality implies that objects for whose protection other men might have fought to the death—their hearths, homes, and land—were not the deepest attachments the Athenians had.

Put in still other terms, they apparently could disengage themselves from and had a relatively manipulable attachment to many of their own objects. Indeed, Pericles tells them, and they vote in concurrence, "We must cry not over the loss of houses and land but of men's lives; since houses and land do not gain men, but men them. And if I had thought that I could persuade you, I would have bid you go out and lay them waste with your own hands, and show the Peloponnesians that this at any rate will not make you submit." [65] However reluctantly, the Athenians do abandon their country properties at the very beginning of the war, and long before their city is in anything like desperate straits.

This diffuse, relatively low degree of attachment to objects manifested in both cases cited above does not, however, seem to be an isolated disposition born of the extremity of war; it appears, rather, to be related to more commonplace and persistent tendencies of Athenian character in particular, and perhaps of Greek character more generally. The open-handed, almost potlatch type of honorific public expenditure which might drive ambitious members of the upper classes to the brink of insolvency is the counterpart, not the antithesis, of the often commented on Hellenic frugality and Spartan austerity.[66] In both cases there is relatively little attachment to material objects. In the latter there is a manifested readiness to do without; in the former, a readiness to use objects up recklessly.

It may be that the Greek's reserved, sometimes contemptuous attitude toward technology and toward economic activities more generally is another manifestation of a relatively low degree of object attachment. Similarly, one cannot help wondering whether this aspect of Greek character was not involved in the Hellenic attitude toward the Sybarites, whom they viewed with utter distaste as somehow alien to the Hellenic spirit because of their love of luxury, of ornamented apparel, and their exceptional fondness for pets. The Sybarites, in short, manifested a strength of object attachment apparently then unusual in Greece. When Croton—spurred by Pythagorean asceticism—destroyed Sybaris in 510 B.C., she seems to have been driven by an animus extreme even for the Greeks and far in excess of the costs of the war she won handily. Upon beating Sybaris, Croton would content herself with nothing less than the city's total annihilation, which was accomplished by deliberately turning the river Crathis upon the town and burying it under silt.

Frequently the Greek's attachment to individual persons or to groups does not appear to be much deeper than their attachment to other objects. We have already observed that Greek men did not commonly make deep emotional investments in women; I have also commented earlier on the precarious character of homosexual unions, while the fragility of friendly relations more generally is proverbial. This is implied in an anonymous drinking song that says, "He who never betrays one he has made a friend shall be given high exaltation among people and gods," and in another that implores, "Oh that it were given to us to open up the heart of every man, and to read his mind within, and then to close it, and thus, never deceived, be assured of a friend." [67]

Again, the reputation the Greeks develop for treachery and duplicity, their taste for Odyssean wiliness, is also noteworthy here, being directed in many notable cases against their own city. Success by treachery, says Thucydides,[68] might win a man the palm of superior intelligence. In Alcibiades' speech to the Spartans, after he has deserted the Athenian cause, he makes it clear that Athens is no longer his city: "I hope none of you will think any the worse of me if after having hitherto passed as a lover of my country, I now actively join its worst enemies in attacking it. . . . [L]ove of country is what I do not feel when I am wronged, but what I felt when secure in my rights as a citizen. Indeed, I do not consider that I am now attacking a country that is still mine; I am rather trying to recover one that is mine no longer. . . ." [69]

In saying that many Greeks had a diffusely low object attachment, I do not mean to suggest there was nothing to which they were positively attached. There is at least one thing to which they manifestly have a strong attachment and which is revealed in the drinking song mentioned at the beginning of this chapter. They are deeply (and perhaps narcissistically) attached to their own embodied person and to their image of it: to health, to beauty, and to youth, which in part implies the first two.

It has long been recognized that the Greeks place a particular value on the body, as evidenced by their magnificent statuary which celebrates the human form in all its graceful musculature and commonly reveals it unadorned, or whose robings only accentuate the body beneath. This attachment to the embodied person can be seen as being related to and expressed in the Greek dismay of death, and in their devaluation of the wraithlike and powerless existence of the remnant "soul," or *eidōlon,* after death.

The Greeks are also deeply attached to their public repute and fame, to the image of self fed back to them by the community and which they win in the course of competing within the contest system. It seems clear that the objects they seek in participating in the contest system are significant as symbols of personal excellence and serve as an expression or basis of a personal claim for public esteem; they are, in short, important as validations of the embodied self.

It has also long been recognized that the Greeks gloried in action: in the doings, comings, goings, and achievements of men, valuing these in particular insofar as they contributed to fame. What men do and the reputation their doings bring them is paramount to the Greeks. It is an aspiration for and achievement of personal repute that sustains them, rather than attachments to the world of inanimate objects.

Believing as they do that a man's fortune can change overnight, raising him up or dashing him down from the heights without warning, the Greeks have a strong sense of the impermanence of their hold on objects. "Men do not really own their private goods," says the chorus in Euripides' *Phoenician Women.* "We simply care for things which are the gods', and when they will, they take them back again." [70] It is, therefore, foolish to make strong object attachments. "I swear I see no wisdom in that man," says Sophocles, who, "though he has watched a decent age pass by, . . . will sometimes still desire the world." [71]

Men's loyalties to one another are commonly feared to vary with their fortunes, and a sense of men's impermanent relation to one another is conducive to an inhibition of attachments to people as well as objects. A fear of losing or of being betrayed by things makes it difficult to invest the self deeply in the world. There is an interesting passage in Plutarch in which

Thales explains to Solon that he has no wife or children because of the grief that their loss would bring him. Plutarch demurs, however, remarking, "[I]t is irrational and poor-spirited not to seek conveniences for fear of losing them. . . . It is not affection, it is weakness that brings men, unarmed against fortune by reason, into those endless pains and terrors, and they indeed have not even the present enjoyment of what they dote upon, the possibility of future loss ever causing them continual pangs, terrors, and distresses." [72]

Under these conditions it is not surprising that the basic locus of security comes to be one's own embodied self, with all its attributes, physical and psychic. Yet if the relatively low attachment to objects in the surrounding world is conducive to a strong attachment to one's embodied self, it is also likely that the process is cyclical, and that in turn the heavy investment in the self inhibits stable and enduring attachments to other things and persons.

The basic point here is that there is likely to be some connection, however complex, among the attachments men make to themselves, to one another, and to other objects. Modern sociology, in particular, is prone to do little with the last and focuses primarily upon the first two, especially upon a "social system" of "actors" who are viewed as both disembodied and propertyless, creating a "sociology of angels." The concept of object attachment is useful, however, precisely because its high level of abstraction subsumes all three possible forms of attachment. It thereby constrains us to consider whether "alienation" from people may not sometimes be part of a more general orientation which disposes men to a similar detachment from other objects. It constrains us also to explore the dynamic processes by which one form of object attachment (or detachment) may be consequential for another.

Individuality, Rationality, and Low Object Attachment

The interrelationship between Greek low object attachment and rationality is of no little importance. In some part, rationalism is an orientation in which the relation between means and ends is subject to deliberate calculation; in which ends or goals are constituted as perceptually organized foci set off from the contextual ground in which they are embedded; and in which other aspects of the surround are also taken from their context and evaluated primarily in terms of their anticipated capacity to realize the goal. In short, the more rational the orientation, the more might it be said that the world is seen from the center comprised by the viewing person, and that elements in it are of significance primarily in terms of *his* purposes. Rationalism thus premises an individual-centered world, in which the self can move easily in and out of the field of objects, choosing some to which it will make more enduring goal attachments, choosing others to use instrumentally to obtain or retain the former and, having used them for its purposes, to withdraw its attachments.

Persons with low object attachments can select goals and means, rather than having these imposed by unexaminable tradition and rather than being bound to them by deeply affective sentiments or by a fear-laden belief in their sacred character. Diffuse, low object attachment means there are fewer objects in the world to which individuals are irretrievably committed or from which they can extricate themselves only with great effort; conversely, it means that there are many more objects in the world that can be used, treated primarily as resources, without being restricted by sentiment in the uses to which they may be put. A diffuse low object cathexis is therefore the characterological counterpart of rationality, facilitating and conducing to its development; indeed, it is this affective disposition of highly rational men that so often leads them to be viewed as "cold."

The Greek capacity to disengage the self from sentimental attachments to persons meant that persons could then be used instrumentally—as, for example, Odysseus treats Philoctetes—or could then be treated as interchangeable parts: "But will you kill your own son's promised bride?" Ismene asks Creon. To which he replies, "Oh, there are other furrows for his plough." [73] The weakening of specific object attachments is an emotional framework also conducive to universalism, that is, to an orientation in which objects may be seen as equivalent members of a class rather than as unique things bound to the self with special ties of affection. They can then be used more rationally as resources for the achievement of one's own ends. Greek tradition and tragedy agonizingly show that men might even sacrifice their own children to their personal aspirations if this seems to be required. The epitome of this is, of course, Agamemnon's slaying of his daughter, Iphigenia, when he seeks ritual assurance of the success of the Achaean expedition against Troy.

It is not, however, that a low object attachment requires men to be rational, but only that it facilitates rationality. Similarly, it is not that rationality requires low object attachment; but it is likely that the emotional costs of rationality are less, and the scope within which it may operate greater, for those with diffuse low object attachment. Above all, the significance of low object attachment is that it facilitates rational action as distinct from rational calculation. It is one thing to make a rational appraisal of a situation or to formulate a rational strategy concerning it; it is quite another to be able to do what is indicated by that strategy. The characteristic thing about the Greeks is not simply their capacity for rational calculation but, as we suggested, their remarkably high capacity to commit themselves in action to their rational diagnosis.

This combination of rationality and diffuse low object attachment does much to make Athenians the restlessly innovating and ruthlessly effective force they are in Hellenic civilization. To a remarkable extent they can see what is needed in their self-interest, and they can do it. Their capacity for rational appraisal enables them often to identify correctly the effective points of leverage; their relatively low object cathexis means they are less bound to traditional ways and means, that their energies are not inhibited or drained off by multiple commitments. Once having singled out their target, they can mobilize their resources and bring them to bear on it in a concentrated discharge.

Social Change and Object Attachments

It is, in part, this fusion of low object cathexis and rationality that not only enables the Athenians to cope with the problems of their international position in Hellenic society but, also, facilitates their development and use of radical solutions to their own internal social problems. The crucial cases in point are the reforms of Solon, Cleisthenes, and Pisistratus, which are not only remarkably clear-sighted and rational in design, but are also remarkable in the relatively ready acceptance given them despite their threat to vested interests and their novelty.

If Athenian rationality and low object attachment are functional in that they promote adaptation to new circumstances by facilitating change, they are also conducive to certain social dysfunctions and entail distinctive costs. These meant that almost any social pattern may be reconsidered at any time, and is always open to critical re-evaluation in the light of changing circumstances and susceptible to modification. Where strong object attachments exist they serve as a brake upon social change. They bind men to established arrangements with nonrational ties of sentiment, and they require that the most compelling circumstances exist before changes are made. In the absence of such sentiments, or when they are weak, changes can be more frequently made prior to the experience of full-fledged crisis and whenever rational assessment promises potential gain.

Consistent with our view of Athenian character structure, particularly its low object attachment, is the often remarked upon readiness of its citizenry to change, to revise, or to revoke their own decrees, at times doing so the day after passing them.[74] Also expressive of low object attachment and similarly conducive to a tendency to social flux is the fact that authority and public officials are held in scant esteem, let alone awe. There is at any rate little or no "mystique" of office, and relatively little development of a public, hierarchical structure, and formal organization. This seems to be the case not only in Athenian civil life but in military organization as well, which, in contrast to the Spartan,[75] is much more loosely integrated, having on the average a larger span of control and fewer ranks. There is a corresponding difficulty in maintaining discipline in the Athenian forces, Nicias, for example, complaining of the "natural indocility of the Athenian seaman. . . ."[76]

Also conducive to the Athenian readiness to change are several other factors. One of these is the tendency, implicit in their conception of democracy, to regard almost any social arrangement as only dubiously legitimate unless it has been initiated by the citizens themselves or sanctioned with their explicit consent. Decisions made by their functionaries in the field are likely to be viewed as suspect, while even their own decisions are subject to rapid revision.

Further, the restraints which could be placed by an older generation upon changes sought by a younger were weakened, insofar as the former could not claim to have committed the younger once the latter had come of age. It seems likely, too, that the ability of the older generation to place a brake upon social change is impaired by the fact that youth is so highly valued. Moreover, the short life span (which averages over-all about twenty-nine years)[77] means that there are relatively few older men available to exert effective pressure for policy continuity. The Greeks seem to have a two-generation cycle, rather than a three-generational cycle like our own; apparently there are no words for "middle-aged" persons; generational turnover is quicker and might, in the context of a group with high rationality and low object attachment, further speed social and cultural change. The past is not treated as sacred, and the Athenians came to feel that there is "no advantage in reflexions on the past further than may be of service to the present."[78]

For these several reasons, change occurs with rapidity among the Athenians. One gains the impression of an all too fluid social organization and culture, where men's attachments to things and persons wander and change course rapidly, where loyalties wear out quickly, and where "old ties give place to new ones."[79] Isocrates catches this character of Athens well: "[T]he city does not present to the mind an image easily grasped or sharply defined," but is, rather, more like a "turbid flood."[80] While this fluidity may confound Athens' enemies, it must surely also exert a strain on the Athenians themselves, making their own as well as their enemies' lives somewhat less predictable and secure, and reinforcing their inclination to view things as sadly lacking in permanence. Though informed by political animus, there is an element of truth in the Corinthians' characterization of the Athenians: "[O]ne might truly say they were born into the world to take no rest themselves and to give none to others." [81]

It is difficult to avoid the impression that Athens is a "quick turnover" society. It is intent not so much on ensuring the long-range stability of its civilization and the continuity of its institutions, but on rationally orienting itself to the more immediate gratification (as the more certain) rather than to gratifications that can be enjoyed in later years or by later generations. The concern is with the here and now, and there is more than a touch of bird-in-the-hand hedonism in it.

Greek pessimism is deeply subversive of Greek rationality, or at least of long-range rationality. The feeling that all things end badly can only inhibit steadfast commitment to long-range goals and weaken the capacity to defer gratifications. Pessimism truncates the time span within which rational planning is felt to be practical and undermines the anticipatory enjoyment of any distant goal: "If anyone counts upon one day ahead or even more, he does not think." [82] The force with which some Greeks pin their hopes for fame upon the verdict of a vague and indefinite posterity is not so much an expression of secure confidence in its ultimate judgment as an alienation from their envious and competitive contemporaries.

The character of everyday Greek rationality is much closer to that of Odysseus than Plato. It is shaped deeply by a concern with self-interest, in which the self is firmly but narrowly bounded, and operates on the assumption that "identity of interests is the surest of bonds whether between states or individuals." [83] In his funeral address, Pericles catches the Athenians' Odyssean character well when he remarks that they trust "less in system and policy than to the native spirit of our citizens. . . . I doubt if the world can produce a man, who where he has only himself to depend upon, is equal to so many emergencies, and graced by so happy a versatility as the Athenian." [84]

Yet the maintenance and stability of Athens' cultural patterns is an endemic problem. The social cohesion and integration of a society is precarious indeed where object attachments are thin, where loyalties and sentiments fade easily under the rational scrutiny of short-range self-interests, where envy is permeative, where human relations are strained constantly by the contest system, and where class conflicts frequently border on civil violence. While, as Pericles puts it, a happy versatility makes the Athenians "equal to so many emergencies," nonetheless, one of the things that holds Athenian society together for so long is the energizing stimulus of these very emergencies: Athens needs the challenge of repeated threats and conflicts to mobilize and hold herself together; in time, she becomes addicted to them.

NOTES

[1] R. Lattimore, trans., *Greek Lyrics* (Chicago: University of Chicago Press, 1955), p. 66.

[2] For the importance of this theme in the Greek value system see L. Pearson, "Popular Ethics in the World of Thucydides," *Classical Philology*, 52 (October 1957), 228–244. On a cognate theme, see J. W. Hewitt, "The Terminology of Gratitude," *Classical Philology*, 22 (April 1927), 142–161, and J. W. Hewitt, "Gratitude to Parents in Greek and Roman Literature," *The American Journal of Philology*, 52, no. 205, 30–48.

[3] For a generalized theoretical analysis of the significance of the cross-cultural prevalence of the norm of reciprocity, see A. W. Gouldner, "The Norm of Reciprocity: A Preliminary Statement," *American Sociological Review*, 25 (April 1960), 161–178.

[4] This point is well documented in H. Kelsen, *Society and Nature* (Chicago: University of Chicago Press, 1943).

[5] A R. Burn's version of this is: "To mortal man, first gift is Health; The next is Beauty; Third is Wealth—Wealth that no shame attends; The fourth is to be young among your friends." See A. R. Burn, *op. cit.*, p. 48.

[6] For an extended discussion of the character and utility of a conceptual distinction between standards of gratification and standards of morality see Gouldner and Gouldner, *op. cit.*, pp. 570 ff.

[7] Translation by Misch, *op. cit.*, p. 81.

[8] Thucydides. 44.

[9] Isocrates i. 131.

[10] *Libation Bearers* i. 104. 313.

[11] Trans. from Adkins, *op. cit.*, p. 119; compare with that by R. Lattimore, *Greek Lyrics, op. cit.*, p. 7.

[12] W. C. Greene, *Moira* (Cambridge: Harvard University Press, 1948), p. 3.

[13] For one of the most thoughtful discussions of Greek pessimism see J. C. Opstelten, trans. J. A. Ross, *Sophocles and Greek Pessimism* (Amsterdam: North-Holland Publishing Company, 1952).

[14] Although I cannot subscribe to its central thesis, I have found the following of great value in exploring this and other central themes in Greek culture: H. L. Finch, *The Greek Idea of Limitation,* unpublished doctoral dissertation in the Faculty of Philosophy of Columbia University, 1951.

[15] E. R. Dodds, *op. cit.*, p. 17.

[16] A. J. White, *op. cit.*, p. 21.

[17] Cf. G. Thomson, *op. cit.*, p. 188.

[18] Sophocles *Oedipus at Colonus* ii. 106. 593.

[19] I am far from the first to have made this observation. R. B. Levinson, *In Defense of Plato* (Cambridge: Harvard University Press, 1953), p. 82, has also remarked upon "the almost unanimous evasion of the topic by the reigning English and American interpreters of Plato" during a somewhat earlier period. Modern scholarship has done little to remedy this lacuna. Some useful materials may be found in H. Blumner, *The Home Life of the Ancient Greeks* (London: Cassell, 1894); H. Licht (pseudo. of P. Brandt), *Sexual Life in Ancient Greece* (London: G. Routledge, 1932); J. A. Symonds, *A Problem in Greek Ethics* (London, privately printed for the Apeoilatitita Society, 1901); J. A. Symonds, *A Problem in Modern Ethics* (London: privately printed, 1896).

[20] O. Seyffert, rev. and ed. by H. Nettleship and J. E. Sandys, *A Dictionary of Classical Antiquities* (Cleveland: World Publishing Company, 1961), p. 431.

[21] Isocrates i. 147.

[22] This quotation from Butcher is cited in F. M. Cornford, *The Origin of Attic Comedy* (Garden City: Doubleday 1961 ed.), p. 30.

[23] Ehrenberg, *op. cit.*, p. 35.

24 E. Friedl, *Vasilika, A Village in Modern Greece* (New York: Holt, Rinehart and Winston, 1962), pp. 75–76. It might be worth adding that the intellectual climate of modern sociology is still so strongly permeated by radical relativism and historicism that, even though I myself have never subscribed to this tradition, I confess it never even occurred to me that there could be many serious cultural continuities between ancient Greece and (even the relatively remote rural areas of) modern Greece. As a result, I first consulted Friedl's study only casually and after the main parts of this chapter had already been written with a focus on the contest system. This, however, is far from the only such continuity implied by Friedl's excellent work. Among others that I would suggest as deserving of closer study are a dramatistic view of life (p. 17); the division of property of the deceased into equal shares among his children (pp. 18, 48–49); an emphasis upon the constraining power of circumstances or "necessity" (pp. 20, 65, 86); a concern with appearances, especially one's own unsightly appearance (pp. 24, 36); a disposition in favor of short-range as against long-range rationality (p. 29); limited attachments to pets (p. 32); a very great value stress upon the importance of maintaining a proper division of labor, to which we will later refer (p. 35); exclusion of women from the public arena (pp. 42, 90); a respect for education and intellect (pp. 49, 51, 76); an enjoyment of town life (p. 49); a view of work as necessary, but not as desirable in itself (p. 50); deliberate regulation of family size (p. 50); female control of dower property (p. 59); the use of lots as a way of allocating certain goods (p. 63); lack of Greek words with the specific and exclusive English meaning of "husband" and "wife" (p. 72); use of shame as a control device (p. 54); a stress on paired male friendships (p. 89); "a . . . compelling distaste for manual labor" (p. 94); "an unwillingness to take orders from anyone" (p. 106). Let me stress that it is not Friedl who asserts these as continuities between ancient and modern Greece. It is, rather, I to whom they seem such.

25 *The Suppliant Women* iv. 157. 549.

26 The next chapter will provide an extended discussion of this concept.

27 Plutarch. 82.

28 Thucydides. 377–378.

29 Ehrenberg, *op. cit.,* 108–109.

30 Plutarch. 116–117.

31 *Andromache* iii. 585. 695 ff.

32 Isocrates i. 87–89.

33 Thucydides. 378.

34 Thucydides. 378.

35 Thucydides. 385.

36 Thucydides. 385.

37 For extended development of the theoretical perspective of which the following is a truncated statement, see J. W. Thibaut and H. H. Kelley, *The Social Psychology of Groups* (New York: Wiley, 1959).

38 *Agamemnon* i. 60. 836.

39 *Heracleidae* iii. 151. 939.

40 *Agamemnon* i. 49. 471.

41 *Orestes* iv. 232. 708.

42 G. C. Field, *Plato and His Contemporaries* (London: Methuen, 1930), p. 111.

43 Good introductory discussions of ostracism may be found in Ranulf, *op. cit.,* and in Glotz, *The Greek City, op. cit.* For some of the more important technical studies, see A. E. Raubitschek, "The Origins of Ostracism," *American Journal of Archaeology,* 55 (July 1951), 221–229; A. R. Hands, "Ostraka and the Law of Ostracism—Some Possibilities and Assumptions," *Journal of Hellenic Studies,* 79 (1959), 69–79; A. E. Raubitschek, "Athenian Ostracism," *The Classical Journal,* 48 (January 1953), 113–122; C. A. Robinson, "The Struggle for Power in Athens in the Early 5th Century," *American Journal of Philology,* 66 (1945), 243–254.

44 Isocrates ii. 279.

45 These two metaphors have been used by Pindar and Sophocles, respectively.

46 ii. 198. 1158.

47 ii. 219. 130.

48 Lattimore, *Greek Lyrics, op. cit.*, p. 6.

49 Here I think the point is more clearly seen with Lattimore's modern translation than with Lang's. *Iliad of Homer* (Chicago: University of Chicago Press, 1962), p. 438. I am indebted to my colleague Professor William Sale for calling this passage and its possible significance to my attention. For Sale's discussion of the heroic value system, see his "Achilles and Heroic Values," 2, no. 3 (Autumn 1963), *Arion,* 86–100.

50 *Agamemnon* i. 60. 832–833.

51 Aristotle, trans. J. A. K. Thomson, *The [Nicomachean] Ethics of Aristotle* (London: Penguin Books, 1956), p. 241.

52 *Ibid.*

53 Ehrenberg, *op. cit.*, p. 198. It seems that women, in particular, were suspected of being poisoners.

54 *Phaedrus.* 232C.

55 *Phaedrus.* 241C.

56 Thucydides. 400.

57 Thucydides. 400.

58 Thucydides. 402.

59 Thucydides. 400.

60 For an excellent popular account of this, see M. H. Jameson, "How Themistocles Planned the Battle of Salamis," *Scientific American,* 204 (March 1961), 111–120.

61 Thucydides. 53.

62 Thucydides. 54.

63 Thucydides. 69.

64 Thucydides. 94.

65 Thucydides. 94.

66 For an interesting if inconclusive discussion of this problem, see H. W. Stubbs, "Spartan Austerity: A Possible Explanation," *Classical Quarterly,* 44 (1950), 32–37.

67 Lattimore, *Greek Lyrics, op. cit.*, p. 48.

68 Thucydides. 209.

69 Thucydides. 424.

70 *Phoenician Women* iv. 480. 555 ff.

71 *Oedipus at Colonus* ii. 134. 1121 ff.

72 Plutarch, *op. cit.*, pp. 85–86.

73 Sophocles *Antigone* ii. 179. 568 ff.

74 Glotz, *The Greek City, op. cit.*, p. 125, is at pains to stress Athenian concern for continuity in policy and legislation, especially through mechanisms such as the *graphe paranomon* which he says "raised law above popular caprice. . . ." I take it that this stress in Glotz's work stems from his desire to defend Athenian democracy; while I share Glotz's sympathies, I feel such a defense unnecessary considering the historical alternatives possible. A little later on, however, in the same work, Glotz himself acknowledges that sometimes "hasty votes were taken, by show of hands, for measures which would be repented of at the end of a few months or regarded with horror a few hours later" —*ibid.*, p. 175.

75 Thucydides. 349.

76 Thucydides. 442.

77 D. E. Richardson, *Old Age Among the Ancient Greeks* (Baltimore: Johns Hopkins Press, 1933), p. 234. Insofar as evidence for this depends upon remnant burial inscriptions, it may well be that the shorter lives of the poor or slaves who were buried without them make the true average life span for the population as a whole even lower than this.

78 Thucydides, 80.

79 Euripides *Medea* iii. 61. 76.

80 Isocrates ii. 283.

81 Thucydides. 51.

82 Sophocles *Women of Trachis* ii. 312. 942; see also 325. 1270.

83 Thucydides. 80.

84 Thucydides. 121.

3

Self and Society in Greece

Socrates: Very good, Callicles; but will he answer our questions? For I want to hear from him what is the nature of his art, and what it is which he professes and teaches; he may, as you [Chaerephon] suggest, defer the exhibition to some other time.

Callicles: There is nothing like asking him, Socrates; and indeed to answer questions is a part of his exhibition, for he was saying only just now, that any one in my house might put any question to him, and that he would answer.

Socrates: How fortunate! Will you ask him Chaerephon——?

Chaerephon: What shall I ask him?

Socrates: Ask him who he is.

—Plato [1]

IT IS widely agreed that Western individualism has one of its great burgeonings with the development of Greek culture. Although one might wish that there was as much clarity about the nature of this individualism as there is agreement about its occurrence, only pedantry would insist that we be clear about the details before acknowledging the broad pattern. The fact is that individualism, in a sense grossly familiar to Westerners, is one of the basic features of Greek culture; in the context of the contest system, it commonly expresses itself as an ambition for personal fame, and in its heroic form it is a quest for a fame undying.

While Greek individualism is clearly evident at the beginning of the classical period, there are tentative indications of its emergence at least as early as Hesiod, who begins his narrative by giving his name and then continues in the first person.[2] Sappho's lyric poetry around the end of the seventh century B.C. also centers attention on the individual, on his situation, emotions, and states of mind. Indeed it may be that the Delphic injunction "Know thyself," echoed in Heraclitus' proud claim, "I have searched myself," serves to legitimate the increasing interest in the individual self. The culmination of this trend occurs in the fifth century when Protagoras avers that "Man is the measure of all things," and when Socrates directs men not only to know their own selves but to take responsibility for reconstructing it.

Bruno Snell's linguistic analysis [3] of Homeric literature suggests that men of that early period still had little knowledge of the self in the modern sense. That is, they did not yet regard it as the source of the emotions (or of the accomplishments of the person), especially of those that were strong or abnormal in some manner. Agamemnon, for example, explains his behavior toward Achilles in this way: "Not I was the cause of this act, but Zeus and my portion and the Erinys who walk in darkness; they it was who in the assembly put wild *atē* [divine temptation] in my understanding on that day when I appropriated Achilles' prize from him." The Homeric Greeks, says Snell, did not yet possess a term for the whole of man's mental equipment or for the mind or soul as an entity in our sense. The soul was not yet regarded as distinct from and, in particular, opposed to the body.

In early Greek art the physical body itself was not, according to Snell, comprehended as an organic unity but as an aggregate of parts. It is not until the classical art of the fifth century B.C. that efforts to depict the body as an integrated organism are found. Homer speaks of fleet legs and sinewy arms, but he has no one word for characterizing the mind or the self. Only gradually do men come to view themselves as the source and author of their feelings and actions, becoming increasingly aware of their powers and conscious of self; only gradually is what we might call the "author-ity" of the self recognized.

It is also well known that Greek sculpture presents an ideal, conventionalized portrait of individuals, as anyone can see who visits a museum in which there is a sampling of Greek sculpture that can be compared with the much more individuated features on the busts of Roman notables. It is not until the second half of the fifth century B.C. that serious literary efforts at individualized characterization are attempted and that Athenians develop a lively interest in personal character.[4]

To understand this emergence of individualism, it must be remembered that from about the ninth to the sixth century B.C. there occurred the greatest social revolution that Europe has yet experienced: the breakdown of tribalism and the emergence of the urban community organized on the basis of territorial propinquity—in short, the state. Men came increasingly to depend upon the state's legal and administrative machinery to protect contracts and right wrongs, and began operating independently of their tribes and families. Important as kinship undoubtedly remains in subsequent Western societies, it will never again be the all-embracing matrix that it was in tribal societies.

In tribal societies kinship arrangements permeate the most diverse and basic involvements: they define a man's fundamental loyalties, determine when and against whom he is to wage war, establish the locales within which he will pursue his subsistence-getting activities, rigorously regulate whom he must or must not marry, from whom he gets justice, and from whom he learns ritual requirements and work skills.

With the decline of tribalism men leave a society in which their diverse activities are integrated within a single institutional framework, in which the bonds between men are multiple rather than segmentalized, and in which the basic paradigm of human relations is that of the family or of kinship ties. Leaving tribalism they come to live among those with whom they are, for the most part, unrelated by real or fictive kinship ties, and thus in effect relinquish the support and protection of a group that is viewed much as if it were a large family.

To leave tribalism is to leave a world in which most decisions are closely regulated by a network of unexaminable rules. To leave tribalism is to enter a world of greater choices—concerning marriage, trade, and personal and political alliances. It is to enter a world in which the very rules governing decisions are themselves regarded as things concerning which decisions may be made. Men increasingly view themselves as rule-makers, as "the measure of all things," rather than simply as rule-followers or rule-breakers. It is a move, therefore, toward an open and unstructured social situation which can be more exciting but, at the same time, more uncertain and anxiety inducing.

In this new world, one way that men for whom established tradition and its interpreters have lost authority may know the right and the real is by referring to the opinion of those around them. It becomes increasingly important for men to secure consensual validation of their impulses, beliefs, and, indeed, of their very worth, when the traditional verities wane and the ways of the world no longer seem ordained.

Under tribalism men might chafe and rebel against the traditional rules but these rules constitute, nevertheless, the visible pivot of their choices. With the breakdown of tribalism the choice is no longer the relatively simple one of conformity with or deviance from received rules, of rules that are taken as given; there is now a question of choices concerning the rules themselves. The rules become problematic. The *dikē,* or "the way," of the group becomes unclear to the detribalized Greeks; they begin to ask themselves: What is *dikē*? What is the right way? What is justice? What rules should we follow? What is the good? Are there any limits to the rules we can make? Is there a latent (or "natural") order underlying and limiting the diversity of the alternative rules by which one might be guided?

The growing concern with problems of ethics and morality—already evident in Hesiod and culminating in Socrates—marks the emergence of men who have to improvise new rules of the game even as they are playing it. With the breakdown of the familiar and complex system of tribal tradition the Greeks face the problem of making decisions in new ways, of reconstructing the very groundwork of decision-making. In particular, they come to assign special importance to the response, the judgment, and the opinion of *others* as a guideline for decision-making.

ON SHAME CULTURE

Greek culture has been characterized by scholars such as E. R. Dodds and Arthur Adkins as a "shame culture," in which the central sanction is presumably "what people will say." In this view the Greeks are, in effect, an other-directed people, much concerned about their reputation.

The very model of this other-directed Greek is portrayed vividly in Isocrates' address to Demonicus:

> Be affable in your relations with those who approach you, and never haughty; for the pride of the arrogant even slaves can hardly endure, whereas when men are affable all are glad to bear with their ways. But to be affable, you must not be quarrelsome, nor hard to please, nor always determined to have your own way; you must not oppose harshly the angry moods of your associates, even if they happen to be angry without reason, but rather give way to them when they are in the heat of passion and rebuke them when their anger has cooled; you must avoid being serious when the occasion is one for mirth, or taking pleasure in mirth when the occasion is serious (for what is unseasonable is always offensive); you must not bestow your favors ungraciously as do the majority who, when they must oblige their friends, do it offensively; and you must not be given to fault-finding, which is irksome, nor be censorious, which is exasperating.[5]

Even Plato, who gives this other-directed orientation a distinctive turn, remarks that "he who has a feeling of reverence and shame about the commission of any action, fears and is afraid of an ill reputation." [6] The worthiness of actions and persons, in a shame culture, is dependent upon the appraisal that others make of them; the important thing is to be successful in one's enterprises and to be judged so by others, rather than having a "good conscience." Merit and excellence are reckoned less by intentions than by results.

One of the central themes in Sophocles' *Oedipus at Colonus* is an opposition to the public condemnation of Oedipus, who says time and again that while his deeds were terrible he is without fault because he did not do them knowingly; he therefore has a claim to and in the end receives God's acceptance. The play may be taken as an expression of a conflict between two moralities, between a shame culture, or "action morality," in which the primary consideration is whether one has done certain things and judgment is made accordingly, and a guilt culture, or "intention morality," in which judgment varies according to the individual's intention. The play suggests, at one and the same time, the prevalence of the former and the emergence of the latter.

In a society having a shame culture, "It is *kalon* [most creditable] for the victors to have won, *aischron* [lowly or shameful] for the vanquished to have been defeated, whatever the circumstances of victory or defeat, and whatever the rights of the case." [7] A man may feel ashamed even if he has not actually done something *aischron* but simply if this is the common opinion concerning his deeds, or concerning what has been done to him or done to (or by) someone with whom he is closely associated. Whatever the reason, failure to do what is expected of a person, particularly if he has high status, is *aischron*. "A shame culture cannot draw distinctions between results and the mental states which produce them." [8]

Shame and Guilt Cultures: Coping with Deviance

The nature of a shame culture may be better seen if it is contrasted with a guilt culture.[9] Both these concepts of culture concern themselves with mechanisms through which men are brought into conformity with the norms shared in their group. Shame and guilt cultures alike have to do with the processes of social control, that is, with the restrictive mechanisms by which deviant dispositions may be brought into conformity with the expectations common to group members. The premise here is that all societies and groups have some system of norms or rules—more or less shared by their members —that constitutes standards for evaluating behavior. When men's behavior is seen to depart from these norms, those observing the departure level terms of reproach or derogation against the behavior and the people engaged in it. Deviant behavior, then, is any behavior eliciting reproach. Deviant behavior is not intrinsically such, but is behavior that someone, using some set of standards, has found wanting and has characterized with a term of derogation.

The basic difference between shame and guilt cultures is the agent or the locus of reproach. In shame cultures the reproachful party is some person other than the reproached; in guilt cultures reproach comes essentially from the *self,* so that the reproacher and the reproached are one and the same person. In shame cultures the person conforms with the norms of the group because of the costs of nonconformity or because of the rewards of conformity, which are—in both cases—created by the judgments of others. In guilt cultures the person avoids nonconformity and pursues group norms because of his desire to avoid self-criticism or to optimize self-approval. In brief, the "shame–guilt" distinction hinges on differences between the imputed sources of conformity, between presumably "external" and "internal" mechanisms of control.

Yet in both cases the mechanisms of control are obviously internal or internalized. Shame no less than guilt is an internal psychic experience that inhibits deviance from group norms. In the case of guilt cultures, however, the standards of evaluation as well as the inhibiting response have also been internalized; the person punishes himself when he observes himself either to depart from—or to wish to depart from—these standards. In the case of shame cultures, the person conforms because he perceives that nonconformity will incur a negative judgment by others—ill repute—and will evoke subsequent punishments from them. He anticipates what the reaction and judgment of others will be and he acts accordingly, either conforming with their expectations or, if not actually conforming, taking their possible judgment into account by preparing to evade the costs of deviance.

In guilt culture, then, what is internalized are various general standards in terms of which evaluations of self and others are made. In contrast, the concept of a shame culture stresses that it is not only generalized evaluative standards that are internalized but, also, a generalized sensitivity to the opinion of others. It seems clear, however, that even in an ideal-typical shame culture a person could not forecast accurately the reactions of others unless there existed some standards or norms—in addition to a generalized concern with his reputation—that he shared with them. The Homeric hero, for example, does not fight with just any weapon; he prefers the spear. A person must know these common standards, even if he does not believe in them, if he is to anticipate correctly the response of others to his own planned behavior. It is not so much, then, that guilt cultures have shared norms and shame cultures do not; it is, rather, that the orientation to the norms in the two cases differs. In a guilt culture, persons are committed to the norms regardless of the public visibility of their own behavior and the sanctions of others—regardless, in short, of the personal consequences of conformity or nonconformity with group norms. In a shame culture, a person's commitments to group norms are affected by the visibility of their behavior, by the presence or absence of others, and by the expected response of others to conformity or nonconformity with these norms.

In a guilt culture, the norms are regarded as intrinsically significant; they are experienced as desirable in and of themselves. In a shame culture, however, the norms—even when well known—have relatively little intrinsic significance, and there is relatively less sentimental attachment to them. The norms are treated by the person as part of the environment within which he operates and are viewed as external to his core self. In one part, a shame culture is an expression of a relatively low (or instrumental) object attachment to shared systems of norms.

The matter might be clarified further by attempting to distinguish more clearly between guilt and shame as such. Both of these are forms of anxiety. Both are "normal" internal experiences or feeling states which, in imposing costs upon the personality, inhibit the pursuit of certain courses of action and dispose toward others. Guilt is that anxiety occurring when a person perceives that, either in action or thought, he is diverging from some group norm that he himself defines as intrinsically desirable; it is the anxiety occurring when he sees himself desiring or doing something that he thinks wrong in and of itself. For guilt to occur at least two things are necessary: the person must define himself as a locus of responsibility and evaluate himself in terms of his conformity with a set of absolute or ideal standards. Divergence from these standards is defined by the deviant himself as "wrong" in and of itself—regardless of other resultant costs or gains to him—and the self is defined as "good" or "bad" when seen to diverge from these standards. Shame, by contrast, is that form of anxiety occurring when a person perceives himself as having failed in some effort at achievement in a manner visible to others whose approval he desires. Shame is the anxiety of being found wanting by others who, either in fact or fantasy, are thought to know of this failure. It is an anxiety about reputation, about the image of the self held by others. The overriding norm here is concern with the opinion of others; and this norm is viewed, not simply as a brute fact of social life, but as a proper principle for the guidance of one's own behavior. The man who knows no shame is flawed. In contrast to guilt—where the self is defined as the locus of responsibility—the occurrence of shame requires that failures of the self be defined as deriving from or imposed by outside forces; failure is taken as an indication that the person is weaker than these outside forces. The public revelation of such a weakness is one of the roots of the Greek sense of shame. Guilt is felt when the person views his failures as being due to something that he defines as part of himself and thus sees his self as tainted. Shame is felt when failures are seen as being due to the self's lacking in a desirable trait and thus being *deficient*.

Shame rests on a concern with one's competence, potency, or power; it is expressive of a desire to avoid an appearance of failure, weakness, or dependency. Guilt rests on a concern with one's goodness or rectitude; it is expressive of a desire to feel right. Guilt is felt when the individual, defining himself along a good–bad axis, appears to himself as bad; shame, when the individual, defining himself along a strong–weak axis, appears to himself as weak. The good–bad and strong–weak axes are, in this view, two fundamental and cross-cultural modalities [10] in terms of which all objects, including the self, may be experienced; they constitute the twin foci around which shame and guilt develop respectively.

Shame as a Mechanism of Social Control

The case at hand rests on two main observations. First, Greeks commonly manifest a pronounced tendency to concern themselves with what others think about them; they "cannot endure to see a circle of condemning witnesses." [11] It is Socrates' mission to redirect and oppose this inclination, telling the Greeks, in effect, "let them mock." Second, the Greeks are deeply concerned with whether they win or lose, with whether they succeed or fail in their individual enterprises. They are unlikely to say primly, "It's how you play the game that counts, not whether you win." "Had I succeeded," says the nurse in *Hippolytus,* "I had been a wise one." [12]

It is essentially these two observations that have disposed some classicists to apply to Greek society the notions of shame and guilt cultures. Being so at variance with the "inwardness" of Protestant conscience and with the inner-directedness of conscientious Western scholars, these two observations have seemed strange and in need of explanation. Yet it may be that the elaborate conceptual apparatus has blurred the really critical problems. Among these problems are the following: Under what conditions do men come to orient themselves strongly to the opinion of others? If people in a shame culture are concerned with the opinions of "others," toward which others are they oriented; are they oriented toward "public opinion" in general, or are the views of some more important to them than those of others? More specifically, who constitutes their reference group, and how does it come to be established? How is it that a strong concern for good repute does not always lead people to conform with prescribed ways of achieving success?

The first question, under which conditions do men come to be highly sensitive to the views of others, can be approached on at least two distinct levels: (1) in terms of the modal life histories of individuals viewed genetically, and (2) in terms of a cross-sectional analysis of their ongoing experiences as adults within Greek social and culture structure.

A Developmental View of Other-Directedness: The Boy and the Slave

Let us consider the former first, but only briefly because it will be returned to later. It makes a difference whether a child is reared, educated, and disciplined by those who feel they embody the standards that the child is expected to obey, or whether the socializing agent's authority is only a delegated moral competence, requiring and allowing him to speak on behalf of values manifestly not possessed by him. In the latter, when a child is reared by a slave—as many Greek children were—he soon learns that the slave's instructions are, "Do, feel, and be as I say, not as I do, feel, or am." In short, the free Greek child can learn his future role neither by spontaneously imitating nor identifying with the slave who helps rear him; for the child's task is not to become a slave but a freeman and master. A child thus reared is punished not because he behaves in a manner at variance with the personal convictions of the superintending agent, except when these chance to be those of the parents. The child will often be punished without personal conviction: when the slave feels it his duty and when the slave fears detection by the parent.

Reared by a person of low status to whom he will someday be superior, temporarily subordinate to someone lacking in esteem and power in the larger society, the child is not expected to "be like" but rather to "mind" the slave; he learns to heed his admonitions to a degree sufficient to avoid parental notice. The slave's instructions and punishments are always subject to review and revision by the parents, and both child and slave know this. The slave cannot therefore be firmly demanding; he must compromise, trying like a jailor to keep order among the inmates without so agitating them that they get out of hand and engage in outbursts that would reflect discreditably upon his management.

The problem for the child is how to live between the immediacy of the slave-nurse and the ultimacy of the parents, between someone who himself does not believe what he says and someone who, often being absent, cannot himself say what he believes. The child must adjust to parental demands that cannot be known with the certainty born of daily testing; he must adjust to demands that are communicated indirectly and known only uncertainly. The slave is unable to punish the child for failure to conform to his own personal standards and is reluctant to punish the child for failing to conform to parental demands which he himself may not accept.

The slave's response to this situation is to punish the child for visible deviant behavior which may come to parental attention. He will be less disposed to punish the child for deviant behavior that escapes the notice of others, for he is faced with the task of sustaining some measure of cooperation from the child. In short, the slave is more likely to punish the child for public misbehavior than for private expressions of belief that depart from social conventions, all the more so as the slave himself does not accept the convention. In this setting, the child learns that it is not his own private convictions that matter; he learns that his punishments or rewards depend less on what he believes privately than on how he acts publicly. It may be in some part through such early experiences that a child first comes to develop a special sensitivity to the opinions of others and is first socialized to be a member of a shame culture.

A Cross-Sectional View of Other-Directedness:
The Man and the Polis

The second level of analysis of factors conducive to a sensitivity to the opinion of others focuses attention on adult experiences within Greek institutions and culture. The breakdown of ancient Greek tribal traditions and loss of faith in its authoritative interpreters disorients men, giving them few fixed standards of prima facie validity. Under these circumstances they are disposed to discriminate the appropriate from the inappropriate by winning consensual validation, that is, the agreement of others. In brief, when the "way" is not clearly given by a stable tradition men will more likely chart their course of action by attending to the opinion of others around them. They may also develop their own internalized standards to which they adhere conscientiously, regardless of the sanction of tradition or the opinion of others. In any event, the dissolution of an ancient tradition modifies the ways of deciding on a course of action. In the Greek case, these new alternatives may have been narrowed by the child-rearing patterns mentioned above, as well as by later adult experiences in Greek society.

Concerning the latter, attention needs to be directed to the requisites of any kind of cooperation among men. The greater the division of labor and interdependence among men, the more, it would seem, they must take account of one another's opinions, views, and judgments; otherwise, their interaction will be subject continually to intrusive frictions. With the growing division of labor accompanying increasing urbanization, the Greek citizen becomes increasingly dependent upon a larger number and variety of others to whose views he has to pay attention.

The heightening effects of cooperation on men's sensitivity to the opinion of others varies widely with the social status of these others. Men are far more likely to attend to the opinion of those whose views can make a difference in their own lives; they are more likely to attend to those opinions which can be expressed in actions that are costly or rewarding to them. Some men's opinions—those of slaves, for example—may therefore count for little or nothing and need be given little attention. In general, the lower the relative status of others—the lower they are in wealth, prestige, and power, the mobilization of which can generate consequences—the less their judgments and opinions need be taken into account, and the less those superior to them need be sensitive to their views. Again, the less that others have access to social or institutional mechanisms through which they can implement their views, the less their opinions need be considered.

Contrariwise, the more that others are our equals, or are superior in status, and the more that they have access to social mechanisms through which they can implement their judgments, the more will we be disposed to pay attention to their opinions. The institutions of franchise and ostracism in Greek democracy are precisely such mechanisms. Available to ordinary citizens, through them the poor could inflict serious costs even upon men of the proudest families. The power with which democratic institutions endow the *dēmos* means that they cannot be safely ignored, and it broadens the range of those whose opinions have to be taken into account; men have to be sensitive even to the views of those they regard as their inferiors when the latter can tax and outvote them. Thus Aeschylus has his king Agamemnon say, "The people murmur, and their voice is great in strength." [13]

The contest system has a similar effect, since it is, in principle, open to all free men and since it incites the dangerous envy of the lowly toward the most successful. In the contest system, judgments of worth are made by many players who have access to institutions through which they can make felt their views about their competitors.

It is not, however, only the social structure that constrains Greeks to attend widely to opinion, but also the culture, the beliefs, and the values they commonly share. At least since the Cleisthenian democracy there is a de-emphasis on the political relevance of differences among men and a stress on men's essential equality in the public sphere. Similarly, in sharply demarcating all men from all members of the Pantheon, the Olympian religion also contains a strain toward egalitarianism. The difference between men and gods is seen to be so radical that the differences among men pale into insignificance. In this sense, all men are equal before the gods, even if the gods do not bestow equal favor upon them.

Several of these themes are conjoined in the dialogue between the servant and Euripides' Hippolytus:

Servant: King—for I will not call you "Master," that belongs to the Gods only—will you take good advice?

Hippolytus: Certainly I will take good advice. I am not a fool.

Servant: In men's communities one rule holds good, do you know it, King?

Hippolytus: Not I. What is this rule?

Servant: Men hate the haughty of heart who will not be the friend of every man.[14]

The threat of punishment for *hybris* is a threat to anyone, regardless of his social status, who by his insolence to any man, even a slave, shows that he has forgotten that all men have a common fate and that all men are, if only in their distance from the gods, essentially equal to one another. The egalitarian stream in the Greek belief system is thus supported both by the newer democratic ideology and the older Olympian theology; and the belief that men are equal in certain basic ways in effect broadens the range of others whose opinions have to be considered.

To the forces moving in this direction may be added the traditional Greek belief that men's fortunes can suddenly be swept away, that the mighty can be humbled at any time. Men of the highest status might therefore be motivated to attend to the opinions of even the lowliest, hoping in some part thereby to store up gratitude for their generosity, in some part to neutralize the envy of the defeated, in some part to avoid the semblance of *hybris,* in some part to win votes, and in some part out of a sense of common human destiny that momentary differences in fortune cannot obscure.

All this, in turn, contributes to and joins with a powerful stream in Greek thought that conceives of social influence—or of victory in contest—as being won in two basic ways, by force and persuasion. To the Greek, force and persuasion are polarized yet intimately related concepts, each defined by the other: Persuasion "means getting a person to do something you want him to do, by the use of almost any means short of physical compulsion." [15] One among many examples that might be cited to illustrate the polar character of these terms is Menelaus' remark to Helen: "I did not come to talk with you. I came to kill." [16] Although ambivalent toward the devices of persuasion, especially sophistic rhetoric and sycophantic flattery, the Greeks come in time to be increasingly sensitive to the dangers of force. Recognizing that force entails the danger of *hybris* as well as the devastation of defeat, they often counterpose to it an apotheosized persuasion, which they prefer at least among those whom they count as equals within their own community and recommend as the instrument first to be tried. But, to persuade, they have to take close account of the opinions of those whom they seek to win over.

In sum, then, Greek sensitivity to opinion is constrained by the institutional enlargement—through democracy and the contest system—of the range of others whose opinions have to be considered because they can affect one's own life and which, in turn, can best be influenced by taking them into account, thus making them susceptible to change by persuasion. Further, Greek sensitivity to the opinion of others is also constrained by Olympian theology and democratic ideology. Together, these all broaden the realm of others who have to be treated as significant persons, a development which is at the root of Greek humanism.

Greek egalitarianism is not, however, an unmitigated boon to Greek society for at least one reason: if it widens the range of empathy it also widens the range of competition, ramifying the melee of the contest system. All who are equal in principle, or who can make a claim to such equality, could be admitted to the contest. As democracy spreads and effectuates aspirations to equality, the contest system spreads with it. No longer confined to a small, heroic elite, who alone could play this hazardous game, the contest system moves out into the city and permeates the citizenry at large.

THE DIVISION OF LABOR AND THE CONTEST SYSTEM

It is in this connection that consideration needs to be given to the Greeks' passionate esteem for the division of labor. For all our view of them as rounded, versatile men, the Greeks, from Homer onward through Pindar, Euripides, and Plato, extolled the virtues of the division of labor. Homer's Poulydamas chastens:

> Hektor, you are too intractable to listen to reason. Because the god has granted you the actions of warfare therefore you wish in counsel also to be wise beyond others. But you cannot choose to have all gifts given to you together. To one man the god has granted the actions of warfare, to one to be a dancer, to another the lyre and the singing, and in the breast of another Zeus of the wide brows establishes wisdom, a lordly thing. . . .[17]

This is echoed centuries later in Pindar's reminder that "One man is excellent in one way, one in another . . . ," [18] and in Euripides' remark that "each has his special excellence. . . . One ought to place a man where he can do most good." [19] Plato's commitment to the division of labor is, of course, expressed in his emphasis on its role in the establishment of cities and, more importantly, in his very conception of justice—with which we will deal later.

More than two thousand years later, Ernestine Friedl's study of modern Greek villagers observed a similar value placed upon the division of labor:

> The householders of Vasilika take it for granted that they will use part of their produce, in kind or in cash, to pay for the services of various specialists. . . . Vasilika's farmers and shepherds consider themselves specialists; they view themselves with pride as experts in farming and sheepherding, and assign the same dignity to the expertness of others. . . . They do not expect a man to know how to do anyone else's work. One specialty is considered enough.[20]

It needs to be stressed that my emphasis here is not on *behavior* or action patterns but on Greek *beliefs* and values. I am talking about the *value* that ancient Greeks place on specialized role activity and the division of labor, not about whether they are in fact "rounded men" or specialists. The latter is a comparative judgment and the conclusion to which one comes about this depends entirely on the group or historical period to which the Greeks are compared. In large measure, the modern appreciation of the Greeks as rounded men seems to stem from the developing critique of alienation in nineteenth-century Europe and the somewhat romantic rejection of specialization that was then current in certain intellectual circles. In a more detailed analysis than can be given here, the Greek value of specialization could be connected with Greek core concepts of *hybris,* "no excess," and *mōira* (on which more shortly). All of these are conducive to the development of values which emphasize limited spheres of competence or authority and esteem for the division of labor.

One function of such a stress on the desirability of specialization is to counterbalance the particularly strong Greek emphasis on personal autonomy; for the division of labor—and the value attributed to it—constrains men to cooperate and seek the services of others, giving part of their own surplus in exchange for these. A second function is its contribution to Greek public life, for insofar as Greeks do not commit themselves to a "do-it-yourself" style of existence, they enjoy a guilt-free participation in extensive leisure which they can spend in conversation at the market place and in political life. A third function of specialization for the Greeks is particularly significant in the context of a competitive shame culture: insofar as men limit themselves to tasks for which they are specially qualified, they reduce the chance of failures that are publicly visible, thus minimizing the risk of ridicule by competitors who are all too eager to put them down.

The transcending significance attached to the division of labor by the Greeks needs fuller interpretation in the context of their contest system. Whether a man's place in the division of labor is seen as due to god-given or inborn skills or to specially trained talents, any division of labor creates and emphasizes functional distinctions among men. As a result, men are not seen as doing the same thing, and consequently the perception of the hierarchical distinctions among community members is blurred, giving less offense to those committed to a view of themselves as any man's equal. With a growing division of labor, those of the same status in the larger community are differentiated into smaller coteries of specialists who compete primarily with others of their own competence and who live immersed in a smaller, culturally bounded social circle. Whatever men's individual motives for valuing or entering into the division of labor, its increase has two vital consequences: it serves to reduce the average number of competitors facing one contestant, and it increases the number of prizes that the community offers.

In this view, then, the social function of the division of labor—as distinct from the motives that individuals have for entering into it—is not merely to heighten economic productivity and in this way enhance the gratifications of individuals, as nineteenth-century political economists had stressed. Nor is it only to make society "organically" solidary by strengthening the mutual dependence of its parts, as Émile Durkheim has described. The division of labor serves also to reduce social conflict by increasing the number of prize-winners and reducing the arena of communal competition. By dividing the larger society into a number of mutually disconnected social circles and establishments, each with its own distinctive standards, the division of labor permits competition to be waged ferociously within each small specialization without embroiling or spilling over into the larger system.

The division of labor reduces the strain of competition in the community as a whole by transforming one big, undifferentiated contest system into many small ones. It does this, in part, by making men ignorant of the very things others hold dear, by making the skills and knowledge which some men acquire unfamiliar to others, as well as uninteresting and unattractive, diverting them from seeking their approval and making them unqualified to give it. The division of labor withdraws men from seeking the approval of many others by involving them intensely with only a few from whom they do wish approval.

Fostered by the contest system, the division of labor enhances communal solidarity by organizing the community as a mosaic of conflicts. It does not induce social cohesion merely by integrating group members by reason of their mutual interdependence, but by separating them and by reducing their capacity to communicate with one another. It fosters social cohesion not so much by encouraging individuals to feel a contrite sense of dependence on the larger whole as by encouraging men to lose themselves in the bitterest of struggles in a smaller and disjoined sector. The division of labor contributes to social cohesion not by giving men a common allegiance and goal toward which they will strive cooperatively and not by eliminating the contest; it fosters cohesion by creating many contests which drain off competitive sentiments in diverse directions and by preventing them from coming together in a single confluence that could overwhelm the community.

As mentioned earlier in discussing the tensions between the man judged most outstanding in war and the one who is titular head of the group,[21] an undifferentiated contest system within the community generates certain strains. A contest conducted at any one time produces a winner; more generally, previous contests establish a rank ordering of all contestants based on achievement. Given the assumptions of the contest system, however, this is always open to disruption and, in particular, the incumbent leaders in the community are open to continual challenge by rising contenders.

In the early Homeric situation, where the contest code stresses military prowess, the question then is: How does an aging king, past his prime physically, legitimate his right to continuing leadership when there are others in his group who are now clearly superior in war? One hypothesis is that the king—or titular head—is said to possess different skills and talents from those of other members of the warrior group and, in particular, to have talents other than those of combat. Military achievement comes to be seen as requiring more than physical prowess; success in war is redefined to enhance the significance of wise counsel and of advice derivable only from years of experience.

Two core specializations would then, on this hypothesis, develop around the differentiation between those who fight well and those who give good advice. Military achievement undergoes a kind of binary fission into two component values, wily planning and effective fighting, each of which can now legitimate a claim to eminence (e.g., the clever Odysseus and the ferocious Achilles).

The generic as distinct from the Homeric form of the problem, however, is to protect any established system of social stratification where contest values prevail. Most especially, how do the leaders of such a community protect themselves against the challenge of new contenders? One possible solution is to stress the value of specialization and the division of labor; they may then go on to define leadership in the group as a whole as requiring, like any other specialization, a special talent or a special training not possessed by other kinds of specialists, and to which, therefore, not all are admissible. (This, as we will later note, is the tack that Plato takes.) With the increasing division of labor, therefore, victory or excellence in any one specialized contest does not necessarily legitimate the claim to leadership in the community as a whole. Competition for leadership in the group can now be defined as a special and distinct kind of contest for which only a limited number of contestants are eligible. The division of labor, through reducing the number of eligibles for communal leadership and by absorbing men in localized contests for leadership within specialized sectors, reduces the disruptive effects of the contest on the community's political system.

THE FAILURE OF SHAME

If the Greeks are so concerned about the opinion of others, how is it that they do not more often behave in ways conforming with the expectations and desires of others but, rather, manifest a strong ability to resist these and to behave in contrary ways? This may be the most difficult and perhaps the most important of the questions about a shame culture, for it would seem that a deep concern with the good opinion of others would make a person subject to their control. It is difficult to reconcile a concern with one's good repute, which the Greeks do indeed have, with the disloyalty and treachery to their cities that men such as Alcibiades epitomize; for this surely must threaten their reputations at least within their native cities if not, indeed, even among those to whom they betray their cities. Why is it that the threat of being shamed by their fellow citizens does not suffice to control such men?

Doubtless the threat of being shamed does to some extent inhibit deviance and does serve as a mechanism of social control; in point of fact it is sometimes only after men's repute has been threatened or injured by their city that they betray it. Nonetheless, it is clear that being oriented to the opinion of others does not, for the Greeks, mean that they will accept any opinion that is rendered. They are ready to accept opinion concerning themselves when it is creditable, when the public judgment is favorable, when it is consistent with what they feel to be their due, and when it is consonant with their own conception of themselves. But when the judgment is unfavorable or at variance with their own self-images they resist it bitterly and they then obstinately pit their own estimate of themselves against that of their judges.

Since good repute is the central objective of men committed to the contest system, they cannot readily accept a negative public judgment. It is in some part because they want victory so much that it matters less to them how it is obtained and cannot accept a negative public reputation. They remain oriented to the opinion of others only so long as they have hope of their rendering a favorable judgment; but once the prize has been refused or given to others, their motive for concerning themselves with the opinion of others is impaired.

In part, then, the two traits that have been held to be elements of Greek shame culture are mutually inconsistent; under the conditions specified above, an intense concern with victory might divert men from a responsive and conforming orientation to the opinion of others. Further, the Greek concern with the good opinion of others is often less important to the Greeks than their own conception of themselves, and when opinion is discrepant with their self-images, it is often their commitment to the latter that governs their course of action. This, of course, premises that the Greeks have the very potent sense of individuality commented on earlier and that they make strong commitments to their own well-bounded and individuated conception of self.

The problem of the failure of the shame mechanism as an instrument of social control, the weakness of public opinion in certain instances, becomes even more complex if we consider the case not of those who fail but of those who succeed in winning the highest laurels. Several things already noted need to be connected here. First, those most successful are also those most subject to envy and hostility. We might say that men of high status are allowed few "idiosyncrasy" or deviance credits.[22] It commonly happens in some societies that highly placed people are allowed some measure of deviance by their group, usually more than that granted to less-highly placed persons. Among the Greeks, however, the opposite seems to be the case. There is a greater readiness to scrutinize the behavior of highly placed persons, in the expectation that they would more likely manifest some form of *hybris,* and there is less tolerance of failure or deviance by them. The slightest failure of the highly placed person is often seized upon as an occasion to punish him. But if envy of someone increases with his increasing repute, and with this goes the increasing possibility of a negative judgment, it would seem that the most highly placed persons would develop some hostility toward their own group and therefore be less influenceable by its opinions and less amenable to its control.

The Alexander Problem: Deviance at the Top

In addition to this problem in coping with the successful, there is another that might be called the Alexander problem: What happens to men when they have "conquered the world" and there are no new worlds to conquer? What happens when they have won all the prizes that their group can bestow? The situation is particularly critical when eminence has been won in a highly aggressive system of competition, for men who have come up this way may still be habituated to achievement; they may continue reflexively to look for other worlds to conquer, going on to reckless adventures. Insofar as their later undertakings are probably the more difficult and risky, it is the more likely they will fail, and they may then be charged with a *hybris* deserving of punishment.

Those victorious in the contest system are subject to still another, but related, contingency that may lead them to behave in ways arousing the hostility of their group. Having won the highest prizes that the group may award, they have nothing left to look forward to. Further rewards provide smaller increments of marginal utility. Since there is little else that a group can hold out as a possible reward, the group's ability to command conformity with its opinions is further impaired. Then, indeed, there is a growing possibility that the victors will behave in ways at variance with group opinion and, along with this, a growing likelihood that the group will view their behavior as manifesting an outrageously overbearing *hybris*. The nurse in Euripides' *Medea* remarks, "Great people's tempers are terrible, always having their own way, seldom checked, dangerous they shift from mood to mood." [23] It is perhaps in connection with the Alexander problem that ostracism may also be understood; to exile the victors is, in effect, to remove the most potentially dangerous men, men whose leadership positions might, on the one hand, enable and motivate them to undertake ventures particularly hazardous to the group and who, on the other, are less subject to influence and control by the group's opinions.

The Uses of Posterity

The tendency of the successful to ignore the opinion of others in their group is further exacerbated among the Greeks because those most intensely involved in the contest system are much concerned with posterity, and are perhaps more concerned with the good opinion of posterity than of their contemporaries. It was "fame immortal" that had been culturally prescribed as the highest goal; it is fame immortal to which the ideal contestant has been oriented—perhaps fortunately so for his own security, considering the pervasiveness of envy and the fickleness of his contemporaries' opinions.

A concern with the good opinion of posterity disposes a man to accept— or at least to suffer—the poor opinions of his contemporaries, caring less for their judgment than for that of those who come after. As Alcibiades remarks,

[P]ersons . . . who have attained to any distinction, although they may be unpopular in their lifetime in their relations with their fellow-men and especially with their equals, leave to posterity the desire of claiming connexion with them even without any ground, and are vaunted by the country to which they belonged, not as strangers or evil-doers, but as fellow countrymen and heroes.[24]

Such a concern with posthumous fame has contradictory consequences for group stability. It is disruptive of group stability by inducing men to ignore the opinions of those around them,[25] but it is also, in important ways, conducive to group stability. An intense concern with posthumous fame may serve to maintain the motivation of men who have won all that their group has to bestow. It may keep them actively striving and prevent them from retiring into private life. If a concern with posthumous fame inhibits leadership apathy at the cost of reducing group control over leadership, it also means that outstanding men will not compare themselves only with their living competitors, and therefore will not rest content—withdrawing their talents from the group—when they have outdistanced them.

The concern with posthumous fame orients men to the achievements not only of living competitors or of those dead, but also to men yet to come and to the unknowable levels of achievement which they will attain. It thus introduces a strain of insatiability into achievement strivings. This lack of measure or limit has been regarded as pathological by Western tradition from Plato to Talcott Parsons; nonetheless, it is this very insatiability that helps maintain the motivation of the highly successful and keeps them participating in group life. While such insatiability is hurtful to the individual and to the group, impairing both the individual's capacity to attain gratification and the group's capacity to control the directions in which gratification will be sought, it also serves to defend both the individual and the group against perhaps an even greater danger: the withdrawal from group life. Insatiability may serve to defend the individual and group against the disorientation and apathy of success. "The sovereign source of melancholy is repletion," said William James. "Need and struggle are what excite and inspire us; our hour of triumph is what brings the void."

Primary Group and Class Influences on Sensitivity to Others

Several other developments that limit the effectiveness of group opinion as a social control in Greece will be mentioned briefly here. These have to do with the state of primary relationships and class involvements.

Even the relatively small and mutually visible community of citizens are not equally sensitive to the opinions of all others. For one thing, men are more concerned with the good opinion of those in their primary groups, their male friends and relatives. Yet with the attenuation of kinship bonds, the precariousness of friendship ties, and a relatively low capacity to maintain strong object attachments, even the opinions of those who would commonly count for most might be less constraining and influential. Further, as noted earlier, the rules of the contest system are such that the good opinion of peers or superiors is more important than that of inferiors. Thus Hippolytus asserts proudly, "I am no man to speak with vapid, precious skill before a mob, although among my equals and in a narrow circle I am held not unaccomplished in the eloquent art. That is as it should be. The demagogue who charms a crowd is scorned by cultured experts." [26] It cannot be expected that public opinion and repute among the *dēmos* would control an aristocrat as effectively as the opinion of other aristocrats; indeed, they might sympathize with those of their own group whom the *dēmos* has punished, deeming the latter's behavior an expression of class prejudice. The sanctions of the shame culture are thus limited in their effectiveness by the existence of a class system and by class loyalties.

For these various reasons, then, while the Greeks are strongly oriented to the opinion of others, this often does not suffice to lead them to conform with others' values and expectations. Concern with the opinion of others is strong, but it is often less strong than the individual's conception of self and of what he owes to it. What the Greeks seek is a good opinion in the view of others. When this opinion is negative, resentment might know no bounds; yet when opinion is supremely favorable, the group might have nothing left with which to reward continued conformity. Within the context of the contest system, then, both defeat and great victory might therefore dispose men to ignore rather than conform to the opinions of others.

MODAL ELEMENTS IN THE GREEK SELF-IMAGE

The Greeks have strong attachments to their selves; which is to say they have a high regard for themselves as persons and they conceive themselves as worthy beings. They are much concerned about behaving in a manner consistent with their own self-image, no less than they insist that others treat them accordingly. As Sophocles' Neoptolemus observes, "All is disgust when one leaves his own nature and does things that misfit it." [27] They conceive of the self as a precarious entity which is difficult but vital to maintain; indeed, they think of the self as an entity that might perish with only one discrepant, unfitting act. Thus after going berserk and killing his camp's animals, the hero Ajax moans, "All that I was has perished with these poor creatures here." [28]

The nature of the self, one's own as well as that of others, is of strong and salient *interest* to the Greeks. The self has become an object to itself, and the importance attached to it is matched by a sense of ignorance concerning its character. The self is felt to contain a mystery that invites a quest to "know thyself." It is not only that the Greeks feel that they do not (but should) know themselves; they also have a nagging feeling—or a fantasy— of being other than what they seem. There are, for example, many dramas that hinge on the concealment, the search for, and the revelation of the protagonists' identity. "I have a brother living," says Iphigenia, "though face to face with him, I should not know him." [29] In Euripides' *Helen,* Menelaus asks, "Who are you? I look, lady, upon your face: whose face?" And Helen counters, "And who are you? The same question for both of us?" [30] In his *Rhesus,* Euripides has the chorus inquire, "Who was the man who was here? . . . Who was it? Where did he come from? What country?" [31] In *The Bacchae* the problem of identity is given various expressions. It is displayed in Pentheus' total loss of identity with his change of clothes and his madness, as well as in Dionysus' appearance as a "god incognito" who tells Pentheus: "You do not know the limits of your strength. You do not know what you do. You do not know who you are." [32] The significance of Oedipus' true identity, of course, needs no elaboration.

The Greek search for true identity is characteristically activistic and outward. Rather than being sought in a reflective inward quest for an ineffable essence, the self is sought in the social relationship with others and in the social role that one has. This might, for example, lead to an effort to determine who one's true parents are, as in *Oedipus Rex,* or to inquiry into whether one's mother is slave or free, as in *Ion.* When Ion asks Creusa to tell him who she is, it is noteworthy how he goes on to specify the original question. "Tell me," he asks, "your family, Your Country. And what is your name?" [33] The riddle of the self for the Greek is characteristically to be resolved by discovering one's true social status; the mystery resides in one's social position and in the social bonds these carry with them.

Yet the Greek search for identity is an ambivalent one; if they are driven to search for it they also fear what they might find: "I am on the brink of frightful speech," says the herdsman to Oedipus who, in turn, replies, "And I of frightful hearing. But I must hear." [34] The hidden or latent identity, it is often feared, may compromise the manifest or seeming identity the individual bears at the moment and may threaten to cast a new and unpleasant light on things. "If by some chance my mother were a slave," admits Ion, "to find her would be worse than ignorance." [35]

The Greek attitude toward the self seems similar to attitudes toward sacred objects; in truth, the self is invested with attributes of the sacred.

There is a sense of mystery surrounding it, there is an impulsion to come close to and know this mystery. There is, at least to the bewildered Cyclops, the near magic of Odysseus' emergence from "Nobody"; there is the disappearance and reappearance of Iphigenia so that she is only seemingly sacrificed by her father; there is a similar intervention of the gods who create a mock Helen and hide the true one elsewhere, leading Menelaus to express wonderment about the uniqueness of individual identity: "I suppose it must be that in the real world a great many have the same name, men named like other men, cities like cities, women like women." [36]

Along with this sense of the mystery—and similarly symptomatic of an attitude toward the sacred—there is also a fear that the self is a powerful, god-involved thing that had better not have human hands rudely laid upon it. This is suggested by one of the most ancient and emotionally charged conceptions of deviant behavior among Greeks, the concept of *hybris*. That the meaning of the concept is especially diffuse and far-reaching is indicated by the fact that there are all manner of prosecutions for *hybris* under Attic law. The charge might be provoked for any kind of bodily injury, for illegal arrest, or for the marriage of a former slave to his master's widow. "[T]he concept of *hybris* is broad enough to include all attacks upon the person or the interests of the person," [37] writes G. R. Morrow. It is a peculiarly abhorrent crime to the fourth-century Greek, he adds, because "it was an affront to the dignity or the honor of the person. . . . An action may be classed as *hybris* if its commission is incompatible with the dignity of the person injured. . . ." [38] That even the self of the slave is protected from acts of *hybris* strongly implies that the self is felt to possess that element of untouchability so characteristic of sacred things.

The Hellenic fascination with the problem of identity and the sense of the precariousness of the self are closely related. The more precarious the sense of self, the more problematic it becomes; conversely, the more problematic it becomes, the more aware may one become of the difficulties of self-maintenance and of the self's varying, elusive character.

The Hellenic world is one in which men have relatively recently lost their tribal involvements and the firmly fixed identities these sustained. There are good reasons to be concerned with identity and to feel that identity is uncertain and concealed. Resident aliens, for example, might and do try to pretend that they are full-fledged citizens and thus share in the latter's perquisites, while citizens fear and resent this intrusion and seek to ferret out the impostors. There is, also, during certain periods, a fear of an inheritable sin or "pollution"; if inexplicable evils befall a man of seemingly innocent antecedents, he might well wonder whether he has other, true parents for whose sins he is being made to suffer. Given a belief in pollution, a man's family identity could be his destiny.

Further, politicians seeking popularity with the *dēmos* might try to conceal or play down their aristocratic heritage. Poor parents also sometimes "potted" an unwanted infant, leaving it in an urn along with identifying amulets, recognition of which, it is probably fantasied, might one day enable parent and child to know one another. Children are sometimes kidnaped from their families and sold into slavery. Again, those brought up on traditional mythology have been taught to believe that the gods might assume human form and cohabit with mortals. And it is widely felt that friends might conceal their true character from one another. From the standpoint of Hellenic custom and assumptions, then, there are many *realistic* instigations to a concern with the identity of one's self and others.

With the breakdown of tribalism and with the emphasis on individual achievement in the context of the contest system, identities are indeed self-created. Men are becoming "self-made." Yet precisely because so much rests on individual achievement in a contest system, the self of the contestant undergoes frequent tests and can be maintained only precariously.

The identity, or self-image, of a person depends in part on his ability to have his claims consensually validated by others. Will others acknowledge him to be what he claims to be, and will they tactfully forego undermining his claims when the opportunity presents itself? While the problems of self-maintenance are the same in a contest system as in other social systems, the chance for a congenial solution to these problems is impaired by the mutual hostility, envy, and distrust that a contest system generates. In a contest system a man's self-image must rest in large measure on what his competitors think of him; thus his view of self must inevitably be precarious. The contest system provides the self with opportunities for an enhanced sense of power born of successful achievement in the face of resistance by others. But each victory for someone is a loss to someone else, and the victors are always under critical inspection by competitors eager for a chance to put them down.

In a competitive, achievement-oriented society, identity is a tense and changing thing because it is always open to challenge and is never once-for-all fixed; it needs to be validated continually in each new trial. In such a society the self is always under assault, always on trial, always dying and being reborn. It can never, therefore, be known fully and finally; one must await the new revelation of self brought by each new trial.

One of the most important elements in the Greek conception of self is a sense of its individual power, the feeling that it is able, or ought to be able, to influence or control things in a sphere around it. To a great extent the Greek image of the person, of what one needs to be and have in order to be a person, centers on the possession of power, on the imputed ability to make decisions governing one's own actions and to live under no one else's constraint. Even if inescapably condemned to die, the Greek ideal requires the self to appear to go willingly: "I offer up my life for them of my own accord," declares Macaria, "but won't be forced." [39] Again Polyxema proclaims, "Of my own free will I die." [40] And Iphigenia states proudly, "Chains are unhallowed things." [41]

In contrast to modern Western judgments about persons—which center far more on their moral worth, or the "goodness" or "badness" of their character—the Greek view focuses more on the weak–strong dimension: "Are you mad enough to think that anyone would choose your helplessness in preference to our strength?" [42] asks Copreus in *The Heracleidae*. Greeks are likely to think in terms of the potency of the person, or of attributes or roles more indicative of this strength or weakness, than of his moral stature seen as distinct from potency. Consistent with this image of the person, if not a projection of it, is the Greek view of the gods which typically focuses on their power rather than on their moral character. Similarly, the Greek idea of life after death is to a large extent a disagreeable or unattractive one precisely because the afterlife is conceived to be a wraithy existence, devoid of power.

Being a person in the Greek sense means that individuals must have autonomy and avoid living under constraint; it also means that they must have the ability to control others. The Greek self was a coin on one side of which was inscribed, "Avoid control of self," and on the other read, "Impose control on others." There is, then, a painful dilemma in the Greek conception of the person: it disposes individuals to do unto others as they would not be done unto themselves; it leads them to behave toward others in a manner that outrages their strongest sentiments. The drive toward control disposes the individual to seek out and manifest his power over others; the drive toward autonomy, however, disposes him to avoid situations that place him in the power of others, make him obligated to them, or show him to be manifestly subordinate to them.

This does not imply, of course, that individuals do not, in fact, enter into social relations in which they are manifestly subordinated, but only that these relationships are not preferred. It is in part for this reason that employment by others is not a preferred mode of livelihood. It is notable that when upper-class Athenians develop the custom of being continually accompanied by a free male companion who is dependent upon them, and who attends dinner parties or symposia with them, these companions are looked upon by other guests with some contempt: they might be referred to as "parasites," and they are "made the butt of much banter to which the invited guests would themselves object." [43]

In a similar vein, Athenians are extremely sensitive not to behave in any way that might imply acceptance of the superiority of another, while they resent any behavior by others which seems to entail a claim of superiority. If a person's mantle falls too low, it is regarded as an expression of pretentiousness; nor must his mode of walking suggest arrogance or pompousness; and bowing, of course, is regarded as a form of oriental obsequiousness, which while appropriate as a way of paying respect to the gods is unseemly behavior between such equals as the citizenry like to think themselves.

Sources of the Greek Self-Image

A central problem, of course, is how the Greeks come to conceive of the person in this way and, in particular, to stress the importance of potency and power in relation to others. Here it is necessary to consider their system of social stratification and, in particular, the significance of slavery and the conceptions they have of slaves. Typically, slaves are defined as those who live under the constraint of another; thus when *persons* are thought of as those free of constraint and autonomous, they are being attributed characteristics complementary to those of the slave. The denial or avoidance of a sense of human insignificance or unworthiness of which the slave is the paradigm in Greek society—disposes the free citizen to define his self (or person) in terms directly opposite to those in which the slave is conventionally conceived.

Olympian religion is also important in expressing and conducing to the Greek view of the person as a potent being. The view of the gods which this religion fosters shows them to be in many ways very similar to men, with the notable exception that the gods are characterized by unrestricted power and immortality. Yet it is not simply that persons may be thought of as potent because they are modeled after these supernatural personages, or because the gods constitute an ideal which men seek to approximate. It is not simply the power imputed to the gods that is related to the Greek view of the person but, also, the ways in which the gods' powers are thought to be used or withheld.

Had the gods been regarded as entirely responsible for all that men do or suffer there would have been correspondingly less scope for the development of individuality, and less of a sense of potency in men themselves. There would have been less opportunity for the development of achievement motivation and concomitant difficulty in justifying a system of punishments and rewards for individual behavior. Many of the unusual deeds and emotions accomplished and experienced by men are, it is true, attributed to the gods. From Homer's Agamemnon to Sophocles' Ajax, the gods are portrayed as inducing strong emotions in men that may lead them to behave exceptionally, in either heroic or irrational ways; they are often shown to lead men astray by giving them a kind of divine madness, or *atē*. Yet the fact remains that, although Agamemnon claims that he wronged Achilles because the gods blinded him, he also offers compensation to Achilles for his deed. Why should he do so if he viewed his actions as the result of divine intervention? The answer would seem to be that when Agamemnon later comes to his senses, he is then subject to a rule which states that a man is, in fact, liable for his actions. The god had intervened, capriciously done his mischief, and departed the scene; other rules then applied.

Clearly a belief system that held the gods active in all spheres of men's lives at all times would subvert the operation of any system of social sanctions aimed at influencing individual behavior, for no one could then be held accountable for the wrongs he had done or be deserving of reward for his good deeds and great accomplishments. In the Greek view, however, the gods are not entirely responsible for all events. Being somewhat like humans—although larger than life in their vast powers—the gods have their own affairs to attend to. There are, therefore, many things they could not trouble themselves with; they do not intervene continuously and completely. Consequently, a zone of contingency exists in which events do depend on men's decisions and actions, and for which they can be called to account.

The divine intention in those areas of life where the gods are thought to intervene also remains uncertain. Pressure is therefore exerted to know the future, and this is expressed in the widespread practice of consulting oracles. These might read the signs from sacrifices, from the interpretation of dreams, from the sifting of sacred salt, or from invocation of the spirits of the dead. Some, like the Apollonian Oracle at Delphi, are consulted on important questions of state by the Athenians and the Spartans (with whom Delphi always had an especially close relationship) and give oral replies to orally given questions.

Within Olympianism there is, then, both a religiously constrained orientation to the future and a realm in which men are free, and in which their actions can indeed make a difference in the outcome. Far from being incompatible with the development of individuality or with a conception of men as potent, Olympian theology induces men to want to know and to shape the future; for men are vouchsafed an area of power and responsibility which, because its boundaries are indeterminate, is all the more conducive to individual effort. Since these boundaries are indeterminate, a man might, like Agamemnon, attribute his mistakes to the gods *after* making them; he could not, however, use the gods as an excuse for failing to make an effort to do the things expected of someone in his position. He could not with impunity shirk his responsibility as an individual.

In such *post factum* use of the gods to explain mistakes, the individual is acknowledging the gods' power over him. That he may thereby be slandering them—as Homer's Zeus complains—is, in a shame culture, less significant than that he admits their power over him, especially under a religious code which condemns *hybris* and which, in any event, never regards the gods as morally bound agents. Furthermore, *post factum* use of the gods to explain derelictions is an implicit denial that the malefactor has behaved out of an abiding enmity from which the victim could expect future injury. Such a use of the gods facilitates the injured party's acceptance of compensation from the wrongdoer, thus short-circuiting the possibility of a continuing feud. In brief, it permits both parties to have second thoughts about their conflict at a time when its costs can be seen more clearly.

Finally, the Greek sense of the self as a potent thing is related to the waning of tribal tradition and cohesion and to the concomitant growth of social differentiation and conflict. Under tribalism, the demands placed upon the individual are relatively consistent and highly uniform and are, in consequence, experienced as relatively powerful. The repeated and uniform demands of others, having a relatively small range in variation, reinforce one another so that they appear as part of an ordained and natural order of things from which there seems to be neither escape nor appeal. In this connection one may recall Solomon Asch's experiments which show that some 33 per cent of individuals will go contrary to the evidence of their own senses when their judgments are at variance with those made by all the other group members.[44] In these experiments, the judgments being made are about something as visible as the comparative lengths of lines and not about intangibles, such as the justice of the gods, which are intrinsically untestable. Asch's experiments are suggestive of the power with which an undivided group can impose its own definition of a situation and can suppress the resistance of individual deviants.

Individuality and Social Conflict

As a tribal belief system breaks down, however, and is no longer shared so uniformly, as there is no longer one "way" but various ways within increasingly differentiated groups, the individual is no longer faced with so united a social reality. Under these circumstances the demands of the group are no longer experienced by the individual as quite so irresistible or natural, and his sense of freedom and power is enhanced. The growth of new technologies, which is associated with the decline of tribalism, also heightens a sense of increasing control over nature and further strengthens the individual's feeling of power.

With the development of conflicting political factions and social classes in Greek society, the individual's sense of potency and his self-consciousness are additionally strengthened. Since his kinship ties no longer give him ready-made alliances, the individual is freer to choose them and, conversely, he is sought out by diverse groups which compete with one another for his support. The individual's sense of potency and worthiness is therefore validated by groups who, in seeking his loyalty and alliance, in effect tell him that *he* makes a difference. The self experiences itself as potent, and is increasingly aware of itself when it is no longer subject to a single blanketing definition of the social situation, and when it can sense its own separation from all the different factions that compete for its attachment. Solon's elegy, describing the state of Athens at the time he came to power, indicates how social conflict may enhance the individual's feelings of a splendid, self-reliant isolation, at once perilous and powerful: "Wherefore, mingling for myself strength from many quarters / I stood at bay like a wolf surrounded by a pack of hounds." [45]

Growing social differentiation and group tensions also increase the likelihood that an individual's impulses will not be spontaneously in keeping with the expectations of others with whom he interacts and, correspondingly, that their responses will not be completely and reflexively in keeping with his. Mutual adjustments will, therefore, have to be made more deliberately and with heightened self-consciousness. It is in some part in contest and contention, when "life is made up of struggles," that the sense of a self-conscious and separate individuality is strengthened. Without some tension with others, the boundaries of the self become more permeable, and the line between self and others grows indistinct. One way the individual experiences himself as potent is by manifesting a capacity to stand up to others, to resist their demands or to overcome their resistance to his. And he may heighten the sense of his own individuality by sharpening tension with others, testing and maintaining the clarity of the self's boundaries by seeking out and entering into contention.

TENSIONS OF INDIVIDUALITY

With the heightening of such individuality and self-consciousness, the person encounters new kinds of problems and tensions, among them a feeling of separateness and isolation. He may feel a certain lonely distance, as expressed in Aeschylus' *Agamemnon* where one of the characters remarks, "far from others I hold my own mind," [46] and becomes disposed to turn inward. In the context of social conflict—of expected differences from and with others—behavior becomes more self-conscious and guarded lest the true self be revealed inadvertently to hostile or untrustworthy persons. Aware of this, Aeschylus' Electra enjoins the chorus in *The Libation Bearers,* "Do not for fear of any, hide your thought inside your heart." [47]

Such concerns help give rise to one of the culturally admired personality types among the Greeks, those who maintain control over their impulses and act on the basis of a rational calculus. This is expressed, for example, in Pericles' Odyssean image of the Athenians as wily strategists who are never at a loss in coping with life's challenges. In contrast to the Spartan self-image, which stresses their physical courage and superiority in the field, the Athenian self-image places greater emphasis on the role of military science, strategy, guile, and craft, and in general gives greater commendation to the rational dimensions of self. Correspondingly, the problem of the propriety of deceit and lying as strategies to gain one's ends is sufficiently unresolved in Athenian society to still be made one of the central problems in Sophocles' *Philoctetes,* although even by Aeschylus' time it appears to have been viewed increasingly as shameful.

Under these circumstances there is a growing sense of the difference between the appearance or social mask presented to others and the "true" self. There is a sensitivity to one's own masks and to the masks of others, the two growing together. This also contributes to the diffuse feeling of distrust in interpersonal relations which both impairs the ease with which persons can enter into mutually revealing or intimate relationships and intensifies the need for them.

Since intimacy entails exposure of the guarded parts of the self, it is felt to be dangerous in the context of mutual distrust. Yet self-conscious persons require intimate relations in which they can be close to others, drop the conventionally required masks, and be admitted to the true self of the other. The individual wants to know what others "really" think, especially about himself. Further, since it takes effort to keep up one's own social disguises, one also requires others with whom he can relax and put these disguises safely aside. This further contributes to the endemic "crisis of intimacy," where the individual needs and wants intimate social relationships, but also fears them.

The Underside of the Self-Image

That there is a gap between the individual's public presentation of his self and his own private experience of it raises the question of what he does with those elements of self or personality that are felt to be at odds with what people expect. There is also the question of which aspects of the self will typically be felt to be at variance with public expectation.

To consider the last first, several suggestions may be made. Where the self is defined in terms of its potency dimension and where its power is highly regarded, then it would seem that feelings of weakness, surrender, impotence, and passive yielding will be denied or hidden from both the self and others. The yearning to be protected by and dependent upon others —so deeply discrepant with the preferred image of the autonomous and powerful person—will be secreted within the person. Conversely, the self will also conceal a sense of superiority and will be cautious about behaving in ways that seem overweaning and arrogant, lest it arouse resentment at its *hybris*. Yet arrogance in interpersonal relations is more likely to be suppressed, that is, more or less consciously concealed, while passivity and surrender are more likely to be repressed, or unconsciously concealed, since they are seen as lowly and therefore more threatening than the former. The contest system permits a greater expression of desires for superiority while it blocks the expression of passive and dependency desires.

Since the Greek image of the proper person or self also stresses the instrumental, deliberative, and calculating sentiments and skills, and since these are among the prized contents of the self, sentiments which are not felt to be under their disciplined control are experienced as unworthy and somewhat dangerous. Not only are the strong emotions often regarded as being at variance with the ideal of temperance, but they are often felt to be mysterious and frightening, somehow external to the person or a part of the nonself.[48] Violent emotion, overt aggression and hostility, lust and abandoned joy, are felt to be dangerous and disorderly presences adjacent to, and yet not a part of, the true or desired self. "Let not their passion overwhelm them; let no lust seize on these men to violate what they must not," [49] says Aeschylus in the *Agamemnon;* and, again, in *The Libation Bearers,* "No, no, control yourself, and do not lose your head for joy." [50]

The Greeks set great store by expressive discipline, or self-control. Their statuary celebrates the serenity of the gods; while the bodies of men are shown exerting themselves strenuously, the faces might be blandly impassive. Yet for all the value they place on expressive discipline, the Greeks often regard it as fragile, and in this we may note still another reason for the Greek sense of the precariousness of the self. There is a problem here, however, for certain strong emotions are appropriate to the contest system and to the performance of military duties. Hand-to-hand killing in open battle, for example, is probably best done by those who can give themselves up to rage; men who have lost control of themselves have lost concern for their own lives and are the most fearful opponents to those who maintain self-control and a concern for their lives. To a soldier-people—and the Greek citizenry are liable for military duty until the age of sixty—who have to kill close up, the thorough repression of aggression might well be fatal. Yet men of hair-trigger temper are also dangerous to their own group, however fearsome they may be to the enemy; they are difficult to discipline and may be too quick to seek satisfaction for some real or imagined slight. Sophocles, for example, shows Ajax—after having been refused Achilles' armor—overcome by a killing mania, leaving a ruin of blood in his own camp. Upon regaining his senses, however, Ajax is horrified at his own deeds and, disgusted with himself, he subsequently commits suicide. The confrontation between Ajax's ideal, heroic self and the suddenly exposed underside of this self becomes an occasion for bitter irony: "Here I am, the bold, the valiant, unflinching in the shock of war, a terrible threat to unsuspecting beasts." [51] Euripides' Medea, too, is shown succumbing to a homicidal mania that leads her to kill her own children in revenge upon her faithless husband. It is noteworthy that a similar danger is feared for Ajax's son; when Ajax is in the grip of his madness, his wife is careful not to let the boy near him. The Greeks, in short, are deeply concerned about their capacity to go murderously berserk. Yet they never relinquish killing as an instrument of city policy and, indeed, the spear-won prize is always highly honorable. The Athenians put to the sword the men of cities that rebel against them during the Peloponnesian War, or who otherwise cause them special trouble; the Spartans, for their part, systematically butcher the Helots.

Given its continuing military needs and involvements, as well as a tradition in which its greatest heroes are renowned for their violence and killing, it is difficult for Greek culture to suppress firmly the violent components of the self. Perhaps it is partly because of this inability to renounce violence that Plato includes in his tripartite anatomy of personality (in addition to reason and to the passions) that elusive third part, the *thymos,* or "high-spirited." Plato allegorically characterizes this part as the "lion," thus, in effect, ennobling a certain kind of violence—especially violence born of outraged self-regard—and preventing it from being condemned along with the other passions.

What happens to the discrepant parts of the self, to those that are experienced as at variance with what the self or others "expect," depends in some degree on the nature of the institutional and role structures that exist, and on the extent to which emotions and sentiments inhibited in one area may find outlets in another. Here several things need to be kept in mind. First, the great value that Greeks place upon a man's political-military (i.e., public) role tends to overshadow other roles. The older, extended kinship ties are attenuated and a man's nuclear family, from which he is frequently absent, forms only a dim background to his public career. As Pericles remarks in his funeral address, "For there is justice in the claim that steadfastness in his country's battles should be as a cloak to cover a man's other imperfections; since the good action has blotted out the bad, and his merit as a citizen more than outweighed his demerits as an individual." [52]

A validation of the self based upon pecuniary success is limited in effectiveness inasmuch as such activities, if not viewed with contempt, are frequently of dubious and low repute and considered of little account in comparison with performance in a public role. To a great extent, then, a man's self-image and sense of worth are shaped by his political-public involvements, and the Greeks, far more than we, tend to conceive of themselves in terms of these roles. The self is invested more heavily in the public roles; it is reinforced by feedback from a small circle of like-minded friends similarly committed to their public roles. Consequently, many of the friendships a person establishes are also dependent upon success or failure in his public role, and on his particular outlook with respect to public policy. When civil tensions are exacerbated, especially by the Peloponnesian War, "blood became a weaker tie than party." [53] That Athenian public issues and policies are discussed so largely in utilitarian and rational ways—indeed, it is depressing to note that no subsequent polity has ever had a higher average level of rationality—is not only expressive of the deliberative and calculating components of the Greek self, but is, at the same time, conducive to the internalization and reinforcement of such components.

The Theater and the Self

One way that expression is given to the underside of the Athenian self, particularly to the strong emotions toward which it is so ambivalent, is through attendance at the regular performances of the tragedies. Most citizens attend and are remarkably knowledgeable about the theater. As Aristotle will state later, the tragedies provide them with a kind of "catharsis"; they permit a controlled release of the repressed part of the self—a relaxation of expressive discipline—which reduces its pressure upon the rational self-image and allows it to be brought back under more reliable control.

Tragedy provides a catharsis for the repressed underside of the self partly through identification with the choruses, many of which are composed of dependent-subordinate personages who give voice to weakness, such as old women or men, slaves, suppliants, lower-class men, or fallen gods. The lowness of the chorus is sometimes accentuated by composing it of those whose social positions are a compound of several subordinate statuses such as female slaves, foreign slave women, or suppliant women.

The choruses of old men also evidence the stigmata of weakness: "But we, dishonored, old in our bones, cast off even then from the gathering horde, stay here. . . ." [54] Similarly, the choruses of soldiers and sailors in *Ajax, Philoctetes,* and *Rhesus* are nonindividuated subordinates commanded by others. All are powerless to direct or to affect seriously the course of events.

The choruses also frequently speak in the whining, complaining voice of people who are concerned and anxious, but doubtful that they will be listened to. They express panicky, uncontrolled fears, as in *Seven against Thebes;* they plead for help as in *The Suppliant Maidens;* they deferentially pledge their obedience and assistance as in *Ajax;* they commonly counsel prudence, temperance, acceptance of the hurt of living, and remind the protagonists that others have suffered before them and have got over it; and they often give sympathetic consensual validation to the protagonists, as in *Orestes,* saying yes, you have suffered terrible wrongs, but do not give up hope, or, as in the *Medea,* saying, "You are in the right, Medea, in paying your husband back." [55]

The exchanges between the choruses and the protagonists often have the quality of an internalized conversation. They often speak to one another when other characters are absent; the protagonist frequently reveals his most secret and hazardous plans to the chorus, as in the *Medea,* with apparent confidence that he will not be betrayed. In short, the dialogue between the protagonist and the chorus is a way in which the former thinks aloud, with both sides acting out different parts of the self: the protagonist acts out the striving heroic, controlling, potent, and ideal components of the self-image; the chorus acts out the underside of the self, the passive, dependent, fearful side.

When this underside of the self comes to the surface—as in Euripides, whose plays more frequently feature subordinate persons such as women, children, and servants—the role of the chorus wanes and sometimes seems superfluous. In Euripides the underside of Greek self and society is beginning to reveal itself openly, and some of the central features of the ideal, culturally prescribed self are subjected to a surgical criticism. Euripides speaks for the antihero; he speaks against the traditional hero's compulsive competitiveness, against his love affair with death, against his self-flagellating striving, against his juvenile presumption that the dirty problems of living may be washed away if only enough blood is spilled. Euripides believes that such victories are empty, and he is, by far, the most antiwar of the tragedians: You are "mindless, all of you, who in strength of spears and the tearing edge win your valors by war. . . ." [56]

In *Heracles,* Euripides shows the "austere culture-hero of received tradition" as the "broken, almost domestic, Heracles fighting back his tears," [57] while *Helen* portrays "the hero in rags and tatters." [58] To marry Achilles—the very prototype of the Greek hero of tradition—he says, is a "wedding which is death." [59] "I saw Achilles' ghost stalk upon his tomb," shudders Hecuba, "howling, demanding a prize from the wretched women of Troy." [60] "Why do you seek after the goddess Ambition?" Euripides has his Jocasta demand of Eteocles; "The worst of all; this goddess is Injustice. . . . It's fine to be looked up to? But it's empty." [61] Relinquish your death grip on repute and fame, Euripides tells the heroic protagonist: " 'The deed' is better if it saves your life: than your 'good name' in which you die exulting." [62] Ambition, eminence, pride—all vanity, he warns.[63] A man is mad "who hunts a glory, . . . who tracks some boundless, superhuman dream." [64] And he lauds the winners in the contest ironically: "Your victory is fair, fair the prize, this famous prize of grief! Glorious the game! To fold your child in your arms, streaming with his blood!" [65]

Power itself comes to be seen as tainting and fragile. "A man whom power has so enchanted," says Euripides' Hippolytus, "must be demented." [66] And his Hecuba warns Odysseus: "[Y]ou have power, Odysseus, greatness and power. But clutch them gently, use them kindly, for power gives no purchase to the hand, it will not hold, soon perishes." [67]

Euripides' savage assault upon the heroic tradition is only the core of a larger attack upon a compulsive conformity with any of the conventional virtues that is mindless of human costs. In his *Alcestis* he satirizes a husband who feels compelled to comply with the traditional requirements of hospitality even though his wife has just died on his behalf. He rejects the ancient Hellenic code of reciprocity, and he calls upon men to have as friends only those who will not "sin to serve a friend as a return for kindness." [68] As against manly physical courage, it is love he extols as the vital source of the strength needed to cope with the senseless suffering to which men are subjected: "For love is all we have, the only way that each can help the other." [69] He praises the love of children, contrasting it invidiously with the love of wealth, as one of the great unifying experiences common to all mankind. "Here all mankind is equal," he insists. "Rich and poor alike, they love their children. With wealth distinctions come: some possess it, some do not. All mankind loves its children." [70] Thus in *Iphigenia in Aulis* Euripides can understand, if not forgive, the Clytemnestra that Aeschylus had condemned; for she had killed the husband who had sacrificed their child. To the ceaseless striving of the contestant, Euripides counterposes and blesses the man "who garners day by day the good of life." [71] To the conventional contempt for the slave, Euripides replies, "A slave bears only this Disgrace: the name. In every other way An honest slave is equal to the free." [72]

Euripides shows human passion and emotion to be as real as reason, and often more powerful; and he cautions those who do not allow it room to live within themselves. In *Hippolytus* his Aphrodite warns, "Such as worship my power in all humility, I exult in honor. But those whose pride is stiff-necked against me I lay by the heels." [73] He transforms the traditional slogan, Nothing too much, from a demand for discipline and restraint to a plea for the expression of the repressed: "[L]earn of chastity in moderation," he says.[74]

In his last tragedy, *The Bacchae,* Euripides makes an effort to confront if not to reconcile the counsel of reason with the clamorous claims of the emotions; he presents Dionysus as the god symbol of an ecstatic passion whose irresistible reality has its own kind of worth and must be acknowledged. Asked what is the use of these things, or of the rites that evoke them, Dionysus is made to reply: "I am forbidden to say. But they are worth knowing." [75] And elsewhere he remarks, "Do not be so certain that power is what matters in the life of man." [76]

Far from having a puritanical loathing for the passions, as has been suggested by some, Euripides' major point is that the passions are real; they will cut a swath of devastation through the lives of those who treat them contemptuously and without respect, understanding and consideration; men must come to terms with life, with all of life, rather than quarantining a part of it on a Devil's Island of the mind. "Is this a poison ointment or a drink?" asks Phaedra in *Hippolytus*. "I don't know," answers the Nurse, "Don't be overanxious child to find out what it is. Accept its benefits." [77] Fondle each day lovingly, says Euripides, accept all of life: "[W]hat the common people do, the things that simple men believe, I too believe and do." [78]

While Euripides fascinates his Athenian audience, he is often more upsetting to them than reassuring; and they, in turn, do not take him to their hearts until he is safely dead. While alive, he is lampooned by the comedians and derided as the son of a greengrocer. Despite his many plays he wins only four firsts in the dramatic competitions and retires, in self-imposed exile, to Macedonia, where he composes *The Bacchae*. If Euripides tells Athenians what they already suspect about themselves, he nonetheless does not tell them what they enjoy hearing.

The very development of the theater itself, which in Western society is an invention of Greek culture, has complex and important relationships with the development of Greek individualism. For one thing, "Old" tragedy is directly indicative of the growing pains of individualism; it is the drama of the individual hero facing his tragic destiny. While it extols the dignity of the person it also exposes his inherent vulnerability, highlighting both his solitary individuality and his potency by setting him against the backdrop of a largely undifferentiated and subordinate chorus.

The Athenian audience's sophisticated appreciation of their theater premises an understanding of the distinction between an actor's performance and his role, or the performer and his mask; it premises an ability to discriminate between the talent of the actor and the excellence of the playwright. The most elemental of the skills required for the writing of drama is a capacity to empathize with a wide variety of persons and to see a situation from their diverging perspectives; it requires a capacity to portray effectively, and thus to some extent sympathetically, perspectives that differ from those the dramatist finds personally acceptable.

The development of the Greek drama premises self-conscious individuals who can do what Agamemnon asks in *Hecuba:* "Put yourself in my position." [79] It means that the individual views himself from the outside, in effect, and sees himself as the defeated in the moment of his victory, from the standpoint of the lowly when he is at his pinnacle, and who feels in his bones "how strange in their reversals are our lives." [80] Plato's *Protagoras,* in which Socrates and Protagoras both (at least seemingly) end their controversy by adopting the view with which the other began, is a philosophical culmination of a long-standing fascination with role reversal. From Aeschylus onward, the dramatists see men engaged in such role reversals:

> You smote and were smitten
> You killed and were slain
> By the spear you killed
> By the spear you died
> Wretched in acting
> Wretched in suffering.[81]

Once the barriers to empathy with the defeated, the lowly, and the enemy are pierced, the capacity to take the role of others can overflow in all directions. The enemy can be seen to possess nobility, and the self can be regarded from the standpoint of its critics.[82]

It is out of such experience and skill in taking the role of the other and the esteem in which this talent is held that some Greeks come in time to abandon the rules of retaliation and reciprocity and to verge on the Golden Rule: "Do not do to others that which angers you when they do it to you." [83]

"You should be such in your dealings with others as you expect me to be in my dealings with you." [84]

The Greek self becomes increasingly aware of itself as it acquires detachment from and becomes aware of the diverse roles it plays, and as it becomes skilled in imaginatively taking or acting out diverse roles. Indeed, the self now takes pleasure in its multiple roles and its role skills; their utilization becomes infused with aesthetic and playlike qualities. When one of Solon's poems has its speaker criticize Solon and then go on to say what he would have done in Solon's place, Solon is not only taking the role of his critic, he is taking the role of a critic taking his own role.[85]

Once the self can adopt the standpoint of widely different others toward itself, the more individuated the person comes to feel; for each of the others sees him in somewhat different ways. It therefore seems more than accidental that a high development of theater and of individuality coincide in classical Greece, and one may well wonder how the subsequent career of the theater in Western society is interwoven with the history of individualism.

The Fear of Death and the New Self-Consciousness

I have suggested earlier that there are important costs associated with the development of self-conscious individuality, including a sense of isolation and separation from others. Another that is noteworthy is a heightened concern with death. Death becomes deeply dismaying, while a concern and longing for an afterlife grows. Even the supreme hero, Achilles, can confess his dismay of death and express a desire for any kind of life on earth, even serving another for his livelihood, without losing his heroic aura. And the popular poet Archilochus confesses that he had once actually fled rather than face death: "Some Saian is priding himself on my shield, which I abandoned reluctantly near a bush; but I escaped death. Let the shield go to perdition—I will get another as good." [86]

Counter to this admission of human frailty, but no less revealing of the attitude toward death, other poets enjoin men to die courageously for their *polis:* "Let us be brave and fight for this land, without heeding our lives." With this, the strange concept of the heroic or glorious death emerges. The Greeks are haunted by a concern with death; it is implicit in their notion that the distinction between men and gods is essentially that between mortals and immortals; on one level, "know thyself" means, know that you will one day die, since you are only a man. Only a people who hate death as much as the Greeks do could have invented the hero who, by risking death valiantly, becomes half a god and wins a purchase on immortality.

The self-conscious individual knows he is a person, and he grasps the nettle of inescapable limitation inherent in this unique estate. He knows he is only a man with an ephemeral self; yet in his heart he wishes it were not so. The Greek abominates death; yet the Olympian underworld is a miserable place, and to wish for immortality is *hybris*. There is a part of the self-conscious person which clings to life with the overriding selfishness of Euripides' Admetus, who allows his wife to die in his place, after his aged parents have refused to die for him. A man will even let those he loves best die for him, implies Euripides, rather than die himself.

Despite the Pythagorean conception of the four ages of man, each of twenty years, death comes relatively early to the Greeks. Their average life span is about twenty-nine years, and it may be even lower for the poor and slaves. Doubtless this, along with the manifest hazards of endemic warfare, does little to mitigate their concern with death. Yet at the same time the culturally prescribed stress on the military virtues, on bravery in particular, constrains men to suppress their fears about it. Whatever their overt expressions of fear, these must conceal an even deeper dismay. When Euripides portrays Admetus as he does, he is unmasking still another aspect of the underside of the Greek self.

The highly individuated Greek self confronts fears that are the mirror image of its ideals and aspirations. The self values potency, self-assertion, and dominance, but these generate an undertow of yearning for the satisfaction of neglected dependent, submissive, and suppliant needs. It relishes conflict and victory but pays a price for this in the social disconnectedness and uprootedness so well reflected in Empedocles' warning that those putting their trust in raging strife are doomed to be exiles and wanderers. It seeks individuation and autonomy yet also wants acceptance and intimacy. It wishes to be brave and dreams of a glorious death with fame undying, but it also detests death and yearns longingly for a significant afterlife. These different sides of Greek individuality are both real; they both need and find expression in various forms, most particularly, perhaps, in Greek religion and in the tension between its "Apollonian" and "Dionysian" aspects.

Apollonian and Dionysian Orientations

In Nietzsche's work initially distinguishing between the Apollonian and the Dionysian—a work which F. M. Cornford says left a generation of scholars toiling in the rear [87]—he indicates some of the implications of these two patterns for the dynamics of the self. In his terms, Dionysianism entails a kind of intoxication, a glorious rapture in which the self surrenders to its feelings, instincts, and intuitions.

Nietzsche argues that the basic function of the Dionysian form of worship is to forge anew the frayed bond between man and man. It generates a vision of mystical oneness in which the individual can lose his self, and it expresses an acceptance of the ultimate dissolution of the self. At certain periods in its history, Dionysianism serves, in effect, to compensate for and overcome the sensed loss of communion with others, with nature and man alike, that grew with the emergence of urban, self-conscious individuality.

Although the general trend of Nietzsche's analysis is to portray Dionysian religious orientations as earlier than the Apollonian, and essentially as corrupted by or syncretized with later Apollonian additions, other scholars maintain that

> The religion of Dionysus entered Greece much later than the cults of the other gods—Zeus, Hera, Athena, Demeter, Apollo—which already had roots in the Mycenean period. It came from the north via Thrace and Boeotia or, according to other sources, from the east via the Peloponnesus and Attica, where it received definite cult forms not before the sixth century.[88]

In discussing the standardization of the Homeric literature—a literature which is Apolline in its basic outlook—Gilbert Murray remarks that even after its radiation from Athens into the Hellenic mainland, there still linger "all through the backward parts of Greece obscene and cruel rites, . . . the darker and worse the further they were removed from the full light of Hellenism." [89] These "cruel rites," however, need not always be earlier patterns antedating Apolline Olympianism but may sometimes have arisen coincidentally with it, in response to new problems; or they may be old patterns adapted to new needs rather than vestigial survivals of ancient customs that were once useful but became functionless. In any event, it seems likely that, regardless of which is historically prior to the other, the Apolline components of Olympianism and the Dionysiac cults each spring from and appeal to the different needs of different sectors of the population, which exist simultaneously during certain historical periods.

I have previously mentioned that Apollo is the god of the aristocracy while Dionysus tends to be a popular god, the god of the *dēmos*. Thomson similarly holds that "Apollo and Dionysus stand at opposite poles, the one for the aristocratic ideal of static perfection, . . . the other for popular enthusiasm, [and in] the last stage of their evolution . . . the cults of Dionysus were popular, non-aristocratic." [90] "There they sit," says Euripides' Dionysus of his entranced followers, "rich and poor alike." [91] To Thomson's judgment that the Dionysiac cults "consisted of a primitive form of agricultural magic [and that] it was natural that such cults should have survived among the peasantry who continued to till the soil, rather than among the aristocracy," [92] A. French has added the suggestion that the growth of Dionysiac rites is a response to a new or, at least, to a growing agricultural crisis and, in particular, to a declining agricultural yield:

> Increasingly elaborate fertility rites are what might be expected in a land of declining fertility, and in Attica we see in historical times art, capital, and human endeavor diverted to the cult of Dionysus, and if the cult was gaining ground at a time of comparative enlightenment, this would imply that the needs to which it corresponded were *still actual*.[93]

In sum, Apollonian and Dionysian elements are probably distributed differentially in the population, the former more likely among aristocratic families, the latter among lower-class strata, the dispossessed or marginal peasantry of the countryside, or the poor, the foreign-born, or the slaves in the *polis*. Furthermore, Dionysian cults have a greater appeal to women rather than men: "[I]n the earliest period these Dionysiac cults were for the most part reserved to women. And so in many cases they remained." [94] In *The Bacchae*, Euripides' Dionysus declares, "Every woman in Thebes—but the women only—I drove from home, mad." [95]

The synthesizing hypothesis then may be that Dionysian cults and orientations are more popular among those who are relatively excluded or removed from the public life of the *polis:* women, hard-pressed peasants, slaves, foreign-born. It is these groups that most especially need the release that Dionysus' fermented gift can bring: "For filled with that good gift, suffering mankind forgets its grief," notes Euripides. "From it comes sleep; with it oblivion of the troubles of the day." It is such depressed groups, in particular, that might feel "there is no other medicine for misery." [96] It is therefore to be expected that Euripides, the dramatist who speaks for the underside of Greek society, begins to express a deep disillusionment with Apollo and, at the same time, a new and deeper understanding of Dionysus. "From now," says the chorus in *The Cyclops,* "our orders come from Bacchus." [97] While in *The Bacchae* Euripides is aware that a thwarted Dionysus is capable of terrible things, he also insists that Dionysus must be given honor by men. In contrast to Sophocles, whose chorus complains that "Apollo is nowhere clear in honour; God's service perishes," [98] Euripides' Orestes is made to say, "I accuse Apollo. The god is the guilty one," [99] and the Dioscuri in his *Electra* speak of the brutal song of Apollo: "Doom is compelling, it leads and we follow—doom and the brutal song of Apollo." [100]

Concerning Euripides' attitude toward Apollo, I concur with Richmond Lattimore, who holds that, in *Ion,* "Apollo emerges in a very poor light as a barbarian god whose ethics are shattered by the probings of a civilized and skeptical mind. . . . *Ion* is an attack on Delphi"; [101] and with William Arrowsmith, who remarks that, in *Orestes,* "Apollo is here transformed from a cool and infallible Olympian into the interested and suspect god of contemporary Delphian politics, neither impartial nor infallible nor even godlike"; [102] and with Emily Vermeule, who maintains that "Electra is another phase in his campaign against Apollo." [103]

F. M. Cornford has suggested that much of the religious history of Greece may be conceived of as a series of fusions between the Dionysian and the Olympian-Apolline orientations. Both the so-called Orphic revival and Pythagoreanism—around the seventh to the sixth century B.C.—involve a syncretization of Dionysian impulses with Olympian-Apolline forms. Orpheus, says Cornford, was Dionysus "tamed, and clothed and in his right mind," [104] that is to say, Apollonized.

Both these cults brought Dionysian elements into civic life, adapting them in Apollonian directions; indeed, the official patron god of the Pythagorean brotherhood was Apollo, not Dionysus. Still another way of viewing these cults is as agencies for the diffusion of Dionysian beliefs which have hitherto been encysted in the coexistent underside of Greek society— that is, among lower status groups such as peasants, slaves, foreign-born, and women—into what has become the overside or leading cultural orientation, Apollonianism, and among the relatively dominant sector of society, the male, urban, citizenry, and especially its elite strata.

The Orphic concern with the salvation of the individual soul, says Cornford, is the psychological key to its understanding.

> The cosmic dualism [in it], with its contrast of the principles of light and darkness, identified with good and evil, reflects outwards upon the universe that inner sense of the double nature of man. . . . It is also the sense of separation from "God," which goes with the intense desire for reunion. We may, perhaps, see the psychological cause of all this in the development of self-conscious individuality, which necessarily entails feelings of isolation from the common life, and at the same time an increasing conflict between self-assertive instincts and that part of the common consciousness which resides in each of us, and is called "conscience." [105]

Such Dionysian cults can be conceived of as a kind of reaction to the demands for autonomy, self-assertion, and expressive discipline—that is, to the demands of the Apollonian self—and as modes of gratifying the suppressed sides of the Greek self. It is for this reason that they may spread from the rural lower classes and come to have appeal to all classes of Greek society. As Nietzsche remarks, "The individual with his limits and moderations forgot himself in the Dionysiac vortex and became oblivious to Apollo." [106] In his view, Hellenic culture is characterized by a titanic dialectic between Apollonian and Dionysian tendencies, each shaping, influencing, and conditioning the other, and each becoming what it does in the course of its polemical interaction with the other. We would add that each expresses and satisfies different sides of the Greek self: the Apollonian, the approved, culturally dominant side; the Dionysian, the disvalued, neglected, and inhibited underside. Each side induces problems that the other in some part resolves; each reduces tensions that the other induces.

In the Dionysian outlook, the paradigm of suffering is dismemberment; that is, there is a feeling of the loss of a larger whole within which the self may be located comfortably: individuation with its separation from others is experienced as a painful alienation. In the Apollonian outlook, however, the paradigm of suffering is a loss of individuality and an inadequate differentiation from others. The Apollonian draws boundaries which contain things in clear-cut forms; he seeks the individuation of persons and the specialization of social roles in a hierarchical organization. The Dionysian is disposed to flow over or through boundaries, seeking the fusion of separate things and stressing the oneness of the universe; he is hostile to individuation, specialization, and hierarchy.

Dionysian ideologies stress a sense of continuity and manifest a feeling for the oneness of time; they stress periodicity and recurrence, the "eternal return," rather than preferring a straight-line imagery of cumulative progression. They stress the connectedness of all things, including the unity of nature and society. The Dionysian seeks mergence with others and with the universe by a relaxation of expressive discipline sometimes attained through orgiastic excitation; the Apollonian, in contrast, is concerned to maintain separateness through the exertion of expressive discipline. The Dionysian's inclination is to surrender to impulse, whether strong feelings or, in terms of his cognitive orientations, "instinct" or intuition; the Apollonian strives to keep strong feelings in check, and his cognitive orientation typically stresses the use of reason, knowledge, and science. Dionysian orientations dispose toward comparative passivity or inactivity in relation to worldly goals, while Apollonian orientations tend to be more actively melioristic.

Nietzsche notes that the Olympian aspect of Apollonianism does not entail an inward striving for moral elevation, spirituality, or loving kindness, or anything of asceticism, but, rather, exults in sheer existence. Whereas Dionysian orientations seem to emphasize an inward striving after perfection, Apollonianism stresses a more external activity, a knowing through doing, and a search for achievement on earth.

Both Cornford and Nietzsche regard Apollonianism as a predecessor of science, while Dionysian movements are seen as a progenitor of later mystical philosophies. The link between scientific philosophies and Apollonianism can perhaps best be seen in the Greek concept of *mōira,* or fate. *Mōira* entails a spatial metaphor of the *cosmos* as compartmentalized, as separated into differently bounded zones which, in the Olympian expression, are under the jurisdiction of different gods. It also stresses the line separating men and gods. Each man is regarded as having a kind of membranous individual destiny which he must not transcend or violate and which, if he does, produces his *nemesis*.

Where man sins, retribution must follow and, indeed, when this happens the whole of nature may be poisoned; thus the "land of Thebes wasteth in the fruitless buds of earth," because of Oedipus' sins. Yet the very possibility that men may in this sense sin implies that they can, somehow, be out of step with the natural order of things. There is an implication of a "slippage" between man and nature, there is an implicit suggestion that man is not totally subject to or merged with it. As Cornford indicates, the concept of the "absolutely impossible" is lacking; the boundaries around various destinies and departments may be stretched and momentarily pierced. Man may exceed himself, but if he does he is certain to be punished. The world limits men but does not make certain proscribed deeds impossible to them, if they are willing to pay the price of violating the ordained order.

The Mōira Mythos

Insofar as *mōira* involves a conception of the universe as embodying an immanent and impersonal order over which even the gods have no control —and who, therefore, need not be invoked to explain it—it is a mythos consonant with a scientific study of nature. In the Olympian mythology, the allotment of different provinces to the jurisdiction of different gods is in the nature of an empowering charter from which they derive their divine rights. As has been commonly noted, the Olympians are young gods who do not claim to create the world. Like the invading tribes who divided up a land they came upon, the Olympians have divided up the departments of a universe that was already established.

The gods, then, are regarded as subject to a more remote and awesome power, *mōira,* or destiny, by which they are limited. Positing a gulf between man and the gods, the Olympian mythology separates men from communion with them; the gods are detached from the group. The characteristic Apollonian or Olympian rite is the sacrifice to the god, from which the worshiper expects some return benefit. The characteristic Dionysian rite, however, notes Cornford, is sacramental, involving an act of communion or reunion with the god. The latter has two different aspects: that of enthusiasm whereby the god enters into his worshipers, and that of ecstasy in which man rises above the prison of his individuality, losing himself in the common life of the whole. It is the function of the orgiastic rite to enable god and man to be reunited in enthusiasm and to permit men to lose themselves ecstatically in god.

Dionysianism and Apollonianism both provide different, indeed complementary, gratifications, and both embody, more or less implicitly, a different paradigm of proper human relationships and individual character. On the Dionysian side is an image of the spontaneous, emotionally expressive person who can discharge his impulses and feelings; he can lose himself without self-consciousness in the group and more readily become intimate with others. On the Apollonian side is an image of the somewhat aloof, more reserved man who does not readily allow others to come too close, and is concerned to maintain his distance and distinctness.

Conceptions of Deviance and Achievement

The Dionysian seeks to avoid loneliness and separation from others; the Apollonian above all seeks to avoid lowness and the contempt of others. The Apollonian values the ennobling differences in men, the differences that make some higher than others. He distinguishes men from the rest of nature, focusing on those common characteristics which he believes make them higher than other species. He values primarily those qualities, such as reason, that set individuals and their species above others and not only apart. Conversely, those qualities which men share with other species tend to be regarded as lowly. Believing that individual men should strive to fulfill that ennobling difference they share with all men, the Apollonian is, in this sense, concerned with the universal in man and with the qualities common to man as a type or class. The differentiating qualities of the class are treated as normative imperatives; that is, individuals should strive to embody more fully the characteristics common to their species or class. Thus Pindar says, "Become what thou art." The emphasis, therefore, is not on the realization of traits peculiar to or distinctive of the individual person; he is encouraged not to be different from all others, but rather to attempt to embody to the highest degree possible a model of propriety which he holds. Thus the emphasis on the Homeric literature in Greek education is in part to provide a fixed and clear set of models to guide the developing youth.

The Apollonian seeks to transcend the commonplace in earthly terms, to behave heroically and to become high in the secular world of respectable men, in the arena of public competition. In the Dionysian orientation, it is not what men accomplish in worldly and public ways that is most important. The Dionysian seeks a transcendence outside the public sphere, in mysteries which are not publicly scrutable and into which only the initiated may enter. It is an unworldly world in which ordinary conceptions of high and low, of the respectably decorous or indecorously deviant, are irrelevant and in which concerns about one's public social status are supplanted by an interest in one's ritual status. To the Dionysian, the relevant categories are grace, sin, and purification rather than prestige, power, and wealth. In its extreme or ideal form, his is a social world in which the customary canons of daily life do not apply, for the central concern is not the relation between man and man but that between men and the divine.

Dionysianism and Apollonianism are alike, however, in inducing man to aspire to and strive toward some kind of higher estate, and to overcome the imperfections under which he presently labors. The Dionysian as much as the Apollonian does not accept man as he is; he views him as a fallen angel who may, with certain laborious purifications, return to the divine. Both regard men as in some, but different, ways exalted; the Apollonian sees reason as the exalting quality, while the Dionysian views all men as possessing a mystical piece of the divine. Both see men as sharing certain universal qualities, though in each case the quality differs. In consequence, neither the Dionysian nor the Apollonian values the concrete, unique individuality of men for itself. The Dionysian values the person because, like all others, he possesses a spark from the divine spirit; the Apollonian values the person because, like others, he possesses an ennobling species trait such as reason.

It deserves to be stressed that the above delineations of the Apollonian and Dionysian are ideal types, ideal types of belief systems, images of social relations and individual behavior; they are theoretical constructions and not historical descriptions of specific belief systems, which usually contain both Apollonian and Dionysian elements. The relation of these ideal types to concrete religious or cultural orientations such as Olympianism, Orphism, or Pythagoreanism is analytical, not historical; it is a relationship of imputed latent forces to manifest and directly observable data. The two poles, the Dionysian and the Apollonian, each entails a syndrome of orientations that seem to be internally consistent and integrated. It does not follow, however, that each is irreducible, and it may well be that underlying each of the two main orientations are a number of still more latent elements.

Pythagoreanism as a Revivalistic Social Movement

Pythagoreanism, like Orphism, involves a mixture of Dionysian and Apollonian elements, but it contains a stronger infusion of the latter. Pythagoreanism moves from the Orphic's passionate identification with the divine to a detached, more intellectually disciplined contemplation: it is the Orphism of the elites.

Pythagoreanism is a social movement; in particular, it is one of the Western world's first great social movements aiming at "cultural revitalization." [107] It provides one of the first examples in Western history of the way in which major shifts in theories about human behavior are often embedded in social movements that arise in reaction to cultural crises. Impulses toward cultural revitalization are responses to cultural crises and constitute an adaptive, tension-reducing effort. Such social movements often center around charismatic persons who are felt, and feel themselves, to be in communication with supernatural or extraordinary powers in some way commensurate with the sensed depth of the crisis. In this vein, Pythagoras is identified by his followers with the Hyperborean Apollo, or, at least, so we have it on Aristotle's authority.

These social movements may take a number of forms, varying with the manner in which they define and seek to respond to the cultural crisis: they are "nativistic" in character when they define the cultural crisis as due to the intrusion of elements alien to the culture, which they call upon their followers to remove; they are "importive" in character when they regard the crisis as due to the failure to build new or to borrow outside patterns, which they then seek to develop or procure; they are "revivalistic" when they define the crisis as due to the neglect and disuse of the old traditional elements, which they call upon men to restore. Pythagoreanism reveals itself as a revivalistic movement toward cultural revitalization in its call for renewed veneration of the gods, of ancestors, and of ancient codes of conduct. In this traditionalistic vein it emphasizes requital or retribution for evil, and it conceives of evil as a form of excess. Conversely, proper behavior is regarded as that which is temperate or restrained and which follows the principle of limit, measure, and of "no excess."

Also characteristic of movements of cultural revitalization is an image (or a fantasy) of the death, disappearance, or withering away of the old and dissatisfying social order, or of the new and threatening social order; new moral codes or new accents are given to older moral beliefs—i.e., there are changes in evaluative standards and orientations; there is, also, an image of a new and more gratifying social order which is seen as a whole; there is a projection of a new or reorganized model of social relations and of the group as a totality which provides a systematic alternative to the presently stressful situation. In the latter connection, it is noteworthy that the Pythagoreans are polemically hostile to any kind of social or political strife: "We must avoid in every way and remove, by fire, knife, or any other means, sickness from the body, ignorance from the soul, a love of luxury from the belly, class struggles from the city, and disagreement from a household." [108]

Its criticism of a love of luxury and social conflict, along with its emphasis on social order, unity, and harmony, suggests that Pythagoreanism is not—at least during certain phases in its development—promercantile, since this form of excess would more likely be charged against the urban rich, whose means might allow them greater self-indulgence. The tone of the entire plea suggests that Pythagoreanism as a social movement embodies a traditionalistic effort to revive an earlier social order whose virtues were austere Spartan simplicity in the individual and social consensus and cohesion in the group. This traditionalistic component, however, is colored with a new, strongly ascetic tinge: the body is seen as evil, pleasures are viewed as corrupting, and man is regarded as a creature whose insatiable wants need to be subjected to powerful controls.

Much of the Pythagoreans' concern centers on the immortality of the soul, which is viewed as passing through various reincarnations. There is, in this conception, a mind-body dualism in which the soul is the higher and exalted part and is regarded as a prisoner of the body from which it needs to be freed to rejoin the universal spirit. This, however, is to be achieved not by conformity to ritual taboos but through a series of purifications taking the form of a dispassionate contemplation of the order in the universe.

In effect, the Pythagorean is enjoined to make a disciplined search for a hidden order in the universe. He is encouraged in the faith that the universe has a knowable order, an order whose harmony of parts is endowed with a sacred quality that is intrinsically superior to conflict, strife, and disharmony. Knowledge of this orderliness is seen as requiring an effort of mind, for it is a latent order not immediately evident to the casual observer. Consequently, Pythagoreanism induces a motivation to know; the pursuit of knowledge about the underlying order in things becomes a way of life through which the individual soul can attain purification, and through this a kind of immortality. Indeed, the contemplative life is now regarded as one of the basic types of existence, in contrast with the traditional Greek emphasis on the life of action; the contemplative life and man are now counterposed invidiously to those who are lovers of gain and fame.

In certain respects, Pythagoreanism also gives increasing expression and sanction to some aspects of the inhibited underside of the Greek self—particularly its passive inclinations—emphasizing as it does the need for each to confine himself to the task assigned to him in the social division of labor, and to give reverent obedience to the gods and lawful authorities. It expresses also, through its emphasis on the significance of friendship—

which term Pythagoras is said to have invented—and through the bond of the Pythagorean brotherhood itself, the need of the self for social connectedness and communion with other men. Similarly, in its stress on the immortality of the soul, it expresses the longing of the Greek self for a vital afterlife.

Bertrand Russell, with his characteristic felicity of expression, suggests that Pythagoras was a combination of Einstein and Mary Baker Eddy, the founder of Christian Science. This could be misleading, however, if we think of the mathematical innovations that schoolboys usually associate with Pythagoras as being incongruous with the mysticism which is suggested by the allusion to Mrs. Eddy. (Indeed, I believe that the sociology of science would be sadly misled if it generally assumed that mysticism and a strong commitment to mathematics are necessarily incompatible.) For the mathematical innovations and conceptions of Pythagoras—and the later Pythagoreans whose contributions are so difficult to distinguish from their master's own ideas—are suffused with mysticism from their inception.

Number is to the mystical tradition what the underlying spatial metaphor is to the Apollonian. In contrast to the Ionian "nature philosophers," who constitute one expression of the Apollonian tradition and who seek the essence of the cosmos in an underlying substance—water, fire, air—and its movement through space, the Pythagoreans see the essence of the universe as resident in numbers. To them, the essential character of things is to be found not in a substance but in structure, proportion, and order. As the order of things in the world is regarded as inherently mathematical, it is something that can be approached through intellectual contemplation, by sheer thinking and logical deduction, without, and indeed apart from, observation or empirical knowledge.

The characteristic thing about Pythagoreanism—like some later schools of thought, such as nineteenth-century French Positivism—is its fusion of mysticism, mathematics, moral reconstruction, and political reform. This combination of elements may be illustrated by some speculations about the ideological implications of the Pythagorean theorem itself—speculations which are by no means alien to the Pythagorean. Considering the fact that the Pythagoreans believe that justice is a square number, it does not seem far-fetched to ask what, if any, political meaning might have been attributed to the theorem? It will be recalled that this theorem states that the sum of the squares of the lengths of the two sides forming a right angle in a triangle are equal to the square of the length of the hypotenuse. The crucial thing about the theorem is that it notes that there is a latent equality underlying a manifest inequality, that is, the sum of the length of the sides of the right angle do not equal the length of the hypotenuse; it is only after the elements on each side of the equation are squared that they become equal. The ideological resonance of the theorem might therefore have moved in two different directions. On the one hand, it might have been thought to imply that things only prima facie seem unequal, but when looked at differently (or more "deeply") are actually equal. The theorem would thus lend ideological support to the existing system of social stratification. On the other hand, the theorem might have been interpreted to mean that existent and manifest inequalities *should* be made equal by some kind of transformation.

It is easy to see from this why the ideological implications of Pythagoreanism—whether it is prodemocratic and promercantile or pro-oligarchical and proaristocratic—have been much debated by scholars.[109] The thing about which there is no disagreement, however, is that this kind of thinking, a kind of politico-mathematical mysticism, is characteristic of Pythagoreanism. Along with others, some of those whose right to an opinion in these matters is better than my own, I am persuaded that many of the characteristically Pythagorean views find their way into Plato's version of the Socratic philosophy. Among the notable points of convergence, as we shall have occasion to observe, is their common emphasis on the immortality of the soul, on the transcendent importance of order, and on the value of a life of contemplation.

Not the least of the convergences is in Plato's stress on mathematics. This, indeed, went to the point, as tradition has it, of an inscription over the door of his Academy—a slogan that should endear him to the most mathematically committed of modern behavioral scientists: *Let Only Those Who Know Geometry Enter Here*. On the face of it, the modern drive toward increased use of mathematics in behavioral science seems to be an unmistakable sign of a hardheaded scientific outlook; those acquainted with Pythagoreanism, and other historical connections between mathematics and mysticism, may wish to think twice about the matter.[110]

NOTES

[1] *Gorgias* i. 447BC.

[2] On this and related issues see George Misch, *A History of Autobiography, op. cit.*

[3] See Bruno Snell, *The Discovery of the Mind* (Oxford: Blackwell, 1953).

[4] Cf. L. Pearson, "Real and Conventional Personalities in Greek History," *Journal of the History of Ideas*, 15 (January 1954), 136–145.

[5] Isocrates i. 23.

[6] Plato *Euthyphro*. 12B.

[7] Adkins, *op. cit.*, p. 157.

[8] *Ibid.*, p. 72.

[9] For some discussions of this set of concepts, see D. P. Ausubel, "Relationships between Shame and Guilt in the Socializing Process," *Psychological Review*, 62 (September 1955), 378–390; R. L. Jenkins, "Guilt Feelings: Their Function and Dysfunction," in M. Reymert, ed., *Feelings and Emotions* (New York: McGraw-Hill, 1950), pp. 353–361; J. Nuttin, "Intimacy and Shame in the Dynamic Structure of the Personality," in *ibid.*, pp. 343–352; G. Piers and M. B. Singer, *Shame and Guilt* (Springfield: Charles C. Thomas, 1953); M. Mead, *Cooperation and Competition among Primitive Peoples* (New York: McGraw-Hill, 1937); M. Mead, "Social Change and Cultural Surrogates," in C. Kluckhohn, ed., *Personality, Nature, Society, and Culture* (New York: Knopf, 1959).

[10] This assumption appears to be supported increasingly by work on the semantic differential by Charles Osgood and his students. See C. E. Osgood, G. J. Suci, and P. Tannenbaum, *The Measurement of Meaning* (Urbana: University of Illinois Press, 1957); see also C. E. Osgood, "The Nature and Measurement of Meaning," *Psychological Bulletin,* 49 (1952), 197–237.

[11] Euripides *Hippolytus* iii. 180. 404.

[12] Euripides *Hippolytus* iii. 192. 700.

[13] i. 63. 938.

[14] iii. 166. 88 ff.

[15] G. R. Morrow, "Plato's Conception of Persuasion," *Philosophical Review,* 62 (1953), 236.

[16] Euripides *The Trojan Women* iii. 645. 905.

[17] *Iliad,* trans. R. Lattimore, *op. cit.,* pp. 290–291.

[18] Pindar. 4.

[19] *Rhesus* iv. 91. 105; *Rhesus* iv. 112. 626.

[20] Friedl, *op. cit.,* p. 35.

[21] See pp. 13–14.

[22] For the first generalized analysis of this concept, see E. P. Hollander, "Conformity, Status, and Idiosyncrasy Credit," *Psychological Review,* 45 (March 1958), 117–127. For a discussion setting this concept into a broader context of sociological theory, see Gouldner and Gouldner, *op. cit.,* p. 602.

[23] iii. 63. 119 ff.

[24] Thucydides. 378–379.

[25] Current theoretical explanations of deviant behavior—perhaps reflecting American liberal ideologies (many of which I happen to share)—are inclined to overstress the role of frustrated aspirations and of the individual's failure, by reason of his lowly social status, to attain goals his group has taught him to regard as legitimate for himself. My own analysis stresses the high incidence of deviance among the highly placed and the successful. In contrast to Durkheim, however, my view of their deviance does not stress the role of the breakdown of individual or group norms, or the inadequacy of old norms in the successful individual's new situation. Rather, my emphasis here is on the difficulties of group control over the successful, seen as a failure of social interaction in the relations between followers and leaders. It is not only that the successful no longer have internalized standards or that the group no longer has rules that effectively encourage its self-control; the followers no longer have rewards which they can use in social interaction with their leaders to keep the latter responsive to group expectations and desires. Moreover, from Durkheim's standpoint, "normlessness" was seen only as contributive to the pathology of individuals and groups. Normlessness was seen as leading individuals to the insatiable pursuit of an endlessly retreating horizon of goals which retreats farther with each success, thus allowing the normless person no gratification. From our standpoint, however, we need to entertain the hypothesis that such normlessness and insatiability may also be functional for the group. It prevents the successful person from becoming apathetic and withdrawing from leadership roles in which his experience could contribute to group gratifications.

[26] Euripides iii. 203. 986 ff.

[27] ii. 436. 902.

28 Sophocles ii. 229. 404 ff.

29 Euripides *Iphigenia in Tauris* iii. 369. 612.

30 iii. 435, 557, 558.

31 iv. 117. 693.

32 Euripides iv. 565. 505 ff.

33 Euripides *Ion* iv. 18. 256 ff.

34 Sophocles *Oedipus the King* ii. 62. 1169–1170.

35 Euripides *Ion* iv. 68. 1383.

36 Euripides *Helen* iii. 432. 496–497.

37 Morrow, *op. cit.,* p. 38.

38 *Ibid.*

39 Euripides *The Heracleidae* iii. 136. 551.

40 Euripides *Hecuba* iii. 518. 545.

41 Euripides *Iphigenia in Tauris* iii. 361. 469.

42 Euripides iii. 119. 56.

43 T. G. Tucker, *Life in Ancient Athens* (London: Macmillan, 1913), p. 142.

44 For a full account of these researches, see S. E. Asch, *Social Psychology* (New York: Prentice-Hall, 1952); for a brief popular account, see S. E. Asch, "Opinions and Social Pressure" *Scientific American,* 192 (November 1955), 31–35.

45 Translation by Misch, *op. cit.,* p. 79. For fuller development, see F. Will, "Solon's Consciousness of Himself," *Transactions and Proceedings of the American Philological Association,* 89 (1958), 301–311. Will's work, which is the most systematic and insightful application of a Meadian social psychology to classical materials, clearly sees the relation between self-awareness and social conflict: "Caught between cross-fires of opposing batteries, he came to realize what he stood for and therefore, inevitably, to have a better idea of what he was"— *ibid.,* p. 305. For our own development of this theoretical point, see Gouldner and Gouldner, *op. cit.,* pp. 59–60, especially the section on "Social Conflict and the Self Image."

46 i. 58. 757.

47 i. 96. 101–102.

48 Cf. Dodds, *op. cit.,* 185 ff.

49 i. 45. 341 ff.

50 i. 101. 232–233.

51 Sophocles ii. 227. 364 ff.

52 Thucydides. 122.

53 Thucydides. 208.

54 Aeschylus *Agamemnon* i. 37. 72–73.

55 Euripides iii. 68. 268–269.

56 *Helen* iii. 460. 1153 ff.

57 William Arrowsmith, in Euripides iii. 272.

58 Arrowsmith, *ibid.,* 486.

59 *Hecuba* iii. 520. 612.

60 *Hecuba* iii. 498. 92–95.

61 *Phoenician Women* iv. 479. 531 ff.

62 *Hippolytus* iii. 184. 501–502.

63 *Hecuba* iii. 521. 625–626.

64 *Bacchae* iv. 558. 398 ff.

65 *Bacchae* iv. 593. 1161–1164.

66 iii. 204. 1014 ff.

67 iii. 507. 283 ff.

68 *Hippolytus* iii. 204. 906.

69 *Orestes* iv. 209. 298–299.

70 *Heracles* iii. 305. 633 ff.

71 *Bacchae* iv. 583. 910–911.

72 *Ion* iv. 45. 855–856.

73 *Hippolytus* iii. 163. 6 ff.

74 *Hippolytus* iii. 193. 731.

75 iv. 562. 473.

76 iv. 555. 310–311.

77 *Hippolytus* iii. 184. 517.

78 *Bacchae* iv. 559. 430.

79 Euripides iii. 531. 861.

80 iii. 531. 846.

81 Aeschylus *Seven against Thebes* i. 296. 960 ff.

82 Thus Solon looks upon himself in the following poem: "Solon is not gifted with wisdom and sagacity. God put good things into his hand, but he failed to grasp them."—F. Will, *op. cit.,* p. 301.

83 Isocrates i. 111.

84 Isocrates i. 111.

85 Will, *op. cit.,* p. 301.

86 Misch, *op. cit.,* p. 80.

87 F. M. Cornford, *From Religion to Philosophy,* "A Study in the Origins of Western Speculation" (New York: Harper, 1957 ed.), p. 111, n. 1.

88 Margaret Bieber, *The History of the Greek and Roman Theater* (Princeton: Princeton University Press, 1961) p. 1.

89 G. Murray, *Five Stages of Greek Religion* (Garden City: Doubleday, n.d.), p. 65.

90 Thomson, *op. cit.,* pp. 130, 151.

91 Euripides *Bacchae* iv. 544. 35.

92 Thomson, *op. cit.,* p. 151.

93 French, "The Economic Background to Solon's Reforms," *op. cit.,* p. 15. My italics, A. W. G.

94 Thomson, *op. cit.,* p. 149.

95 iv. 544. 35.

96 iv. 554. 280 ff.

97 iii. 264, last line.

98 *Oedipus the King* ii. 49. 910.

99 iv. 209. 285.

100 iv. 451. 1301.

101 iv. 3–4.

102 iv. 187.

103 iv. 392.

104 F. M. Cornford, *op. cit.,* p. 195.

105 *Ibid.,* p. 180.

106 F. Nietzsche, *The Birth of Tragedy* and *The Genealogy of Morals* (Garden City: Doubleday, 1956), p. 35.

107 This discussion borrows from and applies to Pythagoreanism the analysis of A. F. Wallace, "Revitalization Movements," in S. M. Lipset and N. J. Smelser, eds., *Sociology: The Progress of a Decade* (New York: Prentice-Hall, 1961), pp. 206–220.

108 Winspear, *op. cit.,* p. 79.

109 The controversy has been waged even among scholars whose basic theoretical position is similar. Thus Winspear and Thomson, though both writing from a Marxist standpoint, come to diverging conclusions concerning the political character of Pythagoreanism, Winspear viewing it as essentially oligarchical and aristocratic in ideological orientation, and Thomson—following Burnet—viewing it as an essentially democratic ideology. See Winspear, *op. cit.,* pp. 78 ff., and Thomson, *op. cit.,* pp. 210 ff. For a closer view of this polemic see A. D. Winspear, "The Social Origins of the Greek Drama," pp. 273–277, and G. Thomson, "Aeschylus and Athens: A Reply," pp. 278–281, *Science and Society,* 6 (Summer 1942). Thomson's argument seems to be that Orphism was historically rooted in a dispossessed peasantry, while early Pythagoreanism represented the rich merchants who were at odds with the landed aristocracy. Although Thomson holds that early Pythagoreanism was democratic in outlook, he also maintains that it was more Apollonian than Orphism and, indeed, that "it was a cult of the *elite* rather than the masses."—*ibid.,* p. 212. He is thus led to qualify his view of the Pythagoreans as democrats, characterizing them in one place as "moderate" democrats and in another as a "commercial theocracy." From my own standpoint, I would wish to keep the Pythagoreans' class linkages—whether mercantile or aristocratic—analytically distinct from their political ideology and orientation—i.e., whether democratic or oligarchical in persuasion. The two did not always go together in a one-to-one manner; politicians of aristocratic antecedents sometimes adopted prodemocratic policies, while rich merchants were marrying into the older aristocracy and sometimes assumed their style of life and outlook. Moreover, I also think it necessary to examine what is meant by a "prodemocratic" policy under varying historical conditions and to recognize that it will have a shifting content. Although not without some ambiguities, it seems to me that the evidence for the pro-oligarchical character of even early

Pythagorean politics is substantial. One of the best summaries of this evidence is provided by Winspear's student, E. L. Minar, Jr., *Early Pythagorean Politics in Practice and Theory* (Baltimore: Waverly Press, 1942). Pythagoreanism, it seems, sought to limit political power to some kind of "aristocracy." Even if this term is defined simply as the "rule of the best" —an interpretation which Thomson emphasizes—it still implies a limitation on the extension of political power. This view can be interpreted as antimercantile only if it is assumed that merchants were always in favor of extending the franchise. To the extent that mercantile groups were reluctant to continue the extension of the franchise to the poorer sections of the *dēmos,* after they themselves had been admitted to the establishment, they were in effect committing themselves to what might be called an "oligarchical" policy. It was oligarchical if we assume that the core of such an ideology entails some sort of *restriction* of the franchise, and is built around an effort to make the political privileges of a group commensurate with its economic position and/or its social standing or prestige. The inherent instability of any oligarchical coalition in Greece derived from differences among its participants as to where to draw the line; tendencies toward "exclusiveness" would threaten some members of the coalition and induce internal cleavages and tensions in it. Kurt von Fritz holds the view that Pythagoreanism was most strongly conservative in its later development, and that this entailed a change from its earlier position when it was much more shifting and ambiguous in political allegiance. Yet he also says, "[C]onservatism seems to have been inherent in Pythagorean doctrine since they always favored order and strict moral principles."—K. von Fritz, *Pythagorean Politics in Southern Italy* (New York: Columbia University Press, 1940), p. 97. Like Thomson, von Fritz regards the Pythagoreans as being, at certain periods, "conservative democrats." Here we have the problem of the half-filled glass of water; is it half full or half empty? Von Fritz, and certainly Thomson, thinking of a Pythagorean connection with rich merchants who wish to extend political privileges to themselves, regard Pythagoreanism as half-democratic, as moderately or conservatively democratic. Winspear and Minar, thinking of the Pythagorean desire to restrict the extension of power, define it in terms of its oligarchical leanings. Perhaps all would agree that at no time did Pythagoreanism seek a continual extension of political privileges to all citizens or adopt a Cleisthenic view of democracy. It sought, in fine, to control and restrict political privileges and to call a halt to a tendency toward a permanent democratic revolution. The pro-oligarchical element in Pythagoreanism, moreover, is only one side of it; this is fused with its polemically traditionalistic and backward-looking character, its self-conscious veneration of ancient ways, and its claim to legitimacy, in some part, because of this. Its social diagnosis was that the city's problems derived, in large part, because it had lost touch with its own *past.* Again, traditionalism is not linked to a specific class in any one-to-one invariant manner and is an element that needs to be kept analytically distinct. It is not only or always the upper classes or an aristocracy that invokes the past, that finds such an invocation appealing, or that uses it to formulate a posture toward current social tensions. One of the latent social functions of such a self-conscious traditionalism is to provide an ideological common ground for diverse social groups, each of whom have somewhat different reasons for opposing certain ongoing or impending social changes. The function of such traditionalism was to inhibit certain dispositions to social change.

110 Although it could only be briefly stated here, this point is not intended merely as a quick polemical thrust. Our seeming digression is actually expressive of one of our central intellectual objectives throughout this work; namely, to find guidelines—deriving from the intensive study of a single case—for the development of a generalized sociological analysis of social theory and social theorists. In short, the point made briefly here is a promissory note acknowledging our intellectual obligations, rather than the repayment of a debt. That there may be a connection between religious and scientific orientations will not be a novel idea to those familiar with Max Weber's thesis concerning the connections between Protestantism and the rise of modern science, as well as with the related re-

searches of Robert K. Merton and Lewis Feuer. In our view, three points need to be added to their discussion: (1) concern with the connection between religious and scientific orientations is, I believe, not simply an antiquarian interest. Our guess is that the connection is not only important historically but continues into the present; (2) the connection deserves to be explored not only in the work of physical scientists but in that of social scientists as well; (3) the further examination of this connection between the religious and scientific orientations of social scientists would, we believe, be facilitated by dividing the later, scientific orientation into two distinctive elements, an empirical concern and a mathematical concern. It is the latter, I suspect, that may continue to have a connection with certain kinds of religious orientation in the work of contemporary social scientists.

4 The War between the Cities

The political experiences of Greece and Rome, no less than their literature and philosophy, are classic. Moreover, being relatively limited in scope and mass, and remote in time, they afford manageable and objective types for the study of causal relationships. If his books and imagination have given a man vicarious experience of these paradigms no subsequent expression of political behavior can disconcert him. But many factors make finality in the exploitations of these paradigms difficult. The ancient record is itself fragmentary, and the loftiest devotion to truth cannot divorce the investigator from the limitations of his own political outlook. . . . The task, then, is laboriously to extend knowledge of antiquity itself by finding new sources of information and exploiting the old more fully, and to bring to bear, for interpreting antiquity and learning from it, fuller knowledge of man and society.

—Moses Hadas [1]

WHILE in their moments of despair the Greeks might blame their trouble on the gods, there is another level on which they know better. When Homer has Zeus complain that men unjustly attribute their misfortunes to the gods, we have to remember that it is, after all, "Homer" who is talking. In having Zeus speak in this way, Homer attests to the Greek disposition to blame the gods and, at the very same time, he reveals their counterdisposition toward self-blame. The Greeks not only recognize but make a point of insisting that much of their suffering comes from themselves; from their own decisions, their own stiff-necked pride, willful blindness, envy, and soaring ambition. From Aeschylus to Euripides, tragedy is awed but never struck dumb by the mystery of self-created doom. In one way or another, tragedy talks endlessly of the death that is in one's own womb,[2] it remarks that self-

133

inflicted troubles somehow hurt the most, and it hears how Hippolytus' own horses drag him to his death.

The Greeks see their world as having an inner flaw and see themselves as the killers of their own dream. To understand this Greek vision of the world as doomed by an inner defect, we need an overview of the dynamics of Greek civilization and a glimpse of its movement as a system. We need to connect the internal tensions of the *polis* with the strains in the relations among city-states. We need to see how this grid of domestic and international tensions traps Hellenic civilization as a whole in that inescapable net to which Aeschylus so frequently refers.

If our analysis is to be focused on that murkiest of historical puzzles —the "decline and fall" of Greek Civilization—we would do well to attend to the obvious. Certainly we would do better to observe the tensions manifestly besetting this civilization as a total system than to dwell on the vagaries of its great art and science which, after all, live and die within that larger whole. The decline of an art, like its growth and efflorescence, is an ambiguous symptom, and the decline of Greek civilization should not be equated with the ebb of its art, philosophy, science, or of its rationalism. Then as now, art and science might spurt from the wounds of a stricken society; their vivid flux may testify not to the serenity but to the agony of a culture.

Greek tragedy, for example, mirrors the struggles and not the victory of Greek shame culture—it is ancient epic brought to terrifying life by infusions from current wars, ongoing class conflicts, political duplicity, personal treachery, and all the pangs of emerging individualism. In tragedy men transcend but never triumph over adversity; they come to terms with defeat. The three-phased flaring of Greek tragedy—in Aeschylus, Sophocles, and Euripides—marks different stages in the growing disparity between the ideal and the reality of Greece. The culminating achievement of Greek philosophy is, at the same time, the crowning Greek treachery—Plato's condemnation and betrayal of classical poetry and science. This Athenian triumph marks the ebb of the Ionian enlightenment.

The decline of Greek civilization is not simply the entropy of an exclusive "high culture," but is the cave-in of an everyday culture, as Thucydides is at pains to show. It is more than the failure of nerve, it is the dead end of a politics and an economics; and what matters is not only the defeat of violet-wreathed Athens but the fate of tradition-proud Sparta and, indeed, of all Hellas. It is the frustration of empire no less than the failure of the city. The decline of Greek civilization is an organic thing; it is the winding down of a total system.

THE GREEK STATE

Although hereditary kingships had all but disappeared by the eighth century B.C., until the end of the seventh century the *polis* was commonly governed by an oligarchy which restricted political privileges primarily to the large landholders and the well-to-do. As noted earlier, at the beginning of the sixth century, in response to growing class conflict, Solon's reforms in Athens began the development toward democracy. This trend continues and by Pericles' time full power is seen to derive from, if it does not in practice always reside in, the Assembly or *ekklēsia*. Greek democracy is, in principle, direct and not representative, each male citizen having one vote in the Assembly which meets at stated intervals and which, in time, comes to have the final decision on all important matters. Only a fraction of the citizenry, however, usually attends meetings of the Assembly. Since rural citizens are loath to leave their farms and since many are often at war, it is rare that more than two thousand to three thousand Athenians—most of them townsmen—sit in the Assembly.

Athenian democracy, however, is not as direct as some friendly stereotypes suggest, and in part for that reason is not as irresponsible and capricious as some hostile stereotypes maintain. While it is true that the *ekklēsia* controls basic decisions, it nonetheless is led by a representative council, the *boulē*, which actually presides over the day to day conduct of foreign affairs and civic defense. The president of the Assembly cannot initiate discussion of any matter that has not been first referred to the *boulē*. The five hundred members of the *boulē* are elected annually by lot, and every reputable Athenian of even moderate means can expect, if he so wishes, to be a member at least once during his life. Over the *boulē*, in turn, there are fifty *prytaneis* who function as its executive committee; and over the *prytaneis* are the *epistatai*, each of whom sits for a day as chairman of the executive committee and who is in effect the president of the republic. The pyramid of power, then, is: *ekklēsia*, *boulē*, *prytaneis*, and *epistatai*.

The administration of civic affairs is shared widely by the male citizens who hold office briefly and then retire. Many minor tasks of civic administration are performed by unpaid volunteers, lesser officials are chosen by lot, and generals are elected by vote of the Assembly. By the middle of the fifth century, the basic principle underlying political leadership is that "no one [is] better qualified than anyone else by breeding, intellectual power, or specific training to direct public policy." [3]

A full-time bureaucracy is scarcely existent. There is, for example, no public prosecutor, and individual citizens themselves initiate legal action concerning both private and civic wrongs. There is no police force or professional military group in the modern sense. The Athenian police consists of a group of mounted Scythian slaves, while the military forces consist of every able-bodied citizen, each of whom is usually expected to provide his own weapons and supplies and is liable to military duty until age sixty. In short, both political decision-making and military power are in the hands of the male citizenry as a whole. The state is, in principle, the citizenry in arms.

Ordinary citizens do not think of the Athenian state in a Germanic abstract or personified way; the state is neither conceived as "the republic" nor even as "Attica" but as "the Athenians"—the community of male citizens. The state is thus not yet clearly distinguishable or set apart from its citizens, and, under these circumstances, it cannot be expected that clear distinctions will be made between the polity and the society or between the political and the social aspects of the community.

The Greek state is in part tacitly modeled after the ōikos. It is, consequently, the state's duty to provide for and to protect its members in all important respects and, in particular, to do so, minimally, by maintaining its own autonomy and, maximally and preferably, by establishing its hegemony over other states.

The state is not only in loco ōikos in terms of its obligations, but also in its rights vis-à-vis its members. Until about the end of the fifth century, there is in principle scarcely any limit on the claims that the state can make upon its citizenry. Their fortunes and their persons are regarded as dependent upon the fortunes of the state to whom, in turn, they have diffuse obligations of obedience regardless of the demands made: Socrates obeys even when he is directed to drink the hemlock. A man's entire life and character are seen as drawing sustenance from the city, which is regarded as the chief educative influence on him: "A city teaches a man," says Simonides of Ceos, later to be echoed by Socrates.

The laws of the city are commonly regarded as the standard of right and wrong, and there is a tendency to view the legal and the ethical as identical. This, in turn, suggests that there is as yet little distinction made between the citizen's private life and his public life. There is a "general unwillingness to allow any other object of political loyalty to be inserted between the individual and the state" [4] and a concomitant distrust of political organizations; indeed, during certain periods, political clubs—which were centers of antidemocratic activity—appear to have been outlawed.

Citizen and State

The nature of the Greek city-state, and the character of the problems that it faces, are better seen when the full magnitude of the support and benefits which it provides its citizens is seen. A mere listing of those provided by Athens during various periods is impressive: the state distributes grain to citizens during times of famine and highly inflated corn prices; it provides pensions for disabled soldiers and for their orphans (indeed orphans are maintained until their eighteenth birthday, when males would be given their military equipment freely and poor girls—if comely, it seems—their dowries); and during some periods the conduct of state-financed public religious sacrifices provides the poorer citizen with an average of one meat dinner a week; citizens are paid three obols or one-half drachma per day for their frequent service as *hēliastai* on juries. If one is correct in inferring from certain passages in Aristophanes that a laborer could support a wife and one child on three obols a day, then Hasebroek is not far wrong in stating that "in the fourth century all full citizens were in receipt of a sufficient amount of food and money to secure them their livelihood," [5] while thousands of other citizens had annual incomes from captured territories which were distributed among them. The "glory that was Greece" was a glory born in the ancient approximation of the welfare state.

As the franchise and other opportunities for political participation are pulled down into the lower reaches of the class structure and as political rights and duties are extended to the masses of the *dēmos,* the civic offices requiring extensive time and energies increase in number and can no longer be manned by those able to support themselves from independent incomes. Not only is there a need to maintain the five hundred members of the *boulē,* but there are also a total of six thousand *hēliastai,* half of whom hear cases during any day, five hundred wardens of the arsenal, and about ten thousand citizens who perform a host of other official duties either in Athens or abroad. Glotz estimates that public affairs require the full attention of about a third of the citizenry at a time when half the citizens do not have an annual income of their own of two hundred drachmae. [6]

If citizens faithfully perform their extensive civic duties, they are unable to support themselves; if they attend to their trades to support themselves they have neither the time to perform their public duties nor to protect their political prerogatives. To resolve this dilemma, Pericles arranges payments (*misthoi*) to all citizens who renounce their professions in order to serve the state. These payments, of course, are not merely a response to the need of the *dēmos,* but also to its political power. The poorer classes use their franchise to better their economic positions by voting themselves various benefits. At certain periods, then, the Athenian citizen can and sometimes does live off the state. To suggest, however, as some writers have, that they are living off the "dole" is mistakenly to equate the *polis* with the modern welfare state. Despite significant similarities between the two, such a view is mistaken because it forgets that the Greek citizens *are* the state; they are not a dispirited group of unemployed but men actively engaged in full-time politics, civic administration, and frequent military service. They are not a pariah group but an elite who feel that what they receive from the state is only a just perquisite enabling them to devote themselves to its affairs. Rather than being a kind of unemployment compensation, the income and other benefits provided citizens are more akin to the dividends paid to stockholders of the modern private corporation. This analogy is far from a limping one, for it is "the ineradicable idea of the Greek that [state] surpluses should be divided between citizens. . . ." [7] "The principle which Athenian democracy worked upon was, however, peculiar neither to Athens nor to democracy. In all times, in all cities of Greece and under all governments, political sovereignty carried with it economic advantages." [8]

It is precisely because the advantages accruing to citizens are so substantial that they are jealous about restricting citizenship to a narrowly limited body. Until about the middle of the fifth century, only someone born of an Athenian father could be a citizen, and in 451 B.C. it is required that both his parents must be Athenian if he is to be a citizen. The citizenry are as loath to share their prerogatives as the managerial group in the modern corporation.

We will not be far wrong, then, in thinking of the *polis* as a private corporation; indeed, Aeschines—Demosthenes' political opponent—uses a similar metaphor, complaining that certain of the political sessions "proceed not as deliberative assemblies, but rather as meetings of shareholders after a distribution of surpluses." Yet if the citizenry are akin to the stockholders of a private corporation, this is a corporation whose stock can often be obtained only by inheritance and which is not always freely purchasable on an "exchange." The *polis* is a closed corporation. It is administered for the benefit of its citizens, who are both its managers and shareholders, and who are often scarcely a majority of the people in the city.

The Greek conception of citizenship embraces diverging values and interests. From one standpoint, citizenship is regarded as a matter of ascription; it is a right which depends primarily upon birth and is not contigent upon residence and is not earned. In this view, citizenship is a kind of property right. There is, however, another view which also influences access to citizenship in very exceptional circumstances. This regards citizenship as a privilege which could be earned, particularly by risking one's life in the military service of the city. Greek democracy, however, commonly takes the direction of extending the political privileges of those who are already defined as citizens rather than of extending citizenship itself to those who did not have it; it does not normally make it possible for outsiders to achieve citizenship by performing some routine service or by attainments that comply with certain universal standards.

Even after the democrats overthrow the dictatorship of the Thirty and restore democracy, notes Walbank, they

> rejected Thrasybulus' proposal to bestow citizenship on all who had fought for Athenian freedom at the Piraeus. . . . In this exclusiveness the middle class had the support of the workers, who saw in the various forms of the state subsidy the one perquisite which divided the poor but free citizen from the slave. Thus, whether rich or poor, the citizen of the fifth century Athens felt himself to be a member of a compact, brilliant, exclusive, and highly conscious community, which was, in fact, living largely at the expense of the resident alien, the slave and the subject ally.[9]

The conception of citizenship as a privilege capable of being earned through one's routine services and performances—although consistent with crucial elements in the Greek value system—is used only rarely; the dominant view regards citizenship as a form of property and a birthright. Those already privileged decline to share their advantages with others outside their own charmed circle. If this undermines the loyalty of those excluded and makes the citizens a narrowly vulnerable elite, this is a price that they are commonly willing to pay for their advantages. They pay another price as well, the betrayal of their own deeply ingrained achievement values, especially of their own conception of *aretē*, or excellence, which in all its forms always emphasizes that a man's worth is dependent on his own attainments. When the exclusive conception of citizenship begins to break down, it does so not because of a new determination to uphold achievement values but primarily because of venality: rich *metoikoi* can and do buy their way into the citizenry.

State Financing

That the Greek state exists primarily for the benefit of its citizens and at the expense of its slaves, resident aliens, and subjects becomes all the more evident if we examine the sources from which the state derives its financing. The Athenian state's surplus during the Empire, Michell tells us, "was created from the tribute of the allies, the receipts from the mines of Laurium, custom duties, and harbor duties, and taxes on *Metics* and foreigners."[10]

As is well known, the treasury of the Delian League was removed from Delos to Athens and was used for the Periclean beautification of Athens itself, making it evident from then on that members of the League were not confederated allies but tributaries of Athens.

In Xenophon's *Ways and Means*—proposals for improving the Athenian economy—written about 355 B.C., he stresses the value that would be derived if the state purchased and employed slaves in silver mining. Xenophon also mentions the value of a more careful handling of the resident aliens: "I can hardly conceive of a more splendid source of revenue than lies open in this direction," he says. "Here you have a self-supporting class of residents conferring large benefits upon the state, and instead of receiving payments themselves, contributing on the contrary by a special tax." [11] In effect, then, even plans for the reform of the Athenian economy assume that the state's surplus will continue to derive from a dependent and subordinated population: from the slaves and aliens in the city and from the people of the subject cities.

Another notable source of public financing at Athens, during the period of democracy, is the taxation of the rich. While Athenians commonly dislike and avoid direct taxation, there are a variety of civic services which the rich are expected to finance. Among these are the *leitourgiai* which, if originally volunteered by the citizen as a way of enhancing his prestige, come, in time, to be regular impositions upon the rich. Among these are the costs of certain religious festivals, the dramas, and the choruses and dances. That these expenses could be draining is suggested in a speech written by Lysias in which one citizen-plaintiff complains that he has spent more than sixty thousand drachmae in nine years. There are, too, the *eisphora,* special taxes on capital levied during times of emergency. Finally, there are the recurrent costs of outfitting or repairing a man-of-war, or *triēres,* which also fall on the rich; these become especially onerous during the Peloponnesian War, even though the state itself pays the initial cost of building and rigging the ship.

Without doubt the endemic tensions between the rich and poor—the "few" and the "many"—derive, in important part, from this system of taxation. In time, some of the rich make determined efforts to conceal the extent of their holdings by keeping much of it in gold or silver treasure or by lending it out for interest—practices that disadvantage those whose incomes derive mainly from visible landed properties. For to be well known as rich is, during certain periods, to court severe costs through the imposition of *leitourgiai.*

One remedy available to a man who feels himself taxed unfairly is the *antidosis.* This provides that someone, on whom a *leitourgia* has been imposed, could name another whom he believes better able to afford it. If this man refuses to accept the *leitourgia* he could be required to exchange all his property with the challenger and would then be given the *leitourgia*. The assumption is that the richer party would rather accept a *leitourgia* than risk an exchange of property. Yet given the prevalent tendency to conceal one's wealth and the lack of a trained bureaucracy to ferret it out, it would not seem that the *antidosis* can work effectively: the person first given the *leitourgia* could never know whether the man he challenges has not been even cleverer in hiding his wealth.

The conflict between the rich and poor over taxation rests on the poor citizen's political power in the Assembly and this, in its turn, leads the rich to oppose democracy and to seek to supplant it with an oligarchy which restricts the franchise. The economic pressure on the rich, along with the resentment of the older families toward the *nouveaux riches,* contributes to the growing alienation of sectors of the upper class. By the end of the fifth century, antidemocratic beliefs are prevalent among them and conspiracies and revolts which they initiate against the Democracy begin to occur. "[A]ll the world over," says the "Old Oligarch" writing about the last quarter of the fifth century B.C., "the cream of society is in opposition to the democracy. . . . [T]here is no state in which the best element is friendly to the people. It is the worst element which in every state favours the democracy." [12]

The economic and the status tensions of the older landed gentry are also severely exacerbated by the prevalence of wars and, in particular, by the Peloponnesian War, which lasts twenty-seven years. War brings direct economic loss through physical damage to landed property; when Athens withdraws behind its walls, the invading Spartans and their allies are free to ravage the countryside, to harry the fields, to burn the crops and houses, and to drive off the livestock. This, in turn, intensifies the poorer peasants' feeling against the gentry, for they could not afford capital repairs and once again they are overburdened with debts and mortgages. The landed gentry is thus politically and economically damaged by war and is, consequently, more inclined toward peace. Paradoxically, at least from a contemporary "liberal" viewpoint, it is not the rich oligarchs but the *dēmos* and the democratic faction that are more inclined toward military adventure and war. For it is these that provide much of the state's surplus from which the *dēmos* derives direct economic support.

Not only might the well-to-do be taxed and outvoted during the Democracy, but their military honor and privilege are also undermined as Athens' military power becomes increasingly naval in character. With Athens' growing reliance on her naval power, the "rowers who guard the state"—the *"rhyppapai,"* as they come to be known popularly from their rhythmic rowing chant—in turn acquire increased political influence. The "Old Oligarch" speaks of this development toward a naval democracy with a detached irony:

> [I]t is only just that the poorer classes and the common people of Athens should be better off than the men of birth and wealth, seeing that it is the people who man the fleet, and have brought the city her power. The steersman, the boatswain, the lieutenant, the look-out-man at the prow, the shipwright—these are the people who supply the city with power far rather than her heavy infantry and men of birth and quality. This being the case, it seems only just that offices of state should be thrown open to every one both in the ballot and the show of hands, and that the right of speech should belong to any one who likes, without restriction.[13]

In the maritime democracy of Athens, notes Adkins, "the poor man, not the rich, mans the navy, the most important striking force of the state, and, his equipment being provided for him, can meet the rich on at least equal terms on that score." [14]

In the last years of the Peloponnesian War the maintenance and repair of ships costs more than can be afforded by a single rich citizen, and groups of two or more citizens, a *synarchia,* are set up for this purpose. By the middle of the fourth century B.C. the size of the ship-maintaining unit is made even larger and comes to consist of sixty members. The growing intensity and costs of war undermine the wealth of the landed gentry as well as the status claims of the rich in general, insofar as the latter are traditionally justified by their contribution to military activities.

WAR AND THE CLASS STRUCTURE

At this point, we may begin to discern some of the relationships between Athens' military adventures abroad and her class struggles and political conflicts at home. During the period of the Delian League, Athens' main source of state financing, and thus of the benefits she provides her citizens, derives from the annual tribute paid by her allies. This had first been fixed at 460 talents, with a surplus of some 3,000 talents accumulating by about 453 B.C. However, with the defeat of Athens at the end of the Peloponnesian War the tribute is eliminated, and in consequence, state financing based upon taxation of the rich assumes more significance. This, in turn, conduces to greater tensions between rich and poor.

The wealthier groups are caught in a grinding cross-pressure in which they face the dilemma of either foreign war or civil war. To avoid being taxed by the *dēmos,* the rich are constrained either to satisfy the demands of the *dēmos* by allowing or leading military adventures from which booty and tribute can be obtained or undercutting the demands of the *dēmos* by eliminating their political power through the overthrow of the Democracy. The first solution means war abroad and the possible pillage of country properties; the second solution invites civil war at home. For both rich and poor citizens, however, war abroad is preferable to war at home and indeed the threat of civil war at home is conducive to conflict between the cities. War diverts the poor from the resources of the rich; it unites both classes against a foreign enemy and provides both a common gain—if they win. Victory produces not only tribute but opportunities for booty as well; it provides new land which is important to the endemically land-hungry citizens and thus reduces discontent and pressure against the landed gentry; it insures control of overseas food supplies which are almost always important to Athens because of her insufficient food production; and it also permits fresh supplies of cheap slaves. Class tensions, within the city and in the countryside, are in some part resolved by war or, more precisely, by victory in war. Defeat, of course, is another matter and results in a continuation and, indeed, an exacerbation of internal class conflicts.

In some ways, the Greek system of stratification is conducive to war but inhibitive to victory. Aside from the debilitating costs of disunity between rich and poor, a city's military position is imperiled by its class system in two other ways: First, her slaves are sometimes a locus of instability; they might revolt or flee during war, in effect contributing to the strength of the enemy. These military costs of slavery are not, however, borne equally by the major contenders in the Peloponnesian War. Sparta, for example, is more disadvantaged by its slave system than is Athens, for a substantial part of her military force is always pinned down at home against the danger of Helot rebellion while Athens,[15] at most fearing desertion rather than rebellion from her slaves, can deploy a larger part of her fighting men abroad. Secondly, since payments to the citizens are in part dependent on the size of the state's surpluses, there is always some question about dividing a surplus or using it to strengthen the city's forces by building more *triēreis.* Defense spending and welfare spending even then compete with one another. The rich, however, cannot wholeheartedly reject the policy of dividing the surplus since, if they do so, this induces the poor to press for increased taxation of the rich. Further, since the rich have to pay for maintaining and repairing the ships after they have been built, a division of the surplus means fewer *triēreis* which have to be kept in condition.

To say that military victory eases the internal conflicts of the city means that war and social disorder between the cities are conducive to social order within the city. In some degree, war is necessary for the internal stability of the *polis*. And there is war aplenty. According to P. A. Sorokin's estimates, during the 375 years between 500 and 126 B.C., some 235 of them, or about 63 per cent, have an occurrence of war. "[I]n the history of Greece," says Sorokin, "frequency of war was much higher than many are wont to think." [16]

"To the Greek mind the normal condition of things was war between state and state, not peaceable coexistence." [17] In addition to the many full-scale wars between cities, piracy and privateering—which are common in most periods of Greek history—provide for the continual and institutionalized conduct of conflict by private parties. Citizens of one state are often the legitimate prey of those in another; foreigners are frequently exposed to seizure on the high seas or coastal waters unless protected by special treaty between cities or by personal privilege. "Greek states went to war with each other almost as part of political routine. . . ." [18] Not peace but war is the condition reckoned as normal; peace is viewed as a time between wars rather than war being viewed as a disruption of peace. Although the ravages of the Peloponnesian War make many long for peace, peace is not viewed as a humane ideal but as a matter of self-interest and, even in 425 B.C., many Athenians still believe that victory in war would ensure their prosperity and enhance their power.

This view of the classical conception of war as the continual and normal state of affairs is by no means a modern ethnocentric projection into the past. In his *Laws,* Plato himself has Cleinias remark, "For what men in general term peace . . . [is] only a name; in reality every city is in a natural state of war with every other, not indeed proclaimed by heralds, but everlasting." [19] In its turn, war is regarded by Plato as having shaped not only Sparta's but also Athens' basic institutions and, indeed, as being their major objective. When Plato has the Athenian remark, in the *Laws,* that it is better to arrange wars for the sake of peace than peace for the sake of wars, Cleinias rejoins that "there is truth, Stranger, in that remark of yours; and yet I am greatly mistaken if war is not the entire aim and object of our own institutions, and also of the Lacedaemonian." To which the Athenian replies, "I dare say. . . ." [20]

It is this prevalence of war and the continuing hope for war's prizes, of war as an ongoing way of life and not simply as the glorious memory of an outmoded Homeric past, that deeply shapes the character of the Greek citizenry. If by the time of the Peloponnesian War the Athenian masses are far from a warrior elite lusting after immortality through heroic military exploits, if their personal taste for battle has dulled and they are no longer so ready to "face the blood and the slaughter [and] go close against the enemy and fight with [their] hands," [21] they yet remain greedy for the spoils of war.

Slavery and War

Endemic war binds the citizens ever more closely to slavery, and slavery, in turn, makes war ever more necessary. An elite engaged in frequent wars cannot take part in the routine conduct of economic affairs; they must be able to live without working if only because they spend so much of their time in the field. Indeed this is one of the reasons that Xenophon adduces for relieving the aliens of military duties; for "the trouble of quitting trades and homesteads is no trifle," [22] he observes. The citizen elite need slaves to help maintain their establishments during their military service, and they need to fight so that they can maintain the slave supply. Slavery and war in Greece are interdependent, each enabling the other to be carried on.

Greek slavery is, indeed, intrinsically inhibitive of the maintenance of a system of peaceful international order among the city-states, because a stable international order tends to reduce the number and to increase the price of slaves. (In a similar manner, when the Roman principate is later successful in establishing social order within the Empire, it eliminates the main sources of cheap slaves, piracy and brigandage, throwing the Romans back on the relatively expensive practice of breeding slaves and thus raising their cost.) Maintenance of a cheap slave supply requires large areas of social disorder between the city-states; it requires kidnaping, piracy, privateering, and above all war. Slavery is thus one of the major inhibitants to the spread of a peaceful international order in Hellenic civilization. Conversely, international disorder is actually useful for the maintenance of Greek slavery, because it allows those outside the basic political unit, the *polis,* to be preyed upon and to be subjugated as slaves. And without the slaves there can be no citizen elite.

The citizen soldiery is the main group in Greek society which can live off unearned income: from payments by the state, from *klērouchiai,* from rents on land that it alone is privileged to own. During certain periods, it is a castelike group whose members are forbidden by law to marry foreigners,[23] membership in which is a jealously guarded birthright, and which has a monopoly of legal and political control.

To be sure, there are many relatively poor citizens—for if they are all "stockholders," each does not hold the same amount of stock—and this is one of the sources of the city's internal tensions. These tensions are all the more aggravated because poverty and routine, continuous work are discrepant with their conception of the ideal citizen. A central objective of

Xenophon's proposed economic reforms is to avoid work and to enable every citizen to "be supplied with ample maintenance at the public expense." [24] As Euripides' Ion, for example, observes, "But father, hear the good points of my life in Delphi: leisure first of all, most dear to any man. . . ." [25]

The ideal citizen is a man of leisure, rich enough to devote himself to the management of the affairs of the *polis* and to its aggrandizement. The citizenry are an elite of politics and war who cannot live as they think themselves entitled to unless others are there to play their parts. The system is a seamless whole: there can be no masters unless there are others who live under constraint.

It is impossible to have an adequate understanding of the Hellenic wars without seeing them in relation to slavery and to the classical system of social stratification common to the city-states. Not only is the Greek class system conducive to war, it also shapes the strategies by which they are fought and influences the conditions under which peace might be sought. When the cities are at peace, they aid one another in maintaining their own slave systems as, for example, in 462 B.C., when Athens sends Cimon with a hoplite army to help Sparta put down a major revolt of the Helots. Conversely, when the cities are at war they incite their enemies' slaves to rebellion or desertion, as in 425 B.C., when Athens seizes a harbor on the west coast of the Peloponnese and Sparta becomes greatly concerned that this will be a locus for spreading rebellion among her Messenian Helots and begins to think of peace.

In the peace treaty signed in 421 B.C. it is agreed that, "Should the slave-class rise in rebellion, the Athenians will assist the Lacedaemonians with all their might. . . ." [26] Something less than a century later, the members of the Hellenic League show that it remains one of the prime functions of international concord among the Greek cities to maintain the established system of stratification by agreeing that there should be "no confiscation of property, no redistribution of land, no cancellation of debts, no freeing of slaves for purposes of revolution." [27]

Powerful groups in the various cities feel a common interest not only in maintaining slavery but, also, in bolstering the larger system of stratification. The tensions of war and, in particular, of defeat in war, exacerbate the strains inherent in the cities' class system; after the Peloponnesian War, in particular, both internecine conflicts and wars between the cities grow in brutality. The poorer classes want the city to be rich enough to support them. The upper classes find themselves economically drained and politically damaged by wars, yet they continue to need war as a way of diverting the *dēmos* from taxing them.

HELLENIC UNITY AND ATHENIAN EXPANSION

One basic solution to this problem is, of course, to promote Greek unity. Stabilizing the relations between the cities and consolidating their forces, the cities can then make a common assault on the "barbarian" empires in the Near East. In this connection, it is notable that Plato objects to the enslavement of Greeks by Greeks because it weakens Hellenic civilization as a whole in its contest with the barbarians. "Do you think it right that Hellenes should enslave Hellenic states, or allow others to enslave them, if they can help?" he asks. "Should not their custom be to spare them, considering the danger which there is that the whole race may one day fall under the yoke of the barbarians?" [28]

Greek unity, however, cannot be attained unless another problem is first solved. This problem is the old one of each of the city-states jealously guarding its autonomy so that none will relinquish leadership to another voluntarily. They could not be unified except by the domination of some more powerful state. Up until the Peloponnesian War, Athens comes closest to consolidating an empire that could provide the power center for an Hellenic peace, but she is finally thwarted by two things: first, by Sparta and her allies, of course, and secondly, by her own inability to assimilate her friends within the subject populace of the empire. In particular, Athens is usually unwilling to consolidate their friendship by giving them citizenship (as Rome later does) because she so jealously guards the prerogatives of citizenship. The exclusive and narrow conception of "community" with which the Athenians operate undermines, to a great extent, their own empire.

It is clear, however, that Athens drifts toward a policy of expansion through conquest and domination. In the fifth century the young Athenian swears an oath that he will recognize "no bounds to Attica save beyond the corn and barley fields, the vineyards and the olive groves"; and by the fourth century he swears, "I will not leave my country smaller, but I will leave it greater and stronger than I received it." [29]

Alcibiades' plea on behalf of the Sicilian expedition indicates that the adventure in Syracuse is seen, by some Athenians, as only the first step in an audacious expansion of empire: "[W]e cannot fix the exact point at which our empire shall stop; we have reached a position in which we must not be content with retaining but must scheme to extend it. . . ." [30] As Alcibiades elaborates after going over to the Spartans, "[I]f Syracuse falls, all Sicily falls, also, and Italy immediately afterwards. . . . None need therefore fancy that Sicily only is in question." [31]

Athens and the Hellenic Class Structure

Athens' expansion is not, however, motivated only by her citizens' avarice. Her power is based not on the needs of Athens alone, seen as a separate social system, but is sustained by larger forces set in motion by the class system common to Hellenic civilization as a whole. The war between the cities, especially the Peloponnesian War, is rooted in the class struggles between the few and the many, the oligarchs and democrats.

No one has made this plainer than Thucydides. The Spartans, he tells us, pride themselves on their oligarchical character; they boast that in Sparta "the many do not rule the few, but rather the few the many, owing their position to nothing else than to superiority in the field." [32] Normally, Sparta's policy is not to exact tribute from her allies (in part because she already has a rich "internal" empire in Messenia consisting [33] of some twenty Helots for every citizen), "but merely to secure their subservience to her interests by establishing oligarchies among them . . ." [34] Of Athens, Thucydides says that "in all cities the people is your friend, and either does not revolt with the oligarchy, or, if forced to do so, becomes at once the enemy of the insurgents; so that in the war with the hostile city you have the masses on your side." [35] In the Peloponnesian War the whole Hellenic world is convulsed, says Thucydides, by this interlocking of class conflict and intercity warfare, "[s]truggles being everywhere made by the popular chiefs to bring in the Athenians, and by the oligarchs to introduce the Lacedaemonians." [36]

What Sparta or Athens become in their international role does not depend solely on their own peculiar internal pressures and character; it constitutes a response to class cleavages and to conflicts that pervade all of Hellas and cut across the various city-states. It is not simply that Sparta imposes oligarchy upon the cities or that Athens imposes democracy; nor is it merely that they both systematically exploit their popular support abroad and use civil war and class struggle as a deliberate device of foreign policy and imperialistic expansion. Athenian support of democracy in the island cities is not "only"—as is sometimes said—a device to exploit class hostilities for Athenian advantage; Athens is not only the creator but the creature of larger forces of a popular character. The class-rooted sources of oligarchy in the cities throughout Hellas create and support Sparta, in part making her what she becomes; the class-rooted sources of democracy throughout the Hellenic cities create and sustain Athens also, making her, in some part, what she becomes in power and political character.

This interpretation need not at all commit us to the view that Athens, always and everywhere, supports democracy and the *dēmos* in other cities, or that she gives support only to democratic cities. Athenian interests of state, the exigencies she faces as a power contending with Persia and Sparta, demand that she give independent consideration to the unity of her empire, and this occasionally leads her to support oligarchic governments and factions. Yet there is no question that in the classical period the Athenian disposition is predominantly prodemocratic, that she relies upon the loyalty of the *dēmos* in the subject cities, and that where there is internal strife in a city or some question of its loyalty to Athens, she commonly throws her power behind the democratic faction. "When she did restore peace or loyalty in a state, she would normally choose the side of the democrats or institute a democratic constitution. . . ." [37]

Certainly, neither Sparta nor Athens can reverse their roles; that each becomes a magnet attracting different class and different political forces is important. Sparta's ecological location makes it somewhat less vulnerable to Persian pressure and also less accessible to stimulation by Ionian trade and science. If her own internal empire is enriched through Messenian fertility, it is also threatened by the abiding and well-earned hostility of the many Helots she controls. Messenia is a precarious and costly prize. Together these reinforce the Spartan tendency to traditionalism, disposing her to a more cautious isolationism in foreign affairs and to conservatism in domestic policy, and making her attractive to aristocratic and oligarchic interests throughout Greece. The democratic forces in Greece are more attracted to Athens than Sparta because of what Athens' great reformers enable her to become and to symbolize. It is not only Athens' selfish ambition but the need for her protection and leadership that lead the *dēmos* of many Hellenic cities to bring their cities into her empire. Conversely, where upper-class oligarchic groups win control of cities, they bring them into the Spartan league against Athens.

Time and again, it is clear from Thucydides' account that the initiative is taken not by Sparta or Athens but by these class-rooted groups in the various cities. It is often they who appeal to and they who seek to ally themselves with one side or the other, rather than having this rule imposed upon them. "Since the fifth century," notes Glotz, "democrats everywhere had fallen into the habit of appealing to Athens for help." [38] It is particularly notable that when, toward the end of the Peloponnesian War, the Athenian democracy is overthrown from within by the conspiracy of the Four Hundred, the Athenian army still at Samos then joins with the Samian *dēmos* to overthrow the oligarchy and restore democracy to Athens. Here, clearly, it is not Athens who is imposing democracy on a tributary, but, rather, it is the latter who, joining with other forces, seeks to defend democracy and to bring it back to Athens.

The power of the Athenian empire is as much created by the need of its subjects as by the greed of its rulers. Despite the shortsighted and overweening ambition of the Athenians, they play a role in Hellenic civilization that transcends their own selfishness and is larger than they know. Although she exacts a price, Athens gives a service in return: she gives protection not only to her own but to the Hellenic *dēmos,* buffering them from their own upper classes. Athens' drive toward empire, her ability to endure the twenty-seven years of the Peloponnesian War against a legion of foes, is empowered and vitalized because she manipulates, exploits and, also, because she gives authentic expression and aid to the Hellenic *dēmos* in their struggles against their own local oligarchical factions.

To hold that the character and strength of the Athenian empire rests on these class forces throughout Hellas does not commit us to a view that Athens is—or is not—popular among the majority of her subjects.[39] A definitive answer to this specific question would require a public opinion poll and cannot be expected. What we have essayed above, however, is an appraisal of the class character of the Athenian empire, an exploration of the relation between the strength and fortunes of this empire, on the one hand, and the system of stratification common to cities throughout Greece, on the other, rather than making an effort to conduct a *post-factum* public opinion poll across the centuries. Even if all social classes in the subject cities had been polled and a majority in each had been found—because of their commitment to the idea of civic autonomy—to be opposed or hostile to Athens, it would still be significant to know whether the *dēmos* was as strongly opposed as the upper classes. It is, in short, still relevant and important to determine whether all classes in the subject cities are equally committed to civic autonomy and equally hostile to Athens.

On this point, the evidence is clear enough: Plato notes in his seventh *Epistle* that the Athenians "maintained their empire for seventy years, because they possessed in the various cities men who were their friends." [40] Among whom were these friends, the *dēmos* or "the better sort of people"? Certainly not the latter, if the testimony of the Old Oligarch is to be believed.

> [E]missaries from Athens come out, and, according to common opinion, calumniate and vent their hatred upon the better sort of people, this is done on the principle that the ruler cannot help being hated by those whom he rules; but that if wealth and respectability are to wield power in the subject cities the empire of the Athenian People has but a short lease of existence. This explains why the better people are

punished with infamy, robbed of their money, driven from their homes, and put to death, while the baser sort are promoted to honour.[41]

A. W. Gomme remarks in his commentary on Thucydides that "nowhere were the majority enthusiastic for Sparta; they generally, as in Mytilene, Amphipolis, Akanthos, Mende, Samos, and elsewhere, stood by Athens, shakily in some places, firmly in others." [42] In my view, the best, most reasoned and judicious statement on this question remains that formulated by Grote more than a half century ago:

> In proportion as fear and hatred of Athens became predominant among the allies of Sparta, these latter gave utterance to the sentiment more and more emphatically, so as to encourage discontent artificially among the subject-allies of the Athenian Empire. . . . [T]he movement for revolt against Athens originated with the aristocracy or with some few citizens apart; while the people, though sharing more or less in the desire for autonomy, had yet either a fear of their own aristocracy or sympathy with Athens, which made them always backward in revolting, sometimes decidedly opposed to it. . . . [T]heir condition was not one of positive hardship, nor did they [the people] overlook the hazardous side of such a change—partly from the coercive hand of Athens—partly from the enemies against whom Athens had hitherto protected them—and not least from their own oligarchy.[43]

The point must be reiterated, then, that in some part the Athenian Empire becomes as strong as it does because of the Panhellenic class conflicts between the *dēmos* and the elite, and because of the support Athens receives from and gives to the *dēmos*.

Athenian Vulnerabilities

Just as Athenian power is linked to the system of social stratification and to the institutions which she shares with other Hellenic cities, so too are some of the sources of her ultimate failure. Athens' defeat derives in large part from her inner flaws, from some of her most fundamental characteristics as a community, and from the image of a community that she holds. Like other city-states, the Athenian image of community is an extremely narrow and exclusive one: it excludes those who are not citizens, and it provides little or no regular basis on which they can become citizens. It is thus difficult for Athens to consolidate the friendly sentiments which are felt for her among the *dēmoi* throughout many Hellenic city-states. Nor can Athens ever pursue a consistent and systematic policy of putting down the upper classes in her subject cities, despite the fact that they are the nucleus of internal resistance to her empire. As the Old Oligarch puts it, "[T]he better Athenians protect the better class in the allied cities. And why? Because they recognize that it is to the interest of their own class at all times to protect the best element in the cities." [44] In short, Athens finds herself in the conflicting position of being able neither to incorporate her friends among the *dēmoi* nor to control or eliminate her enemies in the aristocracy of the subject cities.

Athens' power is in large measure stimulated by the brilliant reforms of Solon, Pisistratus, and Cleisthenes and by the great economic and cultural growth which they foster; but after Athens exploits the opportunities they create, she can go no further without the most radical revision of her own system of stratification.

The Athenian polity excludes vast sections of Athens' own populace, particularly the aliens and slaves. Yet the maintenance of any stable social system requires the motivated performance of social roles; men have to be *willing* to do what is expected of them, otherwise they will not do it reliably. In some part, the citizenry are constrained to exclude the slaves from their polity because, in the nature of the case, the latter perform their roles only reluctantly. Indeed, it is only by excluding them from the polity and from their moral universe that the citizenry can remain "masters."

If, for example, the slaves had been incorporated in the Athenian community and defined as members of it, they would have had to be treated less as tools subject to almost any use and more as persons subject to limited claims and who, in turn, could make claims upon others. In short, they would not have been slaves. The extension of the community to include the slaves or aliens premised the reduction of exploitative attitudes toward them. But if this had been done, where, then, would there have been the advantage to a citizenry who wished to be a leisured, state-supported elite? Athens, like other city-states, therefore, had to accept the liabilities of her social system, if she wished to enjoy its benefits.

The ultimate case, revealing precisely because it is extreme, is always that of slavery: However many the uses to which a slave might be put, there is typically one limit—slaves are not ordinarily used as fighting men. There were a few historical exceptions, such as the battles of Marathon and the often cited case of Arginusae. Yet as Miss Sargent has shown for sea and land warfare, the Athenians "did not permit slaves to take an active part in battles as soldiers." [45]

The reason for this is not simply that slaves lack the skill or the will to fight; it is not only that they could not or would not do battle—for Marathon and Arginusae proved otherwise. There is, in addition, the fact that the price of using slaves as soldiers is prohibitive. For the slave could best be relied upon to fight well when he has the promise, or at least the hope, of freedom. Indeed, tradition calls upon masters to free slaves who fight; for this is what had been done at Marathon and later at Arginusae.

Underlying the classical Greek value system there is, as noted earlier, the lingering premise that military valor is the paradigm of virtue and the corollary assumption that civic rights hinge on the contribution to warfare, so that "military service meant freedom." [46] If the slave fights it is not expedience alone that urges he be given freedom; very deep Greek conceptions of honor and propriety demand it no less. In effect, then, the Athenians are unable to mobilize, to make free and extensive use of their slave manpower, because both morality and expedience make this possible only on the condition that they are prepared to uproot their system of stratification; only on the condition that masters are willing to forego the leisure, convenience, comfort, and superiority of slave owners.

It is only "after the crushing defeat of Chaeronea in 338 B.C., when the statesmen were at their wits' end in a last-minute effort to save an already doomed Greek state, [that] Hyperides brings forward the proposal to enfranchise as citizens and to mobilize all men not normally eligible to serve in the army, namely slaves, debtors of the state, and the disenfranchised." [47] By then it is too late and nothing ever comes of this proposal except that Hyperides is charged and brought to trial for having proposed an illegal measure—a charge of which, however, he is subsequently acquitted.

However much the "school of Hellas," Athens could never make itself Hellas' tribune of freedom; for she was fighting not for an abstract freedom or even for civic autonomy alone; the Athenians fought for such freedom as masters wish, the cherished right to have and to hold slaves without which they are masters no more. Fighting for their liberties and *their* ancient way of life, the citizens of Athens—like those in other places and later times—were never capable of renouncing their vested interests and prerogatives; they were caged within the barricade of their own institutional commitments. Like men under a sentence of death, they would not risk all in a desperate break with their own privileged past, and hoping against hope for a last minute reprieve that history never granted, they were dragged toward their fate.

Had Athens' restless groping toward empire succeeded she might have unified Hellas by imposing an Athenian peace. Suppressing the internecine slaughter among Greeks, she might have marshaled their forces and led them in a commonly profitable attack upon the East. As Rome later did, Athens might have established a peace through domination; but Athens failed.

Even in its most imperialistic posture, however, Athens gave expression to a genuine Hellenic need—the need for a unity among the Greek cities that would somehow halt their interminable wars. That she did so for a price, that she sought her own partisan advantage and had her own private motives, does not refute the collective advantage to all that would have accrued from Hellenic unity.

The drift toward Hellenic unity, toward larger polities that could accommodate diverse cities, is a persistent and deeply ingrained tendency manifested in the Lacedaemonian league no less than in the Athenian confederation, as well as in the various federations such as the Boeotian, Chalcidian, and Arcadian. Basically, however, none of these are expressions of an ideal of Hellenic unity; they are at best alliances for mutual defense against the military threat of other powers, and when this subsides the vitality of the alliance wanes. The drift toward larger polities also commonly founders on the question of leadership: each city is jealous of its autonomy, and the elite of each city is unwilling to diminish its local privileges or walk behind the elite of another city.

THE POWER VACUUM IN GREECE

The question of Greek unity and, in particular, the question of who will lead this unity, is posed in its most desperate form when both the great powers of Greece are smashed: when Athens is defeated by Sparta and when, with classic retribution, Sparta herself is defeated, first in 394 B.C. at the naval battle of Knidos, and some twenty-five years later and much more surprisingly to the Greek world, when this Behemoth of Hellas meets a military genius, Thebes' Epaminondas, who trades on Sparta's inability to improvise and who crushes her finally on land.[48]

These culminating events within Greece must also be placed in the larger context of the developing relationship between Greece and Persia. Persia's power in Greece increases during the Peloponnesian War and especially after 412 B.C. when, in hostility to the democracy at Athens, Persia opens her purse to Sparta. Indeed, it is Persian funds that finance the fleets with which Sparta finally starves Athens into submission.

The fragmentation of Greece and the felt need for unity in it is spurred by the Persian "King's Peace" of 386 B.C. which demands that all the Greek cities—except, of course, those held by Persia—be kept free and independent. Persia, in short, is playing the game of divide and rule. This game, however, is congenial to Sparta since it permits the survival of her Peloponnesian League, which allows its members a nominal autonomy, while it requires that the competitive Theban League be disbanded. In point of fact, Sparta's defeat by Epaminondas is occasioned by Sparta's effort to head off a new Boeotian federation, which had been Epaminondas' first tactical objective in a larger drive toward Hellenic leadership. Thebes' ascendancy itself, however, is also short-lived, and she, too, is removed from the lists when Epaminondas is killed at the battle of Mantinea in 362 B.C. The Hellenic power vacuum, then, is intensifying in an international context in which Persian intervention in Greece is increasingly bold, and when her interest in Greek disunity is manifest and effectively expressed.

The inherent dilemma of Hellenic international politics is this: since none of the cities would agree voluntarily to the leadership of another, unity in Hellas can be won only if one city dominates all the others; yet for a city to win such dominance, she is commonly forced to seek aid from and therefore compromise with the Persians—as Sparta has and, indeed, as Epaminondas also does later. The desire to remove Persian influence motivates the Greeks toward unity, but this unity could be imposed only by a city with sufficient resources. These, however, are often sought from Persia, who is implacably opposed to Greek unity and whose defeat is, in any event, the whole point of such unity.

Panhellenism

It is in this way that two policies—that of war against Persia and that of Hellenic unity—become fused into two sides of the same coin. War against Persia becomes an international and a domestic necessity for the Greek cities. It is needed in order to remove Persia's disunifying influence in Greece. It is needed in order to sack Persia so that the internal class tensions within each Greek city can be reduced; so that the *dēmoi* will have no motive for taxing their own rich, so that the rich will have no motive for violently curbing the *dēmoi;* and so that the two will not rend the city with class war. Conversely, unity among the cities is needed so that the war against Persia can be prosecuted successfully. In order to establish this unity in Greece, however, the Hellenic power vacuum will have to be filled; some city strong enough to impose unity will have to be found.

It is in this context that various elements in Greece begin to search for a political power strong enough to unify Greece and to spearhead the Hellenic push against the East. It is in this context that there is increasing expression of a need for strong men to lead the cities and the idea of a powerful monarchy is rejuvenated. It is in this context, also, that the movement for Panhellenic unity begins to spread and to find its spokesmen.

The sophist Gorgias first raises the theme of Panhellenism at the Olympics, perhaps about 408 B.C., and Lysias takes it up again in 384, shortly after the King's Peace. The fullest and most significant expression of Pan-hellenism is voiced by the publicist and rhetorician Isocrates. Isocrates at first thinks to solve the problem of Hellenic leadership by calling for unity between Sparta and Athens. Since, however, the two are in his view to unite under Athens' leadership, it soon becomes clear that this strategy is hopeless. Isocrates then begins to look outside the core of Greek culture for a strong man who can dominate Hellas, turning at various times to Jason of Pherae, Dionysius I of Syracuse, and, finally, to Philip of Macedonia.

In his *Panegyricus,* Isocrates berates both the Spartans and the Athenians for their "utter madness, not only because we risk our lives fighting as we do over trifles when we might enjoy in security a wealth of possessions, but also because we continually impoverish our own territory while neglecting to exploit that of Asia." [49] The time for war against Persia is now opportune, he pleads; the king's satellites are in revolt and his territories are being overrun by his other enemies. Greece, he points out, is being devastated by wars and factionalism; it is being destroyed by disorganization and anarchy, with homeless men wandering through the land and with many obliged to enlist in foreign armies in order to live. Those who take up the call and march eastward, Isocrates promises, will enjoy a fame undying: "[H]ow great must we think will be the name and the fame and the glory which they will enjoy during their lives, or, if they die in battle, will leave behind them, . . . what encomiums should we expect these men to win who have conquered the whole of Asia?" [50] In the end, Isocrates returns again to the promise of pillage, inciting the Greeks with a conjured fantasy of the riches to be won: "[T]ry to picture to yourselves what vast prosperity we should attain if we should bring the war which now involves ourselves against the peoples of the continent, and bring the prosperity of Asia across to Europe." [51]

Plato in Sicily

It is in the context of the aching power vacuum in Greece that we may also set Plato's adventures in Syracuse, and the ill-starred efforts of certain groupings within his Academy to intervene in Syracusan politics. In this they are, in some part, motivated by a desire to win the rulers of Syracuse to a moral rearmament that can energize and prepare that city to assume Hellenic leadership.

Whatever the historical stereotype, Plato and his Academy are neither disinterested nor uninvolved in the practical politics of their time. Leaving aside the various other expressions of this political interest, nothing better illustrates it than their intervention in Syracuse. The Academy is not only a teaching and research institution, and Plato is not only the first head of a "college"; the Academy is also the first intellectual collegium of rational policy development; it seeks to bridge the policy needs of ancient times with the philosophy, knowledge, and social theory of the period. The Academy is in its own way the RAND Corporation of antiquity. It is, however, "in business for itself" and searches for a client worthy of it.

Not once or twice but three times Plato travels to Syracuse in the hope of educating its tyrants, Dionysius I and Dionysius II, to enable them to become the "philosopher-kings" who could act upon his theoretical diagnosis of the social malaise of the times.[52] After all three of these visits fail ignominiously, some of Plato's younger men in the Academy then give their support to a military expedition to wrest control of Syracuse by force.

Plato himself accepted his first invitation to visit Syracuse shortly after Sparta was defeated at sea in the battle of Knidos and when, because of this, she could no longer as before exert her international influence in Hellas. Plato first turns to Syracuse when the air is beginning to hiss out and the power vacuum in Greece is developing. He returns to Syracuse for the second time, despite the treachery of Dionysius I, who had sold him into slavery, several years after Sparta was defeated by Epaminondas. It is in between these first two visits that he establishes the Academy. Though less traumatic than the first, the second visit is also far from successful and Plato returns to the Academy, where he is exposed to pressure to go once again to Syracuse. Shortly after Thebes' bid for Hellenic leadership is miscarried by the death of Epaminondas, Plato returns for the third time, is again maltreated, and barely escapes unscathed.

Initially, Plato's first invitation to Syracuse had been arranged by Dion, cousin to Dionysius II, who subsequently becomes one of his favorite disciples and students. After Plato's third visit is unsuccessful, Dion entreats Plato to support a military expedition against Dionysius II. Dion is supported in this adventure by an important grouping within the Academy, two members of which are particularly close to Plato; these are Xenocrates and Speusippus, the latter being Plato's nephew who will later succeed him as head of the Academy. While Plato decides against personal involvement in this expedition, he does not commit the Academy against it, and allows the others to make their own individual decisions.

In 357 Dion embarks for Syracuse with an army of some eight hundred mercenaries which succeeds in deposing Dionysius II. Dion's chief opponent in Syracuse then becomes the admiral Heraclides, and, once more, a Greek navy comes to the center of the revolutionary cockpit. Seeing new opportunities in the fluid situation, the reactivated *demos* in Syracuse puts forth new radical demands—the redivision of lands and properties—which Heraclides supports. Not surprisingly, as the scion of an aristocratic lineage,

Dion is out of sympathy with these demands, and Plato's disciple finally finds himself ordering Heraclides put to death. In the end, the traditional Greek paradigm of justice-as-retribution is re-enacted; Dion the murderer is himself murdered. Significantly, however, Dion's assassin is a fellow product of the Academy, Callipus. (Indeed, this is not the only political assassination in which a student of the Academy is involved, another of them, Chion, being the murderer of the prince of Heracleia.) Far from politically uninvolved, then, Plato's Academy seems to have contending, politically animated factions within it; far from politically uninvolved, members and students of Plato's Academy are engaged in the most desperate forms of politics—they teach themselves the postgraduate seminar in politics: military coups, espionage, intrigue, duplicity, and assassination.

Plato's operations in Syracuse had begun when there was no stable rulership in Macedonia, in the interregnum from 399 to 364 B.C. between Archalus and Perdiccas II, and at a time when the Spartan star had fallen. In the end, Plato's ambitions for the Syracusans are thwarted and it is not his but Aristotle's protégés, the rustic Macedonians, who come to dominate the cities of Hellas and it is that prince of juvenile delinquents, Alexander the Great, who finally leads Greece into the treasure house of Asia.

Hellas had at last found a solution to her travail. Only a temporary solution, to be sure; but history knows nothing of permanent solutions. Like all solutions, this, too, was purchased at a price; the price that was paid is what is called, in retrospect, the "decline" of Greek civilization. If this price seems high, what was the alternative? Surely the indefinite continuation of war within and between the cities augured no better.

The only constructive alternative—necessary if not sufficient—would have been a radical overhauling of Greek institutions, especially of its system of stratification and its narrowly exclusive image of community, a change which would have opened the city to the great number who lived in but were not of it. Yet, magnanimous though it may be, can we expect the ancient Greeks to have been wiser than ourselves? Can we expect them to have paid this price when, more than two thousand years later, there are still many who are unwilling to pay a like price, who refuse to open their communities to the outsiders who live among them, who refuse to change their customs in more than trivial ways and who blindly believe that, if only they cling tenaciously enough to their past, history will do for their social system what it has never done for another, give it a grant of immortality.

NOTES

1 "Review: Recent Work in Ancient Politics." *Journal of the History of Ideas,* 13 (1952), 110.

2 See, for example, Aeschylus *Agamemnon* i. 57. 736–736; *Prometheus Bound* i. 319. 228 ff.; i. 344. 920 ff.; i. 350. 1070 ff.; Sophocles *Oedipus the King* ii. 65. 1231; *Ajax* ii. 223. 260; *Women of Trachis* ii. 296. 465; *Philoctetes* ii. 444. 1092; ii. 446. 1163; Euripides *Hippolytus* iii. 211. 1166; iv. 449. 1229.

3 J. S. Morrison, "The Place of Protagoras in Athenian Public Life," *The Classical Quarterly* (January–April 1941), 8.

4 Field, *op. cit.,* p. 81.

5 Hasebroek, *op. cit.,* p. 35.

6 Glotz, *The Greek City, op. cit.,* p. 126.

7 Michell, *op. cit.,* p. 366.

8 Glotz, *The Greek City, op. cit.,* p. 338.

9 F. W. Walbank, "The Causes of Greek Decline," *The Journal of Hellenic Studies,* 64 (1944), 12.

10 Michell, *op. cit.,* p. 370.

11 Xenophon *Ways and Means,* "A Pamphlet on Revenues," F. R. B. Godolphin, ed., *The Greek Historians,* Vol. 2 (New York: Random House, 1942), p. 645.

12 "The Old Oligarch" (or pseudo-Xenophon), "The Constitution of the Athenians," Godolphin, *op. cit.,* pp. 634–643.

13 *Ibid.,* p. 633.

14 Adkins, *op. cit.,* p. 197.

15 For the larger context of these comments, see G. B. Grundy, "The Policy of Sparta," *The Journal of Hellenic Studies,* 32 (1912), 261–269, especially p. 262.

16 P. A. Sorokin, *Social and Cultural Dynamics,* Vol. 3 (New York: American Book Company, 1937), p. 294.

17 Hasebroek, *op. cit.,* p. 118.

18 C. M. Bowra, *The Greek Experience* (New York: New American Library,

1959), p. 35; or again, "Among themselves, of course, the Greek city-states were extremely particularistic, war rather than peace being the normal relationship between them"—Moses Hadas, "From Nationalism to Cosmopolitanism in the Greco-Roman World," *Journal of the History of Ideas,* 4 (January–October 1943), 105.

19 Plato *Laws.* 626AB.

20 *Laws.* 628E–629A.

21 From the poet Tyrtaeus of Sparta, in Lattimore, *Greek Lyrics, op. cit.,* p. 14.

22 Xenophon *Ways and Means.* 646.

23 C. A. Savage, *The Athenian Family* (Baltimore: Lord Baltimore Press, 1907), p. 46.

24 Xenophon *Ways and Means.* 652.

25 iv. 36. 634.

26 Finley, *Slavery in Classical Greece, op. cit.,* p. 65.

27 *Ibid.,* p. 65.

28 *Republic.* 469B.

29 Glotz, *The Greek City, op. cit.,* p. 133.

30 Thucydides. 380.

31 Thucydides. 423.

32 Thucydides. 300.

33 Cf. Carl Roebuck, "A Note on Messenian Economy and Population," *Classical Philology,* 40 (January–October 1945), 149–165. Sparta does, however, exact tribute from Athens after the Peloponnesian War.

34 Thucydides. 23.

35 Thucydides. 189.

36 Thucydides. 207.

37 B. D. Meritt, H. T. Wade-Gery, M. F. McGregor, *The Athenian Tribute Lists,* Vol. 3 (Princeton: The American School of Classical Studies at Athens, 1950), p. 154.

38 Glotz, *The Greek City, op. cit.,* p. 326.

[39] For a brilliant argument in favor of the view that Athens was *not* hated by the "many" or the "mass" of the population in her subject cities, based upon a re-examination of the internal evidence in Thucydides, see G. E. M. de Ste. Croix, "The Character of the Athenian Empire," *Historia*, 3 (1954–1955), 1–41. For an excellent statement of the counterargument, but to me still unconvincing for reasons that I attempt to outline, see Donald W. Bradeen, "The Popularity of The Athenian Empire," *Historia*, 9 (1960), 257–269. Bradeen accentuates the statistical formulation, asking, for example, whether the pro-Athenian democrats are "really representative of the majority . . ." (p. 267), and, again, where he talks of "a large majority" of the Chalcidians (p. 268). Among the several virtues of Bradeen's article is his sensitivity to the "sociology of knowledge" dimensions of the controversy between those classicists who affirm and those who challenge the popularity of the Athenian Empire: "[M]ost of us ancient historians have a sympathy for Athens and her Empire; no matter how impartial we try to be, our whole training as classicists, and possibly our political bent as well, incline us that way" (p. 258).

[40] L. A. Post, trans., *Thirteen Epistles of Plato* (London: Oxford, 1925), the seventh *Epistle*, 332C.

[41] "The Old Oligarch," *op. cit.*, p. 636.

[42] A. W. Gomme, *A Historical Commentary on Thucydides*, Vol. 2 (London: Oxford, 1956), p. 9. Gomme expressly supports de Ste. Croix's position, characterizing it as a "clear and detailed statement about the attitude of the majority in the subject-states of Athens," although adding that he does not agree with de Ste. Croix's interpretation of Thucydides' political philosophy (*ibid.*, Vol. 3, p. 723).

[43] G. Grote, *A History of Greece*, Vol. 4 (New York: Harper, 1899), pp. 517–520.

[44] "The Old Oligarch," *op. cit.*, p. 636.

[45] Rachel L. Sargent, "The Use of Slaves by the Athenians in Warfare, I," *Classical Philology*, 22 (1927), 201.

[46] Rachel L. Sargent, "The Use of Slaves by the Athenians in Warfare, II," *Classical Philology*, 22 (1927), 279. See also

James A. Notopoulos, "The Slaves at the Battle of Marathon," *American Journal of Philology*, 62 (1941), 352–354.

[47] Sargent, *op. cit.*, 211.

[48] Through the fifth century, battles had been fought in fairly traditionalistic ways and with familiar rules of strategy: two columns of hoplites clashed headlong on a plain and to a great extent the outcome was determined by the mechanical force of the differing weight and speed of the columns, which in turn was affected by their size, training, discipline, and generalship. At this battle the Spartan king, Cleombratus, arrayed his troops in the traditional manner. He placed his Spartan hoplites, upon whom he could better rely, in the place of honor on his own right and arrayed his allied troops on his own left. Cleombratus also operated on the traditional assumption, until then used to Spartan advantage, that there would be an inherent tendency for a hoplite column to drift toward the right, each man seeking shelter behind the shield of the man on his right. He therefore expects that his own elite Spartan troops will be moving toward their own right while the Theban troops are drifting toward *their* own right, and hence to the left of the Spartans who can then outflank them and roll up the Theban column by wheeling inward, that is, toward the Spartan left. This traditional Spartan tactic was predicated on the hitherto successful assumption that they could beat the weaker side of the enemy forces, that is, the enemy left, with the stronger side of their own elite forces, before their own weaker allied troops on their left could lose the battle for the Spartans to the enemy elite forces directly before them. Epaminondas, however, anticipates and adapts to this familiar Spartan strategy in the following manner: he builds up and deepens the force on his own left—i.e., directly in front of the Spartan columns—making it into a powerful striking force some fifty deep. He also holds back the weaker forces on his own right, thus creating the "oblique line" with whose invention he is credited, thereby making sure that they do not lose the battle for the Thebans before his own stronger left can win it. In short, Epaminondas weakens and holds back what is expected to be his stronger right and

strengthens what is expected to be his weaker left, moving it forward with greater speed than the Spartans expect and can absorb. Epaminondas is now able to make use of the tendency for the hoplite line to drift to the right; for by this tendency, the Spartan elite columns are drifting toward their right and thus thinning out their center—that is, the left side of their own elite column—which is at the point where they are joined to their weaker allies. Conversely, the tendency for the Theban column directly in front of the Spartan elite column is also to drift toward their own right, which is to say, their own center around Epaminondas; they thus strike most heavily precisely at the thinnest point in the Spartan elite column, spinning it around and breaking it up and, at the same time, disconnecting it from the Spartan allied troops. Several of the assumptions underlying Epaminondas' tactic are sociologically noteworthy: (1) there is a rational utilization of an observed "natural" disposition in the behavior of men—the tendency of a hoplite column to drift toward its right. There is, in brief, an interesting combination of rationalism and empiricism here; but this rational utilization of a natural disposition is also used by the Spartans. (2) There is, also, and this is more distinctive of Epaminondas, a capacity to empathize with, or to "take the role" of, his enemy in instrumental ways. That is, the predictions made possible by empathy with the enemy become a basis for action against him. Here we have a combination of role-taking skills and rational detachment permitting Epaminondas to break free of conventional military tactics and to array troops without concern for the traditional place of honor and solely in terms of their estimated efficiency.

49 Isocrates i. 203.

50 Isocrates i. 239.

51 Isocrates i. 241.

52 For popular and dramatized accounts of these episodes, see G. R. Levy, *Plato in Sicily* (London: Faber and Faber, 1961); and L. Marcuse, *Plato and Dionysius* (New York: Knopf, 1947).

PART TWO

Enter Plato

5 An Alternative to Politics

"Tell me, Euthydemus," exclaimed Socrates, "have you ever been to Delphi?" "Yes, certainly; twice." "Then did you notice somewhere on the temple the inscription 'Know Thyself'?" "I did." "And did you pay no heed to the inscription, or did you attend to it and try to consider what you were?" "Indeed I did not; because I felt sure that I knew already; for I could hardly know anything else if I did not even know myself." "And what do you suppose a man must know to know himself, his own name merely? Or must he consider what sort of creature he is for human use and get to know his own powers." [1]
—Xenophon

NO ONE who has given any thought at all to the life of Socrates can fail to recognize that he was one of those rare men who revitalize the human scene through their sheer power as persons. Though he never wrote anything himself and must be seen through the penumbra of his greatest student, Plato, he still seems human despite this glowing mist. He never entirely overwhelms us either with his cutting brilliance or with his mending wisdom, and he patiently eludes the enveloping mantle of his greatness that he may manifest himself as a man. In the midst of the Athenian love of beauty he lived his life an ugly man—with a squat, bulging face, broad-nosed, and grossly boned—surrounded by people keenly sensitive to the discrepancy between his appearance and his spirit, for the conventions of their society encouraged notice of male beauty, which was often regarded as an outward sign of breeding and virtue. He had a wild and sensual look— some have said an almost Dionysiac appearance—strange for so mild an Apollonian.

In the midst of the Athenian love of cleverness Socrates insisted on patient, serious talk, holding that he speaks well who knows what he is talking about. He was a saintly busybody who ambled awkwardly through the market place seeking and initiating conversation even with strangers, plaguing them for their obscurities and clichés, appealing to them to listen and to talk, to ask and to answer. Born about 470 B.C. to a stonecutter and a midwife, he was penurious and uninterested in possessions. Yet he was listened to even by a people who valued rank and wealth, because they also had an unparalleled zest for challenging conversation, and because in their more generous moments they viewed his passionate intelligence with an almost civic pride.

Indeed, Socrates was a man of the city. He lived his life almost entirely within its walls—except for military service and an occasional pilgrimage—and he refused to flee even when the city's pride turned to bitterness and it meant his life to stay: "[T]he men who dwell in the city are my teachers," he said, "and not the trees or the country." [2] This first great social philosopher of Western society was unmistakably an urban man; his philosophy was one of the first great fruits of urban civilization. The good life, he believed, could be lived only in the city, yet it was clear to him that the city must be made right if the good life was to be attained there. In two of Plato's most important works, the problem directly confronted is that of life in the city, the *Republic* presenting a picture of the ideal city, the *Laws* seeking a compromise between this "utopia" and Plato's subsequent, chastening experience. Since the city as it is, he believed, is sick and evil, but since men cannot attain to true humanity outside it, the problem is to reform both man and the city so that they can be at peace with one another.

Socrates pursued his mission in the city, among men of the city:

> But if anyone likes to come and hear me while I am pursuing my mission . . . he is not excluded. Nor do I converse only with those who pay; but anyone, whether he be rich or poor, may ask and answer me and listen to my words; and whether he turns out to be a bad man or a good one, neither result can be justly imputed to me; for I never taught nor professed to teach him anything. And if anyone says that he has ever learned or heard anything from me in private which all the world has not heard, let me tell you that he is lying.[3]

Although he shunned politics, his life remained a public one, and in the end, having made himself a force to be reckoned with, he was condemned by the city to die: social theorists thus receive the first intimation of their power and their danger.

AIMS AND PURPOSES

This, the second part of our work, consists of a critical case study of Plato as a social theorist.

And here no more than before have I attempted what could be properly called a "history," either of social theory, or—if it needs to be said—of Greece. Indeed, in my judgment there is hardly a serious history of social theory. Those works that have attempted this have commonly been deficient in the virtues of both history and sociology, usually lacking the historian's grasp of documented detail and the sociologist's analytic thrust or imagination. Moreover, social theory today is rarely seen *historically,* as flesh and tissue of its place and time. Social theorists are usually arranged in neat little schemata, lined up like toy platoons, each man treated in his "school" even though members of a school may have lived decades or more apart.

The history of social theory has failed. Perhaps it has failed because the very nature of its enterprise is at odds with science—and social theory today is an arm of social science. Why, indeed, should science need history except for purposes extrinsic to its serious work and remote from its own special functions? Since, after all, anything valuable in the past of a genuine science will be assimilated into its contemporary products, the past presumably needs no recounting, for its true part lives in the present. This outlook is not so much the view articulated by any one miscreant, but it is indicative of the inimical ideological mood within which a history of social theory today has to live.

Those who have worked at the history of social theory in recent times have been caught in this cross fire between history and social science. They have sensed that, to many, history is an antiquarian exercise and that a history of social theory is regarded as the antithesis of a contribution to social theory. Since his contemporaries believe that history has no future, who but the loneliest among social scientists would wish to be seen trudging through the presumably sterile dust of the past?

The task of the historian of social theory is to reveal the different levels on which a theory lives; to show it as a response not only to technical intellectual problems, but also to problems in the larger culture; to appraise a theory by comparing it with alternatives shown and known to be historically feasible; to explore the extent to which the triumphs and the flaws of a theory are not only those of the individual theorist but are culture-linked; and, in revealing this for the past, to press home the point for the present. The task of the historian of social theory is not, as is commonly taught, either to celebrate, to bury—or even merely to understand—the past; its task is to discomfit the present.

Even if it were possible, it is certainly absurd to limit ourselves to a mere description of Plato's (or Aristotle's) theory of slavery. Must we not inevitably—and therefore ought we not deliberately and self-consciously— note and express the ways in which this theory is an apologia for slavery and is manifestly mistaken not only in our view but also in that of certain of Plato's contemporaries. Surely we must be concerned to understand how such ideologically distorted views about slavery came to be held by a Plato or Aristotle. And we cannot help but wonder that if minds of such power and sensitivity could be so grossly wrong and in such utter bondage to their culture, what does this imply about those of us today who must work at the theorist's craft with far less imposing equipment?

Put otherwise, it is the task of the historian of social theory not simply to describe but critically to evaluate a theory in its historical setting. Indeed, sheer "complete" description as such is never possible: to describe is to select; to select is to evaluate; to evaluate is to criticize. The more serious historians of social theory have never, of course, been content to chronicle ideas or events, or for that matter to be mere exegetes outlining another's views. The truth is that when the historian of social theory conceives his task seriously he must be as much the creator as the commentator, and as much the critic as the chronicler. Yet academic social theory and academic history prepare few men to accept that conception of this task or that conception of themselves. The motto among social theorists today is not "criticism" but rather "cumulation" and "continuity," as if the latter were conceivable without the former.

With a very few exceptions, which would be invidious to specify, the history of social theory has failed miserably. With scarcely any exceptions it is intellectually undistinguished. It is hardly of use or interest to anyone except to graduate students preparing for their doctoral examinations. The historian of social theory has failed because he has been unable to resolve the crisis of intellectual identity through which he and his kind have been passing. He has failed because he has been unable to confront the question of his intellectual role and what he really wants to do; because he has been unable to accept that he is, among other things, a *critic* and therefore suppresses—disguising but not eliminating—his critical impulses; because he cannot acknowledge that he is in some part (though in part only) as much a critic as a descriptive historian or sociologist, and because he has had to bury alive this vital side of himself.

It is not possible to write a viable history of social theory today without creating a new intellectual genre—a genre which will be one part history, one part sociology, one part criticism, the whole encased in a membranous boundary permitting the mutual access of facts to values and of technical analysis to cultural interests.

To view the historian of social theory as being partly a critic requires us to clarify the nature of this diffuse role: who and what is the critic? Indeed, the very diffuseness of the critic's role has probably enabled it to perform its most important function—allowing men to do what no one established discipline is socially chartered to perform.

Among the most important of the critic's tasks is the protection of values which are, or have somehow become, precarious in consequence of intellectual specialization. One such value, for example, is that which seeks to safeguard our sense of the intellectual complexity of social theory. If it is the task of the empirical wing of social science to reduce complexity and ambiguity to clear-cut and testable propositions, it must also be someone's task to attempt to preserve a sense of the intellectual architecure from which these propositions are taken. Someone must also be interested in fostering those qualities of mind that encourage the patient probing of ideas, that can await the illuminating understanding, that can explore enriching ambiguities in communication, and that can, in short, appraise the meaning and significance of ideas no less than their empirical validity.

Modern social theorists are in grave peril of losing their *Sitzfleisch* as well as their capacity for passionate involvement. We are in danger of being vacuumed up into a world where work must be completed by a deadline date so that "progress" accounts may be readied for timely submission along with requests for refunding. There is a serious danger today that we will lose our elemental ability to read, even as we learn how to operate high-speed computers. There is a growing atrophy in our ability to ponder the single paragraph, the solitary sentence, let alone the individual phrase. Intellectual qualities such as these are difficult to keep alive today in a world of complexly organized research institutes, where men in a hurry no longer write articles but issue imperious "memos" and "reports." It is precisely such intellectually significant but precarious values that the critic supports.

It is also the difficult task of the critic to probe for those qualities of mind and self—within the theorist he is exploring—that form the intellectual fundament from which the theorist's special knowledge or expertise is only the most visible extrusion. The demanding task of the critic, then, is to link ideas and the man; and then, making the venture even more difficult, to link both to their unique, historical time, cruising that thin atmosphere where biography and history intersect.

In this sense, then, the critic is not a destroyer but a mender; he seeks to negotiate between encapsulated cultures. Under the guise of being a distinct and special something, his task is to reunite those activities that culture has already made too distinct and too special. The critic is not so much a bundle of specialized skills as a conception of how one ought to play an intellectual role.

The critic affirms the creative potentialities of the individual, and he opposes these to the conformity demands of established institutions and of culturally standardized roles. The critic opposes the inherent tendency for any professional role to become routinized and ridden with the smugly self-satisfied; he repudiates the tendency of professionals to prefer sure things with their modest and steady rewards to high variance bets; he prefers men with a capacity for risky intellectual undertakings and with the courage to compromise themselves on behalf of an idea; he detests the domestication of the intellectual life. In truth, the critic is more concerned with the creativity than the reliability of a performance.

The critic speaks against all pedestrian and indifferent performances. He is, indeed, suspicious of the mere capacity to endure routine. He hates the impulse to transform all performances into routines—which, after all, is the essence of sturdy, sober professionalism. The critic is a social nuisance. Obnoxiously serious in the demands he makes on those claiming to lead an intellectual life, he is incapable of talking about things that do not disturb. He insistently demands all the seriousness and all the freshness of response of which a thinker is capable.

The critic knows how very little it takes to be respected in an established intellectual profession; he understands how much the attainment and maintenance of such acceptance depend on social and political skills rather than intellectual products. Always and everywhere, the critic invites the individual creator to remember the difference between his profession and himself; to remember that the profession has a kind of immortality and will survive but that the creator will not. The critic summons the individual to mobilize and expend all the reserves of creativity he has, and to use them whether or not they fit neatly into his professional role. The critic struggles ceaselessly against the self's surrender to routine. It is, I believe, such a conception of the critic's role and of criticism that the new history of social theory must combine with history and sociology.

The historical mission of the social theorist is to assist mankind in taking possession of society. The task of the historian of theory is to assist us in taking possession of our own intellectual heritage, past or present, by appraising it actively—which is to say, critically—in terms of our viable interests.

What follows, then, is not an exegesis, even though it is sometimes unavoidably introductory in character. It is an effort to consolidate the sociologically relevant aspects of Plato's work and to formulate a coherent outline of his contribution to social theory. The main objective is to examine Plato as a case of a social theorist with a view to learning not merely about him as one man or one theorist but about social theorists more generally.

Some social scientists are interested in studying industrial workers; some study physicians; and still others, drug addicts and prostitutes. I happen to be curious about social theorists. They, as the anthropologists would say, are "my people." The ultimate objective is to contribute to an empirically testable social theory about social theorists, as part of a sociology of social science. Certainly no single case study can ever suffice to test general hypotheses, in this or any other area of inquiry. But we are still some way from having hypotheses bearing upon the development of social theory that would be worth testing. The function of a case study such as this is to contribute to the formulation of concepts with which hypotheses can be stated and to contribute to the development of hypotheses which could be tested with proper samples.

In calling this a case study of Plato's social theory I also mean to emphasize my interest in understanding this theory in the context of its culture and society. In some part this implies that certain aspects of Plato's social theory will be viewed as a response to the problems and tensions current during his historical period. More often than not, however, an historical view will not so much require us to relate Greece and Plato as cause and effect but as common participants in a single whole. That is, we may find it illuminating not only to consider Plato's work as "caused" by certain features of Greek society, but to regard it as a distinctive structure made up of tissues essentially similar to other parts of Greek culture. In some respects, Plato's work is no more "caused" by Plato's society than the fist is caused by the wrist.

Our interest in the historical setting of Plato's work derives also from our assumption that social theorists always have some conception—tacit or explicit—of the ills of their society and of possible remedies for them. All social theories, in my view, embody the traces of social diagnosis and social therapy. They are never simply disinterested efforts to describe and explain social reality. One way in which social theories can be understood, then, is as analysis, clear or cryptic, of the cause and possible cures of the ills of the society to which the theorist has been subjected. An effort will therefore be made here to document the utility of this view of social theory by applying it to Plato's social theory and by searching out his specific conception of the ills and possible remedies of the human condition.

Clearly, any of these objectives might have been pursued with a case study of some thinker other than Plato. Aside from his intrinsic interest, however, there are a number of major advantages in focusing on Plato. One is that he happened to be an extraordinarily creative social theorist. A close examination of his work may provide us with occasions to develop ideas concerning the social conditions conducive to theoretical creativity and supportive of theoretical innovation. There are few problems more practically important and theoretically fascinating—from the standpoint of a sociology of social science—and while this interest is not central to us at all times, it is, at least, usually at the edges of our attention.

The most important reason that I have chosen to work with Plato rather than someone else is precisely because I am interested in the present and in coming to an understanding of contemporary social theory and theorists. I believe, however, that we need to take the long way around to come to a more penetrating perspective on who the social theorist today is and what he is in the process of becoming. One way of viewing social theorists today is to see them historically, as part of the long-developing stream of scholarship that has evolved in the last twenty-five hundred years. This exploration of Plato, then, is really the first of a series of historically anchored case studies which I hope to undertake as a form of self-education, with a view to acquiring a better understanding of the social function of the social theorist in Western society.

An understanding of Plato can help in this venture precisely because he qualifies—as much as any one man ever can—as the "first" in an historical series. Plato is the first great social theorist in the Western tradition, and so much of what comes later derives directly or indirectly from him. If sociologists wish to understand the nature of our discipline's accomplishments and prospects today, we need a stable point of historical contrast for which no other theorist serves half so well as Plato.

The historical perspective of many social scientists today is severely stunted. Many modern social scientists scarcely manage to conceive of their work as having nineteenth-century roots, and most of us live in an intellectual world whose historical boundaries usually stop at the Enlightenment. If nothing else, then, it is hoped that this case study of Plato as a social theorist may encourage modern social scientists to reconsider and to expand the boundaries of the historical space within which they now live and work.

Plato's presentation of the philosophy of Socrates and his development of it through fusion with Pythagorean doctrines is the first great coherent treatise on man within the Western tradition. Alfred North Whitehead is probably not far wrong when he says, "The safest general characterization of the European philosophical tradition is that it consists of a series of footnotes to Plato." Since so much in later Western thought manifestly begs, borrows, steals from, and builds upon him, there is almost a prima facie certainty that even modern sociological thought could, in some important respects, be traced back to his formulations. Inevitably so, since both the Platonic and the sociological curiosity are joined by a common interest in the fate of men and a common perplexity about their behavior.

It has been conventional for philosophers to suggest that, with Socrates, Western thought became anthropocentric. With Socrates, it is held, Western intellectual interests moved from the study of nature to the study of human life, from an interest in the outer to one in the inner life. After Socrates, so it goes, a firmer line is drawn between nature and culture, between the realms of necessity and responsibility. While I consider this an overstatement of Socrates' uniqueness, nonetheless his analysis of human behavior is so extensive and rational as to be matchless among his contemporaries and antecedents.

SOCIAL THEORY AS AN ALTERNATIVE TO POLITICS

For a long time many classicists regarded Plato's work as unmarred by an interest in the problems and politics of his era, but opinion in the last fifty years or so gradually has become more sociologically realistic. G. C. Field, for example, stresses that an understanding of Plato's thought requires us to remember that he "grew up in a period when the established order and accepted standards seemed on the verge of dissolution under the pressure of political events and theoretical criticism." [4] Similarly, Alexandre Koyré explains patiently that "no Greek, especially no Athenian, would ever have been able, even had he so desired, to dissociate himself from all interest in political life, least of all, no doubt, the young aristocrat Plato, the son of Ariston, destined by his very birth to the responsibilities and services of the State." [5]

As I discussed in Chapter 4, Plato's philosophy was rooted in the political dilemmas and social tensions of Hellenic society. Moreover, there appears to be evidence—in Plato's seventh *Epistle*—of a direct linkage between his political concerns on the one hand and his philosophical interests on the other. (The seventh *Epistle* is one which many scholars regard as accurate in essentials and even if not, as some believe, actually written by Plato, then by those closely associated with him.) This letter is sufficiently significant to be quoted extensively. Says Plato:

> When I was young I was in the same state as many others: I intended, directly I became my own master, to enter into public life. But it so happened, I found that the following changes occurred in the political situation.
>
> In the government then existing, reviled as it was by many, a revolution took place; and the revolution was headed by fifty-one leaders, of whom eleven were in the City and ten rulers of all. Now of these some were actually connexions and acquaintances of mine; and indeed they invited me at once to join their administration, thinking that to

be due to me. The feelings I then experienced, owing to my youth, were in no way surprising: for I imagined that they would administer the State by leading it out of an unjust way of life into a just way, and consequently I gave my mind to them very diligently, to see what they would do.

And indeed I saw how these men within a short time caused men to look back on the former government as a golden age; and above all how they treated my aged friend Socrates, whom I would hardly scruple to call the most just of men then living, when they tried to send him, along with others, after one of the citizens, to fetch him by force that he might be put to death—their object being that Socrates, whether he wished or no, might be made to share in their political actions; he, however, refused to obey and risked the uttermost penalties rather than be a partaker in their unholy deeds. So when I beheld all these actions and others of a similar grave kind, I was indignant, and I withdrew myself from the evil practices then going on.

But in no long time the power of the Thirty was overthrown together with the whole of the government which then existed. Then once again I was really, though less urgently, impelled with a desire to take part in public and political affairs. Many deplorable events, however, were still happening in those times, troublous as they were, and it is not surprising that in some instances, during these revolutions, men were avenging themselves on their foes too fiercely; yet notwithstanding, the exiles who then returned exercised no little moderation. But, as ill-luck would have it, certain men of authority summoned our comrade Socrates before the law courts, bringing against him a criminal charge of the gravest nature, and one which Socrates of all men least deserved; for it was on the charge of impiety that those men summoned him and the rest condemned and slew him.[6]

It is, then, in part because of these disillusioning experiences with the political immorality of both the "right" and the "left"—of both the oligarchical and the democratic factions—that Plato comes to commit himself to social theory and philosophy. His involvement in philosophy grows out of the failure of his political experience; his immigration to philosophy is an emigration from politics. Systematic Western social theory emerges, then, in Plato's dissatisfaction with politics and in his search for a rational substitute for it:

When, therefore, I considered all this, and the type of men who were administering the affairs of State, with their laws too and their customs, the more I considered them and the more I advanced in years myself, the more difficult appeared to me the task of managing affairs of State rightly. . . . Consequently, although I was filled with an ardent desire to engage in public affairs, when I considered all this and saw how things were shifting about anyhow in all directions, I finally became dizzy; . . . until finally, looking at all States which now exist, I perceived that one and all they are badly governed; for the state of their laws is such as to be almost incurable without some marvelous overhauling and good luck to boot. So I was led to the praise of the right philosophy and to the declaration that by it alone is one enabled to discern all forms of justice, both political and individual.[7]

KNOWLEDGE AS A SOCIAL THERAPEUTIC

To some, it may seem incomprehensible that Plato is anything other than the hoary stereotype of the bumbling, otherworldly philosopher whose abstruse work could today have more than an antiquarian interest. Yet there is a sense in which practically all subsequent philosophy—to leave social science aside—becomes not more but steadily less practical in import, for Plato and Socrates are both passionately interested in how men should live and what they should live for. Socrates, certainly, is the least academic of philosophers. Not yet separated from his city by university walls, he is the theorist of the market place who goes among men to seek and to give guidance in the daily round of life.

One of Socrates' central aims is to diagnose the problems of men and of the communities in which they live. At the very summit of his philosophy, being the whole point to which it is drawn, is a therapeutic aimed at remedying these problems. Indeed, one of the major differences between the Pythagorean and the Socratic outlook is that the former believes that man's life on earth is at worst an imprisonment and at best a preparation for an eternal afterlife. The knowledge of the universe's order to which the Pythagorean aspires is sought as a means of purifying the spirit so that it can be released from its earthly purgatory. Socrates, however—at least in his more optimistic moments—believes that men's lives on earth might be bettered. There is a side of him that believes that knowledge, particularly knowledge about men, enables them to lead better lives in the here and now; and he believes that men should bend every effort to seek such knowledge and that it is, within limits, attainable by them. He believes knowledge will set men free, indeed that nothing else can, and that, in fact, there is little point to knowledge at all unless it can touch and transfigure the daily lives of ordinary men.

TENSIONS BETWEEN SOCRATISM AND PLATONISM

The preceding comments, differentiating the Socratic and Pythagorean outlooks, suggest that it is also appropriate to express my views, however con-
jectural and difficult to substantiate, concerning the difference between the
original Socratic philosophy and the later Platonic accretions. Plato's contribution can in part be thought of as a syncretism of Socratic and Pythagorean beliefs, and, to that extent, Plato introduces a somewhat joylessly
ascetic note into what I take to be the relatively more optimistic outlook
of his master. Perhaps in consequence of these diverse contributing streams
there is a notable tension in the Platonic Dialogues; between those—such
as the *Republic*—that appear relatively more hopeful of some remedy of
the human condition and entail hopes of an earthly fulfillment of the highest
human aspirations, and those—such as the *Laws*—that express a bitter
hopelessness concerning man's destiny and a belief that man must settle
for second best.

There is a tension between an earlier stress on the liberating dialectic,
where men already have within them a potential for knowledge and self-
attained understanding, and a later stress on the controlling laws, which
see men as plastic materials that need to be molded through a deliberate
conditioning. There is also some tension between a belief that the individual
is capable of active and successful strivings toward self-realization and self-
liberation and one that views men as playthings of the gods, best not to be
taken too seriously, who must be protected from their own inherent faults
by a continuing and all-enveloping superintendence.

Whatever the intellectual differences between Socrates and Plato (as
between the early and the later Plato), there were assuredly differences between the historical periods in which the two men lived, and there were also
differences in their persons. Some of these probably derived from their very
different social origins, Socrates' being plebeian and Plato's being highly
aristocratic on both sides of his family—Socrates having married and reared
a family, Plato remaining a bachelor throughout his life. The pervasive
difference in the historical periods in which they lived is also bound to have
had its effect. John Gould suggests that "Socrates, sensing the break-up of
his own society, was at pains to establish a secure foundation for the individual's life, independently of society, in the creation of a self-sufficient
canon of behavior. In the half-century that passed between the death of
Socrates and that of Plato, this became too little as a prerequisite for pur-
posive life; it was Plato's task to construct a whole society that might
weather the storm that was now upon them." [8] (In accounting for the differ-

ences between the earlier and later Plato, however, we ought to be careful not to ignore the obvious or to outsmart ourselves sociologically; banal as it may be, we need to remember that the later Plato is *older* than the earlier, and that when a man ages, it is not only his physical organism that changes.)

Socrates' thought develops during the zenith of Athenian ascendancy, in the buoyant wake of the successful defense against the Persians, the coalescence of the Athenian empire, the vigor of the Periclean democracy, and the glorious rebuilding of Athens. Plato's thought, however, is environed by the climactic experience of Athens' defeat by Sparta, the subsequent destruction of the Athenian empire, and, finally, by the defeat of Sparta itself. If there is bitter conflict within the *polis* that Socrates knew, there is also a sense that one could choose sides and that the choice made some difference. If there is a scent of impending decadence, it is also a time of cultural efflorescence when Athens harvests the preparation of centuries. If there is a lurking fear of retribution, it derives in part from Athens' manifest success and growth. But Plato's is a time when Athens has been humbled; when she is no longer the proud mistress of vast empire, when, with the defeat of Sparta, oligarchical aristocrats no longer have a living embodiment of their aspirations to hold up as a model or look to for political support, and when the Hellenic citadel of traditionalism has crumbled.

THE PROTECTION OF THEORETICAL CREATIVITY

Both the difference and the continuity between Socrates and Plato are repeatedly paralleled throughout the history of social theory; they will be found in the paired relation between Marx and Engels, between Saint-Simon and Comte, and even among some contemporaries. In part, this is a relation between relatively speculative, sprawling, imaginative, and daring innovators on the one hand and their somewhat more disciplined disciples on the other who take the mentor's ideas, sometimes only verbally expressed, and with more or less brilliance diligently codify, systematize, and elaborate their implications in selected directions.

It is notable that major breakthroughs in social theory are not the product of lonely genius but are often the product of a few men working closely together. Some kind of group support is helpful to those striving to elude conventional ways of looking at human behavior; the primary group, whether a *folie à deux* or a love affair, can be a sheltering enclave for theoretical innovations, for these are always precarious and especially need protection during their formative periods. Changes in social theory are always—in smaller, interpersonal influences as well as through larger institutional pressures—a social product. In particular, the master–disciple or teacher–student relation, when close and intense, constitutes a sheltering social system that functions to protect the novel and hence precarious creativity of the older man. The function of the student-disciple is not merely to do the routine, "dirty" work of his mentor, and it is not only in this way that the former obligates the master-teacher to him and wins his subsequent sponsorship. The more intellectually significant function of the admiring and friendly disciple is—through his favorable disposition to his mentor—to give consensual validation to the latter's innovations before they are given over to the public scrutiny of his peers. This enables the master-scholar to overcome his own work-blocking anxieties and provides him with socioemotional support. This support is especially needed when the master's innovation is still precarious, when it is still only half-born, insufficiently documented, incompletely justified, and only dimly perceived, and when, in consequence, the creative innovation could be crushed by a full-scale critique inspired by the competitive animus of the older man's peers.

To borrow Max Weber's terms, Plato is the routinizer of Socrates' charisma. Plato is bound to Socrates but Socrates is bound only by the daemon who speaks to him from within and by his own sense of pursuing a divinely ordained mission. As Socrates explains to the jury in the *Apology,* his mission began when the oracle at Delphi, on being asked if there was a man wiser than Socrates, replied that there was not. Claiming that he has no wisdom, Socrates is confused by the oracle and sets out on his mission so that he might understand and confirm it. He finds that he is wise only in that, unlike the politicians, poets, and artisans, he knows that he knows *not.* "And so I go about the world, obedient to the god," he explains, "and search and make enquiry into the wisdom of anyone, whether citizen or stranger, who appears to be wise; and if he is not wise, then in vindication of the oracle I show him that he is not wise." [9]

It might be guessed that this rather aggressive undertaking is motivated by more than reverent compliance with a divinely ordained mission and that it has more than a little to do with the contest system. Yet Socrates does claim a charismatic legitimation, a sacred justification; he speaks for reason in the name of the god. Far from being the single-minded rationalist that Nietzsche portrays, Socrates has a kind of intense, simple faith and an openness to certain of his own intuitions. In contrast, it is Plato who seems much more of the removed intellectualist and cultured grandee, although even he has strong mythopoeic proclivities.

Socrates uses his sense of a divinely inspired mission to liberate himself from the pressure of contemporary beliefs and from the other-directed Hellenic concern for opinion. "You certainly appear to me very like the rest of the world," he complains at one point, "looking at your neighbor and not at yourself"; [10] and again, "the point is not who said the words, but whether they are true or not." [11] Socrates uses his charisma to release his own intellectual creativity and to defy convention. Indeed, he comes close to an explicit understanding that this is one of its social functions: "Of madness there are two kinds," he says, "one produced by human infirmity, the other was a divine release of the soul from the yoke of custom and convention." [12] Indeed, Socrates uses his charisma not only as a way of legitimating his criticism of tradition and of fortifying reason against convention, but also as a basis for buttressing his own personal intuition against reason itself. When, for example, in the *Phaedrus* he uses "logic" to demonstrate one contention with seeming success, his daemon intervenes suddenly and leads him to affirm and demonstrate the contrary contention. Plato, however, manifests no such sense of a divine mission and personal faith; the charisma is attenuated if not lost in the succession.

Social theories do not develop, however, simply through the cooperative efforts of friendly *epigonoi* who protect and extend their mentors' work in a cumulative and continuous manner. Indeed, theoretical continuity and cumulation derive as much from the mutual hostility of theorists as from their friendly collaboration. Certainly social theory requires a cumulative and continuous development that produces a connected and growing intellectual edifice. It should not be forgotten, however, that theoretical continuity and cumulation refer to the consequences of intellectual effort; they need have nothing to do with the nature of the sentiments with which theorists regard one another. The *epigonos* who admires and respects his master may add nothing at all to his ideas; paradoxically, the critic who polemicizes against him may add much, either directly through his own contributions—animated by hostility for a theoretical opponent—or indirectly by the intellectual defense which his hostility inspires.

Like so many theories that follow it, Plato's derives as much from its polemical animus as from what it learns and borrows in friendly commerce with others, such as Socrates and the Pythagoreans. It is as much influenced by those to whom it is opposed as by those with whom it is allied. In general, there are two types of polemical targets that can influence a social theorist; one of these is the "external" target provided by the conventional views of some of the "ordinary" men in the theorist's society which comprise an aspect of the "common sense." A second type of polemical target is "internal" and is to be found in the work of those who are the theorist's intellectual peers and competitors, who are, like himself, specialists and scholars. The two major internal polemical targets of Platonism are the "nature philosophers" and the "sophists," and some part of its greatness derives from its good fortune in having had such great enemies. The significance of the polemic against each group will be considered in turn.

THE POLEMIC AGAINST THE NATURE PHILOSOPHERS

About a century before Socrates there occurred in Greece the great Ionian "enlightenment," whose nucleus was the mercantile center and port at Miletus, where, from about the seventh to the sixth century B.C., "nature philosophy" and science emerged. The putative father of Greek philosophy, the Milesian Thales (ca. 585 B.C.), was—at least according to a story reported by Aristotle—reproached for his poverty, this being regarded as discrepant with his imputed wisdom. Presumably the discrepancy was taken to prove that his philosophy was useless. The interesting thing about this story is not the triumphal denouement in which Thales, supposedly using his astronomical knowledge, predicts a good olive crop and then, getting a corner on olive presses, makes a fortune. It is, rather, the suggestion that no sooner does a glimmering of science emerge than it is confronted with the direct challenge to demonstrate its practical worth, particularly in terms of economic success. In short, nascent Greek science was confronted almost at once with the ancient Milesian equivalent of the present-day worldly critique of the academician: "If you know so much, why aren't you rich?" It is notable, if the tale is true, that the challenge was taken seriously on its own grounds, suggesting that this was still a time when even learned men were not yet ready to justify knowledge as valuable for its own sake.

Legitimations of Secular Social Theory: The Useful and the Sacred

True or not, the story does dramatize an enduring problem: how does the social theorist, or, more generally, the man of learning, secure acceptance from ordinary men in his society once he is no longer a shaman or magician whose claim of contact with supernatural powers induces awe? For indeed, the outlook adopted by the nature philosophers was a secular one; they were seeking to know the cosmos without theological, magical, or mythological supports or explanations, by reason and by observation alone. How does such a disinterested, secularized intelligence justify its existence? Why, indeed, should the Milesians have condoned Thales in taking something as manifestly useful as the Egyptian technique for measuring plots of land and transforming it into a geometric problem, into a kind of game or play? Why should someone be respected and supported if he is neither blessed by the gods nor useful to men? Being at the very dawn of science, the Ionian nature philosophers could not very well reassure their fellow citizens that their new knowledge would some day prove as useful as their earlier work had already shown itself to be.

Something of the difficulty of the secular thinker in making a place for himself, particularly among an action-oriented people devoted to the contest, is suggested by the poem of Xenophanes of Colophon (ca. 570–480 B.C.), "The Athlete and the Philosopher," which compares the honor given the successful athlete with that given the philosopher:

> Better than brute strength
> of men, or horses either, is the wisdom that is mine.
> But custom is careless in all these matters, and there is no justice
> in putting strength on a level above wisdom which is sound.[13]

It is notable that Xenophanes justifies the philosopher's claim to pre-eminence because of his utility, invidiously observing that "the city will not, on account of this man [i.e., the athlete], have better government" or grow richer.

The new men of knowledge had to secure some societal legitimation of their roles, justifying them in terms meaningful and acceptable to ordinary members of the community, all the more so as they are in close interaction with them. This means that they had to justify their work either as providing sacred services or by claiming to be acting in charismatic compliance with a divine call, and/or by providing some kind of service instrumentally useful to the community. It would seem that it is only when (or to the extent that) men of knowledge are not directly dependent upon ordinary members of the community and when they have succeeded in insulating themselves from it that they justify their knowledge as valuable in its own right.

The tendency to legitimate the contemplative life as a good in itself does not manifest itself most fully in Socrates' life or even in Plato's philosophy. It comes to its clearest classical expression only later in the work of Aristotle, with the waning cohesion and potency of the *polis;* for Socrates, the man of knowledge was legitimated either by his divine mission or by his usefulness to his fellow men. According to Xenophon, Socrates opposed the nature philosophers and was led to declare, "I have nothing to do with physical speculations," [14] in some part because their work was not useful. For what, after all, could men do with Ionian science, centered as it was largely on a cosmogony that aimed at understanding the origins of the universe and its basic constituent substance? Of what immediate use was it to know, even assuming they were right, that the cosmos was made of mist, fire, earth, and water? And, in any event, why worry about the clouds and stars when men knew so little about themselves and their own lives?

In turning from the nature philosophers' concern with cosmogony, Socrates turns from a concern with things past to those in the future, toward a realm in which uncertainty yet hinged; he turns away from a realm in which nothing can be done toward one in which men's decisions might still be useful and count for something.

SOCRATIC CONCEPTION OF THE "USEFUL"

Socrates' conception of the "useful" is not intended, however, in the mercantile sense of an interest in how men may turn a profit; for this implies that they already know the ends that are worth pursuing. The useful, in the mercantile, or more broadly, in the common sense, bears only on means which are capable of realizing ends that are taken for granted. To Socrates, the useful is not simply that which enables men to attain their ends; those things are also useful which enable men to know their ends. He believes, indeed, that there is nothing more useful than a knowledge of the good life.

Socrates takes it for granted that the things men do are done with a view to realizing certain ends. He stresses the difference between means and ends, remarking, for example, in the *Laches,* that "when [a man] considers anything for the sake of another thing, he thinks of the end and not of the means." [15] The means we choose are useful only in relation to our ends, and unless we know them we cannot select appropriate means. The logical prior considerations, then, are the clarification of our goals and determining which of them are worth pursuing. The important thing is to take one's present ambitions as problematic and to subject them to critical examination and rational evaluation. This, Socrates indicates, is eminently practical, for all else depends upon the goals we seek.

In orienting himself to a notion of the useful, Socrates appears to be operating with the concepts of common sense. But he is really operating against them. He is only using their outward form and is filling them with a new content; he is transvaluing them; in a way, turning their meaning upside down. He is speaking the language of his society but asking his contemporaries what they mean by it. You are concerned, he says in effect, with the useful—but do you really know what is useful for men? You are so concerned about getting what you want that you have forgotten the importance of clarifying what you want. Men think of the practically useful as that helping them to get what they want, but it is more useful to know what is worth wanting.

The desires men have and the things they do are arranged with Apollonian care in a hierarchical order of worth and importance: those things that are wanted (or done) are less important than the things they are wanted for. Since man is or should be a rational creature, his intentions and goals should be explicitly examined, and the more explicit and rationally examined, the higher and better the goal. Action is and should be under the governance of some intention of the mind. In fine, action should be governed by goals, and the goals themselves sifted and chosen by reason. The impulsive and spontaneous is inferior to the reflective and deliberate action; habit-ridden, tradition-directed, or passion-driven behavior is inferior to that which seeks clear-cut, critically evaluated goals. The unexamined life is not worth living; the good life is one governed by the mind's design.

THE SUPREMACY OF MIND

Socrates believes that man and the cosmos are of one piece, in that all alike are subject to the direction of mind, and because of this he further opposes the nature philosophers. Since they regarded nature as having its own self-regulating order and as being moved by forces inherent in it, their explanation of the cosmos requires no reference to supernatural entities. Socrates, however, believes that unless things are arranged by some intelligence or mind, they cannot be disposed for the best. On first hearing of Anaxagoras' theory that "mind was the disposer and cause of all," he is therefore delighted, thinking that then "mind will dispose all for the best and put each particular in the best place. . . . For I could not imagine that when he spoke of mind as the disposer of them, he would give any other account of their being as they are except that this was best." [16] But he is grievously disappointed, he explains, for Anaxagoras deals with the "conditions," not the true causes, which are to be found only in mind and not matter.

While Socrates acknowledges his failure to discover "the nature of the best," he holds that he has developed a second-best mode of explaining causes which, he says, is to be found in his theory of Archetypes or eternal Ideas or Forms. Things are the way they are because they "partake" of these absolute Ideas: a thing "can be beautiful only in so far as it partakes of absolute beauty." [17] He retreats from a teleological functionalism to the "second-best" theory of Absolute Ideas or Forms.

Socrates, moreover, opposes the nature philosophers' method of knowing, as well as the assumptions they make about nature, believing that it is not through sensory observation—in the words of Parmenides, the blind eye or the echoing ear—that the truth is to be known:

> I thought . . . I ought to be careful that I did not lose the eye of my soul; as people may injure their bodily eye by observing and gazing on the sun during an eclipse, unless they take the precaution of only

looking at the image reflected in the water, or in some similar medium. So, in my own case, I was afraid that my soul might be blinded altogether if I looked at things with my eyes or tried to apprehend them by the help of the senses. And I thought that I had better have recourse to the world of mind and seek there the truth of existence. I dare say that the simile is not perfect—for I am very far from admitting that he who contemplates existences through the medium of thought, sees them only "through a glass darkly," any more than he who considers them in action and operation.[18]

We perceive through the senses, says Plato, but not with them. It is mind or soul which truly perceives and without which we could not even distinguish one sense activity from another; knowing depends on still other faculties, such as memory and imagination, which are even less linked to the senses. Thus Socrates and Plato seek truth primarily through logical analysis, through making conceptual distinctions and definitions, by advancing hypotheses and deducing their consequences, by appraising whether these are mutually consistent or contradictory, and by seeking the assumptions that are involved in the hypotheses.

THE POLEMIC AGAINST THE SOPHISTS

If we assume that the "practical" side of behavior has two aspects, namely, an interest in the ends of action as well as an interest in means that might realize them, it may be said that Plato tends to focus on the former and to treat the latter as given. It is not that he doubts the importance of means; he believes, however, that they are logically and practically secondary to the clarification of ends, to which, despite this, men somehow give too little attention. This is a disorder he is much concerned to correct.

Socrates' emphasis upon ends, and on the basic values in terms of which they are evaluated, stems partly from his polemic against the Sophists. The Sophists, or at least some among them, seemingly indicate that they are not concerned with ends and that they are, in a sense, ethically neutral. It appears that, as teachers, they sometimes seek to prepare their pupils to realize any end they wish; for example, it seems to Plato that in teaching rhetoric they prepare their students to win any side of a litigation and, indeed, to make the worse side appear the better.

Partly as a result of his polemic against such views, Plato's outlook tends to stress the significance of basic values and goals and, correspondingly, to give relatively little attention to the manner in which men might realize them. Social theory thus begins with a polemic, resonating to this day, between those who focus on the development of a neutral technique and train their students in its use without regard to the ends sought, and those who are concerned about the ends men should pursue and the values worth realizing, often with insufficient regard for the means by which they might be attained. Social theory begins with discord between "technicians" and "utopians."

One crucial issue between Socrates and the Sophists devolves precisely on the question of whether or not men can be taught basic values, or "virtue," in some rational manner. Among several places where this is explored is the curious dialogue in which Socrates is matched against the Sophist Protagoras, in the course of which each seems to end up with a position diametrically opposed to the one with which he began. The dialogue concludes with Socrates' bemused summary: "Socrates, who denied that virtue can be taught, affirms that it is science, that justice, temperance, and courage is all science, which is the surest means of showing that one can teach virtue; while Protagoras, who had first affirmed as a fact that it could be taught, ends by saying that it is anything but science, which deprives it of any possibility of being taught."

Various interpretations have been offered of this seemingly paradoxical conclusion, some classicists suggesting it is meant only ironically and that Socrates never really gets himself ensnared in a true contradiction. (For some, it appears, to be a hero means that one never finds himself in a genuine difficulty.) The paradox is sometimes resolved by suggesting that Socrates is right on both counts: given the different and unexamined meanings of virtue in that dialogue, Socrates is right in denying that it could be taught and right again in concluding that virtue, as he, Socrates, conceives and approaches it, could indeed be taught.

CONFLICTING CONCEPTIONS OF THE THEORIST'S ROLE

It is only at one level of analysis, however, that the difference is a conflict between those—like the Sophists—focusing on techniques and those—like Socrates—concerned with the ends to which they should be put. Another way of conceiving of this tension is to suggest that it reflects a conflict concerning the nature of the role of the social theorist or educator. That is, there are those who believe their roles require educators to transmit anything that their clients or students wish to know, while others feel that educators should make their own estimate of what students require, regardless of the latter's expressed desires, and insist on educating them in this.

The conflict between Socrates and the Sophists is, from this standpoint, a conflict concerning the definition of the educator's role: between those who tend to define education as a sacred activity, responsibility for the content of which must be left to the educator's discretion and must be oriented to the "needs" of the student as the educator defines them, as against those viewing education in a comparatively secular light, the content of which is determined by the desires of the clientele as they formulate them. It is a conflict between those educators who view themselves as obligated to make their own independent appraisal of their clients' or students' "good"—and to do only what they themselves believe is good for their clients—and those who do not regard it as their business to make a judgment of the benefits their clients derive from their services or who take it for granted that their services are, in net balance, beneficial.

This interpretation is at least consistent with the fact that some of the Sophists (who were far more varied in outlook than this single dyslogistic term implies) do not actually deny an interest in the ends to which their skills are put. They merely deny responsibility for them. They deny that they encourage or condone use of their techniques for immoral purposes. Indeed, some state, as Protagoras explicitly holds, that they can and do teach virtue itself and aid men to become better citizens. Others hold it improper for rhetoricians to make the worse seem the better cause and claim in fact that they seek to imbue their students with a sense that their new powers give them an advantage that should not be abused. As Gorgias remarks:

> rhetoric should be used like any other competitive art, not against everybody—the rhetorician ought not to abuse his strength any more than a pugilist. . . . [If] others have perverted their instructions, and turned to a bad use their own strength and skill, . . . not on this account are the teachers bad, neither is the art in fault, or bad in itself; I should rather say that those who make bad use of the art are to blame.[19]

The Sophists, then, do not always reject an interest in basic values. Indeed, some indicate they are willing to teach "virtue"—as well as instrumental techniques—to those who seek it. But insofar as their students take their own ends for granted, since they presumably know what they want, then, given the Sophists' readiness to provide for these wants, they are more commonly engaged in transmitting neutral technical skills than in clarifying and evaluating the ends to which these are to be applied.

Whether or not a social theorist regards his skills as neutral techniques and treats his client's ends as given rather than as problematic depends in part on how his role links him to others; on whether, for example, he is an unattached entrepreneur or whether he is part of a larger protective establishment within which he does business. It would appear that social theorists who are, or conceive themselves as, entrepreneurs *and* who are directly dependent upon the purchase of their skills by various others—who, in short, sell their services on an open market—will more likely disregard the uses to which their clients put their services and, correspondingly, will define their skills as value-free techniques. As a further corollary, the more that theorists define their skills as neutral techniques, the wider and more diversified is the market on which they can sell their services.

In contrast to Socrates, who is in principle opposed to charging fees for education in "virtue," and to Plato, who has some independent means, the Sophists commonly have to charge for the education they provide. The Sophists (a term which originally meant only something like "teacher" or "professor") are for the most part itinerant educators who travel from city to city and make their living by teaching. They earn Socrates' scorn for being itinerants—as "they are only wanderers from one city to another, and having never had habitations of their own, they may fail in their conceptions of philosophers and statesmen." [20] —and for charging fees: the Sophist "buys up knowledge and goes about from city to city exchanging his wares for money; . . . he is the money-making species of the Eristic." [21] Since Socrates regards his teaching as a sacredly imposed mission and not as a source of livelihood, the offering of wisdom or virtue in exchange for money seems profoundly wrong. Indeed, he says, this is akin to prostitution; that is, as prostitution is selling one's beauty for money, so is it a kind of prostitution to offer one's knowledge of virtue for money.

The nature of the relationship between teacher and student, between the "school" and the community, begins to change and to come under the increasing control of the former with the establishment of institutions that are permanently located in one place. Shortly after Isocrates establishes his school in Athens, Plato sets up his own Academy in 387 B.C. in Academia on the outskirts of the city. The manifest function of the new kind of establishment is both teaching and research; its latent function is to insulate the scholar from the pressures of clientele and community.

In some part this insulation is accomplished by separating the Academy geographically from the city. Continued location of the school in one community also enables it to offer and require a longer course of study, with probationary conditions and set prerequisites, subjecting the student to a longer and more effective period of influence by the scholar. Furthermore, not only do the scholars of the Academy work and study together, but they periodically dine together, while some of the members build adjacent cottages in nearby woodland.

In all, these innovations have the effect if not the intention of enabling the institution to resist more effectively the pressures of both the students and the community, of getting the students to adapt themselves to the scholars more fully, and of reducing the extent to which the scholars in turn need to adapt to the students. The school establishes an intellectual community whose members are bound together in a variety of ways. It brings them together in a mutual closeness that provides greater protection from the pressure of "common-sense" views prevalent in the community, and the assembled scholars are better able to defend their own definition of their enterprise against hostile views. Their work can be carried forward in more continuous and cumulative ways because their surroundings provide them with ongoing emotional support and consensual validation, as well as intellectual stimulation and the advantages of a division of labor. It is an apt environment in which that most precarious of things, intellectual innovation, can be more reliably sustained and protected.

THEORISTS AS COSMOPOLITANS AND LOCALS

The variety and diversity of clients to which the Sophists had to adapt was not only due to the economics of operating in an open market, but was also closely related to their physical mobility and itinerancy. Clients were varied not only because Sophists would take any who could pay, but also because they plied their craft in different cities which often had manifestly different customs, constitutions, and beliefs. (In contrast, as mentioned earlier, Socrates traveled hardly at all, although Plato did travel more widely, to Sicily and elsewhere.)

In looking at any community, it is often useful to distinguish between those who are "Locals" and those who are "Cosmopolitans." In the Greek *polis* the various specialized artisans, for example, were more commonly Cosmopolitan in their geographic mobility, while the citizens conformed relatively more to the pattern of the Local, being rooted in and more oriented to their own community by their legal prerogatives, including land ownership. The Sophists may be looked upon as a special case of the itinerant specialist, akin in his mobility to the artists, bards, and rhapsodists of the time, whose style of life and outlook are characteristically Cosmopolitan.

As I have discussed in detail elsewhere,[22] there is reason to believe that scholars' outlooks will be substantially affected by whether or not they are Cosmopolitans, more highly committed to their scholarly activities and less so to a specific community or particular establishment in which they operate. My own research on some contemporary scholars suggests the possibility that even the intellectual outlook that social theorists develop on social problems may be influenced by whether they are Locals or Cosmopolitans.

Some Locals, for example, appear to adopt distinctive orientations to the community; they are

> deeply committed to [it] . . . —and to it as a whole—on the ground that it embodies unique values which they regard as important. They are concerned that those within [it] . . . support this ideology, believing that community agreement is more important than the acceptance of individual differences. They are also more likely to insist that their colleagues possess certain local value orientations rather than technical competencies. . . . Their focus is on the maintenance of internal organizational cohesion and consensus.[23]

Further, one of the clearest findings about contemporary Local scholars is that they—much more than Cosmopolitans—manifest a tendency toward "rule tropism," that is, a disposition to believe that community rules and formal regulations are too lenient and in need of strengthening. This, it is noteworthy, is all the more true of Locals whose influence in their group is low rather than of those whose influence is high.

There is an almost point-by-point correspondence between the social ideology of this ideal type of Local and certain aspects of Platonic social theory, especially with respect to their common stress on values rather than morally neutral technical skills, their emphasis on consensus and unity in the group, and their common stress, notably in Plato's *Laws*, on the use of formal rules and legal procedure as order-maintaining devices. It may be that Plato's emphasis on formal laws, especially pronounced in his later work, is expressive of a social outlook particularly characteristic of powerless Locals, for, as I have noted, his reference groups were probably experiencing an increasing sense of powerlessness due to the defeat of the domestic oligarchical groups with which they were closely connected, as well as their own growing alienation from politics in general.

Because of their birth or longer tenure in a community, Locals are more likely than Cosmopolitans to be attached to its traditional values. For the same reason, Locals are also likely to be more deeply enmeshed in an enduring network of informal relationships with other Locals who can exert influence on their belief systems, while Cosmopolitans, less likely to be caught up in informal networks because of their mobility, are less vulnerable to pressure to conform to traditional community values. Locals are therefore more likely to be traditionalists and to judge the present in terms of the past; they are more likely to criticize the status quo from the standpoint of traditional values while Cosmopolitans are more likely to criticize the traditional values themselves.

SOPHISTIC RELATIVISM: NATURE VERSUS CONVENTION

One standpoint from which an important sector of the Sophists express their alienation from established Hellenic institutions is embodied in their distinction between "nature" and "convention," and, in particular, in the belief that different customs and laws are conventional rather than natural, being the work of men and as such varying with their circumstances. This relativism is congenial to the Cosmopolitan Sophists, whose wide travels have led them to encounter a variety of customs and beliefs. They could see that different cities have different *mores* concerning the same human problems; that some, as Euripides notes, lament at funerals while others make merry. They could see that some cities have differing constitutions and laws and that these are man made; that these are in fact made by contemporaries such as Protagoras, who, at Pericles' direction, drafted the constitution of Thurii in southern Italy. It becomes highly evident to some of the much-traveled Sophists that the cities' diverse laws can no more be ascribed to nature than to the supernatural.

Observation of such cultural diversity leads some Sophists to a criticism of all laws and to a view that laws are merely arbitrary conventions. It leads ultimately, at least in some cases, to a critique of the conventional distinctions between Greeks and barbarians, aristocrats and plebeians, slaves and masters, viewing these as artifices contrary to nature, and, indeed, viewing the gods themselves as men's own invention. The diversified customs and beliefs they encounter lead some Sophists to conclude that when men disagree about institutions, laws, or customs, it does not necessarily follow that some of them must be right and others wrong; and that there is not necessarily any one unvarying standard of truth by which the validity of social beliefs can be judged. Institutions and laws, from this standpoint, have to be evaluated in terms of the differing conditions that prevail in different communities. In contrast to this relativism and to a radical skepticism about any regularity underlying observed diversity, other Sophists believe that some social behavior and relations are "natural," that some things are inherent in human life, and that these could be used as a norm to judge and evaluate existent practices. In varying degrees, these theoretical alternatives are pursued by different Sophists and, of course, by many subsequent thinkers who will become concerned with the implications of cultural diversity.

A significant link with themes dominant in subsequent social thought derives from those whose observation of manifest cultural diversity becomes a spur to search out the latent, underlying regularities in human behavior and who, like Hippias the Sophist, claim that there are unwritten laws which are observed in the same way in every society. Hippias concludes, in a manner discomfiting to Greek slavery, that all men are brothers by nature if not by men's laws.

At least two characteristics of the natural thus conceived are worth noting: first, that the natural is regarded as in some sense the universal, as that which is true and effective everywhere, operating with the same massive effects in all places and times, even if not immediately visible in the seemingly different constitutions and laws made by men. Secondly, the natural comes to be regarded as that which is not made by men deliberately or which is not imposed upon things but is inherent in them. The natural thing is like the free Greek; it is not that which is moved by an external constraint but by an inner impulse.

The latter view is, of course, susceptible to various interpretations. It may mean that the natural is that which is not rationally, deliberately, and consciously made by men but is still contrived by them even if unconsciously or unwittingly. Or it may refer to that which is not at all due to the efforts or intentions of men, conscious or unconscious, but is a gift of the gods or is of divine origin. Again, it may be regarded as both, in that the gods lead men to act in this way by informing them with an unconscious mission, so that, in behaving in these common ways, men are the agents of a higher, divine purpose. In any event, the view that there is a human nature —a nature counterposed to human convention—implies that certain regularities are inherent in human behavior, that certain dispositions are intrinsic to human life. It implies that human life has an inner, even if unintended, orderliness which is not derived from the deliberate designs of men. It implies that that which is not superintended with a view to realizing certain ends, either of men or gods, may yet be orderly.

Once it is held that "convention and nature are generally at variance with one another," it is to be expected that the natural, or natural law, will become a base point in terms of which institutions are evaluated. The natural becomes the standard by which the man-made is appraised, either with a view to the latter's defense, when it is contended that the two are in conformity with one another, or with a view to its derogation, when convention is held to depart from the natural.

In Plato's view, however, ends are not resident in nature but in the universal Ideas or eternal Forms which transcend nature, in which nature only imperfectly "participates" and apart from which it is inherently disorderly. From his standpoint, therefore, nature cannot be self-governing; it must be controlled by the external influence of some regulating end or design. Plato rejects the divorce of nature and custom, believing that both are and should be subject to the absolute, eternal Ideas which, in opposition to some Sophists' relativism, he feels supply a single and unvarying standard applicable forever and everywhere; for "a principle which has any soundness should stand firm not only just now, but always." [24]

These absolute Ideas, he believes, may be discovered or seen more clearly—for they are not invented or created by men, and they exist apart from any man's recognition of them—through the exercise of the dialectic. Wending up and up, the dialectic searches for first principles. It finally gives men a glimpse of the eternal Ideas or Forms, which have been only vaguely and indistinctly imprinted in ordinary practice, and toward which men can strive in remodeling their lives.

Neither to the Sophists nor Plato, however, is law or custom justified on merely traditional grounds; these are not to be obeyed simply because they are hallowed by antiquity. Both Plato and the Sophists seek a standpoint in terms of which the status quo may be critically reviewed. Both believe that tradition must be brought before the bar of reason, where it is to be cross-examined and made to justify itself. In opposition to certain Sophists, however, who believe there is no single set of practices or customs that is best, Plato counterposes the notion of eternal and unvarying Ideas or Forms. In opposition to those Sophists who feel there are latent regularities within human societies, Plato believes that the regulating forces are external and transcendental to human society—God, not man, says Plato, is the measure. In opposition to some of the Sophists who suggest that the "natural" man or natural social arrangements can be discerned through some sort of cross-cultural comparison and observation, Plato believes that the guiding Ideas can be discerned only through the deductive work of the mind and not by the inductive senses.

In contrast to Plato's rationalism, an important group of the Sophists are much impressed by, and rely more steadily on, their *observations* of human behavior, despite the fact that some of them are as opposed to the "nature philosophers" as are Plato and Socrates. The Sophists talk of what they had seen and heard in different places, comparing them, noting their similarities and differences. For all of Plato's continual references to mundane things, to cooks, physicians, and ships' pilots, his use of these is largely analogical. They are taken not as significant in and of themselves but as useful only as guides or models for the development of his logical discourse and for the intellectual clarification of problems. While the Sophists often use sense data as the starting point and test of their reasoning, Plato distrusts the senses and the data they provide. "[T]he unchanging things," says Plato, "you can only perceive with the mind." [25] In this sense, the modern empirical study of men shows more continuity with the standpoint of the Sophists than that of the Platonist.

Plato's attack on the Sophists is reminiscent of Marx's attack upon the utopian socialists: both men are able to make succeeding generations define their opponents as they themselves had; both use a single opprobrious term for opponents who, in fact, hold a wide variety of views. The similarity is noteworthy in that the terms "utopian" and "Sophist" each refer to standpoints that are often nearest to those expressed by Marx and Socrates, respectively. Indeed, Aristophanes' caricature of Socrates suggests that there are many in the Athens of that time who see no difference between Socrates and the Sophists. Certainly if one thinks of the Sophists invidiously, as those employing specious reasoning and "word twisting" or an ingenious but fallacious logic, it sometimes appears that Socrates is neither intellectually nor morally superior to them.

Bertrand Russell suggests that the Sophists are at least willing to follow an argument wherever it takes them, even if it leads to seemingly immoral conclusions and, indeed, that they have the virtue of speaking the truth without regard for its moral consequences. In contrast, Russell holds, Plato is always thinking ahead to the moral implications of his argument, allowing himself to judge matters by their moral and social consequences and twisting the discussion to a virtuous conclusion, rather than reaching it solely by its internal logical consistency or factual basis. There is a good deal of truth in this, for Plato, as we shall see, was a proponent and practitioner of the Noble Lie; but there is also a problem here, to be explored later, concerning the sources of this propensity, and it deserves to be understood rather than letting the matter rest with a condemnation of Plato for his moralizing bent.

ON THE QUESTION OF PLATO'S TRADITIONALISM

It would be a mistake to regard the controversy between Socrates and the Sophists as arising because the latter have no values while the former does; part of the polemic between them stems, rather, from the differences in the values each supports and holds. For example, in taking their students' ends as given, the Sophists tend to service the pursuit of conventional political careers. Plato objects to this, in part, because he doubts the worth of this conventional value, since he believes that "the goods of which the many speak are not really good." [26] Plato is calling Greeks from their other-directed life to an inner-directed existence. He places a stress upon the private, "quiet" virtues, such as temperance and knowledge, in contrast to the other-directed pursuit of a public political career toward which the Sophists aid their students. The contrast is shown when Socrates is made to say, somewhat piously, "I was really too honest a man to be a politician and live." [27]

While the specific value orientations that Plato himself affirms will be discussed more fully at a later point, it may be mentioned here that he objects to the conventional Greek contest system and usual economic virtues: "You, my friend—a citizen of the great and mighty and wise city of Athens—are you not ashamed of heaping up the greatest amount of money and honour and reputation, and caring so little about wisdom and truth and the greatest improvement of the soul?" [28] In particular, Plato opposes certain conventional values in the name of the "soul." He justifies his critique of conventional values by counterposing them to the goods of the soul, which he now infuses with heightened pathos and sacred potency. Indeed, he transforms the traditional Athenian concept of the sacred itself by rejecting, as he does, the conventional Homeric picture of the gods as doing evil to men.

There are at least two different sides to Plato: the side which can celebrate Socrates' loyalty to his own conscience, even against the accusation and pressure of the city; and the other side, which can celebrate Socrates' submission to the city's death sentence and which stresses compliance with the laws. In his polemic against the Sophists, different aspects of Plato's position come forward at different times. Sometimes he seems to compete with them for the wreath of being the most radical and emancipated thinker. Other times he firmly opposes (what he feels to be) their unbridled individualism and speaks out on behalf of traditional communal virtues.

Yet Plato is certainly not at all a "traditionalist" in the sense of one who *uncritically* accepts old, received patterns of belief and behavior; indeed, by his time the authentically traditional ways are all too manifestly decaying. If it be said that Plato is an upholder of the traditional values such as courage, justice, temperance, and wisdom, several things need to be added. First, these are not all equally involved in the core implications of *aretē,* which especially entails excellence and success in contest. While Plato by no means rejects competitive achievement, it seems evident that this is not central to his conception of virtue or of the "good," however vague it may be. Further, it also seems clear that Socrates is in the process of re-evaluating the traditional virtues and of infusing them with new meaning, in particular making them rest on more intellectual or cognitive qualities. Wisdom, he says, is the "one true coin for which all things ought to be exchanged." [29] Indeed, as already noted, Socrates is also engaged in changing the traditional conception of man's relation to the divine: a strange traditionalist this.

What Plato is basically trying to do, insofar as his work is oriented to the social strains of his time, is to reknit the Athenian social structure, to bring forth unity out of disunity, to make the many into one. To the extent that this leads him to stress the importance of social hierarchy, consensus, and social order, he might well be called a "conservative" of sorts; but it would appear misleading to term him a traditionalist. Certainly both of these ideologically resonant labels should be treated with caution since they involve assumptions embedded in a different language and are based upon implicit analogies between Athenian and modern circumstances which should be handled with the greatest circumspection; worse than this, in making the viewpoint seem familiar, such terms often narcotize curiosity at the very point where inquiry should be pressed.

In thinking about Socrates' polemic against the Sophists, there is also the danger that we know the latter primarily through the work of Socrates' friend and greatest disciple, Plato. This amounts to saying that we must rely heavily on Plato for an understanding of Plato's enemies. Indeed, "when one thinks what would become of any modern philosopher if he were only known through the polemics of his rivals, one can see how admirable the pre-Socratics must have been, since even through the mist of malice spread by their enemies they still appear great." [30]

If there is any one greater handicap that we suffer than the ignorance which Plato's antipathies must inevitably impose on our knowledge of the Sophists, it is the ignorance concerning Socrates himself, for there must be some, even if well-intended, distortion of Socrates' character and teaching that Plato's love of him imposes. The difference between the Socrates of the *Charmides* just back from the battlefront—a horny soldier thirsting after knowledge and beautiful youths—and the Socrates of the *Phaedo*— part Pythagoras with a dash of Santa Claus—may well be as much a consequence of the changes that Plato himself undergoes as a faithful report of the transformations that time imposes on the historical Socrates. In the last analysis, Socrates and his adversaries share a common fate: both are Plato's captives, coming alive only in his magic doll's house.

NOTES

[1] *Memorabilia* iv. ii. 24. Trans. E. C. Marchant (Cambridge: Harvard University Press, 1949), Loeb Classical Library.

[2] Plato *Phaedrus.* 230D.

[3] Plato *Apology.* 33AB.

[4] Field, *op. cit.,* p. 91.

[5] A. Koyré, *Discovering Plato* (New York: Columbia University Press, 1945), p. 53.

[6] Here I prefer the version translated in G. Misch, *A History of Autobiography in Antiquity, op. cit.,* pp. 119–120.

[7] *Ibid.,* p. 120.

[8] J. Gould, *The Development of Plato's Ethics* (Cambridge: Cambridge University Press, 1955), p. 130.

[9] Plato *Apology.* 23AB.

[10] Plato *Laches.* 200A.

[11] Plato *Charmides.* 161C.

[12] Plato *Phaedrus.* 265B.

[13] Lattimore, *Greek Lyrics, op. cit.,* p. 25.

[14] Plato *Apology.* 19C.

[15] Plato *Laches.* 185D.

[16] Plato *Phaedo.* 97E–98A.

[17] Plato *Phaedo.* 100C.

[18] Plato *Phaedo.* 99D–100A.

[19] Plato *Gorgias.* 456D–457A.

[20] Plato *Timaeus.* 19D.

[21] Plato *Sophist.* 224A, 226A.

[22] A. W. Gouldner, "Cosmopolitans and Locals: Toward an Analysis of Latent Social Roles, I," *Administrative Science Quarterly* (December 1957), 281–306; "Cosmopolitans and Locals, II," (March 1958), 444–480.

[23] *Ibid.,* 446.

[24] Plato *Meno.* 89C; cf. also *Phaedo.* 78CD.

[25] Plato *Phaedo.* 79A.

[26] Plato *Laws.* 661A.

[27] Plato *Apology.* 36C.

[28] Plato *Apology.* 29CD.

[29] Plato *Phaedo.* 69AB.

[30] Bertrand Russell, *A History of Western Philosophy* (New York: Simon and Schuster, 1945), p. 45.

6

Social Diagnosis: Plato's Analysis of Social Disunity

Regard me not, I entreat you, as a lawless one.
—Sophocles, *Oedipus at Colonus* [1]

SOCIAL theory of power and penetration is not written by the smugly content or by the blasé; nor is it written by those who admire or accept society as it is. Few men would work at the theorist's craft if they felt that theirs is the best of all possible worlds. All social theories, however technical and esoteric, bear the trace marks of some judgment about the social world; all reflect a vision, however dim and indistinct, of a world that is more desirable than the one the theorist knows.

To be a social theorist is not simply to seek out the world that is; it is also to reach for a world that might be, even if this is done with pickpocket fingers. To be a social theorist is not simply to describe or analyze the world that is; it is also to pronounce a judgment on it, even if this is done in a ventriloquist's voice. To be a social theorist is to be the oedipal heir to shamans and priests and to the conjurers of philosopher-kings. It is to be a maker and shaker of worlds that are and worlds that might be.

Underneath the most technically abstruse effort by the social theorist—when he seems blithely to ignore the human condition—and underneath the most playful and irreverent of the theorist's efforts—when he seems callously to toy with the human condition—there is another kind of game being played and another kind of question being asked: Where did things go wrong in our lives, and what, if anything, might be done to rescue them? All social theories involve some diagnosis of human problems and all embody some therapy for them. Plato's social theory differs from many that follow only in that it does this explicitly. Never having committed itself to a value-free conception of its task, Plato's theory never has to conceal or repress its practical interests.

In this chapter I shall limit myself to a discussion of Plato's *diagnosis* of human problems, to the ways in which he conceives these problems, and

197

to what he thinks is "wrong" with individuals and groups. While Plato's diagnosis is linked inextricably with his notions of a remedy or therapy, our grasp of his social theory will be the firmer if we distinguish between questions of diagnosis and problems of therapy, reserving systematic discussion of the latter for subsequent chapters, even if this requires a measure of repetition.

DIAGNOSING THE HUMAN CONDITION

Plato's social theory is, without doubt, the first comprehensive and rational diagnosis of the human condition in the Western tradition. The focus of this diagnosis, as with his social theory more generally, is not, however, with the historically transient or the geographically limited. Plato is not concerned with problems that are peculiar to one time, to one place, or to one nation of people. Plato aims, instead, at what he takes to be the universal problems of human life, at problems that everywhere beset men as men.

In accounting for this ahistorical focus of his social theory, it would be tempting to suggest that, like Greeks generally, Plato lacks an ingrained historical sense because the civilization of which he is a part does not have a long and richly documented historical perspective. Yet educated Greeks are well enough aware, if not of the history, then at least of the diversity of customs and beliefs among the contemporary peoples around them. Indeed, Plato's lunge toward the universally valid is an effort to transcend this manifest diversity; his theory crystallizes in the course of his polemic against the Sophists, who take this diversity as real and basic. He seeks the universally valid in part because he opposes those who, in affirming cultural relativism, have, he feels, opened the door to moral anarchy.

Here we are deliberately focusing on the larger historical conditions as well as the microdynamics of social interaction among theorists, and are suggesting a way in which both may elicit the ahistorical character of Plato's social diagnosis. This is not to deny, however, that other factors dispose to the same result. In particular, Plato's metaphysics would, and probably also do, conduce to a similar level of diagnosis. For Plato the like is "infinitely fairer than the unlike"; for him, true reality resides not in the individual particular but, rather, in the universal class in which the particular participates. The ahistoricism of Plato's social theory is thus of a piece with his metaphysics.

Yet this by no means indicates the irrelevance of underlying social and cultural conditions; it only pushes the problem back farther, for the universalistic character of the metaphysics itself is also in need of explanation.

Indeed, the same existential, social, and cultural conditions shaping the social diagnosis may also underlie the metaphysics. Further, it may be that the social diagnosis Plato makes is as much psychologically supportive of his metaphysics as it is derivative of it. Yet the priorities involved in these several forces need not detain us, for one level of analysis need not refute the other. Our interest in the effects of social and cultural forces on Plato's social diagnosis does not minimize the importance of his metaphysics. Undoubtedly, his metaphysics is also conducive to an ahistorical diagnosis, leading Plato to concern himself with the ways in which men everywhere are alike and to focus on this likeness.

INDIVIDUAL DIAGNOSIS: THE ROLE OF VALUES

Central to Plato's entire method of thinking about men is a stress on the characteristics distinguishing them as a "class." The essence distinguishing a class is usually stated in terms of ordinary human values and interests: for example, the essence of a state that it is just and of a bed that it is comfortable.[2] Plato's analysis of the universal, then, is at once logical and moral: the logically distinctive characteristics of a class tend to be the morally relevant. The moral and existential orders coincide. Moreover, the eternal ideas in which the particulars participate are morally positive. Socrates is embarrassed, consequently, when he is asked by Parmenides, "And would you feel equally undecided, Socrates, about things of which the mention may provoke a smile?—I mean such things as hair, mud, dirt, or anything else which is vile and paltry; would you suppose that each of these has an idea distinct from the actual objects with which we come into contact or not? 'Certainly not,' says Socrates." [3]

Since Plato tends to make the logically distinctive coincide with the morally imperative, once logic reveals the qualities common to men, men are obliged to attempt to transform themselves ever more nearly into embodiments of their distinguishing characteristics. Since analysis reveals that men are commonly distinguished from other animals by the faculty of reason, they must, therefore, strive to submit themselves to it and to live according to its dictates.

Similarly, since men are the only mortal creatures that can attain wisdom and act according to its requirements, it is incumbent on them to become ever more wise. But action based on wisdom, Plato notes, is not simply action based on facts. Men must also know what is worth doing and worth knowing. Socrates thus defines the quest for knowledge as essentially a quest for values—for the "ought" rather than simply for the "is," for the "should be" rather than merely for the "will be." He focuses attention less on questions of fact concerning human nature than on problems of norms or values.

Yet this is an oversimplification, for several reasons. First, as was noted above, the moral and existential orders coincide in Plato; the logically true, if not the observationally reliable, contains value imperatives, and the latter, embodied in pure form in the eternal Ideas, are regarded as real as, indeed as *more* real than, facts resting on sensory observation. Secondly, Plato's conception of the kind of knowledge that is valuable contains elements of the factual, of ordinary technical information, as well as conceptions of the morally appropriate and the good. This comes out clearly where Plato likens the statesman to the ship's pilot, for he refers to and relies on the pilot's technical skill and factual information no less than his probity of character.

Perhaps the point is best expressed by suggesting that Plato takes reliable information as given—he assumes that information can, within limits, be reliable and useful—and focuses on and makes problematic the question of values, the search for the good. He is perhaps driven to this emphasis by his polemic against the Sophists, whose relativism he rejects and who, he feels, dwell too much on the purely technical side of their information. They must be counterbalanced by a concern with the ends to which techniques are put and by the development of a single, unvarying moral standard.

Values are also of crucial importance to Plato because value *differences* are among the main sources of social conflict. Men do not long quarrel about issues that can be resolved by resorting to arithmetic. Rather, he notes, "enmities arise when the sorts of difference are the just and the unjust, good and evil, honorable and dishonorable. . . . And there would have been no quarrels among them if there had been no such differences." [4] Once again, it seems difficult to understand the nature of Plato's social diagnosis except by referring to the diversity of customs and beliefs and to the prevalence of conflict among his contemporaries. Clearly, what he is attempting to find and to provide a justification for is a new value system that can override existent differences in values, to which he attributes so much of the existent social discord.

IGNORANCE AND THE UPSIDE-DOWN EXISTENCE

By itself, a sensory-rooted knowledge of facts does not enable men to know what to do; the data by themselves never provide a program for action. Above all, Plato's is a practical philosophy; it is designed to find out how men should spend their lives. He begins with the assumption that there are some interests which are intrinsically ends and others which are intrinsically means to these ends. The means are inherently subordinate; they have meaning and can be selected properly only with a prior knowledge of the ends. Consequently, the important thing is first to gain clarity concerning the basic ends or values.

The trouble with men, however, Plato notes, is that they commonly lead an "upside-down" existence. Callicles remarks that "if . . . what you say is true, is not the whole of human life turned upside down; and are we not doing, as would appear, in everything the opposite of what we ought to be doing?" [5] Men involve themselves, in their daily concerns, with the means and tools of life rather than with clarifying and appraising the ultimate ends to which they are applied. This is not the exceptional but the usual condition of men, and, on Plato's premises, the condition is no less prevalent in our own time than his.

It is in this sense that to Plato the unexamined life is not worth living; [6] he demands that men subject their ends to critical scrutiny. This means that living according to even the most venerable tradition—accepting things because they have been hallowed by antiquity—is living a life that is less than human. In this sense, Plato's diagnosis is that one source of human problems is traditionalism. Traditionalism, however, is not the only source of the upside-down existence—so, too, is unthinking submission to authority. Plato repeatedly urges his listeners to ignore the question of *who* is saying something: "[A]ttend only to the argument," he insists, "and see what will come of the refutation." [7]

Worse than men's ignorance of virtue, however, is the fact that this ignorance is prideful. Men have an involuntary lie in the soul which entails a double form of ignorance. It is *double* ignorance, first, because they do not know what is worth pursuing and, secondly, because they are ignorant of the fact that they do not know this. Indeed, men imagine that they do know what the good is; they unthinkingly value all manner of things supporting physical life but fail to value the goods of the soul. They give lip service to high values, but, in fact, their daily lives are guided by mean expedience and egoism. And it is because of this ignorance that they do wrong, for knowledge, says Plato, is virtue.

How is it that men are thus ignorant? Here Plato's basic answer refers neither to habit nor to external tradition and authority. The prime source of ignorance, Plato holds, is men's appetites—the "many headed beast" of the passions—which chafe against reason and in most men dominate the psyche. How can man help but be ignorant if his reason, the very part of him that could guide him to knowledge, is enthralled by his passions. Since it is his own appetites that blind him, man is essentially a self-deceived creature; he is an accomplice in his own undoing.

THE CONTEST IN THE SOUL

Plato regards the psyche as having three main parts: first, reason, which he likens to "man" or the true man, and which is the legitimate ruler of the soul; second, desire or the irrational passions; and third, the elusive notion, the *thymos*. Plato conceives of the *thymos* as the "high-spirited" part of the psyche, whose proper function is to accept an alliance with reason and with whose aid reason can maintain order in the soul and restrain the appetites. It is clear that the appetites and the *thymos* are both feelingful impulses; they differ, however, in the concrete impulses assigned to them, and especially in the esteem or value in which each is held.

The appetites are morally "base" impulses: e.g., carnal feelings and greed. The *thymos*, however, contains the "noble" affects: pride, courage, even wrath and violence. In contrast to the Freudian id, in which sex and aggression are jointly located, in the Platonic anatomy of personality they are split, placed in different regions, and are held to be of unequal worth. The *thymos* comprises those affects which are appropriate to the older aristocratic values, stressing the importance of honor, courage, contest, and military skill. The *thymos* is associated with and accommodates the conventional elite virtues. In effect, Plato himself cannot exclude the warlike sentiments or debase them radically, for no more than most Greeks of his time can he imagine a world without war. His anatomy of the psyche betrays an image of man in which, even if sex is to be devalued, aggression is still to be allowed an honorable place.

Plato's anatomy of the psyche also suggests that the integration of personality is expected to require more than the rhetoric of reason, although the main task is seen as bringing personality under the domination of reason. The three parts of the soul seem to correspond to the three types of men in the Pythagorean doctrine, the lovers of wisdom, gain, and honor, but here in Plato the differences are not simply among men but within them: there is a conflict within the soul.

To Plato, the capacity of the soul to attain knowledge is at least the larger part, if not the essence, of virtue. "All other things hang upon the soul," he says, "and the things of the soul herself hang upon wisdom, if they are to be good." [8] The attainment of knowledge, however, depends upon the outcome of the struggle in the soul, for man is not single-mindedly devoted to knowledge and truth. One side of him opposes the efforts of his best and most healthful side. Man needs knowledge for the good life, but he also resists it. He does not and cannot come to knowledge without a struggle, without some effort on his part. Knowledge and ignorance, therefore, are not products alone of man's reason or of his cognitive faculties; they are the result of the relations among the various parts of his soul. They are the outcome of the total disposition of man's character as a whole.

Implicit in this picture of the contest in the soul is a conception of the self as being potent. Each of its sides is seen as having a kind of strength; reason and the irrational appetites are each seen as capable of overcoming the other. The very contest in the soul premises a conception of the self as potent even when divided. What Plato stresses is that the self-conscious and rational part of the self can and must be *master*—i.e., have a controlling force and authority in relation to the other parts. Its influence is not solely a function of its awareness, though this is vital, but also of its power, even if only through alliance with the *thymos*. Plato's theory of knowledge is in this sense a voluntaristic or volitional theory—knowledge being the outcome of a progressive striving, of expended effort and desire. Above all, one must quest after knowledge. Man must want the truth, or he will remain in bondage to his irrational appetites. There must be a commitment of the self to truth.

SOME IMPLICATIONS FOR SOCIAL SCIENCE

In this view of the sources of ignorance we have a kind of psychology of knowledge. The philosopher must begin his quest by examining his own soul to determine whether his own dispositions are so ordered as to enable him to find knowledge and to accept it when he finds it. He must, in brief, first heal himself, by self-mastery of his subversive appetites, and thus come to know himself. There is, then, an interlocking set of notions here: to know the truth one must know oneself, and to do this one must heal oneself.

In indicating that Plato's theory is a psychology of knowledge, we are simultaneously noting that it is not a sociology of knowledge. It does not, for example, lead to a systematic concern with the way in which a person's social role or position facilitates or inhibits the acquisition of knowledge. (One exception to this, however, entails Plato's use of the commonplace Greek concept of the *banausia,* which suggests that men in certain occupations, especially toilsome and menial ones, have little time and energy left to search for knowledge. But this is quite far from suggesting that people in different occupations may have *different kinds* of knowledge and ignorance —a view which, it would seem, Plato might regard as perilously close to, if not identical with, Sophistic relativism or Protagoras' notion that "man is the measure of all things.") In Plato's view, reason is fundamentally the same in character for all men. Differences arise only in the scope and power reason attains in different people; but the premises it employs and the conclusions to which it comes are, when valid, the same for all, because it is directed toward the same Ideas which are unchanging and identical for all. Reason is in this sense a human, but not a social, product. All men are alike in potentially possessing it and in possessing internal forces which could subvert it. Being like other men, the thinker may know them by knowing himself; the truth is basically within him. The man who knows himself has the essential knowledge of others, and he need not, therefore, engage in researches about the customs and behavior of others. He need not commit a social science.

There is another way in which the Platonic viewpoint is inhibitive of the development of an empirical science of man in which issues are at length tested by some form of observation. As noted, Plato is interested not so much in what men do as in what they should do. His observation of their practices is designed not so much to determine and to account for manifest regularities of behavior as to exhibit the ways in which human behavior commonly diverges from logically appropriate and defensible models. Plato regards men's behavior not as entailing an inherent lawfulness but as reflecting or distorting external, transcendental Ideas. Much as the cobbler's shoes reflect the cobbler's imperfect efforts to embody the idea of a shoe in leather, so human efforts indistinctly embody eternal Ideas of justice, wisdom, goodness, and beauty, which, if they were but seen more clearly, could be more fully realized. Man is not the sun but a moon glowing with only a borrowed light.

From Plato's standpoint, men can indeed fail to conform with the moral laws in which he, Plato, is basically interested. And if they do fail, it is because of their ignorance. No one, he says, will knowingly fail to do good or will intentionally do evil: "[N]o wise man, as I believe, will allow that any human being errs voluntarily, or voluntarily does evil and dishonorable actions; but they are very well aware that all who do evil and dishonorable things do them against their will." Plato's theory of social deviance, his account of the sources of social problems, stresses the role of ignorance, particularly ignorance of the transcendental moral Ideas. Men's suffering derives from their lack of knowledge of the true morality. Their need, therefore, is not so much to study the diverse ways of mankind as to obtain a true vision of the one "good."

That the social and cultural differences among men may systematically lead some to see and others to miss certain truths, that the groups within which one is born and lives can hinder the pursuit of truth, is for Plato a secondary consideration. His focus on the characteristics common to men leads him to underestimate the force of cultural and historical differences, which may variously shape the truth available to different groups in different times and places and, indeed, the very categories of thought itself. Plato's focus leads him to concern himself with knowledge solely as a more-or-less-ness, as something more or less reliable and certain, and to ignore the possibility that different men differentially situated are hindered in seeing different parts of the truth because of their social location.

Plato's theory of knowledge, even though fundamentally a psychology rather than a sociology of knowledge, misses the point that men's individual passions, no less than their social roles, may clarify as well as distort the truth and may be a source of knowledge as well as of ignorance. He does stress that reason must ally itself with certain feelings and affections, the *thymos,* if it is to control the passions and acquire the truth. That the malignant passions can themselves be a source of energy for the pursuit of truth is, however, commonly ignored. Thus Plato seemingly takes no note, for example, of the fact that homosexual passions can motivate an ugly man to excel in dialectical disputation so that he may become attractive to and be surrounded by youths noble and fair. That is to say, he does not remark upon this as a philosopher. His artist's eye, however, is truer and the interweaving of homosexual flirtation and logic is obvious enough in several of the dialogues—in the *Meno* and the *Charmides.* (He thus has Socrates say of Charmides, ". . . at that moment, when I saw him coming in, I confess that I was quite astonished at his beauty and stature. . . . O rare! I caught a sight of the inwards of his garment, and took the flame. Then I could no longer contain myself." [9] The dialogue ends with Charmides saying in *double-entendre* to Socrates, "Do not resist me then," and Socrates replying, "I will not resist you.")

Yet, if these criticisms have any worth, it is only because of more than two thousand years of hindsight. That Socrates sees as much as he does in his time, that he understands men are not single-mindedly devoted to the truth but may actually oppose their own efforts to acquire it, is an amazing accomplishment. Of vital significance also is the importance he attributes to knowledge as a tool for the remedy of human problems; he forges an enduring hope that knowledge can lead to the reduction of human suffering. Healing and knowing are brought together.

Insofar as Plato maintains that the source of men's problems resides in themselves, he is saying men can make themselves well, or at least better. They need not resign themselves to eternal despair; they are not simply flotsam that must consent to being tossed about by life. Instead, given the potency of the human self, there is a promise that man can, at least in some measure, control his life and fulfill himself. Yet to see man as inherently cleft—part reason and part passion, half divine and half beast —is to view him in a manner that makes the outcome intrinsically precarious. Man is advised not to hope but to struggle.

SOCIAL DIAGNOSIS: SOCIAL DISUNITY

Plato's diagnosis of the human condition is not confined to an analysis of individual suffering, but also entails a diagnosis of the human community. Although his use of express organismic metaphors is sparing, he draws analogies between the person and the community, and, notably, he regards the community as the person writ large. Plato views the sickness of the one as analogous to the sickness of the other: The best ordered state, he says, "[is that] which most nearly approaches to the condition of the individual —as in the body, when but a finger of one of us is hurt, the whole frame, drawn from the soul as a centre and forming one kingdom under the ruling power therein, feels the hurt and sympathizes all together with the part affected." [10]

Central to Plato's diagnosis of social or communal tensions is his focus on social disorganization and, in particular, social disunity. Do we know any greater evil for a city, he asks, than that which fragments it and makes it many instead of one? [11] The city must be made whole again, and the individual must, as we shall see, be carefully fitted into his proper niche in it; he must be subjected to a set of controls powerful enough to keep him there, willingly or not.

The recurrent, central motif of Plato's diagnosis is that the gravest danger to Greek society is social disunity. The facts of Greek history appear to document this conclusion so thoroughly that the meaning of Plato's diagnosis may seem self-evident, while efforts to clarify it may appear correspondingly pedantic. Yet these are only appearances, for there are many kinds and degrees of disunity and unity. There is the unity of the pile of sand and the unity of the organism; there is the unity of the like-minded and the unity of those who need one another; there is the unity of equals and the unity of the artisan and his tool. That Plato decries disunity because he desires unity is unmistakable: but what kind of unity does he seek?

This is no easy matter to explore, for several reasons. First, Plato's diagnosis of social disunity, like Marx's treatment of social classes, is scattered; no one discussion of it is definitive and comprehensive. Second, his diagnosis of social disunity often has to be inferred from his therapeutic proposals. Thirdly, Plato does not think in cause-and-effect terms; he does not always neatly define social disunity and carefully distinguish between it and the diverse contributants inducing it. Rather, he appears to think in organic terms, treating the various elements as connected parts of a whole; he distinguishes a set of overlapping foci of social disunity. Nonetheless, he does communicate an *image* of social disunity, of a domain common to the various foci, and indicates some of its gross symptoms.

My task in the next pages is therefore a multiple one. First, I will attempt a brief characterization of Plato's image of social disunity, a preliminary view of his conception of it. Secondly, an effort will be made to outline the large variety of foci of social disunity that Plato discusses, without, however, making his analysis seem more systematic than it is and without imposing on it a contemporary and alien order. Plato's own analysis of social disunity is profound, explicit, and comprehensive enough that it may be spared the gratuitous courtesy of being presented as if it were written yesterday.

Without Procrustean reformulation, we will find that his analysis distinguishes and draws upon many of the various levels and elements that are presently regarded as basic to an understanding of social disunity: He examines (1) the role of such external threats as war and the diffusion of beliefs and values from sources external to the community. He explores (2) the effects of internal cultural innovation and invention and (3) the implication of demographic factors; (4) the effects of the integration of the community's value system; (5) the system of power, prestige, and wealth stratification; (6) the implications of role specialization and the division of labor; (7) the relations between individual temperament and character, on the one hand, and the value and role systems, on the other; and (8) the effects of various institutional arrangements, especially those regulating property and sexual and kinship relations. Certain of these areas are more comprehensively treated, and some of the levels of analysis more explicitly distinguished than others; I shall try to give some indication of these variations in the discussion that follows.

Before turning to these, however, it will be helpful to consider Plato's conception of social disunity in a general way. His conception of this is sometimes much more metaphorically rich and suggestive than it is logically clear and precise. He communicates a diffuse image of his meaning that has both organismic and logical resonance. The one has somehow become many and is no longer a single whole; the unity of communities is likened to that of individual persons, and social disunity conveys an image of dissolution, like the dismemberment of an organism after death. Social disunity is also like the separateness of particulars that have lost unifying contact with their transcending communality.

Disunity, in Plato's treatment, suggests a dispersion of parts hitherto connected and their subsequent inability to react to a stimulus in either the *same* way or in an effectively integrated manner. (Plato himself, however, does not make the last distinction systematically; he tends, instead, to treat the two ways of reacting somewhat interchangeably.) Disunity also seems to be associated with the dissolution of the hierarchical arrangements within the system. The old controlling centers no longer control. In the result, the parts behave in an erratic and disorderly manner, in at least two senses: first, that they are lacking in form, pattern, and predictability—they are unlawful and capricious; second, and partly as an implication of the first, that they are mutually inhibitive or injurious—they are in conflict. Strictly speaking, therefore, it is not so much with social disunity alone as it is with social disorganization or disorder that Plato is at bottom concerned; indeed, his is the first comprehensive formulation of the problem of social disorder in Western society.

We now need to look somewhat more closely at the symptoms of social disorganization and the foci around which they grow, moving from diffuse image to sociological specifics. Certainly it is unmistakable that in Plato's diagnosis of social disunity he takes one of its central characteristics to be *dissensus*, in the sense of a diversity of views among the city's population. Much of the trouble, that is, is seen as deriving from the fact that people have different rather than like views.

This conception of social disorganization is as central to the *Republic* as it is to the *Laws*. In the former, for example, Plato remarks that all ought to be ruled by the same principle. Preferably, they should accept or give voluntary consent to this principle, but if they do not, then they should at least be commonly constrained to comply with it: "[E]veryone had better be ruled by divine wisdom dwelling within him, or, if this be impossible, then by an external authority, in order that we may be all, as far as possible, under the same government, friends and equals." [12] In a discussion of the ideal Republic's Guardians, or ruling class, Plato indicates that a community of values—a consensus concerning what is dear—is important because it yields *common* gratifications and deprivations so that one part does not rejoice when another grieves: "All will be affected as far as may be by the same pleasures and pains because they are all of one opinion about what is near and dear to them, and therefore they all tend towards a common end." [13] Similarly, in the *Laws* he insists that the young be trained so that "with one mouth and one voice they must all agree." [14] (Clearly, if the fault springs from diversity of opinions, the therapeutic aim must be to elicit a similarity of views, to unite, in this distinct sense, the city.)

DIFFUSION

The importance that Plato attributes to dissensus can be inferred both from the diversity of the remedies with which he proposes to correct it, and from the variety of diagnoses he makes concerning the foci around which dissensus develops. Diversity of views may, for example, stem from contact with or diffusion of beliefs from other cities. Foreign beliefs may be brought to the city by citizens returning from their travels, especially if the beliefs have not been cautiously appraised. They may also be brought by aliens who come to settle and work in the city (of the *Laws*) and by traders coming to do business. These persons should, therefore, be subject to close surveillance and restriction, lest any of such strangers introduce any innovations.[15]

For related reasons, Plato would require the city itself to be built ten miles distant from the sea, for the sea brings trade and, along with it, new customs that may make the city unfaithful to itself.[16] The habits generated by trade and mercantile occupations are viewed with particular suspicion. The city is to be primarily for farmers, shepherds, and beekeepers.[17] In the city of the *Laws,* the ruling citizen's income is to derive mainly from agricultural activities; in the *Republic,* he apparently is not to be associated with any kind of economic activity but is to devote himself exclusively to ruling.

INNOVATION AND INVENTION

It was, however, not only the importation of diversity through cultural diffusion that Plato saw as disruptive of unity but also the ordinary alteration of established activities by internal innovation and invention. In the *Laws* especially, great stress is placed on fixing the routines established in a variety of areas and on making them as resistant to change as possible. For example, the specification of procedural laws is left to junior legislators; once having laid them down and "having made them unmovable, let them live using these which now have due form." [18]

It is not only for the solemnities of law, however, that Plato seeks fixity. Even the entertainments of adults are expressly held to be unchangeable once they have been developed in detail by the law wardens of the city: "[C]hange nothing pertaining to singing or dancing, and so this very city and citizens spending time in the same pleasures, being as like as possible, live well and happily." [19]

Moreover, it is not only the entertainments of adults but especially the games of children that have to be protected from change, for the latter, too, have serious repercussions upon laws and institutions:

[G]enerally no one has observed that the plays of childhood have a great deal to do with the permanence or want of permanence in legislation. For when plays are ordered with a view to children having the same plays, and amusing themselves after the same manner, and finding delight in the same playthings, the more solemn institutions of the state are allowed to remain undisturbed. Whereas if sports are disturbed, and innovations are made in them, and they constantly change, and the young never speak of their having the same likings, or the same established notions of good and bad taste, either in the bearing of their bodies or in their dress, but he who devises something new and out of the way in figures and colours and the like is held in special honour, we may truly say that no greater evil can happen in a state; for he who changes the sports is secretly changing the manners of the young and making the old to be dishonoured among them. . . .[20]

[A]ny change whatever except from evil is the most dangerous of all things. . . . The legislator must somehow find a way of implanting . . . reverence for antiquity. . . . People are apt to fancy, as I was saying before, that when the plays of children are altered they are merely plays, not seeing that the most serious and detrimental consequences arise out of the change [and] not considering that these children who make innovations in their games, when they grow up to be men, will be different from the last generation of children, and, being different, will desire a different sort of life, and under the influence of this desire will want other institutions and laws.[21]

Plato's attitudes toward change and toward disunity are so closely connected as to be almost indistinguishably fused. Change is feared because it induces dissensus. Further, it becomes a threat almost in and of itself, since the cities of the *Republic* and of the *Laws* will be for the best (or the best possible) and all change will thus be toward, rather than away from, evil. Once the city is established, therefore, all change is prima facie suspect; the citizens, instead of valuing the new or aiming toward progress, should realize that change cannot be introduced freely but must be carefully controlled and scrutinized.

In his desire to cultivate a reverence for antiquity, Plato seems to be a traditionalist; that is, he seems to aim at instilling a respect for things simply because they are old rather than because they are best, or the best possible, considering what men are. Yet he is scarcely the conventional traditionalist, for he proposes profound novelties in the customs and institutions of his planned city, even in the *Laws*. He by no means calls for reverence toward all Hellenic institutions as they are. His basic attitude seems to be: Once we have rationally revised institutions, rationality will further require that we deliberately cultivate traditionalistic sentiments toward the new institutions, lest people change them in ways that can only be for the worse. This, in turn, premises that the rational appraisal of communal disorganization can and will produce only one, unchanging, eternally valid diagnosis and therapy.

DEMOGRAPHIC FACTORS

It is in the interests both of social unity and of permanence that Plato concerns himself with the ethnic character and the population size of his proposed cities. Speaking of population, he remarks, "I would allow the state to increase so far as is consistent with unity." From similar considerations he addresses himself to the city's ethnic composition, observing that "there is an element of friendship in the community of race, and language, and laws, and in common temples and rites of worship." [22] He is also mindful, however, that colonists of common antecedents "are apt to kick against any laws or any form of constitution differing from that which they had at home." [23] It is clear that, in invoking these ethnic considerations, Plato is stressing not the significance of a racially based biological affinity but the cohesion-inducing force of what social scientists would now characterize as a common "culture"; that is, he is stressing learned characteristics rather than those biologically transmitted.

Concerning population size, Plato insists in the *Laws* that the citizenry should number 5,040—this specific number being justified because it has so many divisors—and that to citizens alone, as in classical Athens, should land be given. The "number of families should be always retained, and neither increased nor diminished." [24] This is to be accomplished in various ways. For one, Plato proposes that the ancient testamentary arrangements be changed so that the land is not divided among all sons but, rather, is transmitted to only one of them chosen by the father. The other sons are to be given to families lacking them, while daughters are, of course, to be disposed of by marriage. (It is notable that Plato does not remark upon the possible consequences for the unity of the nuclear family, and especially for the father–son relationship, if the father is to give his land to his one best-beloved son. There is little reason to believe that Plato is unaware of the disruptive consequence this proposal might have for the family but rather more reason to believe that it is a cost he is willing to pay, or to cope with in other ways, on behalf of civic unity.) Birth control measures will also be encouraged by "rewards and stigmas." Should all these measures fail to control the population and prevent its increase, there remains, Plato notes, the long-familiar method of colonization.

INTEGRATION OF THE VALUE SYSTEM:
CONCRETE VALUES

Plato also repeatedly examines the ways in which values and the integration of value systems are implicated in the maintenance of social unity or the production of disunity. As previously noted, he believes that discord is particularly likely where men's values differ—where, through ignorance, men lack true knowledge of the singular nature of the good and, instead, hold diverse notions of justice. For Plato the problem of values derives in part on the practical level, from his polemic against sophistic relativism; he wishes to reconcile differences and conflicts concerning values—to resolve their competing claims—by discerning a single system of values of eternal validity.

The integration of such an ideal value system is not considered problematic but is taken as given by Plato; for being perfect it will have all the attributes of perfection, including integration. The integration of value systems is problematic for Plato not on the level of an ideal and unstipulated "Good" but, primarily—insofar as he accepts and is oriented to them —on the concrete level of the traditional values of Greece. These being various and not one, and being traditional, have not ordinarily been examined in their relations with one another. One way of conceiving of this value-integration problem is as a problem of meshing the quiet values—most particularly, justice—with the older, more traditional aristocratic emphasis on individual competition, in which success or avoidance of failure is deemed paramount. Another and similar way of conceptualizing this value-integration problem is as a problem of reducing the community-disruptive consequences of the individualistic quest for fame by strengthening cooperation-sustaining values, particularly loyalty to the group.

In another way, the problem of value integration presents itself as the problem of reconciling groups that are oriented to different values; for example, the mercantile group, with its greater stress on pecuniary acquisition, and the aristocratic group, with its greater concern for honor and reputation. Still another layer of the value-integration problem is, in more generic terms, the problem of integrating social interaction or individual action when there is a diversity of concrete values, all or several of which may have some claim in a given situation.

Plato's strategy of value integration is diverse, and he moves in on the problem from many directions. First, he seeks to legitimate the newer cooperative values by fusing them with and interpreting them in terms of certain traditional values. For example, he interprets justice in terms of the venerable value placed on restraint and temperance, or "nothing too much." At the same time, he distinguishes his own views from older interpretations of justice as retribution, which would be consistent with the honor-oriented value system; he also opposes an interpretation of justice as equality, which would be consistent with the value-orientations of mercantile or at least debtor groups. Thus Plato seeks a reinterpretation of justice by replacing divergent, conflict-generating conceptions of it with one emphasizing the venerable virtue of temperance.

Similarly, he seeks a reinterpretation of competitive values by calling for a new kind of contest, a competition for true virtue, in which the saving of one's *soul* is the new and highest laurel wreath granted to the victor. In brief, Plato seeks to sublimate the older competitive motivations and to place them in the service of the new, cooperative values.

At the same time, Plato also places an explicit stress on the value of social unity as such, an emphasis which can be understood as in part an effort to inhibit the older values which often subverted civic unity and loyalty on behalf of individual fame and honor. He counterposes an emphasis on civic loyalty and the priority of the group to that of the individual and his private interests and seeks, in effect, to integrate the value system by establishing one value—namely, loyalty to the community—as superior to all others.

In this vein, he expressly proposes that the man who respects and obeys the laws of the city be honored—formally and ceremonially, as well as in other ways—above all others. The honor to be given those respectful of the law is deliberately set above the older aristocratic value on individual bravery:

> Let this then be the law, having an ingredient of praise, not compelling but advising the great body of the citizens to honour the brave men who are the saviours of the whole state, whether by their courage or by their military skill;—they should honour them, I say, in the second place; for the first and highest tribute of respect is to be given to those who are able above other men to honour the words of good legislators.[25]

And, again, Plato holds that the state must not be entrusted to people on the basis of their wealth, their strength, their stature, or even their birth; "but he who is most obedient to the laws of the state, he shall win the palm; and to him who is victorious in the first degree shall be given the highest office and chief ministry of the gods." [26]

It is clear then that Plato is seeking to mobilize the older contest values, stressing individual honor and fame, and to channel them into activities conducive to loyalty to the city.

> Let every man, then, freely strive for the *prize* of virtue, and [he adds with a critical eye on the traditional contest system] let there be no envy. For the unenvious nature increases the greatness of states—he himself *contends* in the race, blasting the fair fame of no man; but the envious, who thinks that he ought to get the better by defaming others, is less energetic himself in the pursuit of true virtue, and reduces his rivals to despair by his unjust slanders of them. And so he makes the whole city to enter the *arena* untrained in the practice of virtue, and diminishes her glory as far as in him lies [27] [My italics —A.W.G.].

LAW AND ANOMIA

Plato's stress upon conformity with the written and positive law—his direct focus on conformity to law as an autonomous concern—rather than only upon the spirit, reason, or values embodied in law, may itself be regarded as a mechanism for coping with the malintegration of the value system. The laws are to hold for all individuals and all groups regardless of their different values or beliefs and even though they have different social functions and roles. The laws thus serve to integrate groups with different values by subordinating them to the common code.

Further, if individual decision-making is oriented first to the laws, instead of to values, it may escape the dilemmas and uncertainties that derive from an unintegrated value system: decision-makers may bypass the malintegrated value system by referring first to the codified stipulations of the law. This analysis of the functions of *positive* law is not, so far as I am aware, one that Plato himself makes expressly. It does, however, seem consistent with the substantive content of the laws he propounds and with the problems to which legislative effort is to be directed.

It is not to be supposed, however, that Plato's concern with law has implications for value systems only in terms of their integration or malintegration; for a diversity and malintegration of values is not the only problem on which value systems can stumble. There is the further, and perhaps more elemental, difficulty of the extent to which men have any values at all; people can in short be normless or *anomoi*. *Anomia*, or lawlessness, is one of the further important foci of social disunity to which Plato attends. He insists that all men, rulers no less than others, must accept and subordinate themselves to the law, for "upon such service or ministry depends the well- or ill-being of the state. For that state in which the law is subject and has no authority, I perceive to be on the highway to ruin." [28]

Nor is the "law," whose lack of authority leads to community ruin, to be conceived of solely as the written, formal law. As will be noted later, Plato is also concerned with the failure of informal, unwritten law, although like most Greeks of his time he often treats the two together. Here, however, I wish to note only that Plato's concern with the development and use of law is in part a response to the declining hold of traditional values, as well as being a response to the malintegration of value systems. Explicated laws serve to provide a framework for individual decision-making and facilitate cooperative social interaction even with the waning of loyalty to traditional values. Laws may thus, in effect, serve in part as a substitute for waning values.

OTHER VALUE-INTEGRATING MECHANISMS

There are still other ways in which Plato proposes to modify the functioning of the community's value system with a view to strengthening it as a source of community integration. In the *Republic,* for example, he assigns the responsibility for certain values to different parts of the planned community—courage, for example, being the special virtue of the soldiery, and wisdom of the ruling Guardians.[29] He further holds that certain other values, such as temperance and restraint, should be common to all groups and classes within the city. In brief, some values are to be productive of social integration by facilitating a division of labor and contributing thereby to an organic solidarity (in Émile Durkheim's sense), while others are to do it by contributing to the similarities of all and conducing thereby to a mechanical solidarity (again in Durkheim's terms).

Thus far I have focused on the rhetorical devices and the proposed social rearrangements through which Plato seeks to remedy the value system, better enabling it to contribute to social unity. But Plato's deep concern with the problem of the value system's malintegration is expressed not only in these practical ways but also in the more purely theoretical aspects of his work. It is one of Plato's intellectual aims to integrate the several historically concrete virtues by organizing them hierarchically in some rank order of merit. In the *Laws,* for example, Plato remarks that wisdom is the leading virtue, followed by temperance, and the two together are held to give rise to justice, which is followed by the fourth virtue, courage.[30] (This aristocratic, *agathos* value is clearly given a place, but a subordinate one.) In another connection in the *Laws,* he again stipulates the "greatest virtue," characterizing it here, however, as "loyalty in the hour of danger." [31]

Plato also seeks to integrate the various concrete virtues by searching for their communality, the single shared dimension which distinguishes them as "virtues." Indeed, many of the dialogues are concerned with the way in which the several virtues can be both "one and many" and in the *Laws* it is emphasized that the rulers of the city must be persons who know "what that principle is which is the same in all the four [virtues]." [32]

SOCIAL STRATIFICATION: THE POWER, PRESTIGE, AND WEALTH HIERARCHIES

Plato also pursues his effort to account for social disunity into an analysis of the system of social stratification. He commonly associates social disunity with the failure of the once central and leading social agencies, and he clearly regards their inability to retain effective control over the formerly subordinate parts of the community as a key focus of social disorganization. Disunity of the system is especially evidenced by the dissolution of its inner hierarchical arrangements. Indeed, much of the community's lack of integration is seen as a failure of the system of authority along with a corresponding default of obedience. In this vein, Plato remarks, in the *Republic,* that in a democracy "the son has no respect for either of his parents; and that is his freedom, and the *metic* is equal with the citizen and the citizen with the *metic,* and the stranger is quite as good as either." [33]

If social disunity for Plato means the dissolution of the community's authority hierarchy, it also means disunity and *dissensus* most particularly within the ruling class itself. Although he conceives of the community as an organic entity, as a system of interdependent, mutually influential parts, Plato never assumes that all the parts are *equally* influential in their effects upon the system as a whole. He consistently maintains that the character of a State is especially influenced by the character, aims, and competencies of its ruling class and that, correspondingly, the city-state's problems, as well as its attainments, depend more on its rulers than on others. Indeed, it is because of this assumption that the larger part of the *Republic* and the *Statesman* center on the disposition, selection, training, and organization of the ideal city's ruling elite.

As Plato remarks, even a small ruling elite can maintain a stable polity if it is united. Changes result from *dissensus* among those holding office: "Clearly, all political changes originate in divisions of the actual governing power; a government which is united, however small, cannot be moved." [34] It is on the ruling element, both in the city and in the soul, that so much of the outcome depends.

Plato is also deeply concerned with the interplay of the power, prestige, and wealth hierarchies and with their role in the maintenance or the disruption of communal integration. In particular he wants prestige or honor to be given primarily on the basis of individual achievements, in terms of the basic virtues previously mentioned, and—later in the *Laws*—on the basis of conformity to law itself. One of the net effects of such an arrangement is to disjoin the prestige from the power hierarchy and, most especially, from wealth, and there is no question but that Plato deliberately intends the latter separation in particular. Although not in the manner of primitive Christianity, Plato regards wealth and virtue as incompatibles: "I can never assent to the doctrine that the rich man will be happy—he must be good as well as rich. And good to a high degree and rich to a high degree at the same time, he cannot be." [35]

Wealth as such, he says, is indifferent to virtue; it can be acquired or spent in a manner that is both just and unjust. Although critical of the pretensions of the well born, Plato never says anything quite so caustic about *their* virtue, and it is evident from his subordination of oligarchical governments of the merely rich to timocratic governments of the nobility—about which, more later—that he does not regard them as equally degrading.

While Plato seeks to disjoin the prestige from the power and wealth hierarchies, his conception of the relation between the last two is somewhat more complex. In the *Republic,* his tendency is to isolate the ruling Guardians from all economic activity, and indeed, there is a similar tendency in the *Laws.* In the *Laws,* however, it appears that the ruling class may have certain limited economic involvements, particularly agricultural, although the actual physical labor required by them is to be done by slaves. The citizens in the *Laws* are, however, expressly and firmly excluded alike from mercantile or trade activities and from the crafts; their vocation is to be the pursuit of virtue and governance.

In the *Republic,* the Guardians are simply to have their needs provided for them, and are to be similar in wealth or class status. In the *Laws,* however, wealth differences among the citizenry itself are provided for and permitted. Plato insists, nevertheless, that firm limits be placed on the economic differences to be allowed, retaining his emphasis on the need for common experience and unity within the ruling class. Specifically, no citizen may have more than four to five times as much wealth as the poorest, and anyone obtaining more than this is to assign the surplus to the city. If he does not make this disposition voluntarily, then he becomes liable to legal charges which, if proved true, require him to surrender half of his excess wealth to the person initiating the charge.

As noted, Plato's *Laws* provide that the citizenry will be the only landed group within the city, and in this manner he links the wealth and power hierarchies. This linking is explicitly reinforced by the provision that wealth is to be made a criterion for voting and for holding certain offices; offices in the city, taxes, and civic benefits must be allocated in a manner "proportioned to the values of each person's wealth, and not solely to the virtues of his ancestors or himself, nor yet to the strength and beauty of his person, but also to the measure of his wealth or poverty." [36] The net effect of the stratificational plan in the *Laws* is a somewhat closer correlation of the established wealth and power hierarchies than that in the *Republic,* where the stress is on the insulation of the rulers from wealth in particular and from economic activities in general.

On the other hand, in the *Laws* power and prestige (or honor) are not so closely connected as they are in the *Republic,* although some positive correlation is expected and is regarded as desirable. Both in the *Republic* and in the *Laws,* however, a separation between wealth and prestige is insisted upon polemically. In both dialogues, Plato's intent seems to be to bring the prestige system and the value system closer together. Honor or prestige is to be given primarily for individual performance in conformity with the prescribed values, rather than for possession of wealth or high birth. Stated otherwise, the prestige system is increasingly differentiated and made more autonomous from the other two stratificational systems, wealth and power.

ROLE SPECIALIZATION AND THE DIVISION OF LABOR

Another of the central foci in Plato's analysis of social disunity is that of role differentiation and specialization. Plato never employs the term "social role," and it should be remembered constantly that we are always groping for his meaning through the dim devices of translation. However gifted the translator, these are at best approximations, and there are often no really suitable English equivalents of his Greek. Nor, of course, does Plato engage in role analysis on the same, explicitly generalized level that is found in modern anthropology and sociology. Nevertheless, he does get well beyond a start in distinguishing role analysis from other levels. He notes, for example, that the mercantile and menial economic or occupational specializations and certain stratificationally located roles, such as the slave's, are conducive to distinctive styles of thought.

Much of Plato's role analysis takes place through his emphasis on the division of labor. Indeed, he is at pains to *generalize* the significance of the division of labor, stressing its fundamental importance as a requisite for the maintenance of the urban community and applying it not only to the economic sphere but to political activities as well. He repeatedly indicates that social integration no less than economic efficiency depends directly upon (what he construes to be) a proper division of labor. Like Durkheim some two thousand years later, Plato is fully aware that a highly specialized division of labor contributes to social cohesion by creating a mutual interdependence; and like Durkheim, Plato is also aware that the effects of the division of labor upon social integration depend heavily on the way in which the specialized roles are assigned.

There are, of course, many expressions of Plato's concern with the last, ranging from his interest in the selection, testing, and training of the Guardians to the mechanisms of upward or downward mobility in the ideal Republic for those who have been misplaced in the class structure. Equally important in this connection is Plato's maxim "one man, one task." He insists that in their economic or political activity men should do only one thing. He holds that if the city's division of labor follows this rule, individual men and the city as a whole will *be* one thing, or integrated. Failing this, they will be disunited and disrupted. Plato's focus is on the specialization of *persons*—particularly in their roles as rulers or ruled—rather than solely on the specialization, or the limitation of authority and competence, of the *roles* themselves, which he tends to regard as given. Plato not only holds that certain roles require special aptitudes and competencies, and that persons lacking in them should be excluded from the roles, but also and more importantly that a person should perform only that one role for which he is best suited by nature and training. In particular, Plato opposes multiple role involvements in the public and economic spheres.

It is particularly in his analysis of justice that Plato clarifies the place of the division of labor as a focus of social disorganization. And since it is in connection with his analysis of justice that he makes the single most probing diagnosis of the problem of social disorganization, we should give this extended attention here.

ON JUSTICE

The Greek concept of justice, or *dikē,* referred in its early Homeric usage primarily to the way things were. It meant the "way of" things, the "way of" the world. In short, at first it meant the mores, and it could refer to either men or nature, without distinction. One could speak of the *dikē* of a colt, which might be to run playfully, or the *dikē* of a king, which was to rule pridefully. Only gradually did the concept lose its predominant meaning as the customary and come to take on an implication of moral obligation, of what should be. Gradually, as custom was no longer given the wide consensual validation that it had in the viable tribal society, and as social differentiation brought increased conflict, *dikē,* the traditional way, also came to mean that which is right and proper; it came to refer to a man's due, to what is owed and owing. What *has* been done comes to mean what *should* be done, when men were no longer so likely to do it.

As early as the Homeric literature, there were indications that the customary way, *dikē,* and the desired way were beginning to diverge. In the *Odyssey,* for example, Penelope remarked that her lord was not " 'overweaning' as is the *dikē* of lords." Also, Eumaeus spoke of the *dikē* of serfs like himself, "who go ever in fear"; apparently fear was the expected but not the preferred or desired thing to a serf. Out of this growing tension between the desired and the customary—and as a way of bridging them—emerged the conception of *dikē* as desir*able,* as the ought to, the should, and the right. That which was "*ordained*" was beginning to split into two parts: necessity and morality; constraint and propriety.

That which was desired, when at variance with current practice, was given force by the claim that it was not the individually arbitrary or the selfishly advantageous. Its suprapersonal, nonpartisan validity was vouchsafed by an imputed divine sanction. After Hesiod, *dikē* came to be associated with a religiously or supernaturally sanctioned principle. Those who failed to do *dikē* received punishment from Zeus, who, as Hesiod warned, had "thrice ten thousand spirits, watchers of mortal men, and these keep watch on judgments and deeds of wrong as they roam. . . . Keep watch against this, you princes, and make straight your judgments, you who devour bribes." The appeal to justice in Hesiod came to be an appeal from, and an effort to remedy, the social status quo. The appeal to justice was a *rhetoric* of exhortation to those whose behavior in the here-and-now fell short of what was desired.

I previously noted that the Pythagoreans conceived of justice as being a kind of equality, a squared number, and of retribution as the remedy for injustice. Democritus also tended to treat equality and justice as interchangeable and to interpret the latter in terms of the former. Plato, however, comes to stress the transcendence of justice over equality, conceiving what is just to be equal rather than what is equal to be just.

Plato opposes the traditional Greek emphasis on reciprocity and retribution—on paying one's debts and returning good for good and evil for evil—with his own concept of justice. In reply to Simonides, who says that justice is "to pay back what one owes," Socrates, interpreting this as entailing retribution, replies that it is always unjust to harm someone, whether friend or foe. He is essentially, at least in this connection, conceiving of justice as "goodness," that is, as doing no harm to others, rather than as behavior that varies with the behavior of others toward oneself. This seems in part to be an effort to oppose other-directedness and serves to extricate the individual's behavior toward others from control by factional pressures, perhaps thus mitigating the development of vicious cycles of social conflict.

Plato also tends to associate justice with lawfulness: the man who acts in accordance with law, or *nomos,* is just. Socrates therefore emphasizes that, although the law has been mistaken in condemning him, he still feels obliged to conform to its decision. Yet there is still an element in his outlook that is not yet entirely removed from the claims of reciprocity, for Socrates indicates—in the course of a dialogue with the law incarnate—that the law has a right to demand conformity from him in part because of all that it has given him: because it provided a sheltering framework for his parents' marriage and his own birth and because it educated him.

ANOMIA AND JUSTICE

If, in the Platonic view, there is the assumption that justice and conformity with law (*nomos*) have certain communalities, there is also the corresponding assumption that injustice is linked with the unlimited, unbounded, or lawless and that the unjust man is the *anomos* man and injustice is *anomia.* Plato uses *anomos* as a synonym for anarchy, or lawless and disorderly social organization. (This relationship between *anomos,* on the one hand, and the lawful and just, on the other, is also found in Herodotus, who used *anomos* as an antonym of justice.) [37] It is in some part because Plato associates democracy with anarchistic liberty, with an *anomia* bordering on the licentious, that he opposes it. "They cease to care even for the laws, written or unwritten," [38] he complains of democratic cities. Clearly, what Plato seeks is not so much liberty but the elimination of *anomia* and the establishment of social order and restraint, in political as in other matters. "Anarchy," he insists with the fervor of a Pythagorean, "must be extirpated from the entire life of all mankind and from all the breasts of men." [39]

Linked to his distinction between justice and injustice is a series of more or less explicit and corresponding dualisms: order versus disorder, temperance or restraint of the appetites versus intemperance and emotional excess; lawfulness versus lawlessness, anarchy, or *anomia.* (These affect-laden polarities also resonate with our own previous distinction between the Apollonian and the Dionysian. Indeed, from the Platonic viewpoint, the very quintessence of vice is intemperance, a lack of emotional discipline, the concrete paradigm of which would seem to be the orgiastic ecstasy sought in the Dionysian tradition.)

THE DIVISION OF LABOR

So closely linked is self-restraint (or "limit") to justice, in Plato's view, that he further explicates justice to mean confining or limiting oneself to one's own tasks. The city, in his view, has its origin in the advantages accruing from the division of labor and from the mutual need that men with different abilities and skills have for one another. If justice is to reign in the city, each man must confine himself to his own specialization; each must mind his own business, doing no more than what his natural talents and his education permit him to do well. This aspect of Plato's conception of justice as entailing a division of tasks among different persons is similar to views apparently current among Pythagoreans of the late fifth century and fourth century B.C. "Every man has a duty which it is his regular task to perform and he will by performing it preserve the harmony of the universe." [40]

It is assumed here that an individual can do only one thing well. Doing justice, therefore, is limiting the person to the place and station for which he is best suited. Being just is knowing your place and doing your best in it, leaving others to perform the roles for which they are suited: "You remember the original principle which we were always laying down at the foundation of the State, that one man should practice one thing only, the thing to which his nature was best adapted; . . . justice was doing one's own business, and not being a busybody." [41] The ideal class system that Plato recommends in the *Republic* is, therefore, one in which there is a firm and clear specialization among the classes, such that one should rule, decree, and judge; a second assist with armed might; the third obey and work. In effect, Plato accepts and adapts the traditional Greek value on specialization to the entire system of stratification and authority—allocating dominance, enforcement, and obedience to different groups—rather than limiting or confining it to the sphere of occupational differentiation.

Not all failures of specialization are equally crucial to Plato. Those occurring in economic activities are unimportant in comparison with improper specialization along authority or class lines:

> Suppose a carpenter to be doing the business of a cobbler, or a cobbler of a carpenter; and suppose them to exchange their implements or their duties, or the same person to be doing the work of both, or whatever to be the change; do you think that any great harm would result to the State?
>
> Not much.

But when the cobbler or any other man whom nature has designed to be a trader, having his heart lifted up by wealth or strength or the number of his followers, or any like advantage, attempts to force his way into the class of warriors, or a warrior into that of legislators and guardians, for which he is unfitted, and either to take the implements or duties of the other; or when one man is trader, legislator, and warrior all in one, then I think you will agree with me in saying that this interchange and this meddling of one with another is the ruin of the State.[42]

There are, consequently, two levels in this analysis of justice. On the more general level, Plato is saying that injustice, with its concomitant discord, derives from men's failure to confine themselves to one public role—"public," for clearly he is not referring to men's familial or friendship relations—which they are competent to perform. In contrast to those Sophists who took a radically relativistic position, Plato holds an absolutist position concerning justice. It does not vary in its essential character from place to place. It is certainly not to Plato, as it is to Thrasymachus the Sophist, simply the will of the strongest; nor, again, has it to do with equality.

Justice is, rather, acting out one's communal station or role and fulfilling the obligations incumbent on anyone in that role. On a different and lower level of analysis, Plato conceives of injustice as an attempt by incompetents to exercise public authority or leadership. In this view, then, the city's problems are seen as residing in the system of public authority—in the ways in which men are recruited or gain access to authoritative roles and in the grounds on which incumbency in such roles is legitimated.

Plato's discussion of justice is the central way in which he deals with the conditions conducive to social unity. The problem of justice is the problem of social order put forward in the framework of ethical discussion. It is the problem of social conflict analyzed mainly through a discussion of what men must and should do if they wish to lead orderly lives in the city. Holding that value differences conduce to conflict and wishing to remove this conflict, Plato searches for the source of the value differences. He regards this source as primarily in men's ignorance of the nature of true universal justice and, more generally, in their neglect of ultimate values.

Clearly, then, Plato's diagnosis deals with the social problems of a community and involves a sociological interest. But even though the problems are intrinsically sociological, nowhere does Plato raise the question of the social or cultural conditions that are conducive to injustice or *anomia*. Having identified these disorders as a potentiality of humans everywhere, he does not consider whether, or in what ways, differing social systems or cultural patterns are more or less conducive to *anomia* or injustice. Most particularly, what he fails to see is that differences in power, wealth, or status may allow one party to exploit and behave unjustly and intemperately to another. (He misses this because he is committed to the polemic against the demand of certain sections of the *dēmos* for "equality.") For Plato such status differences are significant primarily as sources of divergent values—and of experiences that are conducive to disunity—rather than as creating a social framework in which one man can impose himself on another whose values and beliefs may be no different than his own, with resultant conflict and disunity despite their agreement in beliefs.

Basically, Plato conceives of injustice and *anomia* as a kind of falling away from and failure to conform with the laws that is attributable to certain individual attributes, such as men's appetites, which subvert their reason. Injustice and *anomia* are not seen as due to the specific nature of the laws or, again, to the varying opportunities for conformity with them diversely available to individuals located in more or less advantaged sectors of the social structure. They are attributed primarily to things inherent in individual character.

Although Plato does not analyze the ways in which different kinds of social arrangements are more or less conducive to temperance or *anomia,* he does regard the latter as associated with different political forms or types of states. In the *Republic,* for example, Plato arranges various types of states in a rank order of worth depending upon their correspondence with the ideal state, in which, of course, wisdom and those who possess it rule. There is, first, the rule of the best, an aristocracy, which in his view is not the rule of a hereditary nobility but a rule of the wise; beneath this type he locates the timocracy, the rule of the high-spirited—those under the sway of the *thymos* (which symbolizes timocracy as reason symbolizes true aristocracy)—whom he regards as the pursuers of fame and honor; beneath the timocracy, in terms of virtue, he places the oligarchy, the rule of plutocrats governed by a lust after wealth; then comes the democracy, in which men will do as they like, anomically pursuing one chimerical passion after another and completely at the mercy of their own vacillating appetites, until, finally, a tyranny ensues, in which one man subordinates and sacrifices all others to his selfish impulses. (Although Plato's later formulations somewhat upgrade the place of democracy, they can be disregarded for the purpose at hand.)

These successively inferior political systems correspond to progressively unworthy types of individual characters. Plato, however, does not maintain that the political system causes the individual character type, nor, again, that the two are mutually influential, each affecting the other. Rather, for Plato, *it is the individual character type that determines the type of state:* "[G]overnments vary as the dispositions of men vary, and there must be as many of the one as there are of the other; . . . we cannot suppose that States are made of 'oak and rock,' and not out of the human natures which are in them, and which in a figure turn the scale and draw other things after them. . . . [T]he States are as the men are; they grow out of human characters." [43] Indeed, earlier in the *Republic* he makes this even more explicit:

> Must we not acknowledge, I said, that in each of us there are the same principles and habits which there are in the State; and that from the individual they pass into the State?—how else can they come there? Take the quality of passion or spirit;—it would be ridiculous to imagine that this quality, when found in the States, is not derived from individuals who are supposed to possess it.[44]

It may be added that the progression from the perfect to the most debased states is not presented as an historically real, temporal regularity; the transition from the more- to the less-perfect manifestations of the ideal type state is a logical, not an evolutionary progression. In it, step by step, a valued quality of mind is stripped from the inhabitants until, as in tyranny, all depends on the irrational vagaries of only one man.

INFORMAL NORMS

A notable aspect of Plato's analysis of injustice and *anomia* is that it dwells little on the informal, unwritten norms or customs and it does not examine at any length the differences and relations between them and the formal, legal regulations. Plato makes little distinction between deviance from the formal laws and deviance from the informal norms of the community. In some part, this is so because the difference between these types of norms is not yet clearly perceived in Greek society at large; there is no separation of church and state or of religion and polity in Athens, and, correspondingly, no clear-cut separation between impiety to the gods and disloyalty to the state. Morality and the laws tend to be seen as one.

The relative neglect of informal, unwritten norms may, however, stem also from other historical conditions important to Greek development. The demand for written, formal laws was one of the first put forward by the *dēmos* during their urban development and was used as a device for extricating themselves from the arbitrary use of power by the early tyrants. Access to the law was from then on available to all for independent scrutiny, and the law could no longer be twisted to the shifting needs of rulers.

The development of urban law served also to liberate the individual from the older kinship arrangements—the *genē,* the *phratriai,* and the tribes—and from the authority of their heads, who had earlier been invested with an arcane knowledge of the sacred *themistes,* or principles of family rule. In effect, the norms involved in the *themistes* are the nucleus of the community's unwritten traditions which might on occasion conflict with the decrees of civic authority, as suggested, for example, by Antigone's insistence on burying her brother in opposition to the king's order. The unwritten and informal traditions are essentially the viable remnants of the *themistes,* or family-centered traditions; they bear on things that are the family's. Plato, however, is primarily concerned with the city and its unity, which required the subordination of the family and was built not around the *themistes* but on the laws.

Yet Plato does note that "there is something over and above law which lies in a region between admonition and law; . . . in the education of very young children there were things, as we maintain, which are not to be defined, and to regard them as matters of positive law is a great absurdity." [45] These ancestral traditions, although unwritten,

> are the bonds of the whole state, and come in between the written laws . . . if they are rightly ordered and made habitual, [they] shield and preserve the previously existing written law; but if they depart from right and fall into disorder, then they are like the props of builders which slip away out of their place and cause a universal ruin —one part drags another down and the fair superstructure falls because the old foundations are undermined.[46]

It is notable that, as important as they are for Plato, the unwritten traditions are not to be given unthinking loyalty. They must be inspected and judged in terms of their orderliness of functioning, which, in turn, depends on whether they conform with or "depart from right." That customs are old is no supreme justification. Plato notes that people will defend almost any strange practice, even the licentiousness of their women, by saying, "Wonder not, O Stranger; this is our custom." [47]

FUNCTIONS OF FORMAL LAW

Though second best in comparison with the rule of a wise man, a rule of laws is needed; for wise men are rare and power corrupts individuals unless they serve some master such as the law. Formal laws are needed because good men may profit from instruction concerning the manner in which they can live on friendly terms with one another, says Plato. Laws are needed even more, however, because there are evil men in the world who refuse such instruction and who violate the most ancient of the unwritten traditions, as in striking their mother or father. Fearing no divine punishment in an afterlife, they need the "punishments of this world" for which the law makes orderly provision. In short, the law serves to explicate expectations and to facilitate punishment. Thus the rule of law must be developed and extended, says Plato, because men have become heedless of even the most "ancient and universal traditions," and less fearful—as, in fact, the Greeks increasingly had become during this period—of divine retribution and, indeed, less inclined to believe in the very existence of the gods. Most basically, laws are needed because

> no man's nature is able to know what is best for human society; or knowing, always able and willing to do what is best. In the first place, there is a difficulty in apprehending that the true art of politics is concerned, not with private but with public good (for public good binds together States, but private only distracts them); and that both the public and the private good, as well of individuals as of States, is greater when the State and not the individual is first considered. In the second place, although a person knows in the abstract that this is true, yet if he be possessed of absolute and irresponsible power, he will never remain firm in his principles or persist in regarding the public good as primary in the State, and the private good as secondary.[48]

All this rests, once more, on Plato's estimate of the strength of the evil inherent in man, a strength which seems to grow in Plato's estimation as he himself ages and becomes more pessimistic: "Human nature will always be drawing him into avarice and selfishness, avoiding pain and pursuing pleasure without any reason, and will bring these to the front, obscuring the juster and the better; and so working darkness in his soul will at last fill with evils both him and the whole city."[49] Here, in the *Laws,* the assumptions are that human nature's predominant disposition is toward evil and that, when unchecked by fear of divine retribution, it will overthrow ancient tradition, leaving man without a master. It is for these reasons that laws are needed. Moreover, it is in part for these reasons that laws are linked to the divine. Those who serve the laws, admonishes Plato, are in "the service of the gods";[50] while he who deserts justice is "left deserted of God; and being thus deserted . . . in a short time pays a penalty which justice cannot but approve, and is utterly destroyed, and his family and his city with him."[51]

In the *Laws* the key diagnosis of social problems is the same as it is in the

Republic: that they ultimately derive from attributes inherent in individual men—that is, from men's appetites and passions. By the time of the *Laws,* however, the dream of reason and the belief in its potency has faded. The theory of the passions is worked out in greater detail in the *Laws;* men are seen as having three basic desires, which do not include a wish for knowledge but rather involve food, drink, and "the fire of sexual lust, which kindles in men every species of wantonness and madness." [52] Man's nature is seen essentially in terms of a behavioristic psychology, as being governed by the quest for pleasure and the avoidance of pain, the two strings that the gods pull to make man, the puppet, move. Men must therefore be trained to want the good by a right conditioning of their earliest desires; their passions and the disorders they bring are to be opposed by "fear and law and right reason." [53]

TEMPERAMENT, CHARACTER, AND ROLE

Plato's diagnosis suggests then that, in part, social disunity derives from a lack of integration between the temperamental or characterological dispositions of individuals and the demands of their various social roles and values. Plato assumes that men have differences in their natural aptitudes that make them unequally suitable for different roles: "[W]e are not all alike; there are diversities of natures among us which are adapted to different occupations." [54] Indeed, he regards and deliberately uses such imputed differences (as indicated by the myth of the earthborn men of different metals) as the basic legitimation for assigning men to different social classes.

Much of the process through which the Guardian class is sifted and readied for rule is a process of testing the candidates, of exposing them to various pressures and temptations, such as alcoholic beverages, to discern whether they possess the character or temperament—e.g., gentleness to friends, harshness to enemies, keenness, swiftness, and strength—appropriate to rulers. These tests of character are above and beyond the purely educative functions of their novitiate. Education is seen as cultivating native dispositions—as polishing, tempering, and refining them—which are assumed to be transmitted hereditarily. Access to successive and superior levels of training depends upon continuing manifestation of such traits of character or temperament.

It is largely because Plato assumes these traits to be hereditary that, in the *Republic,* he stresses the deliberate manipulation and state control of mating arrangements. The Guardians in power are to pretend that matings take place by lot or pure chance alone; but in point of fact, Plato says that they would be arranged secretly so as to produce the mating of eugenically desirable couples. Those demonstrating exceptional valor in war are, in part for a similar reason, to have, as one of their prizes, more frequent opportunities for sexual intercourse, so that "such fathers ought to have as many sons as possible." [55]

So important is hereditary constitution, in Plato's view, that it may in some cases actually prevent men from leading lives of virtue. In the *Timaeus,* for example, Plato suddenly dons a physician's learnedness and pontificates:

> He who has the seed about the spinal marrow too plentiful and over-flowing, like a tree overladen with fruit, has many throes . . . and is for the most part of his life deranged; . . . his soul is rendered foolish and is disordered by his body. . . . The truth is that the intemperance of love is a disease of the soul due chiefly to the moisture and fluidity which is produced . . . by the loose consistency of the bones; . . . the bad become bad by reason of an ill disposition of the body and bad education.[56]

This brings us to education and to defects in education as a source of social disunity; for in making the previous comments on the role of native dispositions, it was not intended to imply that Plato ignores defective education as a source of pathology, but only to show that he stresses the importance of education within the unspecified and unknown limits allowable by hereditary temperament and constitution.

EDUCATION AND SOCIALIZATION

In the earlier dialogues, much stress was placed on the use of the dialectic as an agency of education or re-education, particularly of mature, adult minds. In the *Laws,* however, it is held that one of the basic functions of education—or, perhaps more properly, of socialization—is to mold character from the earliest childhood years onward so that it will be reflexively disposed to conform with the city's values and laws and will shun deviance from them. It is emphasized that this is to be accomplished by a behavioristic regimen of reinforcing appropriate responses and, also, by punishments aimed at extinguishing the inappropriate. Plato premises that the manipulation of pleasure and pain is the key instrument through which the child's mind may be educated.

> I mean by education that training which is given by suitable habits to the first instincts of virtue in children; when pleasure and friendship, and pain, and hatred, are rightly implanted in souls not yet capable

of understanding the nature of them, and who find them, after they have attained reason, to be in harmony with her. This harmony of the soul, taken as a whole, is virtue, but the particular training in respect of pleasure and pain, which leads you always to hate what you ought to hate, and love what you ought to love from the beginning of life to the end, . . . will be rightly called education.[57]

Similarly, the child's character is to be shaped by deliberately controlled chants, plays, and games, and by more formal tuition with increasing age. It is through education that men are to be shaped, *so far as they can be,* to fill the roles and to perpetuate the institutions awaiting them in adult society.

Here the emphasis is on communicating and transmitting a previously composed vision of virtue through a controlled education and socialization. The earlier dialogues, however, appear to have placed a greater emphasis on the self's own quest for an unstipulated good, through the friction of the dialectic. The emphasis was then on an open-ended search of a mind seeking its own way to a communion with the eternally perfect forms. By the time of the *Laws,* however, education is conceived as a production of minds rather than as their stimulation. It is conceived as the structuring of the person through a communally organized and rigorously controlled conditioning. In the time between the earlier dialogues and the *Laws* there seems to have been a growing transition from the stimulation of a venturesome, deeply dedicated, and relatively autonomous self toward the training of a self that has to be paternalistically protected from its own errors. From education, conceived as a challenge to an engaged and involved individual through a provocative appeal to reason, there is a transition to a training of men by the total mobilization and wrap-around of a culture bent on deindividuation.

INSTITUTIONS: PROPERTY AND FAMILY

Men cannot, however, be deindividuated so long as they make attachments to, or have possession of, things that differentiate them from others. To reduce diversity and disunity, especially among the ruling class, the discord-generating distinction between "mine" and "thine" has to be eliminated. If the Guardians are to give dedicated service to the community, the range of things to which they can make distinctly private attachments must be limited. Private vices are not expected, as a much later ideology will hold, to produce public benefits. Clearly, Plato assumes that private wealth, property, monogamy, and the nuclear family system would subvert the Guardians' dedication to the public weal, and he is therefore constrained to propose further changes on the institutional level. In the *Republic,* the Guardians are to be divorced from wealth and economic activity, while wives and children are to be in common. There is, in brief, no longer to be "my" property, "my" wife, or "my" children to divert loyalties from the community as a whole. There are to be no particularistic attachments strong enough to undermine devotion to the basic virtues or obedience to the law and civic authorities. The Guardians are to give no hostages to fortune.

This aspect of the *Republic* is commonly regarded as among the most extravagantly utopian of Plato's proposals, which is to say it is widely felt to be so greatly at variance with "human nature" as to be unworkable. Yet, there have been societies or groups in which some men have been divorced from economic institutions and activities and are devoid of wife and children, and some of them, such as the Catholic Church, seem to have manifested exceptional effectiveness and survival ability. Indeed, I suspect that it is sometimes precisely when he is being most utopian that Plato comes closest to the jugular and is being most sociologically perceptive.

Plato is not unaware of the difficulty and the resistance that would confront his proposal to deny the Guardians private property and families. He proposes this not because he expects to be popularly applauded or because he has become compulsively attached to the dreams of a fanciful imagination. He takes this tack because, *given his assumptions,* it seems that such institutional changes are sociologically necessary. If what Plato seeks is unswerving loyalty to the community as a whole, and unbending dedication to its laws and values, then he is quite right in supposing that both private property and the nuclear family will frequently be inconsistent with these objectives; for men will seek to use their economic advantages to gain preferments for themselves and for the property, the children, and the wives they regard as "mine", and they will all too readily persuade themselves that what is good for them and their families is also "good for the country."

Finally, it might be added here that Plato's proposed family and property changes are probably not so outrageous or utopian in terms of Athenian values as they are with respect to our own. Athenians were long disposed to restrict family size and tend to have only one child; moreover, their males are not so emotionally invested in females and in their wives as ours are. Plato's attitudes toward economic involvements are also more congenial to Greek values and, especially, to the aristocracy, who often regard economic pursuits as vulgar.

These, then, are some of the crucial foci and sources of social disunity, as Plato conceives them. Although he does not present them systematically, they are comprehensive in range, touching on almost all the basic levels of analysis currently considered significant in exploring the problem of social order. Now, however, I wish to stand back from the particulars of Plato's diagnosis of social problems and attempt to view the diagnosis in a somewhat more coherent manner. To do this it will be helpful to note that, although he ranges widely over a variety of social problems, he does not regard them all as equally important and does not treat them all as intellectually problematic. His central concerns can be highlighted by attempting to notice what he does not focus on and what he does not treat systematically.

NOTES

[1] Line 142 (Sir Richard Jebb).

[2] I have found the discussion of this problem in the following to be of particular value: H. L. Finch, Jr., *The Greek Idea of Limitation* (New York: Doctoral dissertation in the Department of Philosophy, Columbia University, 1951).

[3] *Parmenides*. 130C.

[4] *Euthyphro*. 7CD.

[5] *Gorgias*. 481C.

[6] *Apology*. 38A.

[7] *Charmides*. 166D.

[8] *Meno*. 88E.

[9] *Charmides*. 154C. 155D.

[10] *Republic*. 462D.

[11] *Republic*. 462A.

[12] *Republic*. 590D.

[13] *Republic*. 464C.

[14] *Laws*. 634DE.

[15] *Laws*. 953A.

[16] *Laws*. 704E.

[17] *Laws*. 842C.

[18] *Laws*. 957B.

[19] *Laws*. 816CD.

[20] *Laws*. 797ABC.

[21] *Laws*. 798BC.

[22] *Laws*. 708C.

[23] *Laws*. 708D.

[24] *Laws*. 740B.

[25] *Laws*. 921E.

[26] *Laws*. 715BC.

[27] *Laws*. 731BC.

[28] *Laws*. 715D. Cf. *Republic*. 561D.

[29] *Republic*. 431 ff.

[30] *Laws*. 631BC.

[31] *Laws*. 630BC.

[32] *Laws*. 965BC.

[33] *Republic*. 545C.

[34] *Republic*. 545C.

[35] *Laws*. 743A.

[36] *Laws*. 744BC.

[37] Both *nomos* and *anomia* seem to be increasingly used from the time of Herodotus onward. In many usages *anomia* seems to imply godlessness and impiety, and that which is irregular, inconstant, and wild, as well as being synonymous with anarchy, as Plato uses it. Among the key lexicons for tracing this development the following might be consulted with profit: Bailly, *Dictionnaire Grec-Français;* Liddell, *Lexicon of Greek and English;* Woodhouse, *Lexicon of Greek and English;* Prellwitz, *Etymologisches Worterbuch der Griechischen Sprache.*

[38] *Republic.* 563E.

[39] *Laws.* 492C.

[40] As cited in Winspear, *op. cit.,* p. 87.

[41] *Republic.* 433AB.

[42] *Republic.* 434ABC.

[43] *Republic.* 544D.

[44] *Republic.* 435DE.

[45] *Laws.* 822E.

[46] *Laws.* 793C.

[47] *Laws.* 637CD.

[48] *Laws.* 875BD.

[49] *Laws.* 875BD.

[50] *Laws.* 762E.

[51] *Laws.* 716B.

[52] *Laws.* 783A.

[53] *Laws.* 783A.

[54] *Republic.* 370B.

[55] *Republic.* 460AB.

[56] *Timaeus.* 86BC.

[57] *Laws.* 653ABC.

7

Social Diagnosis: Lacunae and Assumptions in Plato's Diagnosis

> Combinations are wholes and not wholes; drawn together and drawn asunder.
>
> —Heraclitus [1]

FROM the standpoint of a modern, there are several lacunae evident in Plato's diagnosis of the human condition. It is clear, first, that Plato does not regard war as a problem in anything like the sense that he does a dissensus of beliefs or values, disunity in the ruling class, failure of the authority system, or flaws in the social division of labor. His diagnosis centers persistently on the conditions internal to social systems or cities—on the forces that make them inwardly cohesive or disunited—rather than focusing systematically on the sources of breakdown in international or, more properly, intercity relationships.

Plato believes that civil war in the city is of greater consequence than wars between cities,[2] and that a man's conduct during a civil war is the supreme test of his character and virtue. He views wars, at least between Hellenic cities, as a kind of civil war and believes that the factors conducive to civil wars also dispose cities toward foreign wars. Plato's social theory no less than his legislation aims primarily at the prevention of civil rather than foreign wars.[3]

In this respect, modern social theory, and especially modern sociology, is all too continuous with his conceptions. It has only been recently—and under the unprecedented threat to planetary survival occasioned by nuclear warfare—that international relations have become a growing focus of research and theory in the behavioral sciences. From Plato onward, the central problem of social theory has been that of the war within cities and within societies rather than war between them. Social theory has very largely been born of civil strife.

That Plato does not make the avoidance of foreign wars his central concern by no means implies that he likes war, or seeks a society bent on military aggrandizement. From his standpoint, which is similar to that of the war-exhausted, landed upper class of Athens, neither civil nor foreign wars are desirable and, indeed, he deplores both.[4] He believes that the love of war is dangerous, and he tends to associate it with the policy of tyrants. Military victory is regarded as a necessity, not as a good,[5] and is to be arranged to contribute to the city's enduring peace. To this end, the spoils of war are to be rejected.[6]

Plato's central attitude toward intercity war seems to be that it is largely unavoidable, and it is perhaps in part for this reason that he does not make analysis of it central. Wars, he holds, derive from the cities' wish for luxury; when "they exceed the limit of necessity, and give themselves up to the unlimited accumulation of wealth," [7] they go to war. In his view, then, wars spring from the "love of money." Plato's pessimism about eliminating war is not peculiar to the *Laws;* it is also manifested earlier in the *Republic,* in which, of course, one of the main classes is to be the soldiery.

It may be that this pessimism derives in some part from his assumption that wars are rooted in men's universal bodily needs and lusts, which he regards as the ultimate source of their greed for money, wealth, and luxury. But if bodily needs are so irresistible, how then does he imagine that the whole style of life of the Republic's Guardians—which premises that effective control over the appetites can be developed—is possible? If Plato assumes that such a conquest of the body is possible only to a few, who then deservedly become the ruling elite, why are they, the effective and self-disciplined rulers, unable to lead their state away from war? The reason can only be that the other city-states surrounding Plato's ideal city will not allow it. Still living in the old way, they will behave in the old way and wage war.

This, I believe, says something obvious but important about the social unit to which Plato restricts his social diagnosis: the city-state is still the center of attention. In his view, it is to remain and indeed to become the increasing focus of men's loyalties, for the political community has to be large enough to satisfy its needs, but not too large to maintain its social unity. His diagnosis of the effects of size on social unity and his overriding concern to maintain an intense degree of communal integration, joined with traditional Greek values stressing city autonomy and reinforced by his observations of what had happened to the ambitions of the expanding Athenian empire, dispose him to diagnose Greek problems on the level of the city-state and to seek for remedies within it.

This conception of the ideal city-state as an autonomous group has, in turn, at least one interesting implication in that it disposes any realistic appraisal to assume that war is, in fact, unavoidable. Plato can only barely believe that even one of the cities of his time will be transformed according to his proposal. Indeed, this is one of the reasons why he moves from the "best" city of the *Republic* to the second-best but more feasible city of the *Laws*. Consequently, he certainly cannot think that all or most of the Greek city-states will be transformed simultaneously into either of these two cities. Plato must therefore expect that the model city will be surrounded by potential enemies. He faces the problem of building an isolated utopia in one city-state, which is not unlike that faced by those who much later will wish to "build socialism in one country."

This problem involves issues basic to any form of rational social planning. Ideally, the planners would like to control everything capable of effecting what they wish to change, an ambition especially likely to appeal to those who employ a system model of thinking or an organic metaphysics. Yet at any given moment this is "unrealistic" and well beyond the planner's resources; there are always outside influences coming from the environment which may be inimical. As a result, the planner is constrained to make his plans for internal organization even more extensive and total than he may have initially desired. Either that, or he must isolate the unit for which he plans from its surroundings, so that he can either control or exclude undesirable external influences.

The more the planner succeeds in either effecting his plans—thus differentiating the "client unit" from those surrounding it—or in isolating the client, the more his client will be perceived by its surroundings as threateningly different or "deviant." The surrounding units may come to distrust or dislike the innovating unit, at the same time that there are fewer constraints that could inhibit their hostile action toward the innovator. Conversely, the innovating unit that has sought security through isolation continues to feel dangerously surrounded and threatened, particularly if it believes that continuing influences stemming from its environs are inimical to its planned changes and, all the more so, as the environing units vindicate their anxieties by behaving in hostile ways. Certainly it is obvious to Plato, as to any Greek, that the influence of one foreign power in the domestic affairs of another is an ever-present possibility.

By focusing on the city-state and by premising that it is to remain an autonomous unit, Plato's own plans assume the continuance of an international arrangement in which war must be expected. They make the expectation of war realistic and thus reinforce the pessimistic assumptions about war with which he begins.

Though not a warmonger, neither is Plato a pacifist. Rather than focusing attention on arrangements that would prevent war or make it unnecessary, Plato aims primarily at enabling the city to fight if it must, and to win. He by no means believes that a life of virtue will suffice to protect the city. His solution to the problem of war is to prepare for it intensively—a strange utopian this.

Indeed, in the *Laws,* his preparations are so minute it almost seems that, when Cleinias characterizes the institutions of Athens and Sparta as having war as their primary aim, Plato is in effect speaking also of the city planned in the *Laws.* In the *Republic,* war seems to be the activity of a limited and specialized soldiery; or, at any rate, this aspect of it is stressed there. In the *Laws,* however, the fear of war and the preparation for it permeate the entire community.

Even children are to be given military instruction. In fact, they are to be prepared for war in the most realistic way by being taken to witness it. They are also to be taught the ambidextrous use of weapons, so that an injury to one arm will not incapacitate them as warriors.[8] Children's supplications to the gods are also to be made with military solemnity, when they are dressed in arms. For adults, gymnastic instruction and athletic contests are to be organized with a view to cultivating military skills;[9] races, for example, are to be run with weapons and armor, and there arc to be archery and javelin-throwing contests.[10] Women also are to be given military training, so that they too may aid the city in the event of invasion.[11] On one day of every month men, women, and children are all to engage in a variety of realistic war games, in which, it is expected, some will be killed. Cowardice in war is to be socially defined as so reprehensible that not even capital punishment is regarded as sufficient punishment, and the coward is, rather, to be left to live so that he may know the worse punishment of living amid the continuing contempt of his fellows. There is more than a trace of Spartanism here. Conversely, of course, the hero is to be given full honors before the gods.

The city is to live in constant preparation for war. Stores are to be kept for use during military contingencies, and a civic militia—again in the Spartan manner—is to scour the countryside and borders of the city continually to find weaknesses in its defenses and to grow familiar with its terrain. The city, in brief, is to live as an armed camp with guards ever on duty. The spirit of the military is to pervade the city's entire life. All are to give obedience to their rulers, says Plato, as if they were soldiers at war. It should be clear, then, that Plato does not regard war as unimportant. In saying that he takes it as given, we mean not that he is unaware of or neglects it, but, rather, that he gives little systematic attention to its specific sources; that he tends to reduce and assimilate these, insofar as he does examine them, to tensions internal to the city; and, finally, that he proposes to arrange matters so that wars will be won rather than removed.

POVERTY

A second lacuna in Plato's diagnosis of communal problems, which is again especially noticeable to a modern, is in his treatment of poverty, which is neither systematically attended to nor defined as a central social problem. Plato proposes no "war on poverty." As in the case of war, Plato is not unmindful of poverty's existence, nor does he deem it acceptable, let alone desirable. For Plato, however, poverty is not undesirable because it dehumanizes men or makes them suffer, or because of its physiological effects, or because it violates humanistic sentiments or involves a particularly objectionable form of social inequality. He does not regard poverty as a stigmatic emblem of an inner unworthiness or, in and of itself, as a form of injustice. After all, Socrates himself voluntarily chose a life of poverty, believing it consistent with the pursuit of wisdom. To Plato, poverty is objectionable because of its moral consequences—its effects upon social morality—rather than because he feels that it is in itself morally undesirable.

Plato dislikes poverty both because it makes men "vicious" and "mean" and, in particular, because it conduces to social disunity and civil war. He remarks that primitive or early men engaged in little or no social conflict, in part because they had an abundance of pasture and other material necessities. Since it is poverty's effect on social integration that concerns him most, he finds it comparable in consequence to, and no more objectionable than, great wealth. Poverty as such is not distinctly problematic to Plato. From his standpoint, great wealth and great poverty are alike; both are conducive to immorality and disunity, wealth leading to luxury and indolence as poverty does to meanness. Both thus generate civil discontent.[12]

Where there are extremes in either condition, the city is divided into two conflicting factions of rich and poor: "[T]he community which has neither poverty nor riches will always have the noblest principles; in it there is no insolence or injustice, nor, again, are there any contentions or envyings." [13] The primary significance of poverty for Plato, then, is not that it contributes to the cultural deprivation or physical suffering of individuals, but that it is conducive to the disruption of communities. Whatever judgment one makes of such a diagnosis, it is clearly an acute specification of the sociological significance of economic differentiation for the maintenance of social order, even if it ignores the effects of other power differences.

Essentially, then, Plato subsumes the problem of poverty under the problem of social differentiation, seeing it, together with wealth, as another concrete contributant to the disruption of social solidarity by inducing diversity and dissensus. It would appear that such a conception of poverty is most likely to be congenial to those of aristocratic origin or orientation, those who are in some measure "above the conflict" between the mercantile rich and the urban poor, or who are at least somewhat detached from, if not impartially disposed to, these two competing interests. The diagnosis contains a touch of "a plague on both your houses."

I imply above that Plato is not equally opposed to both these classes, despite his detachment from their conflict. This is so for several reasons, one being that the vices he attributes to the poor and to the wealthy do not seem equally opprobrious. In setting the luxury and indolence of the rich alongside the meanness and viciousness of the poor, he suggests that the poor are more actively detrimental to the community. Indeed, he remarks in the *Laws* that legislators must be prepared to cope with poor men who attack the property of the rich by shipping them off somewhere to form a new colony.[14] The rich, however, are merely to be chastened to behave with due moderation to the poor. Further, as previously mentioned, in the *Laws* offices are to be allocated in proportion to wealth.

Insofar as Plato has a distinct remedy for poverty, one solution is to get rid of the poor when they seek a redistribution of wealth. His second solution, if less direct, is more radical and more deeply linked with his basic diagnosis of human problems. It is to remove poverty by removing desire, for "poverty [is] . . . the increase of a man's desires and not the diminution of his property." [15] If men would only rid themselves of their bodily desires, or, at least, confine themselves to basic necessities, they would not, in effect, be poor.

This last, of course, is just a special case of Plato's general conception of bodily wants as the ultimate source of discontent and of both individual and social problems. In this sense, poverty is problematic to him in much the way that sexual passion, homosexual or heterosexual, is problematic. Plato does not, as a modern would, regard the problem of poverty as solvable by increasing the productivity of the community any more than he would regard the problem of sexual lust as remediable by increasing the number of orgasms. His solution, rather, is to restrain and control desire. Plato apparently assumes that the tensions induced by the distinction between "mine" and "thine" would not be mitigated by a general reduction of scarcity.

The strategy of increasing abundance is inhibited for several reasons. First, Plato assumes that men's bodily wants are inherently insatiable and unsatisfiable. Second, he believes that a general increase in wealth would not necessarily narrow the gap between rich and poor and thus need not reduce the tension-inducing differences among them, which is one of his central concerns. Third, a commitment to a general increase in wealth and, more generally, material objects is not only different from but incompatible with the style of life that Plato wishes men to adopt, one centering on the pursuit of virtue and the goods of the soul and an emancipation from the bodily appetites. Fourth, the effort to increase wealth would, especially if successful, produce ramifying changes in the community which, as such, are at variance with his desire to stabilize and fix its patterns. Fifth and finally, an increase in wealth would require a developing technology and a readiness to apply it for such purposes; it would require that an enhanced value be attributed to technology and its economic uses, as well as increased status and other rewards for those involved in developing and applying it to production. This last prospect is resisted in some part because it is at variance with a disdain for the "*banauson*" and with the view that participation in the industrial arts is fitting for *metoikoi* and slaves but not for free citizens whose prime occupation, as Plato says in the *Laws,* should be the production of virtue or *aretē.*

The citizen's prime activity—a life of governance on behalf of virtue—is assumed to require leisure, which in turn, Plato believes, can be supported sufficiently by the employment of slaves in agricultural enterprise. The use of mathematics and science is, from his standpoint, mainly for the cultivation of the mind rather than for the development of a wealth-producing technology. Given the existence of slavery as an institution and sufficient slaves to enable the citizen to live as he believes himself entitled to live, and so long, in fact, as use and development of the industrial arts are defined as work for slaves and *metoikoi,* then their cultivation by citizens tends to be regarded as degrading and unnecessary. It should be remembered that, when he addresses himself to the problem of poverty, Plato is not concerned with the poverty of all within the city. He is primarily concerned with the poverty of the free citizens, who may remedy their condition by the use of slaves rather than by the development of technology and the industrial arts.

In the ancient world, a notable increase in wealth could commonly derive from trade or craft manufactures and to a lesser degree from successful agriculture; but it most often and dramatically came from booty and tribute incident to success in war. In opting for an agricultural basis for the citizenry, as he does in the *Laws,* Plato is seeking a stable rather than an expanding economy. This is sought not for its productivity but for its compatibility with the style of life he believes appropriate to an elite citizenry.

In opposing trade or crafts as the work of citizens and war as a preferred policy of the ideal city, Plato rejects the swiftest route to riches in the world of antiquity. Since a central aim of his policies is to circumscribe the role of economic interests and activities, there can be little question of alleviating the poverty of all within the community by routine and peaceful methods of industrial and technological development. Under these circumstances, if one segment of the population is to be comfortable without working—as Plato believes the citizenry must be if they are to govern properly—it can be done only at the expense, deprivation, or poverty of another. But this suggests a surprising paradox: such an economic arrangement would be conducive to the very internal tensions, the very disunity in the city, whose elimination is presumably central to Plato's entire program.

SLAVERY

This issue, of course, brings us to the problem of slavery, another crucial omission in Plato's diagnosis of Greek social problems and, once more, so striking to a modern. Again, to speak of this as an omission is not strictly correct; rather, Plato makes no serious and systematic examination of it. Slavery is discussed, but from a very limited standpoint as still another indication of the weakness in the current system of social stratification and authority. Plato's basic complaints concerning slavery are that the slave is not being kept properly in his place and, as mentioned earlier, that Greeks are enslaving Greeks instead of joining together against the East. Slavery as an institution is never questioned; neither is it seen as a basic factor in the breakdown of the Hellenic social order.

Yet it might have been thought that, just as Plato resists too great a differentiation between rich and poor—because it contributes to civic conflict—he would also object to slavery as inducing an internal differentiation similarly inimical to the maintenance of civic integration, and as providing a treacherous fifth column that can be manipulated—as it is in Greece—to the advantage of a foreign enemy. Although this is consistent with Plato's other views, it is revealing that he never sees slavery in this way.

It seems clear at this point that there is something about Plato's diagnosis of social problems that still escapes us; that there is another, deeper layer to it that we can reach only by probing beyond the prima facie meanings of social unity or disunity. This becomes particularly evident when we recognize that Plato does not regard the sharp differentiation between slave and master as a hazardous source of social disunity. This is a differentiation that Plato believes must be made ever more pronounced; that it is a necessary and natural aspect of the division of labor; and, indeed, that it is an expression within the social system of a cosmic principle of hierarchy by which all things are either rulers or ruled. Far from seeing slavery as a source of

Hellenic problems and as an institution requiring radical remedy, Plato believes that it requires tightening up, so that it may better serve the citizen class and provide them with the wherewithal for the life of leisure required for governance.

Plato assumes that the citizenry's livelihood will be derived from the work of slaves, whose continued presence is taken for granted. The important question therefore is not the economic one, but rather, "What will be the manner of life among men who may be supposed to have their food and clothing provided for them in moderation, and who have entrusted the practice of the arts to others, and whose husbandry, committed to slaves paying a part of the produce, brings them a return sufficient for men living temperately." [16] It is particularly notable that Plato's conception of the slave system in the projected city of the *Laws* is not the traditional Athenian, but rather the Spartan one: the slaves will be involved in agriculture and will pay "a part of their produce." In short, the plan is modeled on Spartan helotism.

Although Plato recognizes the tensions between masters and slaves— indeed, he has no doubt that slaves will, given the chance, murder their masters—these are viewed as within the nature of things. Slavery is not regarded, as other tensions he discusses, as a source of disunity to be remedied or as a diversity to be mediated; for his entire view of the economy and the system of stratification—particularly the privileged and leisured position of the citizenry—posits slavery. In one way, he does not even view the tensions and differences between slaves and masters as an expression of a communal disunity because his image of the desirable community simply does not include the slave as a member of it. In keeping with the Hellenic citizen's image of the community, the slave, and to some extent the *metoikos,* is to be excluded from it; he will no more be a member of it than the cows, tools, or metal treasure. The community is to be the community of and for the citizens.

Plato assumes that an effective instrumental use of slaves requires not less but more social differentiation between slaves and masters, reinforcing, not mitigating, their mutual diversity and social distance. The instrumental use of slaves is further assumed to be improved if the slaves themselves are disunited deliberately by arranging it so that they speak diverse, mutually unintelligible languages.[17] It may therefore be seen that the social disunity that Plato diagnoses as the community's central difficulty is the disunity of its ruling class of slave-holding citizens. Indeed, it is they and they alone who are to be the community.

The slaves are to be diligently disunited so that they may be more effectively controlled by their masters. Slaves are to be integrated with masters by being made more usable by them through external mechanisms of control, rather than by fostering sentiments or values that will be assimilated by and common to them both—with the possible exception of the value on restraint or "measure," which means here, in effect, knowing and keeping your place. The slaves' integration with their masters is to be an integration of tool and craftsman. When Plato speaks of unity it is always implicitly unity within a slave system. Despite the variety and changes in his plans of social reorganization, this aspect is never changed in essentials; its continuance is presupposed in even the most optimistic of his plans. The social unity of the ruling citizen class functions to facilitate the subordination of the slave and the maintenance of slavery as an institution, while, conversely, the maintenance of slavery will contribute to the cohesion of the ruling citizenry.

That Plato takes slavery as a given cannot be repeated too often: this limits the range and penetration of his diagnosis of the Hellenic community's problems; this cramps the character of the remedies he proposes for them; and indeed, as we will note later, this cripples his conception of the very role of reason itself in society. If there is anything that hobbles his sociological analysis, it is his inability to be more, not less, of a utopian, and to expose slavery to systematic examination. Plato simply cannot imagine a world without slaves.

Plato's, then, is only apparently a neutral theory of social order, of society as a whole, of order-in-general; it is only seemingly a theory which impartially seeks the benefit of all. It is, rather, a partisan theory, a theory of the distinctive requisites of a society of a very specific kind, to certain of whose institutions it is tacitly, but firmly, committed. As such, Plato's social theory is the prototype of all subsequent "oligarchical" theories whose central value and problem is "order" and whose hallmark is their nominal concern with social order-in-general, even as their underlying interest is in the preservation of specific institutions that maintain the special advantages of some groups and the corresponding liabilities of others. (Similarly, "equality" is the focal value and interest of "democratic" social theories.) To look at society as a whole is not necessarily to look at it from the standpoint of all its parts. Underneath the generalizations of formal social theory there is always a concrete image of a specific, good society. In the case of oligarchical social theory, there is always some underlying image of a specific kind of elite-managed society. It is the distinctive, if unstated, requirements of this elite that establish invisible (but no less constraining) restrictions on the thrust of sociological imagination. The sweeping generalities of "large scale" social theory are the systematizations of a latent and concrete image of a good society. It is a function of modern "middle range" social theory—

where each piece of the mosaic is revealed one at a time—to conceal the existence and nature of this larger image.

PLATO ON LOVE

There is another conspicuous lacuna in Plato's diagnosis that may be considered here; and this can also tell us something about the nature of the social disunity he deplores or of the unity he seeks. Although Plato speaks well of friendship and regards it as desirable among men, nowhere does he indicate that the disunity he dislikes is due to a lack of love. For him, it is not that "love is not enough," but that love is, in itself, downright suspect. Neither in a Christian nor in any other sense does he call upon men to love one another. Essentially, Plato strives to strip love of its Dionysian qualities and to make it a thing of the mind, rather than something of the deepest emotions or of the whole, embodied man. For him the best kind of love is not the love of men for one another, but the love of pure beauty, or the contemplation of the beauty of the eternal Forms.

Rather than thinking of love as a way of making men whole again, as others of his time do, Plato regards it as akin to the pursuit of fame, as basically expressive of a quest for immortality. Like the fame won in a contest, love is man's hedge against his mortality:

> The mortal nature is seeking as far as is possible to be everlasting and immortal. . . .[18] Think only of the ambition of men, and you will wonder at the senselessness of their ways, unless you consider how they are stirred by the love of an immortality of fame. They are ready to run all risks . . . for the sake of leaving behind them a name which shall be eternal. . . . [A]ll men do all things, and the better they are the more they do them, in hope of the glorious fame of immortal virtue; for they desire the immortal. Those who are pregnant in the body only, betake themselves to women and beget children— this is the character of their love; their offspring as they hope will preserve their memory and give them the blessedness and immortality which they desire in the future. But souls which are pregnant—for there certainly are men who are more creative in their souls than in their bodies—conceive that which is proper for the soul to conceive or contain. And what are these conceptions?—wisdom and virtue in general.[19]

Plato's rejection of love as a way of mending men and making them whole reveals still further his conception of social disunity and unity: disunity does not entail a sense of individual isolation, of experienced social distance from others, or a felt loss of communion with them, or of a separation between man and man. Essentially, Plato speaks here as an Apollonian. He rejects the Dionysian quest for communion among men through love or, for that matter, through alcohol. He rejects the bond of strong feeling in favor of temperate, friendly admiration and on behalf of a measured coordination among specialists arranged in a hierarchical manner. What Plato seeks is not love but respect.

The crucial text here, of course, is the *Symposium*. To my mind it is one of the most poetically brilliant of the dialogues; it is also one of the most curious. It opens with an expression of confusion concerning the time at which the events and views reported in it are supposed to have occurred. Plato is apparently trying to say something through the point he makes of this uncertainty, but what it is remains unclear to me. It may have to do with his view of the historical authenticity of the events presented or with an uncertainty concerning the accuracy with which he renders Socrates' ideas on this matter.

The setting is a dinner party at which the speakers are to render a series of speeches in praise of love; a friendly after-dinner contest in rhetoric. The speeches are introduced by Eryximachus, who reminds the others how strange it is that all the other gods have had their encomiasts except the god of love. In this he remains essentially unchallenged by those speaking later, suggesting the Apollonian tradition among this stratum of Athenians.

Love, says Phaedrus, is great because it makes men behave honorably, for who would wish his beloved to see him behave dishonorably. Love's value therefore is that, even more than the ties of family and friends, it disposes men to virtue. It will make men dare and die for their beloved and, Phaedrus surmises, an army composed of lovers would be unconquerable. (Apparently, neither Spartan nor Theban efforts along this line confirm this view.)

Pausanias reminds the company that there are two kinds of love, the common and the divine. The divine springs from heavenly Aphrodite and is a love among men only; the common form of love is heterosexual. In some cities, we are told, in an oligarchically slanted *aperçu,* homosexual love is disliked because it is incompatible with tyranny; for the tyrant recognizes that this brings men closer together and thus enables them to resist him better. The general assumption here is that homosexual love creates cohesive bonds, among some men at least, and this in turn is incompatible with certain kinds of political arrangements.

In his own formal remarks Eryximachus makes a similar comment, suggesting that love dissolves dissensus through a reconciling of opposites. The theme of love as unifier is carried forward by Aristophanes. He relates a myth in which humans were originally animals of a single sex, from which the two sexes were split by Zeus when humans displeased him. Love, then, is the split animal's quest to find his other half, to be whole again; it is a kind of healing that leads men back to their unified and true natures. Agathon also sees love as eliminating discord, as emptying men of their disaffections; being the opposite of force, it produces an agreement that is voluntary.

Against this eulogy of love as unifier, Socrates rises to dash cold water on the impassioned encomiums. Praise, he says somewhat arrogantly, should speak the truth, and since this has not yet been done, he will do it. Love is the expression of an insufficiency and an incompleteness, he says, for it is a desire, and we can desire only what we do not possess. Those who love are those who lack. Socrates declares that he will tell his listeners what he has learned of love from Diotima of Manintineia. She taught him, he relates, that love is neither mortal nor immortal, neither fair nor foul, but something in between. Socrates acknowledges it as a mediating or unifying force, but the bridge it builds is not one between men—as the others had stressed—but between men and the gods, between the mortal and the immortal. Born of the union of Plenty and Poverty, love is poor like its mother, Poverty; it is therefore not tender or fair, but rough and squalid and always in distress. Like its father, Plenty, it is always plotting against the fair and the good, and is bold, energetic, and intriguing. It is half ignorant and half wise, always in flux and lacking in stability. It is not the other half of themselves that men seek in loving, but the continuance and reproduction of themselves in immortality. "And I am persuaded of their truth," says Socrates, speaking of Diotima's views.

In remarking that love is neither fair nor foul, Plato is saying that it is beyond good and evil. From the standpoint of one who believes that men should ever be concerned to seek and do the good, this clearly removes love from the Pantheon of virtues. In thus stripping it of moral relevance, he also casts it beyond the pale of reason and essentially leaves it, particularly in its ordinary earthly manifestations, in the laps of the gods, a divine madness which is theirs to bestow. From Plato's standpoint, ordinary love between men is tainted with every weakness that he ever sought to escape: it is expressive of the discontent of desire; it is linked to the body's imperatives; it is devoid of formful stability and is ever in flux; and it gives rise to the intemperance of lust. From a love of one another, Plato calls men to the love of the Forms, of wisdom, and of beauty eternal. It is not the feeling which unites that he seeks, but the understanding that transcends all desire.

PLATO'S DIAGNOSTIC ASSUMPTIONS

Given the comprehensive range of Plato's diagnosis of human problems and the variety of levels on which it operates explicitly or resonates implicitly, it would be easy to make it appear eclectic, that is, as deriving from diverse and disconnected diagnostic assumptions. This impression, however, would be unfortunate because for the most part it would be mistaken. Plato's diagnosis is an integral one. It stems from and entails the self-conscious use of a set of assumptions which, if never presented in single, architectured outline, are nonetheless visibly organized and relatively consistent, despite what I, along with others, take to be his increasing pessimism as he grows older. In the next few paragraphs I will briefly outline what I take to be the main assumptions he employs.

Diagnostic Rule One: Wholism

Human groups constitute some kind of a whole, and each of them, as a whole, has certain dominant tendencies that pervade it. Groups as such differ from one another because, or in terms, of these dominant tendencies. Cities which are democratic, timocratic, or oligarchical, for example, have different dominant tendencies even though, in changing from one form to another, the same men may remain members. Conversely, democracies (like timocracies or oligarchies) in different cities are essentially alike, each having recognizably common characteristics, even though each is composed of entirely different persons. In short, groups have certain distinctive properties which permeate and influence their several parts.

Yet the dominant tendencies of the social whole depend on and derive from the characters of its individual members and on the kinds of persons their characters dispose them to admire and follow. These tendencies depend particularly on the characters of those who rule. In some part, those who come to rule do so because the characters they have are congenial to the characters of the others, and, being more influential, they can guide or crystallize certain tendencies in the whole and make them dominant. The social whole, then, is seen as particularly shaped and characterized by the nature of its controlling stratum, and this in turn is viewed as dependent upon the individual properties of the members.

Diagnostic Rule Two: Relations among Parts—Hierarchy

It must be emphasized, however, that regardless of how often Plato's metaphysics lead him to stress the priority of the whole over the part, they also lead him to emphasize the principle of hierarchy, perhaps the most basic principle of organization to which the whole is seen to be subject. All wholes are so constituted that they have or require a differentiation of parts into rulers and ruled. The integrity or "wholeness" of the whole depends on the maintenance of the division of labor among these parts and on the proper performance of their respective functions of command and obedience. Plato's metaphysics thus dispose him in two directions, one stressing the priority of wholes and the other stipulating parts and their relationship in hierarchical terms.

While committed to viewing groups as wholes composed of hierarchically related parts, Plato also, and quite insistently, wants to make the point that the state of the whole is not dependent equally on all the parts but is contingent particularly on one of them, the ruling part, with whose abilities and character he most associates the fate of the whole. It is in this vein that he stresses that cities will not turn from evil until philosophers become kings and kings, philosophers. On the most general level, then, Plato is led to a somewhat ambivalent position, to stress the whole as such and to stress not only the whole's parts and relations but, most particularly, the ruling part.

There is, as a result, some theoretical tension between Plato's view of the whole as having a distinctive, indeed a superior, kind of reality to that of the parts, and his view of the whole as being dependent on the characters of its individual members. Both views are given expression, but they are not clearly integrated with one another. Certainly there is no question but that Plato sees a whole as entailing parts and their relations. In his group analysis, for example, he exhibits the social roles and strata, the specific occupations and social classes and the individual persons of which they are composed, and the ways in which they are related. Yet beyond a doubt he also believes that these parts, whether social structures or persons, are or should be subordinate to the whole. This emerges with particular clarity in the *Laws,* where Plato returns with insistence to his teleological functionalism and has the Athenian remark:

> Let us say to the youth—The ruler of the universe has ordered all things with a view to the excellence and preservation of the whole, and each part, as far as may be, has an action and passion appropriate to it. Over these, down to the least fraction of them, ministers have been appointed to preside, who have wrought out their perfection with infinitesimal exactness. And one of these portions of the universe is thine own, unhappy man, which, however little, contributes to the whole; and you do not seem to be aware that this and every other creation is for the sake of the whole, and in order that the life of the whole be blessed; and that you are created for the sake of the whole,

and not the whole for the sake of you.[20] . . . [T]he Gods . . . make all things work together and contribute to the great whole.[21]

GROUP AND INDIVIDUAL: THE PRIORITY PROBLEM

The city, then, is seen as an organic entity akin to the human person, involving both a subordination of its parts to the whole and especially to its intelligent center and, conversely, a sensitivity of the soul center to each of the parts. But health requires that the part remain subject to the center and to the needs of the whole, "for the part can never be well unless the whole is well." [22] Plato's strategy of diagnosis requires that specific social problems be seen in their context and, as an outgrowth, of the condition of the whole. A higher value and priority is given to the welfare of the whole, and there is a pronounced tendency to subordinate the individual to the larger community. Yet there is difficulty in interpreting Plato here for, vital as the whole is, he is equally emphatic that the whole group derives its character from the properties of its component parts.

The matter is further complicated because this seeming confusion is expressed on two levels. One is the most generalized, metaphysical analysis of wholes and parts discussed above. The other is a more substantive analysis of human behavior as such. Here the problem is whether Plato's conceptions of social or group structure give rise to his conceptions of personality and the individual psyche, or the other way around. With respect to the latter, more sociologically specific problem, it seems clear, even where Plato stipulates that the condition of the whole derives from that of the characters of the component members, that he himself is thinking about individual character on the model of the group or city as a whole. His argument moves from the characteristics of the state to those of the individual, from the tripartite system of social classes to the tripartite division of the soul. His argument runs that if the state is acknowledged to have or require such a class system, are we not then bound to admit that each person must have similar elements in his soul? Moreover, the strife in the soul between its higher and lower elements is regarded as akin to the strife of political factions in the city. Indeed, Plato even says that thinking, in general, is "the unuttered conversation of the soul with herself." [23]

Of similar import is our earlier suggestion that the *thymos,* the part of the soul standing between reason and the passions, needs to be distinguished from the latter two because it entails the nobler affects and sentiments, which are appropriate to the contest system and to conformity with the military virtues. The *thymos* is a characterological requisite for the proper performance of the still highly valued role of the soldier. Plato also believes that certain menial or *banausoi* occupations affect the moral and mental characteristics of their incumbents, and thus, for example, the status of the slave has a profoundly injurious effect upon his reason. Finally, in his discussion of justice, Plato asserts that the rule "one man, one task" will if followed have the beneficent effect not only of integrating the city as a whole, but of integrating the individual person.

In numerous places, then, where Plato analyzes specific instances of the relation between social structures or social processes and individual psychic or mental qualities, his assumptions seem to be, first, that the psyche reflects and is influenced by group structures, role needs, and modes of social interaction (such as strife and conversation) and, second, that the psychic states may be viewed on the model of the qualities of the group. Yet these assumptions remain unintegrated with his explicit statements to the effect that the group's character derives from that of its individual members.

Rather than pursue some logical but Procrustean solution in which both of Plato's views are allegedly integrated, I am inclined to feel that this is a genuine difficulty in his work and allow it to stand. There remains, however, the question as to why this difficulty occurs. Several not mutually exclusive reasons may be advanced, one of which may be a "geological strata" solution: the emphasis on the priority of individual attributes and the contrary tendency to explain these in terms of group structures may reflect unresolved tensions between Socrates' original stress on the individual and Plato's own greater emphasis on communal integrity and cohesion. Second, the clearest expressions of Plato's view that the character of the state derives from that of its individual members is found primarily in the earlier *Republic,* while the subordination of the individual to the whole is most accentuated in the later *Laws* and may thus reflect a genuine transition in Plato's own ideas, whatever their origin. Third, and on a different level, the tension between these two views concerning the relations between psychic and group properties may be unresolved because Plato does not use a clear-cut distinction between cause and effect and lacks a distinct analytic notion of the interdependence of variables. He thinks aesthetically, in terms of a *gestalt* or of the eternal Forms seen as wholes. If the individual person and the *polis* each have their own, separate ideal Form, there inevitably arises the difficulty of how the two are to be integrated.

On a totally different level of analysis, it may also be suggested that Plato's vacillation between the group and the individual levels is related to his social-action interests, to the fact that he not only has purely theoretical interests but is also concerned about the practical remedy of certain social problems. These action interests confront him with certain dilemmas which may be mirrored in this intellectual ambivalence.

SOCIAL THEORY AND SOCIAL ACTION

Certainly there are strong tendencies in Plato's metaphysics and in his ideological orientation that dispose him to assume that the individual is a political animal, a man of the *polis;* that a man is, has been, and can further be shaped by his community. The problem is that if men are molded by their community, how can they ever be made to seek a better city than they know? How can the sick men of a sick city build a healthy one and themselves become healthy? How can men be held responsible for living as badly as they do if the way in which they live and their total character is merely the product of heredity and a corrupt social environment?

A commitment to rational social change imposes its own imperatives. Like any thinker committed to a program of social reconstruction, Plato must hold it possible for individual men to transform themselves and their social surroundings to some extent and to make themselves and their groups somewhat different from and better than they are at present. The assumption that the characteristics of the state derive from the individual is a way of supporting the hope that men can improve themselves and their group, and it is also consonant with Plato's belief that men are to be held responsible for their actions. It assumes that there is some slippage between the individual and the group—that the individual can in some degree transcend his environment—and it thus provides some rationale for efforts to change the community. But the very objective of changing the community implies that the group affects the behavior and the minds of men, for why change the group structure unless it does? Plato's assumption that the group exerts a potent influence on individual attributes is necessary to the entire enterprise of social change. The point is that such an enterprise intrinsically assumes that planned social reconstruction can benignly affect the individuals involved and that it can be brought about or be affected by (at least some) individuals.

Plato's tendency to assume that there is a correspondence between the nature of the state and that of individuals entails, however, more than the general assumption that the individual can or does influence the state. Plato's premise is even more specific than the assumption that the kind of state that exists will in some way depend on the kind of men that exist; his narrower premise is that there is a kind of correspondence between the characteristics of the group and those of the individual, and that the group's tendencies are the mirror image of those in individual psyches. This in turn implies a conception of the way in which individual minds and their dispositions influence social outcomes: it implies a strategy of social change. It implies that the "good" state can be built only by "good" individuals—philosopher kings—whose inner condition is not only properly but previously established. Although the "road to hell" can in Plato's view be paved with good intentions in the sense that good men can be thwarted by external circumstances, the road to paradise cannot be paved with evil intentions. It is therefore very important to Plato that things be begun rightly, that innovation be started with a clear and correct model in the minds of men, and that it be preceded by an effort to delineate in detail the desired social organization.

Diagnostic Rule Three: Relations among Parts— Consensus and Interdependence

It is necessary here to return to Plato's key diagnostic assumptions and particularly to some implications of his wholistic view of groups. Although they are not necessarily mutually exclusive in all cases—indeed, he himself does not always distinguish them—it can be suggested that Plato focuses on three basic kinds of relationships that the elements or parts of a group may have with one another: (1) Hierarchical relations, in which certain parts are subject to and controlled by others that are superordinate and dominant. Since we have already discussed this at some length, it need not be reviewed in this connection. (2) Consensus, that is, possession by the parts of some like properties, such as holding the same beliefs or values; (3) interdependence, that is, a relation in which the functioning of the parts provides mutual benefits to one another, as in the division of labor. Consensus and interdependence, like hierarchy, are relations among parts which constitute them as a whole. A characteristic case of concrete sociological analysis in which both the assumptions about consensus and interdependence are implicated can be found in Plato's discussions of friendship, where he explores whether it is the like or the unlike that become friends. This example is particularly notable, as are his discussions of family relations, because they clearly reveal that his diagnosis of human relations is not to be applied only to the largest autonomous groups such as city-states or communities, but also to various other social relations and most probably to all of them. In modern sociological terminology, Plato does not limit his analysis to the "societal" level but extends it to the "social-system" level. This inference is supported by his belief that the relations between city-states can be analyzed in terms of, and depend upon, the same elements as the relations within them.

Diagnostic Rule Four: The Open System

This is not to say, however, that Plato *applies* this fundamental diagnostic precept with equal frequency to all kinds of groups, or that he regards examination of them all as equally important. On the contrary, impelled by his stress on the rule of "wholistic" analysis, he focuses on the larger social systems—most notably the *polis*—for the other, smaller social groupings are implicated in them as parts. Again, because he interprets the wholistic assumption in a realistic way (in both the technical and popular senses), he does not treat social systems as autonomous. Plato sees social systems as implicated in and affected by ecological, geographical, and, in particular, biological systems. (Notably, however, he does not concern himself with the involvement of social systems in technological systems.) In short, while he treats human groups on the most generalized social-system level of analysis, and although he treats this level of analysis as distinct and central, he does not treat it as autonomous. He does not regard the social system as closed but rather as open to other analytically distinguishable systems which, together with it, constitute the total universe, or *kosmos*. It should be remembered, however, that wholism for Plato is not a heuristic or working hypothesis, employed for its convenience, for the analytic or empirical gains it yields. Plato believes that wholism truly describes the nature of all reality, social and otherwise. In brief, Plato's wholism is a part of his metaphysics.

Diagnostic Rule Five: Functional Connectedness

Because the problems reside in a whole which consists of parts having relations with one another, Plato also employs the diagnostic assumption that a change in any one part may ramify and affect other parts. Thus, even changes in children's games or music, says Plato, may produce changes in political institutions. Conversely, a change in any one part may originate in changes in various other parts, particularly if the controlling centers do not maintain effective control over the whole.

In some sense, and Plato acknowledges that it remains obscure to him, his diagnostic precepts assume that things within the system have been arranged for the best. In the *Timaeus,* for example, this apparently applies to the original arrangement of the system by God; but it is not altogether clear whether, in the subsequent "forgetting" or corruption of the system, this remains the case.

Diagnostic Rule Six: The Inner Flaw

This last is related to Plato's further diagnostic assumption that, insofar as change occurs in nature, nature's basic drift, in contrast to the influence of

God, is toward disorder, entailing either entropy or some manner of conflict. Moreover, the disorder that develops within a whole stems primarily from its own internal characteristics, and each whole has its own distinctive vulnerabilities and pathologies.

The development of disorder is mediated by another diagnostic principle, the principle of dialectical alternation, "the truth being that the excessive increase of anything often causes a reaction in the opposite direction." [24] It is in the natural order of things, for example, that an excess of liberty passes into the excess of slavery. This point is generalized in the *Phaedo:* "Are not all things which have opposites generated out of their opposites? . . . [I]n all opposites there is of necessity a similar alternation. . . . And in this universal opposition of all things, are there not also two intermediate processes which are ever going on, from one to the other opposite, and back again?" [25] As an implication of this principle of dialectical alternation, change in the whole is seen not as having a progressive or evolutionary character, but a cyclical form in which all natural systems are born, decay, die, and are born again: "If generation were in a straight line only, and there were no compensation or circle in nature, no turn or return of elements into their opposites, then you know that all things would at last have the same form and pass into the same state, and there would be no more generation of them." [26]

These are some of the most general and metaphysical premises that Plato makes about groups as wholes; they form the basis of his more specific assumptions for diagnosing the pathologies of human systems. Thus, for example, all pathologies derive from and must be interpreted in terms of the larger wholes in which they are implicated. This is as true for headaches, which, he says in the *Charmides,* must be examined in reference to the total organism, as for political pathologies. Conversely, any localized pathology is likely to be system consequential and in time ramify outward into the whole unless corrected by the controlling center.

SOCIAL-SYSTEM ANALYSIS AND SOCIAL PROBLEMS

Several other points can be made, or deserve to be reiterated, concerning the general strategy of Plato's diagnosis of human problems. The first is that Plato concerns himself with social systems on the highest level of analysis, clearly indicating what he regards as some of their basic and distinctive requisites. Consensus or diversity in values and beliefs, of unity or disunity among the ruling class, and of the division of labor or the allocation of roles are analytic abstractions. Changes or variations in these may, depending on their direction, disrupt or stabilize the system as a whole. Plato makes a distinction between these analytic elements and such concrete phenomena as poverty or population growth, which he thinks of as "precipitants" that effect system cohesion through their effects on the above-mentioned requisites. In other words, Plato sees a distinction between manifest and concrete social problems and the intervening variables through which they affect the state of the social system as a whole. Specific, concrete, and manifest social problems are significant, but only as starting mechanisms for changes in the basic system requisites. Two different concrete social problems may disrupt a social system in the same way by their influence on the same intervening variable. Thus, for example, both poverty and population growth may produce diversity and dissensus in beliefs and, through this, social conflict or disorder.

Although Plato treats the requisites of stable social systems as a problematic and distinct level of analysis, he does not, as previously emphasized, regard the social system as autonomous. Indeed, in the last analysis, all social problems are seen as originating in bodily appetites. War, for example, derives in his view from a greed for money, which is in turn sought for bodily gratification; the quest for fame is regarded as a search for immortality to compensate for and overcome man's mortality. Men are regarded as endowed with a set of drives which, if not always specifically tissue-linked, are viewed as contingent on (what I will call) their "embodiment" and which, left to their own devices, are insatiable.

The influence of these drives is also seen to be dependent on their relation to the other parts of man's psyche, especially their reason; the root difficulty of all human troubles lies in the failure of reason to exert proper control over the bodily passions and appetites. In effect, when Plato describes how he believes human problems are generated, he focuses on and ascribes their development to the dominance of material conditions or forces over the higher and proper controlling centers of reason and mind. This, in turn, results in failure to conform with true values, to know and to do what is best. It is, therefore, not that Plato as an idealist is unmindful of the influence of material forces; it is, first, that he indeed believes that they are in fact especially potent, but only under certain conditions, and, secondly, that he disvalues them because in his view they are subversive of the good.

Plato's basic strategy for diagnosing human problems, then, is concerned not with the historically contingent and limited, but with the historically invariant and universal sources of pathology. Plato is concerned with the way in which men and groups, anywhere and at any time, can come to grief.

SOCIAL DIAGNOSIS AND PESSIMISM

Such a focus on the ahistorical sources of individual and group pathology is, in its turn, conducive to pessimism and passive resignation in the diagnostician and in his client. These can be dissonant with the distinctive role requirements of each, for these roles require their incumbents to have some hope of an improvement through active striving in accordance with a rational diagnosis.

"Diagnosis" not only attempts to define the nature and the sources of pathologies—to this extent it would differ in no way from the hypotheses of pure research—but it also involves a social relation in which the diagnostician gives some promise of help to the client. Diagnosis aims not only to understand pathology but to do something about it; it is preparatory to remedial action. It is linked to the provision of services which can in some way rationally remedy or alleviate the problem. At the very least, the diagnostician promises to do no harm to the client and to ease or remedy his travail wherever possible. To maintain his own morale and to fulfill his role responsibilities, the diagnostician must have some confidence that his knowledge and technical skill are sufficient to aid the client more than the latter could do for himself. The diagnostician's morale is, in part, a function of the extent to which he believes his own skill and knowledge will suffice to provide a remedy.

Plato's concern with the ahistorical and universal sources of human problems conduces to a view of them as massive and as eternally recurrent, ever present and always the same, and to a view that regards efforts at remedying them as running on a treadmill. Such views are a deep instigant to pessimism and passivity. To the extent that any diagnostician believes the sources of client pathology to be essentially unchangeable and rooted in the natural conditions of the system with which he must deal, and to the extent that he believes the client to be perpetually vulnerable to an essentially unalterable hazard, he may well despair.

The diagnostician who, in contrast, focuses on the manner in which a historically specific state of the system is conducive to its problems may seek for a remedy by proposing fundamental system changes and by helping the old system move from its present flawed state to a superior one. (This, for example, was Marx's response to the problem of the "internal contradictions of 'capitalism.' ")

The kinds of problems to which Plato's ahistorical diagnosis orient him, however, are not susceptible to remedy in that way; for they are not problems specific to Hellenic society which can be transcended historically, but are problems of men universally, which cannot be. Such universal problems cannot be remedied; they can only be held at bay. There can be no lasting improvement in the things that matter. Society comes to be seen as a huge sick ward composed of patients who all have terminal diseases; life itself comes to be viewed as one long illness. This, indeed, is an implication of Plato's diagnosis for which Nietzsche will not be able to forgive him. Nietzsche will see it implied in Socrates' last words, in his request that the debt he owes to Asclepius be paid—which carries the suggestion that the god of medicine has at last cured him of life, with death.

Though not solvable here on earth, ahistorical human problems can be transcended; in particular, they may be believed to be transcended in an afterlife. If Plato's pessimism is not derived from it, it is, it would seem, at least reciprocally reinforced by and related to the ahistorical character of his social diagnosis. He seeks a radical transcendence of men's universal problems by separating the soul from the body, by conceiving of the soul's survival apart from men's embodied persons, by focusing his remedies upon it, and by promising the soul a deliverance in an afterlife or another world.

CONTEMPORARY POSTSCRIPT

The issues considered above are worth exploring precisely because their relevance is not limited to Plato; they have a bearing for all social diagnosticians, for all those who today hope to use knowledge and theory about human behavior for the relief of human suffering. Clearly, those succumbing to pessimism will have their ability to realize their aspirations crippled. Either they will resign from the effort or else the ways in which they pursue it will be irrationally warped. Yet at the same time those with therapeutic ambitions for the use of social science are peculiarly susceptible to pessimism; for in contrast to "pure" social scientists, who aim only to understand, but not to remedy, human problems, the "applied" social scientist has undertaken a particularly difficult task. It is harder to change the world than simply to comprehend it, and it is, therefore, easier to fail as an "applied" than as a "pure" social scientist, at least in terms of the different standards and aspirations that matter to each. It can be conjectured, then, that seizures of pessimism are one of the serious occupational hazards of those who—like the applied social scientist—want to change the world. If his work is to be developed in a self-conscious manner, with an awareness of its contingencies, then we need extended and systematic study of the ways in which the therapeutically ambitious social scientist maintains his morale and learns to manage his own inclinations to pessimism and resignation, or fails to do so.

The development and training of serious applied social scientists who are more than facile technicians would also require that they be exposed to the human issues involved in their enterprise, among which is the balance of optimism and pessimism, and the attitudes toward these, that they are to cultivate in themselves. The social scientist who believes that his discipline can and will ultimately solve all human problems and who encourages others to believe likewise is an immature enthusiast unworthy of his calling and lacking in any sensible appreciation of the human scene. In the end he is likely to encourage expectations so nearly impossible to realize that their inevitable frustration will generate as much despair as pessimism would. The difficulty on the other side stems not so much from the compulsive pessimist as from those who, prematurely and without rational or empirical justification, allege that certain specific problems are inherent in the human condition or, for that matter, are presently unsolvable. Certainly there are such problems. It is well, however, to be sure, very sure, which are of this sort, before venturing to douse human hopes with the charge of utopianism.

I think it not too much to ask that social scientists, especially those most concerned with alleviating human suffering, strive to be men of cultivated sensibility as well as technical proficiency. One may hope that, while they will be realistically aware of the acute limitations of their own knowledge and skills and of the limits within which all men live, they will yet possess the stamina to do all they can toward the relief of human suffering, neither underestimating the possibilities nor glibly glossing over the difficulties.

NOTES

[1] Fragment 59 (Bywater).

[2] *Laws.* 629.

[3] *Laws.* 628BC.

[4] *Laws.* 622C.

[5] *Laws.* 622C.

[6] *Republic.* 422D.

[7] *Republic.* 373D.

[8] *Laws.* 795BC.

[9] *Laws.* 831D.

[10] *Laws.* 833D.

[11] *Laws.* 814AB.

[12] *Republic.* 422.

[13] *Laws.* 679BC.

[14] *Laws.* 736A.

[15] *Laws.* 736C.

[16] *Laws.* 806DE.

[17] *Laws.* 777D.

[18] *Symposium.* 207D.

[19] *Symposium.* 208–209.

[20] *Laws.* 645.

[21] *Laws.* 647.

[22] *Charmides.* 6.

[23] *Sophist.* 263E.

[24] *Republic.* 564A.

[25] *Phaedo.* 70–71.

[26] *Phaedo.* 72B.

8

Therapeutics: Planned Social Change in Plato's Theory

Whoever concerns himself with the Greeks should be ever mindful that an unrestrained thirst for knowledge for its own sake barbarizes men just as much as a hatred of knowledge.

—Nietzsche [1]

AS PLATO has a diagnosis of man's disorders, so too has he a conception of what might be done about them. He has, in short, a therapy. He has a vision of a new social order to supplant the old—indeed, as noted, he has several of them—where the old ills might be controlled if not remedied, and where human life would be better, as he views it, if not perfect. Plato also has some more or less explicit strategies as to how human ills could be alleviated; how men might seek and perhaps arrive at the truth and come to know what they do not know; and how they might increase their value consensus, establish social justice, control discord, and become more integrated men living in more integrated communities; for an integrated life, no less than a life of reason, is central to Plato's basic image of the new social order.

For Plato, reason is not only a cognitive orientation. It is not solely a way of knowing about the social world, but it is also infused with certain affectively laden sentiments not strictly required for cognition alone. Platonic reason is not "pure reason." It embodies a desire to be practically relevant, to influence and to change the world in tangible ways. Plato has a strategy and a tactics of change. Both of these are at many points complex and vague, yet not so much so that their general outlines and component elements are indiscernible. To be understood, both his strategy and his tactics of change must be related to the social diagnosis he makes, and to the goals and values that underlie it.

In outline, Plato aims to have individual lives, and the communities in which they are lived, integrated by the governance of reason and by the surrogate of reason, law. The proper community is like an organism; it is one thing, yet it is also many things requiring a division of labor among the parts. Like an organism, the whole suffers when any one part is injured. Yet there is no mistaking that the part exists for the whole, not the whole for the part. The part should, therefore, be subordinated to the direction of the highest elements—the most conscious and rational sectors of the whole—to the soul and reason in the body, and to the rational polity and law in the community, if not to a philosopher king. Plato's goal is integration through the governance of men by reason. Reason must, therefore, be somehow emancipated from its thralldom to other forces and must impose its dominion on them for their own good. Reason must play the directing part proper to it. Each of the parts must also play the role they are competent to perform, leaving the others to play theirs. Remedial changes must aim at integrating the parts in this manner and at restoring mastery of the whole to its proper locus in the rational centers or in their surrogates.

In the following, an attempt will be made to describe both the tactics and strategy of remedial social change in Plato's theory. First, an effort will be made to understand Plato's change tactics, particularly his use of dialectic as a change method. In viewing the dialectic as a deliberate tactic for changing human beings, it is not intended to suggest that this is all it is, or that this is the only way in which it must be construed. The aim is rather to distinguish the dialectic from Plato's larger, many-faceted scheme of social change—of which it may be regarded as a part—which I shall term the "Model-Guided Strategy of Change." Nor is it intended to suggest that the tactic of the dialectic and the strategy of the Model-Guided Change are both necessarily of one piece, that they are built upon identical conceptions of planned social change. On the contrary, I am inclined to think that the flux of the dialectic and the fixity of the Model-Guided Strategy are rather dissonant, and that the former may express the more authentically Socratic or earlier dispositions of Plato, while the latter may embody his somewhat later, more pessimistic inclinations. Correct or not, however, it would seem useful to distinguish between these two aspects of Plato's approach to social change and to attempt to clarify the characteristics of both.

THERAPY AS DIALECTIC

The quest for the liberation of man's reason is seen by Plato as a matter of intense individual effort. Although different people have different natural potentialities for attaining truth, every man who hopes to succeed must strive for truth actively and his success depends on his own individual effort allied with his natural endowment. Yet however dependent on the striving individual, man cannot find truth in isolation or solely through individual meditation. In the pursuit of truth, men need the aid of others: "[A]ll men who have a companion are readier in deed, word, or thought; but if a man 'Sees a thing when he is alone,' he goes about straightway seeking until he finds someone to whom he may show his discoveries, and who may confirm him in them." [2] It is not surprising to find that a member of an other-directed, shame culture believes that to find and know the truth men need the agreement of another; that they need a companion with whom they can interact in the quest for knowledge; that they need some consensual validation.

Men also need two other things in the quest for knowledge. First, they must adopt the right sentiments or attitudes; second, they must use the right method, which is to say they must use reason in a disciplined way. This fusion of the right sentiments and method, within the context of social interaction, is the dialectic.

There is no one place in Plato's work to which we can turn to clarify the character of the dialectic. In this, as in other respects, any synthesized statement depends on the interpreter's skill in meshing various discussions, bridging these by what he takes to be reasonable inferences, making certain emendations of his own which seem consistent, and codifying the whole in a manner inescapably shaped by the interpreter's own ultimate purposes and interests.

Dialectic: The Contest of Minds

The dialectic is a struggle of minds. It is a contestful way of achieving "truth" congenial to those who think of it—as the Greeks do of *alētheia*—as that which is not-concealed or not-forgotten, or as something without deceit. The would-be knower, therefore, does not simply arrive at or find truth, but engages in a struggle to vanquish and to remove the concealment and distortion by which it is assumed truth has been disguised by other persons or forces. Truth is born of a contest, a contest of minds.

But the dialectic is not just any kind of friction of minds. To understand Plato's dialectic, it is helpful to contrast it with what he regards as its polar type, the eristic, or contentious discussion. The eristic has certain outward similarities to the dialectic in that it, too, entails a conversation, involving two or more persons, nominally aimed at intellectual clarification. Yet, notes Plato, the eristic is primarily a conversational contest in which commitment to the truth has been subverted by the aim of ringing up debater's points. The contenders in the eristic strive to vanquish one another, each seeking to put the other man down and to manifest dominance over him.

Above all, the eristic is a dialogue in which men have lost sight of the proper end of intellectual discussion, the attainment of truth, because they have been blinded by their desire to win public acclaim. In contrast, the dialectic, ideally pursued, seeks one thing only, the truth. Thus in the *Philebus,* Socrates says ironically, "for surely we are not simply contending in order that my view or that yours may prevail, but I presume that we ought both of us to be fighting for the truth." [3]

The search for truth requires that individuals commit themselves to it, and this above all is the sentiment needed for successful dialectic. Men must want to know the truth more than they must wish to win or to be judged victorious in the conversational contest. They must be lovers of truth rather than lovers of fame. In short, to win the truth they must partially extricate themselves from the contest system; for what Plato is saying is that the conventional contest system is, in certain ways, inimical to wisdom.

As anyone who has ever heard contemporary academic conversation can testify, Plato was not talking about some peculiar Greek failing but of a still prevalent inability of discussants to separate their purely intellectual interests in the truth from their interest in maintaining a creditable image of themselves, in their own view and in the view of others. Plato recognizes that men would often rather sacrifice the truth than admit error or defeat in public discussion. This being so, why then does he not propose that men seek the truth in isolated meditation, where in the privacy of their own thought they can acknowledge error without at the same time having publicly to acknowledge defeat? Does not the very insistence upon a dialectical method—inherently requiring a public exchange of views—incite men with the very ego-protecting motives that corrupt the quest for knowledge?

Plato sees that the dialectic easily elides into the eristic and that it always possesses this truth-defeating potentiality. Yet this danger must be risked, for men when alone commonly assume that they already know the truth. How, then, may they be made to recognize their ignorance and remedy it in private meditation? Moreover, men are self-deceived by their own passions, so how can a man whose understanding is already distorted by his appetites release himself from their bondage? Plato assumes that, left to his own devices, a man will tend to think as he has in the past. It is precisely because a man can and does get deeply involved in the friction of dialectic, because he is exposed to the pressure, surveillance, and criticism of another, that he is constrained to re-examine and to change his established views.

The friction of minds in the dialectic requires a man to defend his views; his very involvement in the dialectic, indeed his very desire to win, may motivate him to comply with the impersonal method it imposes and, in this different manner, to enhance his public and his self-image. The dialectic, in short, is not a radical rejection of the contest; it is an effort to sublimate contest motives to the interests of increased knowledge. It is an effort to control and rechannel competitive impulses, placing them in the service of knowledge. The dialectic is the strategy of forcing an alliance between reason and *thymos* by placing the individual in a social interchange where, in order to avoid shame, he must be reasonable.

STRUCTURE OF THE DIALECTIC

Since Plato assumes that men are commonly mistaken in believing they already know the truth, one of his central objectives is to make them aware that they do not. Yet a dialectical confrontation often does not begin with direct denials and mutual refutation by the participants. Rather, they often start by finding points of seeming agreement and making these explicit. The contestants make an effort to find a level at which consensus already exists, then to bind one another to it and proceed from there. There will commonly follow a series of short questions and brief answers. At any rate they will be brief if they heed the Socratic prescription, for few habits of discussion more excited Socrates' wrath than having a question answered by a lecture. "And will you continue to ask and answer questions," he asks Gorgias hopefully, ". . . and reserve for another occasion the longer mode of speech which Polus was attempting?" [4] Long answers enable the participant to beg the question, to conceal from himself and onlookers that he is either not answering the question or does not know the answer. Long answers also increase privatization and reduce the mutual interaction of the participants. There is, also, in the *Protagoras*, an indication that Plato associated brevity with traditional Spartan austerity; their wisdom, he says, was admirably terse, "consisting of short memorable sentences." [5]

In principle, there is no rigid division of labor and no status difference between those asking questions and those answering them. Both men take turns doing each. There is a ready role reversal between those who, for the purpose at hand, treat one another as peers. Dialectic is not the giving of advice by an expert to a client. One person is not the teacher or doctor, and the other is not the patient or student; in principle, both parties are on a par. Both also enter the relationship voluntarily with a view to mutual learning. "I am one of those," says Socrates, "who are very willing to be refuted if I say anything which is not true, and very willing to refute any one else who says what is not true, and quite as ready to be refuted as to refute." [6]

Step by logical step, through asking and answering questions, a partial agreement is sought and secured. In this manner the parties gradually come to be committed to the process of clarification and to the preliminary conclusions that it yields. Having started from assumptions with which both concur or having applied methods and standards they commonly accept, both parties tend to be constrained to accept the conclusions to which they lead. At length, one of them aims to convince the other that the assumptions with which he began are either inadequate, in the sense of being unclear or ambiguous, or that they lead to contradictory conclusions; that is, the assumptions themselves are shown to be mutually contradictory or insufficient. In particular, the dialectician astonishes conceit and embarrasses prideful ignorance by producing a manifest contradiction in the other's chain of reasoning, showing him that the conclusion which follows from his own premises disagrees with other opinions he now holds. The argument has, in short, led to a conclusion that is manifestly disagreeable to the discussant. And now he must, if he is to appear rational, reject either the opinion he once held and change, or he must deny the validity of the conclusions to which he has come and which he had publicly acknowledged to be correct.

In this regard, then, the dialectic is a controlled form of intellectual contention; it is a contest conducted according to the rules of logic. It is a form of contention, however, whose very method entails a search for the areas of initial agreement, that seeks to make explicit these elements of latent consensus, and uses them as the beginning of a strategy of partial and successive commitments to constrain the parties to accept the conclusions finally arrived at. In the end, the areas of mutual consensus are thus enlarged or, at least, the nature of the unresolved dissensus has been clarified. The objective of the dialectic, then, is to generate concord by constraining one or both parties to change their initial views in a direction that entails greater mutual agreement.

DIALECTIC AS METHOD

This is facilitated by defining the changes that occur as a response to the requirements of an impersonal logic, as obedience to a suprapersonal truth to which both must bow, rather than as the submission of one party to the personal superiority of the other. That such a consensus does not in fact always result from a dialectical discussion is dramatically highlighted in the *Protagoras,* where each party changes in the direction of the other's initial view, leaving both in the end as much at odds as they were in the beginning. The very poignancy of this paradoxical ending ("for if the argument had a human voice, that voice would be heard laughing at us [7] ") underscores the fact that it is not just any change that is sought in the dialectic, but one that entails increased consensus.

The Platonic assumptions are that a truth exists to be uncovered, that it is a hidden reality, and that a properly conducted search will lead to a single conclusion for both parties. If they end by differing, it can only be because either or both has not used the proper method. The method seeks to appraise ideas, stressing the need for a critical examination of even the most familiar and commonly agreed-upon beliefs: "first principles, even if they appear certain, should be carefully considered." [8] Neither a sense of intuitive certainty nor the cultural pervasiveness and wide acceptance of a belief in any way validates it. Only if critical examination demonstrates that the assumptions made lead to consistent conclusions can they be acceptable. Ideas are to be tested by their intellectual consequences alone. Neither tradition, inner conviction, nor the senses can be trusted with respect to positive doctrines. Only the conclusions of a purely logical method are valid. The emphasis, then, is upon the dialectic as a constraining *method* of discovering truth.

Socrates' message was that only a method, not a positive doctrine, can produce agreement among men. Men will at length agree on positive doctrines if they begin by agreeing to use a proper method. If two men see the truth, they must agree because the truth is one; consequently the important thing is to use a method enabling them to unearth the truth. Nonetheless, each cannot know it as a truth unless they both agree concerning it. Each success is dependent upon the other; knowledge of the truth requires consensus, and consensus requires knowledge of the truth. Method is the lever for prying open and entering into this circle. The assumption is that men can agree on method more readily than positive doctrines.

The dialectic, then, seeks a common commitment to method in order to bridge value differences. This same intent is involved in Socrates' frequent use of an analogy with productive craftsmanship. Although the analogy was seen to be incomplete, moral skills were conceived of on the order of technical skills, both entailing a rational and dependable technique or method. The dialectic was the method specific to the reliable production of valid moral beliefs. Akin to the techniques of the craftsman, skillful use of dialectic makes men practically competent in the most important business of life: clarifying and knowing their ends.[9]

Despite the emphasis on the dialectic as impersonal method, it is also intrinsic, even if implicit, to the Platonic dialogue that Socrates himself makes a difference as an individual. His person and character are deeply involved in the whole change process and in the outcome. We get involved in trials, dilemmas, anxieties, and ambitions that we are made to feel are Socrates'; and it makes a difference who he is and that it is he, rather than someone else, who feels them, for it is through our identification with him that we become increasingly aware that these problems are also ours. The dialectic as method is never presented as a machine which produces identical results without regard to the character of the men who operate it.

DIALECTIC AS REPOSSESSION

The truth sought by the dialectic is not a truth about nature or about the way men do in fact live; it is, rather, a vision of the way men should live. The aim, in short, is a practically efficacious virtue. Socrates, however, does not believe that this can be taught like arts or skills, such as rhetoric or medicine. It cannot be transmitted from one mind to another, like passing a cup from one hand to another. People cannot, indeed need not, be taught virtue in that way; but they can be helped to learn it.

In Plato's work this view of dialectic as the context for learning, not teaching, is associated with the doctrine that learning is remembrance. The job of the dialectic is "purification" in the sense of removing impurities; it is the overcoming of forgetting; it is the removal of encumbrances on a knowledge that already exists within the person but from which he has been alienated. It is not transmitting something new, but enabling the person to recover what he already knows: it is a technique of repossession, for all enquiry and all learning is but recollection. Says Plato, "there is no teaching, but only recollection." [10]

The idea that learning is remembrance is associated with the Pythagorean doctrine of reincarnation; the remembrance secured is a knowledge of what was learned in a previous life. Indeed, Socrates is told this by one of his disciples, Cebes: "Your favorite doctrine, Socrates, that knowledge is simply recollection, if true, also necessarily implies a previous time in which we have learned that which we now recollect. But this would be impossible unless our soul has been in some place before existing in the form of man." [11]

From a contemporary perspective Plato's doctrine of learning as remembrance seems, if taken literally, to be sheer twaddle. Yet the more general problems in which it is embedded endure; that is, that there are different kinds of learning and knowing, some having to do with the learning or knowing of facts or techniques, on the one hand, and of values, on the other; that there is also a difference between learning things for the first time and being able to recall and verbalize information and orientations one has previously acquired; that there is a difference between the role of the senses and the role of the other faculties of mind in determining truth.

In part Plato is saying that there are some things that men learn by virtue of having lived. Here the problem is not to give them something new or something which they do not yet have, but to enable them to take hold of and to use efficaciously their own life experiences. Plato is also saying that just because values cannot be taught in the same manner as rhetoric or medicine does not mean that they cannot be learned with the aid of some method which, if used in common, can build common values among men.

KNOWING AND AWARENESS

Plato's concern with values is part of a larger domain of interests; it is part of his concern with a distinctive type of knowledge, *epistēmē*. *Epistēmē* embraces a broad range of mutually implicated powers; it includes intellectual insight and rational understanding, a capacity to apprehend a hidden reality, to articulate in explicit ways a stable awareness of this reality and of its relationship to the knower. *Epistēmē* is a knowing in which there is consciousness concerning the nature of the method used by the would-be knower and of the relation of what is uncovered to the self of the knower. *It is a knowing in which the object discovered is implicated deeply in the self of the knower,* to whom it is no mere academic thing or a matter of idle curiosity.

To know, in this sense, is to have more than isolated and reliable bits of information; it is to see the connectedness and architecture of reality. It is to be able to organize, to account for, and to explain what is seen; it is a rational assimilation of sensory data. To know in this sense is not simply to acquire a view of the world outside, but to see it in its relation to and personal meaning for oneself as the knowing subject. To know, in this sense, must mean to have insight into and understanding of the self—to know oneself. Finally, to know in this sense means to have overcome resistance; to have engaged in a successful struggle against active forces that conceal, disguise, distort, or forget reality, whether these forces are external or internal. To know in this sense therefore requires that intelligence be united with valor, with a willingness to undergo high risk to the self. Knowing in this sense is the prize for an intellect that is not only skillful but is also courageous.

Plato's concern with values is an aspect of his concern with the examined life, with the self-conscious and aware existence. He is committed to searching for the kind of knowledge that is difficult and hazardous to secure and which most resists knowing, the self's knowledge of the self in its involvement with the world. Plato's concern with values is an aspect of his vital interest in awareness.

Plato is concerned not merely with an awareness of various values. Awareness to him is not simply one among many goods; awareness has a special place in the Pantheon of values. As he views it, it is clearly not enough for men to do the good; in order for it to be good, they must also do it deliberately. They must know what it is that needs doing and that they are doing it.

There is in Plato a kind of polarization between the true and highest knowledge, *epistēmē,* which embodies awareness of the known, of the knower, and of knowing, on the one hand, and another but lesser form of knowledge, *technē,* to which it is counterposed and which, on the other hand, consists of the lessons of experience, of trial and error, of clever skills refined through diligent practice. This dualism is developed in Socrates' polemic against the Sophists, Socrates symbolizing the aware person, the Sophists epitomizing the unaware, caught in the absorbing exigencies of daily life and trapped by their double ignorance, not knowing of their ignorance. The dualism expressed in counterposing *epistēme* and *technē* reflects an interest in two forms of knowing with two correspondent, larger styles of existence:

Knowing $_1$ *(technē)*	Knowing $_2$ *(epistēmē)*
as being informed	as being aware
having facts and skills	having understanding, insight, values
acquirable from and held by: experts and technicians	not acquirable from but manifested by: "theorists," philosophers, wise men
extrospective	introspective

Far from being archaic, the distinction between these two different forms of knowing is at the root of many major controversies in the social sciences today and, particularly, in sociology. Indeed, it has been implicated in these since the nineteenth century, when a distinction was formulated between the natural and the cultural (or human) sciences, each presumably having its own different object and appropriate method, corresponding to the two forms of knowing. This nineteenth-century distinction between the natural and the cultural sciences generated a polemic, echoing to this day in the social sciences, concerning whether sociology was a natural science, like biology or physics, and was to be pursued with the same methods as these disciplines employed, or whether sociology required a special and distinctive method and training, for example, *verstehen,* clinical intuition, or some kind of awareness.

Those conceiving of sociology as a natural science tend today to think of it also as developing cumulatively and continuously, with each new generation progressing beyond the previous. Those regarding sociology as a cultural science often conceive of it as a historical discipline, as a science "to which eternal youth is granted" and which does not, in basic respects, manifest continuous progress.

The naturalists characteristically believe that a contemporary specialist —for example, a Robin Williams—"knows" more about race relations than even the best of the classical American contributors to the study of race relations, say, a Robert Park. Conversely, the humanists are more likely to believe, despite the cumulation of researches since Max Weber's time, that he "knew" more about systems of social stratification than a modern specialist in this area, such as W. L. Warner. In some part, this polemic between the naturalists and the humanists derives from the fact that they are each seeking different things when they seek "knowledge," and that they each mean different things when they talk about "knowing."

The humanists are, in effect, seeking awareness when they seek knowledge; the naturalists mean something much more like "information" when they speak of knowledge. That they are talking past one another becomes clear when one notices that the naturalist seeks to account for the "variance" in some variable, and the more he does so the more successful he counts himself; yet even if a piece of research accounted for 80 to 90 per cent of the variance in an important variable, the humanist might well not find the research of interest because he is not merely seeking a change in the information supply as such but a change in the quality of mind of the supplier.

This distinction between the knowledge sought by the humanist and the naturalist suggests that the argument over whether or not the social sciences can progress is a specious one. There are some ways—for example, in terms of the information supply—in which social science can progress cumulatively, and other ways—in terms of awareness—in which social science may not progress cumulatively. Certainly, there is no prima facie reason to suppose that the progress of social science is an all-or-none matter; that it either has to be cumulative and progress in all ways or that it can progress in none whatsoever.

The humanists, I have suggested, are seeking a quality of mind rather than the enlargement of a body of information. In their polemical opposition to the naturalists, what the humanists oppose—for example, "methodology" —is often clearer than what it is they favor. The awareness that they seek is a residual category; in it everything not mere information, or not methodology, or not facts, is lumped together. "Awareness," therefore, needs some conceptual clarification.

Awareness as a form of knowing, I would suggest, is a capacity to discern the boundaries of information. We are aware when we have a capacity to distinguish between what we do and do not control intellectually; between the empirical generalization based on practical experience and the rational appraisal and stable discrimination of the limits of this experience—it is a capacity to distinguish between what we know and do not know. Men have awareness when they know that they know not; when they apprehend the kinds of things about which they do not have reliable information; when they know that these are not random but are in some way patterned; when they know that there are some kinds of information that are distasteful, if not actually hurtful, to them.

The humanistic proponent of awareness is hypersensitive to the weaknesses of sheer information. He knows, for example, that such knowledge cannot of itself indicate what information is worth possessing. The humanistic proponent of awareness seeks wisdom, not information. He seeks an attitude toward information, a knowing about knowing, an awareness.

Does this awareness have continuity, cumulation, and does it manifest progress? Can it be transmitted, taught, and studied with success? Here the answer can by no means be given as confidently as in the case of information. While I, at any rate, am confident that a Gunnar Myrdal, a Robin Williams, or a Melvin Tumin have a great deal more information than had Robert E. Park about ethnic or race relations, I am not certain that they have greater awareness, understanding, or wisdom concerning race relations.

Yet does this mean that such awareness cannot be increased over time? Information, of course, is capable of being increased as it is transmitted from one person to another, from one generation to the next, and from an earlier to a later time in the same person. Awareness, however, seems far more precarious and discontinuous. Although it can certainly be increased within the lifetime of one person, awareness may not be permanently consolidated even in a single lifetime. It is even more questionable if there is a sense in which awareness increases over generations or can be passed on from one person or generation to another.

A man can, of course, lose information just as he can have a dulling of awareness. Information may, for instance, be forgotten or somehow misplaced. For example, as a sociologist grows older or less interested in the area he may simply remember fewer of the facts or theories concerning race relations. But he can always find them again easily enough; he can always consult some storage bank: a card file, a book, a library, a colleague. For information to exist, it does not have to be recallable by a specific knower; it does not have to be in the mind of any particular individual. Indeed, information as such may be in no one's mind, and all that may be known to anyone is its location. Information is not the attribute of an individual, it is the attribute of a culture. Since it does not even have to be held or possessed by a mind but can simply be stored in libraries, the quality of information does not depend upon the quality of the minds that possess it at any given moment.

Awareness is quite another matter, for it has no existence and no value apart from the individuals that possess it. Awareness is the attribute of an individual, not that of a culture (even though it may derive from or be caused by living in a specific culture or by being located in a specific part of the social structure). While a culture may assist or hinder men in attaining awareness, understanding, insight, or wisdom, a culture as such cannot *be* aware.

To return to the direct question, what is awareness? It has to do with a person's access to "hostile" information, while, conversely, lack of awareness has to do with his resistance to hostile information. Information is hostile when it is discrepant with a man's purposes. For example, the stability of a government is hostile information to a revolutionist who lives in hope of a revolution; the fragility of government is hostile information to the conservative who supports the status quo. It is not the state of the world that makes information hostile, but the state of the world in relation to a man's purpose. The knowledge and use of information inimical to one's own desires and values is awareness (and, perhaps, some part of wisdom, too). Awareness is access to hostile information born of a capacity to overcome one's own resistance to it and cannot, therefore, simply be "retrieved" without a struggle—as can information. Since such resistance is always based in some part upon the pain or fear of knowing, the struggle to overcome resistance and to attain awareness always requires a measure of valor.

In arguing that men already had knowledge within themselves and that this needs to be repossessed, Plato stresses the importance of awareness— especially self-awareness—as the characteristic of the person that achieves that high knowledge he calls *epistēmē*. From the classical standpoint, the paradigm of hostile, fear-inspiring information is the knowledge of man's mortality. To the Greek mind, men must be constantly aware of and never allow themselves to forget their mortality and their inevitable death. Indeed, the Greeks go out of their way to ensure that no one overlook or slight this bit of information. It is certain, however, that they regard it as hostile information: men are not expected to view their mortality as glad tidings.

From the Platonic standpoint there are, then, at least two different kinds of knowing which it is possible for men to seek and attain, the knowing that is an apprehension of facts and a grasp of practical skills, and the knowing that is awareness, the capacity to acquire and to hold hostile information.

It seems much more likely that the progress and cumulation which the social sciences make will be in terms of the first kind of knowing, while the second —knowing as awareness—is a fugitive achievement that must be won and rewon by each person and each new generation and which, while it can be learned, cannot be transmitted like property that passes from one man to another. Awareness, therefore, is no man's legacy. He cannot give it to or receive it from others. Although others may help him, each man must win it for and preserve it in himself, and it is won not by bloodless intellect alone but by struggle and courage.

These two forms of knowing, with their corresponding conceptions of what the social sciences should be like, each have their own corresponding pathologies. For example, knowing as naturalistic information-gathering tends toward narrowness. Its characteristic product is the brief and direct technical article capable of being understood only by a few other specialists. Its tendency is to commit itself to a metaphysics which believes that the complexity of the world is undesirable and unnecessary and that things are really simpler than they seem. It consequently has a more hopeful and optimistic view of human ambitions. It is intolerant of intellectual ambiguities and builds intellectual structures into which all things can be fitted neatly, seeking for the simplest and most elemental units of which things are composed. It can, in brief, be naïve and simple-minded.

Knowing as awareness also has its own if different form of pathology; it enjoys the shiver induced by a sense of mystery. Loving the smell of incense, it has a tendency toward mystification and a preference for mood-resonating obscurities. Awareness is committed to a metaphysics in which things are felt to be much more complex than they seem, in which simplicity is only appearance deep, and awareness seeks to capture and portray the complexity of things. Enjoying the mystery of life, it seeks to protect it, and it can therefore become the enemy, not only of science, but of reason as well. Believing the mystery impenetrably complex, it easily sinks into pessimism about the human prospect.

The function of *epistēmē* and of the dialectic through which it is obtained is not, however, simply awareness for its own sake, in the sense of a mere apprehension of the truth; it is also concerned with changing behavior; it is a practically effective knowledge, a knowledge manifested in everyday behavior and choice.

The dialectic seeks more than a cerebrally insulated knowledge; it is not simply a tool of inquiry but a therapy. Indeed, it is explicitly regarded by Plato as a kind of healing. "Answer, Polus, and fear not," says Socrates, "for you will come to no harm if you nobly resign yourself into the healing hand of the argument as to a physician without shrinking." [12] The dialectic aims at changing men's lives, behavior, relations with one another, and, indeed, the deepest layers of their selves.

DIALECTIC AS A SMALL-GROUP THEORY OF KNOWLEDGE AND CHANGE

Yet the dialectic is not an instrument for changing people in any way; it seeks to change them in the course of a quest for knowledge. In particular, the dialectic has special reference to certain of the conditions under which knowledge may be sought and generated: the small-group conditions, the microsocial, face-to-face relations. As noted, Plato indicates explicitly that a man needs others to confirm him in his views, that he will not regard an idea as true unless some others concur with him. The dialectic, therefore, is tacitly premised upon a belief in the *special potency of intense face-to-face interaction in the shaping and reshaping of ideas.* It is characteristically Platonic, however, in its implicit focus upon ahistorical conditions. It deals, that is, with influences upon knowledge that transcend local or particular times and places; it deals with certain universal conditions conducive to the critical refinement of thought.

The dialectic focuses on the role of everyday conversation in particular. It attends to the frictionful conversation of intellectuals as the ongoing, scarcely noticed social matrix within which distance from old ideas and involvement with new ones is generated. The dialectic premises that the development of social theory does not usually emerge solely from the meditations of an isolated scholar—in which he takes counsel only with himself —or from reading books or doing research alone, or, again, from the special congresses of scholars in solemn assembly. Social theory is seen as continually enmeshed in, and emergent from, the ongoing stream of scarcely noticed conversation in a community of adjoining scholars, and it is this that provides the local social matrix of creativity. It is here that new ideas are tentatively exposed, casually debated, informally refined. Here there is a play of thought in which imagination may leap beyond proof. Here there is a chance to be warned off, or to secure support, permitting the final product to be polished in advance of the time that the scholar's public reputation will ride with his work.

The ongoing conversation among adjoining colleagues is the "backstage" where the participants may interact in spontaneous ways: pursuing hunches, sharing fantasies, exchanging scraps of potentially useful information, revealing ignorances, or exposing intellectual or personal antipathies and sympathies that would be deemed inappropriate by the conventional canons of their craft or be discrepant with their desired public image. This is the arena within which serious things may be played with, or in which they may be treated with playful pretense. This is the arena in which a man may gauge the degree of receptivity, understanding, and tolerance that colleagues may have for intellectual novelty, and in which novelty may be rehearsed and learn to make itself acceptable. This is the arena within which men who claim to know may continue to learn. It is also the setting from which the larger, uninformed public is excluded and where social theorists may be partially protected from the press of conventional values, experimentally revising the larger system of beliefs within which their own more specialized ideas operate. It is here that work and play are fused.

The conversation of scholars, however, is not only work-significant, but it is also status-relevant. The intellectual play of scholars, like their intellectual work, has implications for their social position within the stratified community of scholars. It is a source of all manner of extrinsic rewards (as well as of intrinsic satisfactions), much of which depends so heavily on the display of verbal quickness and wit and an imputation of intellectual originality or "priority."

In the earlier relations among members of the Pythagorean brotherhood, all possessions, including intellectual innovation, were held in common. As F. M. Cornford relates, "no individual member of the school was allowed to claim the credit of any discovery he might make." [13] It was believed that all intellectual inventions by members of the school derived from the daemon of Pythagoras himself, even after his death. The relations prevailing among the intellectuals of Plato's Athens, much like those current among scholars today, are, however, regarded as based upon an individual talent; their relationships are shaped by the pressures of the contest system which govern the subcommunity of scholars as much as any other sphere.

The disciplined quest for knowledge occurs within a community of scholars who are socially stratified and where position is determined by work (and play) in a competitive context. The scholar's position depends much on the judgment of peers who have the significant peculiarity of also being his competitors. Each man is both the judge and competitor of others. Each is to some degree motivated to seek knowledge by a quest for recognition from some of the very men with whom he is also competing.

It is partly because of this unique role system that a scholar's rewards will not always neatly correspond to his merit and that carefully measured packages of recognition are not meticulously handed out in balanced return for impersonally appraised contributions. Given this role structure, there will inevitably be some socially constrained slippage between the value of a man's contribution and the prizes he is awarded for it. There will be the "evil" of meanness and envy even within the community of science.

To attempt to critically refine the work of another scholar is, in a way, to tamper with it. Although the theorist or scientist has a license to do so, this may still be taken as an attack upon the other's earlier contribution—in fact, it is often enough exactly that. On a fantasy level, the older thinker sometimes experiences the critical work of his juniors as an attack upon himself and, indeed, upon his very claim to immortality. While theorists and scientists may be sedulously socialized to view the obsolescence of their own work by the surpassing contribution of another as an inevitable, expected, and proper part of the intellectual process, they do not take its actual occurrence with benign serenity.

This, of course, is one way in which theory and science do grow cumulatively. Yet this very triumphal growth of the institution may be experienced as a tragic supersession by the contributing individuals: developments that mark institutional milestones may be individual tombstones. As a result, intellectual creativity, originality, and novelty are not always as warmly welcomed or impersonally appraised as the scholar's code enjoins. They may be resisted bitterly, sometimes especially so by powerful men whose prior contributions have earned them a leading place in the community of scholars and a right to sit in judgment. It is, in part, because it occurs within a contest system—in which men are both judges and competitors of one another—that the dialogue of scholars at work or play often takes on an eristic quality. This, in turn, induces both resistances to intellectual novelty and attacks upon intellectual convention. The contest system both inspires individual intellectual creativity and impedes its acceptance by the community of scholars.

Much as a dam channels an available water current to produce usable electricity, the dialectic harnesses the enormous intellectual energy inherent in the conversation of competitive men. The dialectic seeks to make their contention productive. It motivates men to overcome resistances to intellectual innovation, while restraining their sheer contentiousness by subjecting contention to certain rules and constraining participants to abide by a common method. The dialectic tends to formalize the normally informal, catch-as-catch-can quality of conversation, to bound its boundlessness, to impose some control upon it while at the same time removing the restraints of mere tact and sociability.

In making the conversational process more orderly and its outcome more reliable, the dialectic, however, sometimes dams up its lively imaginative quality. Often demanding a premature precision and arresting productive intuition and fantasy, it intimidates what Gilbert Murray has called "those fainter powers of apprehension and surmise and sensitiveness." [14] There is a juggernaut tendency in the dialectic. It transforms conversation from a nimble organ of discovery into a lumbering machinery of proof, and it repeals conversation's charter to play. Socrates himself, it appears, was aware of this danger in the dialectic; at any rate, there are times when he backs off from its prescriptions, seeking exemption in the name of his daemon, the unpredictable inner voice which warns him away from certain logically stipulated courses. Of similar import is his occasional use of myth and, most notably, his turn to poetry during the last days of his life.

INTELLECTUAL CREATIVITY AS A PRECARIOUS PERFORMANCE

The theorist committed to the critical refinement of thought cannot accept something as true simply because others around him believe it. At the same time, he cannot properly regard something as true if he alone believes it. Intellectual creativity is a precarious performance requiring a man to detach himself from the conventional view and to find support for his own unconventional innovations, to disentangle himself from old involvements and to make new ones that can elicit and sustain his creativity. (It is quite clear in Plato, where he speaks of the need that a man has for a companion to whom he can show his "discoveries," that he refers to ideas which are new or at least not already part of the common sense.)

The problem of creativity—of generating and sustaining valuable novelty—is particularly precarious, given the intellectual assumptions and the social conditions within which Plato works. First, the need for a companion from whom the consensual validation of novelty can come is intensified when there is a devaluation of sensory evidence. It would seem that even isolated thinkers who employ and value sensory evidence—and whose work can elicit it by repeated studies—would be more able to sustain faith in their own novel discoveries than isolated thinkers concerned primarily with a complex chain of reasoning and logical inference. Second, the ability to escape the pressures of convention and to innovate intellectually would appear particularly difficult for an isolated person in an other-directed culture such as the Greek, for the innovating person must be socially supported in his intellectual novelty or insulated from the pressures of conventional views. Thus Socrates may be found repeatedly attempting to divert his discussant from an orientation to the common view. "But why, my dear Crito, should we care about the opinions of the many?" asks Socrates, "Good men . . . are the only persons worth considering." [15] He also warns Crito to take note that the view toward which he is tending diverges from the common view and that he ought to commit himself to it with an awareness of its unpopularity. "But I would have you consider, Crito, whether you really mean what you are saying. For this opinion has never been held, and never will be held, by any considerable number of persons." [16]

However "solitary" intellectual creativity is always a social process. It requires some detachment from the pressures and expectations of the larger public or colleague group, while maintaining a supporting involvement with some others (who may also need a similar detachment from conventional views). This, too, is the task of dialectic, for the intense mutual involvement in a dialectical discussion serves to create ephemeral, yet sheltering, group boundaries. The discussants' need for intense concentration on the complex argument, combined with their competitive and defensive impulses, temporarily distracts and insulates them from their social surround. It is in this vein that Socrates speaks of the "intoxication of argument." [17] Each discussant works on the other, generating the cyclical build-up of an intense absorption in one another as well as in the argument, an absorption that seals them off from others and surrounds them, as it were, by an almost membranous boundary.

At one and the same time, dialectic enables a discussant to extricate himself from the common-sense view and to orient himself to the view of the other discussant, requiring it to be taken seriously. When Polus tells Socrates to "ask the company," and inquires, "Do you not think . . . that you have been sufficiently refuted, when you say that which no human being will allow?" Socrates rejects this argument. He replies,

> [I]f, as I was saying, you have no better argument than numbers, let me have a turn, and do you make trial of the sort of proof which, as I think, is required; for I shall produce one witness only of the truth of my words, and he is the person with whom I am arguing; his suffrage I know how to take; but with the many I have nothing to do, and do not even address myself to them.[18]

The efficacy of the Platonic dialectic depends upon a number of conditions. It usually requires, for example, that discussants have a relatively high level of education, at least in the elements of logic. Conditions must also be such that discussants feel free to say what they truly believe—to follow the argument wherever it leads—without concern for community sanctions or political reprisals. Further, the men involved must be social equals or else must be prepared to ignore their status differences and regard them as irrelevant to the discussion at hand. Which is to say, they must be prepared to exclude their normal communal roles and the immunities or privileges to which these usually entitle them from the dialectical dyad. They must, for example, accept that a generally high communal status does not necessarily endow them with the special qualifications and skills required in the game of dialectic and for which alone it pays off.

At least one other hidden source of leverage in dialectical discussion deserves mention, and this is the nature of the discussants' self-images. If the dialectic is to succeed, the discussants must think of themselves as rational men. This self-conception must be important enough to them so that they can recognize and accept the force of another's argument, even when it is opposed to their own views. They must also learn to feel pain when their own views entail some kind of logical contradiction, non sequitur, or ambiguity. "I would rather . . . that the whole world should be at odds with me, and oppose me," says Socrates, ". . . than that I myself should be at odds with myself, and contradict myself." [19]

It is when intellectual consistency becomes a potent basis of self-regard that it generates motivations powerful enough to revise previously held views and provides an inner locus of vulnerability to the rational appeals advanced by others. The intense pressures of sustained and frequent dialectical discussion serve to heighten, if not to imprint, a rational self-image so that the discussant becomes increasingly what the rules of the game—as enforced and expected by the other—premise he will be. In some part, then, the conduct of dialectic in time produces the kind of men upon whom it is dependent for its success and who, in particular, possess a capacity to control their own competitive impulses and *eristic* contentiousness.

THE PATHOLOGIES OF DIALECTIC

The *eristic* is the pathology peculiar to the dialectic; it is the Achilles' heel or special vulnerability of the dialectic; it is the disorderly state to which dialectic is peculiarly prone and into which it is continually eliding. Indeed, we can note Socrates himself frequently slipping into the very *eristic* sentiments which he deplores, becoming interested in putting the other man down or of not being put down himself, becoming involved with defense of the ego rather than single-mindedly devoted to the truth. Socrates is all too human and Plato knows it. Indeed, there is substance in R. Robinson's claim that "Socrates seems prepared to employ any kind of deception in order to get people into . . . *elenchus*," [20] or refutation.

Plato shows Socrates describing his encounter with Protagoras in a manner that manifestly reveals his conception of it as a contest. "I could not help fearing that there might be something in what he said, . . ." confesses Socrates, "And I felt at first giddy and faint, as if I had received a blow from the hand of an expert boxer." [21] Again, in the *Phaedo,* Socrates is made to confess, "For at this moment I am sensible that I have not the temper of a philosopher; like the vulgar, I am only a partisan, . . . anxious only to convince his hearers that what he says is true." And he warns his hearers to "withstand me might and main, that I may not deceive you as well as myself in my enthusiasm, and like the bee, leave my sting in you before I die." [22]

There are other dangers of the dialectic, other ways in which, at least from a modern standpoint, it has pathological potentialities. For one, the dialectic is, by virtue of its ingrained tendency to inquire into all assumptions, apt to degenerate into a form of methodological perversity, in the sense that it may become endlessly concerned with the quest for knowledge and disinterested in its culminating capture. It becomes an unending regression and an eternal search for the assumptions behind the assumptions, so that one is continually moving backward into the mind, without pausing to move forward into the data and without seeking confirming inference from sensory observation. In Plato's view, however, this is not a pathology but the method proper to the search for eternal verities that can be apprehended only by the mind. It is a pathology only from the standpoint of an empirically oriented social science that wants to know about the world of men as it is, in its persistence and its change.

Plato himself, however, seems to have felt that there was a pragmatic or social danger, if not an intellectual one, in this continuous process of critically evaluating one's own assumptions, in that it may lead immature men mistakenly to relinquish commitments to all beliefs and values. In fine, the dialectic may induce *anomia*. It is largely because of this fear that Plato proposes to defer the dialectical training of the Republic's Guardians until they have reached the age of thirty and have passed other preliminary tests. And then, he warns, great caution is needed:

> "Why great caution?"
> "Do you not remark," I said, "how great is the evil which dialectic has introduced?"
> "What evil?" he said.
> "The students of the art are filled with lawlessness." [23]

This, says Socrates, is not so very unnatural, and he seeks to illuminate it in terms of an analogy which involves an interesting fantasy of hidden identity: compare a young man's experience with the dialectic, he says, to the experience of a popular and rich young man who suddenly learns that those whom he supposed to be were not, in fact, his real parents. While ignorant of the truth, he honored his parents. Once knowing the true relationship, however, he will be less disposed to give them honor and will now devote himself, instead, to his friends and flatterers. In similar manner, there are traditional beliefs about justice and honor learned in childhood, and when these are refuted in dispute, the young man is "driven into believing that nothing is honorable . . . or just and good any more than the reverse. . . . Can he [then] be expected to pursue any life other than that which flatters his desires? . . . And from being a keeper of the law he is converted into a breaker of it." [24] Thus while dialectic aims to elicit new beliefs, to which conviction may properly be given and on which social consensus may be based, it also has the very danger it is seeking to remedy—discord and normlessness.

The dialectical discussion, I may add, is also subject to veiled use as an instrument for the expression of hostility. This possibility has already been implied in saying that it can easily elide into the eristic, where the objective becomes dominant over the other rather than truth. This is suggested in Socrates' own description of the dialectic in the *Apology,* where he characterizes it as entailing both cross-examination and accusation, implying that he is taking the role of a God-appointed litigious prosecutor acting punitively on behalf of the public interest.

It needs to be borne in mind—as, indeed, is evident from the Platonic dialogues—that a dialectical discussion is commonly conducted before an audience of onlookers, a troupe who often revel in and egg on the contest-like character of the interchange. The presence of this live audience serves to exacerbate the eristic quality of a discussion by making the discussants more mindful of the dangers to their public image. Conversely, because of an audience's presence, the discussion may be used as a vehicle to undermine the other's public image and make him lose face. The dialectic is thus susceptible to misuse as an instrument of intellectual sadism and refined hostility.

THE MODEL-GUIDED STRATEGY OF CHANGE

In the following, an attempt will be made to characterize the larger Platonic strategy of remedial change that encompasses the tactic of the dialectic. The focus here, however, will not be on the particulars of the Utopian cities or on the specifics of their proposed social organization. Many of these have already been indicated in previous chapters and need no repetition here, except as they help us understand and clarify the more general features of Plato's change strategy. The structure and elements of the change strategy to be outlined, however, are not peculiar to Plato, and many elements in it are to be found in subsequent and even contemporary efforts at social change. In some part, this is because later change efforts derive from the intellectual tradition to which Platonic thinking gave so profound an impetus and, in some part also, because there are certain generic problems that are encountered in all efforts at planned social change and for which, it may be suspected, there are a limited number of solutions.

THE OPTIMUM SOLUTION

The most characteristic aspect of Plato's approach to planned social change may be highlighted by terming it a "Model-Guided Strategy of Change"; for this appropriately focuses attention on the way it emphasizes the detailed specification, in advance, of a set of social arrangements that are deemed best. In Plato, of course, these take the form of outlining the characteristics of several utopian communities. Platonic dialectic begins to function therapeutically by discerning and explicating the desired pattern, the rearrangement that is regarded as the one best plan. Various alternatives believed equally appropriate are not presented, although different plans which more or less approximate the one best plan may be formulated. (For example, the city of the *Laws* is not regarded by Plato as being as "good" as that outlined in the *Republic* but seems, rather, to have been regarded as a more feasible approximation of it.)

In the Model-Guided Strategy of Change, the assumption is that every problem has only one best solution, that the planner should aim to determine what it is and strive to attain it, so far as he can. The good or the best arrangement is not felt to be a personal invention but the discovery of a suprapersonal truth, attained or glimpsed through the application of impersonal method. This truth or solution exists apart from the planner who searches for it and cannot be formulated in more than one fully accurate manner.

The Model-Guided Strategy of Change begins by attempting to clarify what would be ideally desirable rather than first attempting to provide an adaptation to the status quo. It tries to minimize those features of the status quo which are taken as given and to reduce the constraints within which it must plan. Its underlying attitude is, in this respect: why settle for less than the best; why cling to the past. This strategy has a readiness to make a great break with the present and with things as they are; it rejects, at least in the beginning, considerations of "practicality." Since "the way things are" is not felt to be as important as a clarification of the way they should be, it is less disposed to engage in systematic empirical study of existent social arrangements and more inclined toward a primarily intellectual clarification of the projected future rearrangement.

The Model-Guided Strategy of Change premises that it is possible to clarify this once and for all and in advance of efforts at implementation. Little emphasis is placed on preparing alternative strategies to be activated in the event of various contingencies. The basic plan, with its incorporated end-states, is not viewed as open to a continuing reappraisal in the light of emerging experience with it. This is so because it is regarded as the one best plan. Experience in applying it is at most relevant for suggesting adjustments in the mode of realizing it, just as bad weather may lead a pilot to reroute his course without changing his intended destination.

This conception of the plan as the one best, once-for-all design has the paradoxical implication that, although the plan is to be formulated rationally and is to be based on the best possible information, no improved ways of reasoning or no important new information of relevance to the plan is expected to emerge. The premise is that the planner already knows all that he needs for his purpose. Although the world in which the planner acts is in need of and susceptible to improvement, it is assumed that the instrument through which he acts, namely dialectical reason, is not. This assumes, also, that the planner can extricate himself from the social situation with which he deals. It assumes that he can rid himself of any distorting personal pathologies in advance of formulating and implementing the plan.

ELITE TRANSFORMATION

In the Platonic case, however, it is not assumed that the planner is invulnerable to the pathologies of the systems for which he is planning. He, too, has the "many-headed beast" within him, but it is expected that he must and can control it. Implicit, then, is a conception that a change effort has two major phases. The initial phase is one in which there is the development of an elite who will first extricate themselves from the distorting pathologies. They will be those who first discover, as Plato indicates in his metaphor of the cave, that men have not been looking at reality but at its shadow. The ultimate instrument of self-transformation of this elite would appear to be the dialectic. The next phase then begins when the newly enlightened elite, through compassion and pity, elect to return to the cave to liberate the others from a life of illusion, enabling them to see and live by the plan.

The plan is not a partial or piecemeal one, focusing on this or that limited pathology, for any pathology is seen as shaped by the environing system and as resonating throughout it. The pathology is therefore not seen as an isolated morbid entity but as a state of the system as a whole. Since it is a state of a system—which is composed of mutually influential parts—any one part is potentially susceptible to infiltration from the port of entry, or initial locus, of the pathology. Conversely, all parts are potentially usable as bases of operation against the pathology.

SYSTEM MANAGEMENT

From this standpoint, any pathology is a potential danger to the whole system, and the response required is a response of the whole system. No part of the system is excluded from rational appraisal, either as a port of entry for a pathology or as an instrument to be used, correctively or preventively, against the pathology. All system elements are to be weighed, appraised, and used. All parts, therefore, are conceived of as resources in that all may be deployed to realize the plan. There is nothing untouchably sacred except the goal and the plan; there is nothing that is exempt from use on principle. Everything is material that may be manipulated.

This is not to say, of course, that the planner is unaware that the human materials may be recalcitrant and unwilling to be used in this manner. Recalcitrance, however, is an attribute intrinsic to the materials—comparable to the resistance of the sculptor's stone—that is also to be rationally planned for in advance and managed as far as possible. Where persuasion seems unpromising there is the "noble lie," and failing this, there is force. The Model-Guided Strategy of Change conceives of the materials with which it works not as infinitely malleable or as capable of being worked into any form, but as possessing a sufficient plasticity. They are viewed as suitable enough for the planner's purposes, or at least capable of being made so by some sort of preliminary softening-up; those parts of the materials which prove unduly refractory are to be discarded. While the materials are far from perfect, it is supposed that they can be worked and, at any rate, that the planner must make do with them.

FOCUS ON SYSTEM-STARTING

The Platonic concern with the detailed formulation of a plan is partly expressive of and partly legitimated by his emphasis on the importance of good beginnings. A good beginning, stresses Plato, is more than half of every task.[25] Indeed, "beginning" is apotheosized as "a God dwelling in man [who] preserves all things if it meet with proper respect from each individual." [26] This stress on beginnings is noticeably different from the dominant focus of much of contemporary and, especially, "functional" social theory where interest centers not on "starting mechanisms," as I have elsewhere called them, but rather on the self-regulating mechanisms that serve to maintain the equilibrium of already on-going systems. Perhaps it is to be expected that a "Eupatrid" such as Plato would feel that being "well-fathered" is an advantage not to be taken lightly. But his concern with good beginnings also seems indicative of the practical bent of his social theory, being the kind of interest that would more likely impress itself on those oriented to social reconstruction and who do, in fact, often have to initiate new systems.

It is clear that Plato's Model-Guided Strategy of Change has a definite conception of what a good beginning is not: it is not one that feels its way cautiously, step by step, pausing on the way to assimilate its new experiences and to modify its plans accordingly. For him, a good beginning is a rapid one to be made in a bold manner. It is, in fact, to be a fresh start, "taking the State and the manners of men, from which, as from a tablet, they will rub out the picture and leave a clean surface." This, he acknowledges, "is no easy task." [27]

The "they" who would do this are apparently the philosopher-king(s) who, once in power, will rid the city of its adults and begin immediately to re-educate the remaining children. Those older than ten will be sent out into the fields, and the younger will be taken and raised apart from the present habits that their forbears have, resocializing them immediately into the new patterns.

ALL-AT-ONCE CHANGE

Plato develops his detailed plans in advance because, in some part, his change strategy implies an all-at-once, fresh start. He hopes to launch the new system in operating condition almost from its very beginnings, conceiving of it as an ongoing concern soon after its launching. The changeover, it seems, is to be made within one generation at the least, this generation bringing the new institutions into existence at once. It is not conceived of as a "seed" which passes through successive and distinct changes in structure before reaching maturation; it has no evolutionary or genetic phases.

This all-at-once conception of change is consonant with Plato's deepest feeling that change is deeply hazardous, particularly that the natural drift of things is toward disorder. Even the fully formed and best state would be precarious. Surrounded by external enemies and permeated by internal threats, its life would be perilous, and even this best state is doomed to ultimate dissolution. What chance, then, does slow gradualistic change have? How can the new state ever survive if it has a long period of adolescence and transition?

CONSENT AND IMPOSITION

The emphasis throughout the Model-Guided Strategy of Change is on clarifying the desired end-state, and, correspondingly, the question of how the plan is to gain initial acceptance or conformity is not systematically explored. In particular, the question of whether it is to be imposed or given voluntary consent is unclear. Plato's stress on reason as an element inherent in the human psyche assumes that men are in some part open to persuasion. Certainly there is no doubt that he regards persuasion as preferable to force. In the seventh *Epistle,* he states explicitly that the reform of the state must not be based on force. Repeating the conventional Greek theme, he holds force to be a method appropriate for dealing with slaves rather than freemen. He indicates that men must seek advice on their own accord from the philosopher and must change voluntarily, and he holds that the philosopher will avoid interfering in affairs of state if he finds his advice disregarded.

Yet Plato also stresses that men are continually vulnerable to baser appetites which they commonly cannot resist and to which they are, indeed, all too often enslaved. He consequently stresses that controls must be imposed upon them and that they must be trained by those who know what is best. Further, it is evident in the *Republic* that he believes it is better for the human materials to be relatively malleable and for the trainers to start with the young, on whom appropriate habits may be more readily imprinted.

Two other considerations are, however, relevant here. One is that Plato's vacillation between imposition and consent may be resolved insofar as he thinks of different groups as amenable to different methods. It may be that it is the elite, who are to rule the ideal state, that are to be won over at first by persuasion through reason and that it is their consent which is to be sought. Others, upon whom the elite, in turn, work, may be those subject to a greater measure of imposition and constraint. Persuasion may be seen as especially preferred and used with those few exceptional men who are to become the lawgivers, while constraint and imposition may be regarded as required for the common run.

A second relevant consideration would indicate that this Model-Guided Strategy of Change does not regard the plan as justified or legitimate because it is in conformity with most men's existent wants or stated desires. Rather, it is legitimate because it conforms with their needs as reason has discerned them. The plan is regarded, as noted previously, as a suprapersonal truth glimpsed through reason, not as the summary score of a public opinion poll. In brief, the interests of men are to be formulated by the theoretically informed, by the social theorist or philosopher-king; they are to express their conception of the ordinary actors' requirements rather than the latter's own expression of their desires or wants. The elite know the truth and what is best for the others. Whether they secure compliance through imposition or persuasion is, from this standpoint, a somewhat secondary question. The vital thing is that some are to be set over the others as their natural rulers. How they get their power is of little importance in comparison with the importance of their having it. Since they know what is best for the others, the important thing is that this be done somehow, not whether it is accepted voluntarily or imposed. If imposition is not preferred, neither is it rejected on principle nor deemed inadmissible; if necessary, it is to be used, and to be used without qualm.

In the end Plato believes that men can be conditioned to want and to give consent to what may, at first, need to be imposed upon them. Suppose, however, persuasion and consent to be the only or main change devices employed; this makes the transition chancy at best. Even if once accomplished, it remains unstable, for men may be blinded by their irrational passions and may never even come to see the good life. Even if they are, at one time, persuaded to establish it, there is the danger that their commitment will be temporary, and there is the certainty that it will be precarious. The passions subversive of reason abide, ever ready to assert themselves and to overthrow their natural ruler.

Such security as can be hoped for—and it is little enough—can come not from putting reliance on the wisdom of men's choice but, so far as it can be arranged, by seeing they have no choice but to do what is best. Given no choice, men cannot choose wrong. In the end, therefore, the appeal to reason comes to be seen as less secure in its results than the manipulation of costs and rewards, and most men are to be confined in a carefully contrived stockade of pleasure and pain where they will be given no choice but to do good.

SYSTEM ISOLATION

One of the central strategies by which this is to be accomplished is by isolating the new system from dissonant stimuli by insulating it from competing beliefs and alternative images. To do this it is to be sealed off in time and space. The impulse to cut the system off from the past is suggested by the radical breach in generations that Plato proposes in the *Republic* when he recommends the separation of children from their parents. In a way, the system is also cut off from the future by conceiving of the newly established city as fully formed almost from its inception, as requiring no evolutionary development to perfect itself, and, indeed, by cultivating traditionalistic sentiments of respect for the new system and of suspicion toward all forms of change. The city is, also, obviously to be insulated from its surrounding environment by controlling and limiting travel to and from it.

The city, however, has to be isolated not only from discordant stimuli that might travel across time through generations or across space through voyagers. The city must also be sealed off from the inherent disruptants carried by embodied persons as part of their natural constitution. Men must be cut off from their animal nature by the inhibition of their impulses and bodily wants and desires. Intrinsically insatiable, these are the root of men's trouble, and men must cast them off if they are to cease from evil.

THE TENSION BETWEEN GRATIFICATION AND MORAL STANDARDS

Here one may note a fundamental difference between the Platonic—and indeed the classically Apollonian view of the good life—on the one hand, and that of the modern, on the other, for the modern world is permeated by the assumption that human troubles derive from an inhibition of impulses or from a subsequent shortage of gratifications. On this basis the modern world's distinctive (not necessarily its most frequent) remedial strategies are oriented to facilitating the expression of impulses and to gratifying wants and desires.

In their largest cultural import, as distinct from their diverse intellectual complexities, both the Freudian and the Marxist movements are in this respect alike. Although oriented to different needs, both endorse the legitimacy of men's tissue-linked wants and desires; both tend to view the frustration of these desires as a source of human problems rather than seeing their gratification as the source of individual or social pathology. Rather than fearing it, both seek more gratification. In this regard, however, Freudianism and Marxism are expressive of a still larger cultural transformation; they are both in some part outgrowths of nineteenth-century Romanticism, as well as of certain aspects of the French Revolution, which underwrote the desirability of expressivity and sanctioned the possibility of worldly happiness.

In contrast with some features of our contemporary ethos, the Platonic and Apollonian standpoint prefer self-restraint and deferred gratification as against immediate enjoyment or "fun." They seek impulse control as against expressivity, the performance of duty and the long-range pursuit of the good life as against the life of ongoing gratification. One way of formulating this distinction is to suggest that the modern standpoint typically stresses standards of gratification, while the Apollonian and Platonic are, in contrast, oriented to standards of propriety and morality. Plato wants men to be good, not happy. It is this that he stresses and makes problematic, however much he alleges that a good life will also make men happy. In contrast, modern men typically stress the importance of happiness, although they may claim that this is not at variance with the demands of morality, and they may seek to accommodate the two by conceiving of the pursuit of happiness as among their rights.

TOTAL CONTROL

Since all aspects of men and their behavior are viewed as materials and resources commonly available for rational utilization, and since the dangers to the new social system are regarded as ubiquitous, the new system can and must be made subject to a total set of controls and to close supervision even after it is established. As indicated, this is to begin with the youngest children, whose socialization is carefully planned and superintended.

The adult round of life is similarly to be governed by numerous social controls, both legal and traditional. In a way that illustrates the tension between standards of gratification and standards of morality (and Plato's emphasis on the latter), the *Laws* will require that the marriages contracted by a man are to be those that will be "beneficial to the state," [28] and not those most pleasant to him. Indeed the wedding ceremony itself is to be officially regulated so that it is conducted in a solemn manner, with specified expenditures for the celebration (varying according to wealth),[29] and with limitations on the number of guests to be allowed. There is to be control over reproductive practices, and the children are to be educated at the direction of the city rather than of their parents.[30] In addition to controls over family life, there are also controls on wealth, economic activity, occupational and career pursuits, military training, and the arts. Some kinds of music, such as the Lydian, are forbidden,[31] as are certain musical instruments such as flutes,[32] while drama and poetry are also to be subject to careful censorship.[33]

The distinction between private and public life is to be minimized as far as possible, and what, in our view, are considered some of the most intimate aspects of private life are to be governed by legislation. Plato suggests that in the best of societies, "the private and individual is altogether banished from life." [34] Indeed, there are specifications concerning the manner in which people should sleep and have sexual intercourse.[35]

Plato specifies that sacrifices are to be done only in public. The law will also forbid the private possession of sacred objects or of shrines at home,[36] thus inhibiting men from attempting secretly to placate the gods. In providing that "no man shall have sacred rites in a private house [and no] one shall possess shrines of the Gods in private houses," Plato, in effect, requires men's relation to the gods to be mediated through public institutions. He places their ritual status, or state of purification, under the direction of the public authority, thus monopolizing its access to sacred forces, and in fusing this with its secular powers, he constitutes the public authority as a theocracy. The individual has been expropriated from the means of worshiping and propitiating the gods, and he is divorced from direct access to the sacred.

The administration of this tight system of control is to be organized on the basis of a correspondingly severe hierarchical system arranged on a military model. The system is to be as authoritarian as it is total. Perhaps the culminating expression of this is to be found in Plato's well-known remark in the *Laws* where he holds:

> [T]he great principle of all is that no one of either sex should be without a commander; nor should the mind of any one be accustomed to do anything, either in jest or in earnest, of his own motion, but in war and in peace he should look to and follow his leader, even in the least things being under his guidance.[37]

THE UTOPIANISM PROBLEM

While Plato may manifest a "failure of nerve" he manifests no corresponding failure of imagination however "conservative" its form. It is this that evokes the common, indeed stereotyped, estimate of him as the "utopian" *par excellence,* the man whose imagination ran away with him. Indeed, any appraisal of Plato as a social diagnostician and a therapist must at some point address itself to and take its stand on the meaning of Plato's utopianism. I have deliberately delayed confronting this issue because it all too often serves to divert analysis from a detailed inspection of Plato's change strategies. Labeling him a utopian commonly implies that he had no change strategies, rather than encouraging us to search out the distinctive character of his approach to social change. While we are not yet done with an analysis of Plato's therapeutic orientation, I believe that our previous examination of his approach to planned social change should at least inhibit any inclination to feel that, once one has called Plato a utopian, nothing more needs saying.

From a modern standpoint it is certainly not Plato's specific vision of the ideal society—it is not his totalitarianism, authoritarianism, or even his restricted kind of communism—that disposes us to view him as utopian.

From the standpoint of a generation that has witnessed the rise of modern Fascism, Nazism, and Soviet socialism, all these are at least readily conceivable, if not familiar. They certainly do not make the modern imagination stagger. From a modern standpoint, the utopian character of Plato's work does not reside in his ends; for us, Plato's utopianism has its locus in the means he proposes to employ, or, rather, in the seeming insufficiency of his means relative to the radical character of his ends, and indeed, in his neglect of these means. The mechanisms that could bring about the new society are never given anything like the systematic analysis and detailed presentation that he gives to the character of the new society itself. In particular, Plato does not pay attention to the kinds and degrees of social power that would be necessary to realize his new state. It is this seeming neglect of power that makes the modern mind uneasy.

To understand this, it needs to be remembered that Plato's cosmology conceives of "generation" as requiring two things which are coexistent and autonomous. One of these is, indeed, power which, in the *Timaeus,* is God; the other is the Forms, eternal Ideas, laws, or plans according to which power is to operate. From Plato's standpoint, it is not power but the laws which are problematic.

This is so because power already exists in the Hellenic world; Greece has many cities and these, many rulers. Plato may allow himself to conjecture that perhaps a son of philosophical disposition will be born to one of these rulers and adopt his plans, or, as he himself attempts with Dionysius II, perhaps a ruler will be converted to them. Plato does not regard power as mysterious, peculiarly scarce, or especially inaccessible. Power is certainly familiar, even in its most intimate workings, to those of aristocratic lineage such as Plato, who communicates with and has access to some of the powerful men of the time.

Power is, after all, continually being mobilized, brandished, and used in the see-sawing struggles between the cities and in the continuing internecine conflicts between oligarchs and democrats. Power is manifest in the occasional *coup d'état* of one party against the other, and, indeed, as we saw, Plato's own uncle had participated in one of these in Athens. For these reasons Plato might well feel that the sheer mobilization of power as such is not the problem. The problem is what to do with power and how to use it.

It is this conception, Plato undoubtedly feels, that is lacking; and it is this that his plans for the city may provide. Witnessing as he does many radical changes in the fate of different Greek cities and rulers—and sensitized to the imminence of such dramatic changes by traditional Greek beliefs concerning the fickleness of fortune—it is by no means fantastic for him to hope for a sudden acquisition of power through which he may enact the projected city. At least it is not quite so alien and utopian an expectation for him as it would be for those such as ourselves with a longer and ingrained historical sense and with a predilection for evolutionary conceptions of change. Looked at from within, Plato is never quite so wildly utopian as he may seem to us, looking at him from the outside. Our modern invidious judgment of him as a utopian is, to a large extent, an expression of our own ethnocentric tendency to view him in terms of current beliefs and standards and of our failure to see his work in its own cultural context.

In one part, then, the mobilization and the use of power is neither inconceivable nor mysterious to Plato. It is familiar to him. He has seen it done time and again and has lived close to those who have done it. The trouble, from his standpoint, is that he has not seen it done successfully, in the sense of leading to a stable and desirable polity. Power brought forth counterpower, and what one side did, another undid. Further, power was used incompetently and for selfish ends. Plato concludes that the customary use of power in Greek society is a corrupt and corrupting thing, a kind of dirty politics at its worst. Time and time again he remarks that power corrupts those who have it, and the more so the more they have of it, especially when they are not themselves subject to a restraining authority such as the laws. "[T]he very bad men," Socrates says to Callicles, "come from the class of those who have power." [38] Again, "if anyone gives too great a power to anything, . . . everything is overthrown," [39] and excess and injustice result. "No human nature invested with supreme power is able to order human affairs and not overflow with insolence and wrong," [40] unless they are themselves governed by laws. Where it is submissive to laws, the state will have salvation "and every blessing the Gods can confer." [41]

It is thus not only that Plato, knowing the ways of power, feels free to neglect it. There is the further consideration that he does not like what he knows about power. Plato has lost confidence in the ability of the established loci of power to use it wisely. From his standpoint, the major conventional power centers are morally bankrupt. Neither oligarchs nor democrats, neither aristocrats nor the *dēmos,* neither the poor nor the rich, are expected to use power for the moral purposes he sought. Indeed none of them has even been able to maintain Athenian power; the city is defeated by Sparta while Sparta is, in its turn, vanquished. Thus Plato's utopianism is in some part also to be understood as a result of his despair about the proper uses of power.

So far as sheer power is concerned, he sees it as a diseased old drab available to all comers; it has lost its lure for him. Power, therefore, has to be transformed and purified before it can be touched without risk of contamination. It has to be used by philosopher-kings who will be beyond temptation, and it has to be controlled and mastered by laws embodying reason and wisdom. There is no problem in getting power, but who wants it as it is? To make and keep it honest requires the scrupulous care and planning to which Plato turns his attention. Using power wisely, from his standpoint, requires the utmost resolve and intelligence if it can be done at all. In one part, the detailed planning of the utopias is an adaptation to this hazard; it is an effort to minimize it in advance as far as possible. The details of planning constitute a response to threat, as we have said before, but this is a threat that resides in one of the two basic conditions that Plato sees as necessary to reorder society—in power itself.

In one respect, then, the detailed, busy planning of the utopias is a rational adaptation. It is a practical preparatory response to prevent blind politics from stumbling once more to failure. The detailed planning of the utopias, however, is more than the precautionary specification of useful arrangements that might bypass the difficulties inherent in using power. It is a consummatory as well as a preparatory activity, for the detailed plans also permit an immediate if vicarious enjoyment. The sensuous evocation of the ideal city in concrete and fulsome specification permits gratification now. The city sought takes on reality in the imagination and thus reduces the tension between the ideal and the real, between what Plato longs for and the frustrating limitations of Greek society as it is. The highly detailed utopia is a kind of wish fulfillment, a hope realized in fantasy, a dream in which fulfillment may indeed be had without power.

To say this, however, is not to say that the outline of the new cities is nothing but a form of escape literature depicting a society that it is never intended or believed possible to realize. Simply because it permits vicarious and consummatory satisfactions does not perforce demonstrate that they are a sheer entertainment. Indeed it may be suspected that any detailed plan or model will permit such consummatory gratifications. There is, however, a crucial contingency here in that such satisfactions may, on the one hand, serve to reinforce the planner's efforts to carry his plan forward and realize it, or, on the other hand, they may serve as substitute gratifications diverting energies from their practical realization. Perhaps, for Plato, the plans for the cities have both elements in them. It is certain, however, that he regards them as desirable, and there is little doubt that he views them as possible. "There is no impossibility in all this; that there is a difficulty, we acknowledge." [42]

In the accusation of utopianism—a cafeteria of complaints if there ever was one—there is an implication of a well-intentioned but soft-headed idealism that lays out colorful but impractical plans. This bill of complaints commonly contains two distinct charges: first, that what is planned cannot be realized and, second, that this is at least in part due to the planner's overestimate of the benign qualities of men and their institutions. The implication is that men are unrealistically regarded as more idealistic, altruistic, and reasonable than presumably they are in fact. So far as Plato is concerned, I believe that the latter cannot at all be maintained. Everything that has so far been said of his estimate of the subversive effects of the bodily passions—of men's greed, lust, and selfishness, and of their downright incompetence—must without further repetition acquit him of such a charge. Furthermore, the man who took slavery for granted, the man who believed that an approximation to the ideal society required preferential concessions to men of wealth, and the man who proposed to set up a vast and comprehensive network of authoritarian controls can, it seems to me, scarcely be accused of having thought too well of his fellows. Far from being tender-minded, Plato, it would appear, was among the more tough-minded of social theorists ever to write. He may have wanted the best from men, but he certainly expected the worst.

We need to ask here from whose standpoint and within what period of time were Plato's plans practically unrealizable. I have already indicated that, from Plato's standpoint and, indeed, in terms of certain of the characteristic assumptions of Greek culture, his utopias could well have been felt to be more feasible, however difficult, than we with our very different premises might judge. It is all too easy and profitless to say from the vantage point of several thousand years of hindsight that what did not happen could not have and is therefore utopian.

If by utopian we mean that the proposed social rearrangements would not and could not be accepted and work at the time they were proposed, then we must ask what is the time unit to which we should confine ourselves in making such a judgment, and would this not vary with the depth, the scope, and the inherent difficulty of the proposals? Sometimes it seems that utopianism is in the mind of the beholder. It entails a tacit judgment that is based on his own, often questionable conception of what is a "long" time. In this connection, it seems appropriate to remember that Plato was by no means the only writer of utopias in Greek antiquity. Cratinus, Aristophanes, Phaelus of Chalcedon and Hippodamus of Miletus also wrote them. Among his "visionary" plans, Phaelus provides in his utopia for equal and uniform education for all citizens. Hippodamus, for his part, dreams of the division of cities into square blocks by intersecting roads. From a modern standpoint, perhaps we had best define as utopian those whose plans have not to the moment been realized. On second thought, perhaps we who live in cultures that are blueprinting plans for trips to the moon and the planets have no right to call anything utopian.

CONTEMPORARY POSTSCRIPT

There is indeed scarcely any innovation of physical science and technology that today puts amazement in us, and there are few now envisaged that we can confidently proclaim impossible. After our own fashion, we ourselves have become as utopian as any people ever were. Our utopian impulses seem, however, to center largely on our expectations of physical science and technology. We plan for remarkable new machines, factories, buildings, vehicles, and indeed for the material framework of total cities and more. But we seem to have lost our taste, our nerve, and our imagination for conceiving new forms of social relationships, new structures of social organization and community—in short, new social solutions to the problems of living. American foreign policy in the early 1960's, for example, congratulates itself as daring and brilliantly imaginative if it has the courage to propose the export of the New Deal policies of the 1930's to the "underdeveloped" areas of the rest of the world.

In large measure this failure is due to our widespread cultural preoccupation with the purely technological and with our understandable proclivity to exploit to the fullest its profusive potential. In smaller degree it derives also from our training of social scientists and from the conception of themselves which we induce them to adopt. Modern social scientists have been trained to analyze, study, and understand modern social problems, and, in my opinion, they do this with no little skill and success. They have not, however, been well trained or much encouraged to try their hand at "solving" social tensions if, by this, we mean not simply understanding their sources or causes but also proposing possible remedies for them. Such solutions always entail proposals for changing existent conditions, and, in turn, they require an image of alternative social relationships and institutions, of new organizational and community forms. In short, they require that there be imagined a mode of behavior—a way of life or a form of human relations—which differs from that which already exists in the group experiencing the problem.

Commonly, social scientists today feel that their roles require them to act in a value-free way—though this is far from the clearest of prescriptions—and they believe that the stipulation of specific social arrangements, alternative to those that exist, cannot be justified by or deduced solely from the facts of the case. And they are right in this. Most social scientists, therefore, hew to the description, analysis, and explanation of "what is." They plan neither manifestly practicable alternatives nor daring utopian designs.

Yet if a sociologist or other social scientist is not as such licensed to pre-scribe what ought to be for others, or still less to impose it upon them—and there are few social scientists, if any, with such aspirations—neither is he less qualified than others to do so. Certainly if he cannot say what ought to be, he is as much and often more qualified than most to say what could be. The social scientist has no right—and none I know are Platonist enough to claim it—to tell others what they should or must do. But it would seem that they do have a right, if not a responsibility, to inform men about what they *might* do to relieve human suffering and to discover alternative social arrangements.

Yet what does it mean to speak of discovering alternative social forms of social organization? Does it mean that through a careful study of the natural variability of existent beliefs, institutions, and social relations, sociol-ogists may come upon some that promise to serve as a useful remedy for current problems? But why need these social forms be presently existent in order to be worthy of consideration? Would one feel inclined to disqualify arrangements that had once existed but no longer exist? A proposed alterna-tive can only be decided on by appraising its appropriateness for the pres-ent, and it is this, of course, that is the germane consideration. It makes no difference whether or not this alternative already exists somewhere, once ex-isted but no longer survives anywhere, or never existed at all. If social scien-tists have a right, let alone a responsibility, to propose social arrangements alternative to those in existence, they also have a right to invent new arrangements that never at all existed and which are, at least in this sense, utopias.

Indeed, what good reason is there for a social scientist to restrict his pro-posals to the satisfaction of needs that already exist or for tensions that are already felt? Why should social scientists be required to withhold their pro-posals until after the need occurs or has become unpleasantly evident? Why should they be confined only to suggesting proposals that reduce tension; why cannot they propose social alternatives, so far as they can, simply to make good things better?

To do these, social scientists require two necessary conditions: the first is that very knowledge of human relations which they are now increasingly coming by and which is their special business. The second is a quality of mind which habitually leads them to conceive, to play with, to formulate, and to entertain various solutions for social problems rather than simply to describe and explain them. They need a constructive quality of the imagination which can sense what might be. If some of their proposals turn out to be extravagant, needless, wasteful, outrageous, or even utopian, no one needs to buy them; but let them at least be freely available on the market place of ideas—rather than being self-inhibited—where they can be compared with the shopworn social worlds that are presently up for sale.

N O T E S

1 *Philosophy in the Tragic Age of the Greeks,* pp. 30–31.

2 *Protagoras.* 348CD.

3 *Philebus.* 14C.

4 *Gorgias.* 449C.

5 *Protagoras.* 343A.

6 *Gorgias.* 458A.

7 *Protagoras.* 361A.

8 *Phaedo.* 107C.

9 J. Gould, *op. cit.,* p. 30.

10 *Meno.* 82A.

11 *Phaedo.* 73A.

12 *Gorgias.* 475C.

13 Cornford, *op. cit.,* p. 202.

14 Murray, *op. cit.,* p. 164.

15 *Crito.* 44D.

16 *Crito.* 49C.

17 *Lysis.* 222C.

18 *Gorgias.* 474A.

19 *Gorgias.* 482C.

20 R. Robinson, *Plato's Earlier Dialectic* (Ithaca: Cornell University Press, 1941), p. 9.

21 *Protagoras.* 340E.

22 *Phaedo.* 91C.

23 *Republic.* 537DE.

24 *Republic.* 538E–539A.

25 *Laws.* 753E.

26 *Laws.* 775E.

27 *Republic.* 501A.

28 *Laws.* 773B.

29 *Laws.* 775A.

30 *Laws.* 804D.

31 *Republic.* 398C.

32 *Republic.* 399C.

33 *Republic.* 378E; *Laws.* 801A.

34 *Laws.* 739A.

35 *Laws.* 775BC; 807EF.

36 *Laws.* 909.

37 *Laws.* 942AB.

38 *Gorgias.* 526A.

39 *Laws.* 691D.

40 *Laws.* 715D.

41 *Laws.* 715D.

42 *Republic.* 499D; *Laws.* 502C; *Republic.* 540D.

9

Therapeutics:
Law and Universalism

> . . . we must not be annoyed if, in the course of
> legislation, we have enacted some things, and have
> not made up our minds about some others; for as
> yet we are not legislators, but we may soon be.
> —Plato, *Laws* [1]

WHERE men have good laws to which they submit, says Plato, they have
the blessings of the gods: here I turn to two specific aspects of Plato's therapeutics—to changes in law and changes in the value system. In concerning
himself with law, Plato is concerned with the kinds of norms, written and
unwritten, needed to govern men and to avoid *anomia*. Among the more
obvious concerns that dispose Plato to the use of law as therapy is his
interest in the problems of authority. He seeks some arrangement by which
all will be governed and to which the master no less than the man will submit. He seeks a solution for the problems of governance which he views
very largely from the standpoint of those who govern.

LAW AND AUTHORITY

It is among the most elemental dispositions of men in authority—and not of
them alone—to appraise their social relations in terms of their own expectations or plans and to evaluate subordinates in terms of the degree to which
they obey. Authorities concern themselves with increasing the correspondence between their own expectations and their subordinates' behavior. They
take special note of the divergences that exist, and they advance some kind
of explanation for them. Finally, authorities take some kind of action
intended to reduce such divergences by exerting various kinds of influence
on their subordinates. Indeed, to be in authority is to have the right and the
power to rectify a discordant social relationship by initiating action to
modify the other's behavior.

Certainly the problems of authority are among the most crucial with
which Plato is concerned. He regards authority's effective functioning as

vital for a stable community, and he views its failure as central to the disunity of Hellenic society. Indeed the problem of maintaining a proper authority is at the core of his metaphysics, for it is not only the social world but the universe as a whole that rests upon authority and hierarchy. There is little question but that Plato sees social disunity within the city as deriving in important part from the failure of authority—from the double failure of the natural rulers to rule correctly and of the subordinates to obey. Indeed it is more important to obey than to command well. "Every man should remember the universal rule," says Plato, "that he who is not a good servant will not be a good master; a man should pride himself more upon serving well than upon commanding well." [2] The problem, of course, is how such obedience is best to be procured.

CONCEPTIONS OF DEVIANCE

The answer that will be given depends upon the alternative solutions that are seen as available, and these, in turn, depend on current beliefs about why men fail to conform. One of the basic responses to disobedience is some form of close supervision, where the authority watches his subordinates closely, tells them very explicitly what he wants, and carries on a continuing inspection of their behavior. Such a strategy premises that authorities have come to view subordinates as essentially unwilling or unmotivated to do what they want done, rather than, for example, as simply incompetent or unskilled.

Authorities may, however, define nonconformity with their expectations as due to the ignorance of the subordinate, as entailing an involuntary and unintended disobedience. This, of course, converges with one of the strongest Socratic themes, that no man does evil voluntarily, an assumption concerning social deviance that Plato never expressly rejects. This definition of deviance conduces to remedial action along educative rather than punitive lines. It seeks to bridge the gap between the superior's expectations and the subordinate's behavior by implanting some kind of information or new beliefs in the subordinate which, in turn, brings his behavior into line.

The first definition of deviance from authoritative expectations—a "voluntaristic" definition—conceives it as in some part deliberate, while the second, which I have termed a "utilitarian" definition of deviance, conceives it as an unintended by-product of ignorance. The voluntaristic conception is conducive to a punitive response, to close supervision backed by the threat of coercion and force. The utilitarian conception of deviance, in contrast, is conducive to the use of persuasion or education as a remedy. It is clear, however, that close supervision entails serious difficulties. For one, it is often inexpedient and costly, even if possible, for an authority to watch all his subordinates all of the time. In his absence or in the absence of those to whom he has delegated this task, the authority cannot rely on the continued obedience of subordinates. Indeed, to the extent that an authority is disposed to define deviance from his expectations in a voluntaristic way, he may not even feel he can rely on his junior officers to watch the others.

Under certain conditions, close supervision can in fact heighten the resentment of subordinates and may only further impair their motivation to obey. Rather than mending the disparity between the subordinates' behavior and the superior's expectations, close supervision may intensify it. This vicious circle is more likely to result when group members conceive themselves as basically equal and autonomous persons to whom subjection to the visible authority of another person is degrading. Without question, both these conditions were present among the Greek citizenry. From the citizens' standpoint, obedience to the visible, directly given orders of another person was suitable for slaves, but it was discrepant with their salient image of themselves as free and equal men.

The Greeks felt that a personal form of submission was characteristic of an Eastern subject's relation to his rulers. They long remembered seeing Persian officers drive their men into battle with whips and had viewed this with amazement and contempt. In the course of the Hellenic struggles against Persia, this self-image of the free and equal Greek was sharpened by national chauvinism against the barbarian. Indeed, Greeks came to think of barbarians as natural slaves for submitting to such a form of authority and for allowing themselves to be ruled through coercion rather than by their freely given consent.

Close personal supervision is discrepant with such a self-image and is therefore not a stable remedy for the failure of authority. In part because of this, another method of coping with the failure of authority must be found. This new method is a system of impersonal and formal rules—the rule of law.

Law and obedience to law is a functional equivalent, or substitute, for personal orders by and obedience to men. Indeed, Plato expressly thinks of the law's relation to the citizen on the model of a system of command and obedience, associating the notion of obedience to law with that of obedience to men. For example, in the passage cited above—where he remarks that a man should pride himself more for serving than commanding well—he adds, "first upon serving the laws; . . . in the second place, upon having served ancient and honourable men in the days of his youth." [3]

Plato explains that laws are needed to educate men and to inform them of what is best, for men are by nature driven to pursue their own private interests rather than what is best for the city. In the terms used above, Plato is operating with a utilitarian definition of deviance, conceiving of it as due to ignorance. In a utilitarian vein, he remarks that the citizens cannot "properly observe the laws by habit only, and without an intelligent understanding of them," [4] and that legislators or rulers should first seek to obtain compliance by "persuading men." [5] It is partly for this reason that laws ought to be written in the "long form," in which reasons are given for their stipulations.[6] Mankind also needs laws because "no man's nature is able to know what is best for human society; . . . there is a difficulty in apprehending that the true art of politics is concerned, not with private but with public good . . . and that both the public and private good as well of individuals as of states is greater when the state and not the individual is first considered." [7]

He adds, however, and this time in a voluntaristic vein, that laws are also needed because, while a man may know these things in the abstract, "Human nature will be always drawing him into avarice and selfishness, avoiding pain and pursuing pleasure without any reason, and will bring these to the front, obscuring the juster and the better; and so working darkness in his soul will at last fill with evils both him and the whole city." [8] Men ought to be converted from such ignorance and intemperance "as far as their evil minds can be healed, but to those whose web of life is in reality finished, giving death, which is the only remedy for souls in their condition, as I may say truly again and again." [9]

Formal rules or laws are also needed because they specify the citizens' obligation in definitive form. Clarifying fully his tasks and his relations to others, they serve as educative instruments: "[T]he laws when once written down are always at rest; they can be put to the test at any future time, and, therefore, if on first hearing they seem difficult, there is no reason for apprehension about them, because any man however dull can go over them and consider them again and again." [10] More specifically, laws are impersonal forms of education, neither exposing the superior to the strain of personally repeating his instructions nor subjecting the subordinate to the embarrassment and indignity of a tutelage that makes visible another's superiority to him.

The formalization of rules into laws authorizes the superior to command without requiring him to imply a personal superiority. Conversely, law permits subordinates to comply without implying a merely personal submission that would betray their image of themselves as free men equal to any other. Personal superiority and subordination are masked insofar as superior and subordinate alike are governed by and subject to law.

Plato is at pains to insist that rulers no less than subjects must comply with the law, for no one can "sustain the temptations of arbitrary power." In obeying the law, rulers benefit themselves as well as the city, avoiding, for example, the ruin to which the kings of Messene and Argos brought upon themselves.[11] It is notable that Plato counterposes the rulers' conformity with law to an arrogance and invidious display of personal superiority that would be most objectionable to *hybris*-sensitive Greeks who view themselves as equals and free men:

> To justice, he who would be happy holds fast, and follows in her company with all humility and order; but he who is lifted up with pride, or elated by wealth or rank, or beauty, who is young and foolish, and has a soul hot with insolence, and thinks that he has no need of any guide or ruler, but is able himself to be the guide of others, he, I say, is left deserted of God.[12]

The law, then, creates a sphere of equality. It establishes and distinguishes an area outside of the discord-generating differences of the system of stratification; it controls the competitive and prideful sentiments of the contest system. It does these, first, by establishing cultural boundaries around power, wealth, and prestige, confining and limiting their influence in the public sphere; and, second, by defining these as irrelevant in appraising the parties' claims or liabilities.

Insofar as there is a governance by laws, the expectations which they embody are also widely and publicly known. This enables many members of the group to know how and when *others* are deviating from them. The ordinary citizen, therefore, may augment the enforcement efforts of the formal authorities by directly intervening to inhibit or punish infractions, or by informing to the authorities. Both are held in the highest esteem by Plato, and informers especially are lauded.[13] In his new society, ordinary citizens who intervene directly to uphold the laws are to be the prize winners in *aretē,* or civic virtue.[14]

Not only do formal rules or laws serve an educative function, they also legitimate punishments for violation of the expectations they incorporate. Punishment, of course, is not regarded as legitimate under any and all circumstances, and in classical Greece lack of willful malice is widely viewed as a basis for mitigating punishment. As Euripides remarks, "Ignorance acquits you." [15] Conversely, punishment is deemed particularly legitimate for a lack of those valued qualities that may be learned, or, as Protagoras states, for a want of "those good qualities which are attained by study and exercise and teaching." [16] Plato himself apparently concurs, remarking upon the heinousness of crimes committed by those "receiving such an excellent education and training from youth upward." [17]

In a somewhat tortured discussion in the *Laws,* Plato comments "that ignorance is a third cause of crimes," [18] along with passion and pleasure. Men may, of course, do injustice because of the latter two, but even individuals bent on doing good may "be sometimes mistaken," [19] and their behavior can hurt others. Such an action should, however, be defined by the intention, not by the consequences, and is a just one, he remarks, although some think of it as an involuntary injustice.

Despite the murkiness of this discussion, born largely of Plato's desire to champion the Socratic principle that no one does evil voluntarily rather than the popular practice of legislating differently for voluntary and involuntary crimes,[20] it seems clear that Plato also believes that ignorance extenuates. Crimes committed because of ignorance of the good, though with the intention to do it, are viewed as less onerous than those committed out of passion or a quest for pleasure. Men can rise above pleasure and passion, he observes, but never above ignorance.[21]

Insofar as the laws educate and inform men of what is desired, making this available for study, in effect the laws constitute a warning in advance of the consequences of infractions. In this way laws serve to legitimate punishments, safeguarding the community from discord born of a divergent judgment of the punishment. (And, indeed, Plato is admittedly concerned that "everyone may understand our proposal, and be able in some way to judge whether the penalty is fitly or unfitly inflicted." [22]) Finally, on this point, it may be observed that the need to provide a strong and unmistakable legitimation for punishments is all the greater where the punishment prescribed is stringent, when it is believed that "the best kind of purification is painful, like similar cures in medicine," [23] and when there is expected to be a class of incorrigible and great sinners who, unable to profit from instruction by the law, must be executed or exiled.

Basic to the proliferation of laws and the severe sanctions for their enforcement is the assumption clearly made by Plato that men ought to be regarded with an abiding distrust. Formal rules, then, are a way of communicating obligations to those who are viewed as ready to evade, avoid, or withhold full and proper performance of them. Laws are an instrumentality congenial to those whose ambitions do not generate the ready and full consent of others. In effect, laws serve to diminish reliance upon persons, particularly those whose involvement is needed but who are viewed as incompetent or insufficiently motivated to do their part.

Clearly, however, if formal laws are to perform these functions successfully, they themselves must be deemed positively legitimate. This is to be accomplished in several ways: first, the laws are to be the product of reason, which at least in some part is expected to discern what is "best." The laws, in fine, are reason surrogates and are to be relied on and respected because they embody man's highest faculty. They have been arrived at in a manner most likely to ensure knowledge, or the clearest vision, of the good. Second, they aim at and help realize what is most desirable, not for this or that individual or for the selfish interest of any one person, faction, or class, but for the community as a whole: the laws are to stand above the interests of persons and classes. Plato undoubtedly regards the law's nonpartisan character as one of its strongest claims to legitimacy.

SACRALIZATION AND THE RITUAL STATE

The third and perhaps most powerful strategy that Plato uses for legitimating the laws is to sacralize them. To serve the laws, he holds, is to serve the gods.[24] The strategy of sacralization takes the form of defining the laws as God-given, and almost the entire institutional apparatus provided by the law—governing land allotments, contests, contracts, marriages, births, and deaths—is intentionally interwoven with ritual and religious observances.[25] Plato seeks to stabilize the new institutional order by stressing the power and the pervasive involvement of the gods in the civic order. He does this indeed to the point where conformity and nonconformity with law is almost coextensive with piety and impiety. Plato's proposals would also make men increasingly dependent on divine power and favor, thereby heightening their dependence upon the civic authorities who, in his society, mediate relations with the gods.

Feelings toward the institutions of the new community are to be fixated through a binding-in process that defines them as sacred. The new institutions are to be viewed as a god-touched, divinely ordained order imbued with a sacred power and majesty; they are to be regarded with a sense of awe and are to be untouchable on threat of a terrible punishment. This combined view of the law, stressing its meticulous explication of requirements, on the one hand, and its impregnation with sentiments of reverence and sacred awe, on the other, is reminiscent of nothing so much as the stereotypy of ritual. And when these two characteristics are seen in conjunction with the pervasive extent and total jurisdiction of the laws, we may well think of the proposed community as a "ritual state." It is to be a ritual state in that men are to be oriented to prescriptions that are meticulously detailed and sacredly sanctioned. Each man is to have his place in a scheme of things that is defined as divinely ordered. Each is to occupy a social space structured and boundaried by a sacred force, and to act out an unchanging part in an unchanging passion play.

Men's behavior in this society is not to be differentially adapted to varying individuals and events, or to the reciprocal gratifications and mutual aid they provide for one another, or, as much as formerly, to the good opinion of others. The behavior of men in the new society is, rather, as far as possible to be single-mindedly oriented to the devoted enactment of their own part in the sacred service. Looking neither to the left nor right, they are to speak their lines as they were ordained, regardless of how others may falter and miss their cues. In Plato's view, this is to be a society in which God, not man, is to be the measure of all things.

The society is to be pattern-oriented rather than person-oriented. Its basic orientation is to be toward pattern maintenance rather than the mutual accommodation of persons. Insofar as men are to take notice of one another, this is to be in terms of their ritual status, appraising or dispraising, rewarding or punishing one another largely for their conformity with or deviance from the hallowed laws. Otherwise each is to mind and do his own business. The people of the new city are to be as model-oriented as the planners who prepare for it. It is in this way that Plato proposes to overcome the flux and fluidity of the Greek society he knows. To Athenian changeability he counterposes a commitment to pattern maintenance that will fix and bind in the desired forms of behavior through their sacralization.

Underlying the model-oriented change strategy that culminates in the ritual state is a sense of threat, a threat that surrounds and permeates the planners and those for whom they are planning. The whole world—inner and outer, within and between men—is felt to be in enormous hazard. Since all is in great peril, everything that can be made subject to influence must be controlled. Man is seen as essentially frail and vulnerable to fortune; "man never legislates, but accidents of all sorts, which legislate for us in all sorts of ways. The violence of war and the hard necessity of poverty . . . the power of disease . . . pestilences . . . a succession of bad seasons . . . in human affairs chance is almost everything . . ." [26] The world, then, is viewed as immanent with the frustration of human hope and subject to many forces that are uncontrollable.

Perhaps the most relevant theory that social scientists have that bears on the institutional consequences of such a sensed loss of control is that of the anthropologist Bronislaw Malinowski, who holds that ritualization is more likely to occur when men lack realistic or technologically adequate means for realizing their ends and controlling their environment. Magical ritual, he says, "arises and functions in situations of emotional stress: crises of life, lacunae in important pursuits, . . . [and serves to] open up escapes from such situations and such impasses as offer no empirical way out." [27] The detailed explication of ritual prescriptions serves to reduce anxieties, doing this in all the ways accomplished by formal rules. Rituals, like laws, state precisely what must be done, and hence do not exacerbate anxieties with new doubts and uncertainties. Knowing exactly what is required in each area of life enhances the sense of control, for the things that ritual requires *can* be done.

In endowing the rules with a sacred significance they are made so compelling a requirement that the actor's attention is externalized—in focusing on the rules he is distracted from his inner anxieties. If properly performed, the sacred prescription mitigates feelings of powerlessness by promising assistance from extraordinary powers. At the same time, transformation of rules into rituals by sacralization makes conformity with their requirements fraught with heightened solemnity and hazard; for now deviance from the prescription may incur the wrath of gods as well as the displeasure of secular authorities. Ritual thus induces a new anxiety, but this, unlike the other diffuse and pervasive sources of anxiety, is controllable. In effect, then, ritualization exchanges a controllable source of anxiety for an uncontrollable one. If the old world is threatening and unmanageable, ritualization creates a new social world which is or seems to be humanly controllable.

METAPHYSICS AND SOCIAL PLANNING

Plato's metaphysics both expresses and heightens this sense of threat. In conceiving of all nature as intrinsically hostile or indifferent to mind—having, that is, an abiding disposition toward disorder—the planners' proposed changes are felt to be made and maintained only against nature, not with its cooperation. Change can be made only by overcoming and controlling the ingrained recalcitrance of things, a recalcitrance that never ceases and which makes change, even if once accomplished, perpetually precarious. Greek that he is, Plato cannot imagine life without a continual struggle.

Like every social diagnostician, Plato must distinguish at least two characteristics of the system he proposes to modify: its pathological and its benign features. He needs to discern the enemies and the allies of the change he wishes to initiate. From Plato's standpoint mind and reason, and therefore orderliness, are not in but above nature and need to master it. From Plato's standpoint there is nothing in nature that may be relied upon to ally itself with reason to remedy pathological states and to bring about the desired state. As mentioned, Plato at one point looks for an alliance between reason and *thymos;* the aristocratic sentiments of pride and competitiveness are to be placed under the direction of reason. But as his discussion of timocracy makes plain, Plato also believes that the *thymos* itself is, like other natural forces, susceptible to corruption. While the *thymos* may be used, it, too, may not be trusted or relied on.

Insofar as nature is seen as inherently disposed to disorder, the planners' situation is desperate, and he has a sense of perilous isolation. The planner can respond to this in various ways, each of which is manifested by Plato: by looking to assistance and support from supernatural forces, from the gods; by succumbing to pessimism and withdrawing from practical efforts to bring about the desired change; by designing a solution commensurate with the extremity of the situation as he has defined it, that is, by seeking to impose a total control and an eternal vigilance over the system to be changed; by solving the problem on a fantasy rather than a reality level. Far from irrelevant, the planner's metaphysics profoundly influences his social diagnosis and therapeutic efforts. The problems he sees in society, like the remedies he proposes, will be shaped by his most general feelings about the world and, in particular, by his broader concept of nature.

From Plato's standpoint, embodied human beings are a part of the world of nature, and as such they comprise materials which, if left to themselves, possess no desirable inner drift. They will not of their own accord develop into or remain something sought by the planner. They therefore need to be transformed deliberately in accordance with the model specified by reason. They need to be worked on from the outside if they are to realize the desired pattern. Once formed into the desired pattern, they will not of their own accord retain this form, for the inner drift that they are believed to have is an undesirable one, entailing inherent tendencies toward entropy or disorder. They are inclined to behave at variance with the design, in ways that are random relative to the desired pattern (although these need not be random relative to some other standard). In consequence, once shaped into a copy of the desired pattern the materials need, first, to be kept under close and continual surveillance, and, second, corrective influences need to be kept ready to counter the inevitable tendencies toward pattern blurring or "forgetting."

A planner operating with these assumptions does not regard himself as working together with his materials, but sees himself as imposing something upon them. Something of a lion trainer, he does not cooperate with the innate dispositions of his beasts, but aims to override and control these. It is around this central issue that some of the important differences between the change strategies of the nature philosophers and those of Plato devolve. As he remarks, the nature philosophers believe that everything exists by nature and chance rather than by the action of mind, God, or art. Plato further characterizes the nature philosophers as believing that certain of the serious arts, such as medicine, husbandry, and gymnastics, and, in less degree, politics, "cooperate with nature." [28] In brief, the nature philosophers do not regard themselves as operating in isolated opposition to nature. They view themselves as working their changes by augmenting, strengthening, and moving in the direction of certain of the natural processes already and continually present. In some part they see nature (or history) as being "on our side."

From Plato's different standpoint, forces internal to the system cannot be relied on either to bring a disrupted social system back into order or to keep it there. Indeed, even shortly after it is perfectly arranged by God, the world is not regarded by Plato as self-maintaining and self-regulating. It is instead seen as vulnerable to disorganizing influences inherent to it and must, therefore, be subject to close and continual superintendence, mechanisms for which must be built into it: "Let everything have a guard as far as possible." [29]

There is, I suspect, no issue of more fundamental importance to understanding planned social change (or applied social science) than that involved here. Whether the social theorist views society, or any group with which he is working, as having built-in dispositions of its own, and how he conceives of these dispositions, are fundamental to the change strategies he develops. The more he regards the natural disposition of social processes as at variance with—either opposed or indifferent to—the solutions he conceives for social problems, and the more powerful he regards these inhibiting forces, the more will he be inclined toward pessimism, supernatural solutions, compensatory fantasies, and planned remedies requiring a total and continual superintendence of the system. The theorist's image of the new society will depend greatly on whether he conceives it to be supported by or at variance with dispositions he takes to be inherent to men and societies.

As suggested earlier, however, it is not only that Plato expects all men everywhere to resist the new order out of a common human failing. They require superintendence also because he tacitly expects that certain human institutions, most notably slavery, generate an unyielding recalcitrance among those subject to them. The pith of the matter here is that Plato believes that reason can work wonders in men; and, surely, it is man's best hope. Yet he knows in his bones that not even reason will reconcile men to slavery. For while slavery is natural from the Greek standpoint, so too is it natural, again from their standpoint, for men to hate and resist it. The appeal to reason is Plato's first and preferred strategy of change. Yet in assuming that slaves are necessary to the good society but that they are not open to change by an appeal to reason, Plato is constrained to limit the reliance he places on reason, and he must in turn strengthen coercive mechanisms to control those whose consent to the new order is not voluntary.

THE DEVELOPMENT TOWARD
UNIVERSALISTIC ACHIEVEMENT NORMS

The development of law in ancient Greece moves along two parallel lines: first, toward universalism, that is, equal treatment for persons identified as belonging to the same category or class, and, second, toward individual as against family responsibility for crimes. Individual responsibility means that punishments can be inflicted only on the person doing them and that there is no imputation of the collective responsibility of the *genos*. The individual alone becomes the legal agent who, by himself, can make claims and who, by himself, is to be punished for his wrongs. There is, for example, an increasing tendency not to exile entire families (or to confiscate their property) but only the offending individuals. Justice becomes something that only the individual can seek and that only the individual can earn.

The former trend, toward universalistic law, entails the constitution of a public authority. It implies that all those belonging to the same legal category shall in principle have the same obligations toward, and the same privileges to influence, the public authority. Thus, following Cleisthenes, all males in the legal category of citizen were in principle entitled to an equal opportunity to vote and to hold office, and all were obligated to do military training and service at age eighteen.

Legal categories, as well as legal obligations and rights, are those explicitly stipulated by a public authority, and in the Greek case they are commonly regarded as those that are written down. The action of public authorities, such as the magistrates and *hēliastai* (jurors), is to be based on an imputation of the individual's legal identity and the rights and obligations which are expressly stipulated for this category. All other aspects of the individual's social status—his kinship or friendship ties, his position in the system of social stratification, his relation to the judging authority—are defined as irrelevant to the legal decisions of the public authority. In its mature development, this implies that a firm distinction has been drawn between the public authority and the family system and in which public authority is not the special privilege of a leading family or families.

All persons publicly defined as belonging to the same legal category are to be treated in the same manner by the public authority and are defined as having the same relationship to it, and it is in this sense that Greek legal arrangements are increasingly universalistic. At any rate, this is the direction in which Greek legal institutions were drifting, though, in practice, the defendant in a trial often believes it legitimate to win the jury's sympathy by indicating his many services to the state or by pleading that a verdict against him would impose severe hardship on his family.

A universalistic conception of law is common both to the oligarchical and the democratic viewpoints in Greece. It is common to the Spartan no less than the Athenian, and even the Spartan conceives himself a "free man" because he lives under this system of laws. Such a view of the law is one of the shared premises pervading Hellenic culture and contributes importantly to the maintenance of social order within the *polis*.

UNIVERSALISM: OLIGARCHICAL AND DEMOCRATIC

Although both democrats and oligarchs concur on the importance of a rule of law universalistically conceived, they nonetheless differ in how they conceive universalism. In general, democrats stress an egalitarian conception of law; they more typically want all citizens to have equal rights, and to this extent theirs is a larger and more open conception of the community. Oligarchs, in contrast, commonly seek to establish a more stratified and differentiated set of legal identities in relation to the public authority, and tend to establish property qualifications as a basis for defining different legal statuses among the citizenry. To this extent, theirs is a narrower and more closed conception of the community. Basically, oligarchs are concerned to limit the public influence of those with less property—of the many—so that they cannot use their franchise to tax the property or impair the privileges of the upper classes.

The democratic view of legal universalism stresses the equality of all citizens and minimizes the number of legal identities that will be established. It insulates the public domain from influence by the upper classes and utilizes the legal system as a way of redressing existent social disadvantages. In the oligarchical view of legal universalism, emphasis is on maintaining the existent socioeconomic differences among citizens and on developing diverse and unequal legal categories. In general the oligarch seeks to establish legal rights and categories isomorphic with established social differences. He uses the legal system to protect the established system of stratification.

To democrats, all reasonable men of mature years are seen as belonging to the same legal category and are viewed as entitled to the same relation to the public authority. Here, in the democratic interpretation of universalism, emphasis is on the similarities among men in one category. If the democrat leans toward a Dionysian oneness, the oligarch has an Apollonian impulse to separate men and to establish boundaries that keep them apart. To oligarchs, the spirit of legalism is in the making of distinctions among classes of men; at its political root, these distinctions are aimed at separating those who vote or rule from those who do not. The oligarch's interpretation of universalism has an exclusive disposition; governed by an elite impulse it continually restricts the group to whom political power is available. The oligarch presses toward distinctions between those classes of men who have full political powers and those who have second-class membership in the polity.

If the democratic interpretation of universalism focuses on the similarities among all those in one category, the oligarchical interpretation focuses on the multiplicity of categories and on the differences between men who belong to different categories. In the oligarchical view, any category of public identity is legitimate, even though its members have more or less political power than those in others, so long as all those in one category are treated alike. From an oligarchical standpoint, then, a property qualification or an ethnic category is not felt to be intrinsically dissonant with legal universalism.

The oligarchical interpretation of universalism in Greece permits a compromise to be effected. Under the slogan of "equality of laws," *isonomia,* it provides a kind of partial compliance with the demands of the *dēmos* for distributive equality, i.e., *isomoiria;* for now all those within one legal category are indeed to be aided equally by the public authority. At the same time, however, it formulates a system of unequal categories which reflects and safeguards the established system of social stratification.

In one sense, *isonomia* seems to mean equality before the law, which implies that whatever laws exist are to be upheld equally and impartially. In another sense, *isonomia* may also be taken to mean equality upheld through the law; here the laws do not sanction unequal political powers but insist on and protect the equality of all within the public domain. In the oligarchic sense of *isonomia,* there is an implication that whatever social and economic differences exist should be upheld and protected equally by the laws. In the democratic sense of *isonomia,* the implication seems to be that all citizens should share equally in governing the state. If, on the one hand, the oligarch's view of *isonomia* conceals his intent to maintain social and economic inequality under the guise of allowing legal and political equality, *isonomia* is probably useful also to "liberal" democrats by allowing their demands to be distinguished from those of the "radical" democrats who seek *isomoiria.* "If this interpretation is correct," says Gregory Vlastos, "*isonomia* is the record of a defeat for the poorest section of the *dēmos.* It signalizes the paradox of Greek democratic society: the astonishing fact that the man who, as citizen, shares the kingly dignity, the sovereign power of the *dēmos,* may yet as a private individual labor under the indignity of utter destitution." [30]

UNIVERSALISTIC ACHIEVEMENT VALUES IN PLATO

For the most part, there is little question but that Plato favors the oligarchical interpretation of legal universalism. Universalism and individualistic achievement are also central to the system of *values* that Plato formulates. This system is individualistic insofar as it is concerned with the behavior of individual persons, and it is achievement oriented in that it calls upon individuals to strive toward certain goals. In some measure, Plato intends individualistic achievement to be a substitute for rewarding men in terms of their birth, wealth, or electoral popularity, thus providing an alternative to conventional aristocratic, plutocratic, or democratic systems.

The basic social identities in terms of which men are to be categorized, in Plato's system, are moral ones. That is, the most significant identity of a man is not whether he is high- or baseborn, rich or poor, popular or outcast, but whether he is good or bad, which is to be judged independently of these other identities. Plato maintains—for example, in his discussion of friendship—it is these moral identities that shape men's social relations.

Since moral identities are to be assigned in universalistic-achievement terms, a man can now be good or bad regardless of his other social positions, his lineage, wealth, or power. The Platonic value system thus *creates distinctions among men that cut across those established by the class system.* It is no longer to be these worldly differences by which men are to be separated, it is their moral character that now counts. Moral character brings men into new solidarities that bridge old divisions while separating them from those with whom they might otherwise be allied because of their shared worldly condition. Universalistic achievement values then function to attenuate class cleavages and class conflicts and, in this way, reduce tensions in the established system of stratification.

An interest in men's moral identities—with whether they are good or bad men—premises, in turn, a concern with rewarding men differentially according to their differential moral status. A concern with men's virtue or moral status can then become a justification for inequalities of reward for those who may otherwise be viewed as similar. Isocrates makes this clear: "It is altogether monstrous," he remarks, "that the good and the bad should be thought worthy of the same privileges. . . . [I]t is of the essence of justice that distinctions should be made between them, and that those who are unlike should not be treated alike but should fare and be rewarded in each case according to their deserts." [31]

Although endorsing an achievement orientation, Plato's value system is not behavioristic. It strongly seeks to assign different rewards to men, not only in terms of what they do, but also in terms of what they intend—although these two elements, intention and accomplishment, remain together only in uneasy juxtaposition. As a result of Plato's emphasis on the significance of intentions, however, a man can now be good or bad regardless of his success or failure in the public contest.

Plato's value system is also an effort to purify the contest system, by inhibiting its tendency to withhold eminence enviously from one's competitors. Plato is at pains to indicate that "if a society is to be rescued from disaster and, in the result, judged happy, there is one indispensable requirement: that it should, within the bounds of what is possible for humanity, be scrupulously exact in its distribution of honor and dishonor." [32] Plato seeks an arrangement in which honor and prestige (not office) will be awarded solely on the basis of individual merit. In a manner that resonates the competitive sentiments of men committed to the contest system, Plato conceives of virtue as a prize to be awarded in the contest of life. (In this vein Euripides also has it said, "Oh a mighty quest is the hunting out of virtue." [33])

FUNCTIONS OF SPIRITUAL VALUES

There are some ways in which certain universalistic values—those that public orators today commonly eulogize as "spiritual" values—mitigate communal tensions deriving from the compulsive competitiveness of the contest system, and there are other ways in which these values serve also to reduce this very competitiveness itself. Universalistic values do the latter by sanctioning the pursuit of certain goals—particularly those which may in principle be obtained successfully by all men or by all in certain categories—so that one man's success does not necessarily require another man's failure. In contrast, many of the values of a shame culture—such Odyssean virtues as expedience, shrewdness, or "never being at a loss"—are intrinsically competitive, for one man can be shrewd only at the expense of another. But the virtues that Plato extols, justice, wisdom, and temperateness, do not necessarily require men to pit themselves against one another. Indeed, a man cannot be wise at the expense of another, for actions injurious to others are deemed by Plato to be intrinsically at variance with the very nature of these values.

While one man's wisdom can be greater than another's wisdom, a man cannot be wise at the expense of another's; nor can he be just at the expense of another's justness. Such values, therefore, serve to reduce competitively exacerbated interpersonal hostilities by orienting men to a class of "goods" that are not intrinsically limited in supply. Moreover, the supply of these goods does not diminish with the length of time that individuals possess them or the more that they use them. This is much of what Isocrates has in mind when he counsels men to seek such gifts "that even though you make hard use of them every day without fail, you will never wear them out, but will, on the contrary, enlarge them and increase their worth." [34] Insofar as competition occurs because goods are scarce, Plato's strategy is to reduce competitiveness by defining as good things which are not intrinsically scarce, the goods of the soul, whose salvation he defines as the highest of goods which may be won by all. As it develops historically, then, a system of universalistic, "spiritual" values emerges as a solution to the dilemmas of an economy of scarcity, and serves to ameliorate the tensions of social relations which, partly because of this scarcity, were organized in a quasi zero-sum manner.

Plato's universalistic achievement values are functional not only by reducing group-disruptive competition, but also by enhancing the security of the individual's ego system. Many of the things central to the heroic or classical value system of everyday Greece—health, wealth, youth, beauty, and power over others—do not entail desiderata that the individual can effectively control. They are evanescent body values which the person cannot hope to retain through the means at his disposal. One can do little or nothing, for example, about controlling or attaining youth or beauty. The Greeks also recognize that people can be born with constitutional impairments to health and, although they know that a proper regimen and medical treatment can improve or protect health, their medical knowledge is still relatively slim, as is borne in on them by the devastating plague in Athens during the Peloponnesian War. While they believe that wealth and power may be greatly enhanced by utilizing resources within the individual's control, they are also deeply pessimistic about its security, believing that men's fortunes can be overturned in a day. Virtue, however, says Isocrates, contrasting it directly with beauty, wealth, and strength, "is the one possession which abides with us in old age." [35]

Plato's development toward universal spiritual values—his emphasis upon the goods of the soul—is part of a larger cultural drift which he shares with the Skeptics, Cynics, Stoics, and Epicureans. This development is a response to strains endemic to the traditional value system, and especially to its focus on desirables that are intrinsically unstable or not reliably controllable. The traditional Greek value system induces men to want things which they commonly find themselves unable to obtain or retain. This endemic gap between many of the goals endorsed by Greek culture, and the institutional means that it makes available to achieve them, is, of course, critically heightened after the collapse of the Athenian Empire and of Sparta's power.

THE RETREAT FROM WORLDLY VALUES

Although Socrates lives through the fall of Athens, he does not experience the decline of Sparta or the Hellenic power vacuum that follows. This, however, is central to the life experience of Socrates' chief disciples, Plato and Antisthenes, the latter of whom seemed likely to become Socrates' successor, till overshadowed by the former. Antisthenes, "the Skeptic," loses faith in traditional worldly values and comes to believe that nothing matters but to do one's best. He loses faith as well in the intellectual means of realizing the good life, dialectical speculation. Unlike Plato, who stresses conformity with the laws as such, Antisthenes counterposes virtue to the enacted laws, and he holds that men should obey the former rather than the latter. Antisthenes is the bridge from Socrates to the Stoic and Cynic schools, the leaders of each of these, Zeno and Diogenes respectively, having been his student or disciple.

The career of Antisthenes' greatest student, Diogenes, spans the lifetimes of the key figures in Socrates' intellectual circle, on the one hand, and the rise of Epicurus and Zeno the Stoic, on the other; it thus encompasses the subjugation of Athens by Macedonia and the rise and fall of Alexander. Diogenes calls for a complete renunciation of earthly interests and for a self-sufficient life that will permit independence of external worldly conditions. Extolling ascetic poverty, he mocks the pursuit of wealth, power, marriage, comfort, hereditary nobility, and public games. To the traditional, polis-limited loyalty of the Greeks, Diogenes counterposes a kind of cosmopolitan individualism. To the traditional focus on religious ritual and temple worship, he counterposes an emphasis on the inward life. He calls men to the direct pursuit of goodness and to the things of the spirit that he believes obtainable only by rejecting all earthly desires and by living a simple, natural existence.

The Stoics and Epicureans later reject conventional worldly values in a similar manner. The Stoics believe that all that matters is the goodness of a man's soul. The Epicureans believe that men can obtain a measure of happiness only if they cease torturing themselves with false beliefs, such as their fear of death, whose true nature they held to be akin to sleep, and only if they turn their backs on the world with its sterile passions and empty prizes to seek a private existence with quiet enjoyments and temperate affections. While there are, of course, important variations in their several viewpoints with which we cannot deal here, they all commonly agree in seeking independence from the conventional earthly values and rewards.

While Socrates does not reject conventional values with anything like their absoluteness or push his philosophy toward a radical individualism or cosmopolitanism, his outlook, like theirs, does emphasize goals and values that are more fully within the control of the individual; and, like them, Socrates does subordinate the pursuit of wealth and power to the goods of the soul. The Socratic value system increases an orientation toward goals that any person may successfully realize alone. It directs men toward aspirations that they may supposedly realize in this life or in an afterworld, regardless of the cooperation or opposition, the success or failure, of others. In one part the Socratic value system is the ethic of a self-sufficient loneliness.

Yet while Plato believes that the lone individual can pursue virtue, his conception of human nature does not dispose him to believe that he will normally persevere and succeed in this if he remains alone and uncontrolled. Further, Plato seems to doubt that virtue will be seen as its own reward, and he continues to believe that a good man will be concerned to have a good reputation among the good. Consequently, while he remains committed to the *polis,* Plato believes that it must be reorganized so that the pursuit of virtue will be supervised closely and rewarded by proper recognition. In seeking to make men less other-directed, Plato means to detach them from a dependence upon the many so that they might be the more attached to the few who were good, and to the laws on whose behalf the latter ruled.

Rather than rely solely on a spontaneous and informal recognition of virtue, Plato provides for legally stipulated rewards. In placing some responsibility for awarding prestige or honor in the hands of public authorities, he reduces men's dependence on the mesh of their immediate interpersonal relations with their peers. Yet Plato does not seek to reduce such interpersonal dependence as an end in itself, but only so that the community will be more integrated hierarchically and men more responsive to their betters.

Plato organizes the pursuit of the new universal values to allow room for some of the conventional values and institutions rather than in a way that radically renounces them. Conversely, he aims to use certain traditional sentiments, particularly those centering on the contest system, to reinforce the new values. Plato's stress on universalistic and especially spiritual values is one way of increasing the autonomy of the prestige hierarchy vis-à-vis the other two basic status hierarchies, wealth and power. The proposed strengthening and the greater autonomy of the prestige system is in turn a way of ensuring that there will be resources available to reward conformity with a universalistic value system.

Such rewards, however, do not require that property institutions be changed, that wealth be redistributed, that debts be canceled, or that the class system be changed in a manner threatening those already advantaged by it. It would seem, then, that the increased autonomy of the prestige system conceived by Plato's *Laws* serves to mobilize and provide noneconomic rewards. It aims at reinforcing the new value system while still protecting the established class privileges and institutions. The goods of the soul can be obtained, it seems, without impairing vested interests or shaking the class system. Spiritual reform is to be a substitute for earthly revolution.

DYSFUNCTIONS OF UNIVERSALISM

Yet this is not entirely successful, for certain consequences of universalism are indeed injurious to community cohesion and irritate rather than reduce some class tensions. Insofar as universalistic achievement standards are used to distribute prestige in the community at large, they generate a number of difficulties. In particular, it has been known to happen that those who are the most powerful and wealthy, or even most popular, may not also be the best or most prestigious in terms of universal standards. The high and the mighty may be neither competent nor good men, a discovery that comes as something of a blow to most social orders. This is no surprise to Plato, however, and it is precisely what he is trying to avoid. But since he is also seeking accommodation to parts of the class system he cannot give full rein to "meritocracy." It is because he sees that these tensions will remain that he paradoxically confesses that cities will not cease from evil until philosophers and kings are one—until, in short, the claims of universalistic values and class privileges are reconciled somehow.

This dissonance would seem especially likely to the extent that prestige is assigned scrupulously on the basis of the individual's own achievements; that wealth and power are transmitted by hereditary succession; and that public offices are elective. Under these conditions, those judged most meritorious by universalistic achievement standards may not be those who are most powerful, popular, or rich. Indeed, it is possible even for slaves to be known as better men than their masters and for the baseborn and poor to be better than the nobility and the rich.

There is consequently an ever-possible disparity between a prestige hierarchy, where status depends on individual behavior appraised in terms of universalistic standards, and power and wealth hierarchies, where status is assigned on the basis of hereditary arrangements. When this status disparity develops, the merely rich or powerful come to be regarded as only dubiously legitimate and are viewed ambivalently. Something of this tension is evident in Euripides' *Ion,* when he notes that, save for his name, the honest slave is equal to the free man.[36] And as is so often the case, Isocrates sees and reveals the issue with a lean clarity: "This thought you must lay to heart, and see to it that in proportion as you are above the others in rank so shall you surpass them in virtue." [37]

There are, of course, various strategies by which social tensions born of such a status disparity may be mitigated and by which compromises can be effected among the different standards for allocating status. One is to make upward social mobility in the power or wealth hierarchies open to those judged to have more of the appropriate virtues or competencies. Plato's recognition that children of "gold" talents may be borne to parents of "bronze" talents (and must be reclassified upward) is one way he proposes to accommodate the ideal Republic to this pressure. Again, the various public offices may, like other occupational specializations, be defined as requiring a special competence derived from special talent and training. In this vein Plato requires that the Guardians of the Republic possess a rational knowledge of the art of ruling as well as a mastery of the keystone of all the sciences, the dialectic, in addition to other virtues deemed appropriate to rulers.

Plato, then, is concerned with the adjustments that are required if the class system is to be accommodated to universalistic achievement standards. He is concerned to safeguard the new value system from subversion by the existent wealth and power hierarchies. He also wishes to revise the system of stratification to safeguard the application of universal values to public authority. It is partly to protect the effectiveness of universalistic achievement standards that he seeks to insulate the Republic's Guardians from particularistic ties to women, children, and property, by having them held in common. In the *Laws,* however, Plato seeks a compromise from the other, more realistic direction, extending special political perquisites to those of greater wealth, utilizing the strategy of oligarchical universalism.

In the end Plato has to face two ways at once, particularly in his conception of authority: authority must be open to those with reason and virtue, but it must be totally closed to slaves. Unless Plato does the former, his plan would involve a basic betrayal of his Socratic heritage, since it would provide no mechanisms for rewarding virtue or for influencing government by good or competent men. Unless Plato does the latter, however, he will undermine the operating effectiveness of slavery along with the whole system of stratification, and he will alienate the upper classes.

It is perhaps for this reason that Plato moves from an earlier stress on the individual's proper orientation to the good to a greater (though not a novel) stress on the importance of formal laws. In the *Laws* Plato stresses that the highest communal prestige is to go to those who give the fullest obedience to the laws. It is such obedience, rather than conformity with the underlying values (of which the laws are supposedly the surrogate), that is now regarded as crucial. Indeed it is the laws that authoritatively define the very character of both the virtues and of God himself: "the Gods are such as the law ordains (and this may be extended generally to the honorable, the just, and to all the highest things, and to all that relates to virtue and vice)." [38]

Plato employs another strategy which would also preserve the established wealth and power hierarchies from the disruptive effects of a universalistic allocation of communal prestige: he tends to stress the intrinsic significance of virtue, the ways in which virtue is its own reward and vice its own punishment. This argues, in effect, that any slippage between the power–wealth hierarchy and the prestige hierarchy is fundamentally trivial. (It is notable that, although he stresses the intrinsic significance of virtue, he hastens to reassure his listeners that virtuous men will also find their earthly rewards, but undermines this reassurance by adding that even if this were not the case he would assert it was.) From this standpoint the virtuous slave need not be freed or the virtuous poor man enriched; for they are amply enough rewarded by their sheer possession of virtue.

Yet in what sense can virtue be its own reward? This remains obscure until we answer the question of to whom or to what is virtue its own reward. To say that it is so to the embodied person is manifestly unconvincing, for this denies the testimony of everyday life that there is all too often a discrepancy between men's worth and their rewards. There is, however, another answer which is impossible to discredit on the basis of experience: it can be said, as Plato does, that virtue is rewarding to the *soul* of the person, not to his embodied being. In brief, Plato draws a firm distinction between the soul and the embodied person, arguing that the former is immortal and can be benefited in some afterlife or other-worldly way, if it lives a virtuous existence in the here and now. Since the soul is the highest and best part of the person from Plato's standpoint, then that which rewards it is the highest and best of rewards. Furthermore, since they are given in an afterlife, the soul's rewards are not visible here and now, and in fact their exceptional worth is heightened by their extra-worldly, nonvisible character. It is this enjoyment of the soul which even the slave and the poor, if they live virtuously, may anticipate. Even the lowest may have the highest of rewards, rewards which have the convenient property of requiring no serious change in the system of social stratification and in the allocation of scarce goods.

Plato essentially conceives of the laws as reason surrogates, and from this standpoint the ultimate justification of all rulership is the possession of reason in its higher forms. Yet so long as authority is thought to be ultimately legitimated in terms of universalistic achievement values, particularly reason, then in principle anyone manifesting such values, regardless of his wealth, birth, or popularity, has a claim to authority. In principle, then, it is possible even for the slaves or the poor to merit and claim rulership. It is in this connection that Plato's analysis of justice in the *Republic* is most apposite. It will be recalled that there Plato interprets justice in the state to mean that each will do only the one thing for which he is best suited and that none will meddle in another's business. From this standpoint it is unjust for a slave to wish to be a ruler. The slave who would wish to use his possession of reason or his successful performance in terms of other universalistic achievement values to claim authority reveals an intemperance that manifestly disqualifies his claim.

This, however, bears only on the claim to authority that the lowly may wish to advance on their own behalf. Nonetheless, even if the poor and slaves themselves modestly lay no claim to authority, it may still be felt by others that the slaves should be given authority commensurate with their conformity to universalistic achievement standards. It is in this connection that Plato's remark about the implications of slavery for the "reason" of the slave takes on a special interest. Zeus, he says, quoting Homer, and without in any way accounting for it, impairs the reason of those enslaved: "he takes away half the understanding of men whom the day of slavery subdues." Since possession of reason in its higher forms is, for Plato, the ultimate legitimation of all rulership, the slave's very status disqualifies him for authority; and the laws excluding him from authority are, therefore, rational and legitimate. However Plato came to such a view, it serves as a ground to withhold authority from slaves.

Plato is aware that universalistic achievement standards, and a prestige hierarchy derived from them, would be dissonant with the established arrangements for allocating wealth and power, especially insofar as these are based on private property and hereditary transmission. Indeed, it is a mark of his sociological penetration that he sees this as clearly as he does. However extravagant or insufficient his solutions, there is no mistaking the depth of his diagnosis. He sees that universalistic achievement standards are a crucial source of tension for, and are in turn threatened by, the conventional power and wealth arrangements.

PLATO'S REFERENCE GROUP

To whom is Plato's value system directed? In what social context is it fostered? These questions lead us to explore the character of the audience to whom his work seems tacitly oriented. The nature of this audience or reference group emerges in greater clarity if we contrast it with those who are in a way Plato's closest intellectual competitors, Antisthenes and Diogenes.

These two derive from and are oriented to groups quite different from those to which Plato and Socrates himself are sensitive. Antisthenes, whose mother had been a Thracian slave, establishes his school in Kynosarges, a gymnasium for those of lowly or base birth, and he himself, dressing in beat-up workman's clothes, is reputed to have made friends with the "bad." Antisthenes' disciple, Diogenes, is the son of an ill-esteemed money-changer; he lives a mendicant existence and—no account would seem right without its mention—sleeps in his renowned tub, a large earthen pitcher.

Plato and Socrates, in contrast, seem to associate with youths "noble and fair" who appear to be essentially a segment of the *kaloi k'agathoi,* as suggested almost explicitly by Xenophon.[39] Many of the aristocracy think of themselves as *kaloi k'agathoi,* though later this term will not be confined to aristocrats and comes increasingly to be a term of commendation for individuals whose style of life or "culture" manifests the older graces and traditional virtues. *Kaloi k'agathoi* has a variety of implications; perhaps the most familiar for us is "noble and good," or "gentlemen." But it also resonates with aesthetic implications of fineness, gallantry or flair, gracious-ness or knightliness, and it possibly implies youth and beauty. The *kaloi k'agathoi* are perhaps younger aristocrats, or others whose style of life has not become dissolute and who manifest a refinement and education which encourage them to a sense of their own social superiority. If not them-selves highborn, they have a respect for the "better" traditions. They tend also to be antimercantile, critical of the democracy, and pro-Spartan in tendency. It would seem that they are often the "we" or the "they" who will do the various things required for planning and implementing Plato's utopian cities. At any rate the contrast between Socrates' and Plato's well-born reference group and the baseborn *dēmos* to whom Antisthenes and Diogenes orient themselves is evident enough.

Certainly these different social groups experience the political crises and social disorganization in Athens after its defeat by Sparta in significantly different ways. The lowly, who comprise Antisthenes' and Diogenes' refer-ence groups, must experience this as even more threatening and frustrating than the elite to whom Plato and Socrates are oriented. The gap between what the lowly want and the means they have available to attain it is bound to be particularly great, and their response takes the form of a more radical escape or retreat from the conventional institutions and the worldly values of Hellenic society.

Having an aristocratic lineage or leaning, the *kaloi k'agathoi* have tradi-tions of political rule and responsibility, or at least conceive themselves as having a claim to leadership. Viewing society from a superior position in it, they see the crisis as a failure of authority, and the solutions to which they are disposed require a political renovation, often in the direction of an oligarchical reinvigoration of authority. Such a group's sentiments would be congenially resonated by the repeated emphases on hierarchy and authority in Plato's projected cities. No more than Dion after his invasion of Sicily, few of the *kaloi k'agathoi* will be attracted to a radical reform of property institutions and the system of social stratification. Nor does it seem likely that the *kaloi k'agathoi* will usually be inclined toward cosmopolitanism.

It is noteworthy that Plato's social theory, unlike Diogenes' and Zeno's, is not cosmopolitan in orientation. Certainly Plato never regards himself, as Diogenes does, as a *kosmopolitēs,* as a citizen of the world rather than of a single *polis.* For Plato, the *polis* with its laws is still to be the center of men's earthly loyalties. I have previously suggested that Socrates' reference group, and Plato's somewhat less so, was strongly "local" rather than "cosmopolitan" in character. In particular, the suggestion was made that Plato's outlook is especially convergent with the ideological orientations of those whom I have termed "powerless locals." They may also be thought of as dispossessed or declassed locals, locals whose privileged class position has been threatened or reduced.

It may be that the conjunction of these two factors—that is, its upper-class outlook and its localistic orientations—specifies Plato's reference group somewhat more precisely. It needs noting, however, that these two characteristics are not always mutually compatible but may, under certain conditions, generate conflicting cross pressures. In general the Greek upper class may be expected to stress the local autonomy of the individual *polis* because it is within its restricted framework that their traditional prerogatives are viable. Given larger federations of cities and territories, the pre-eminence of a local elite is overshadowed and their former influence is limited by the elites centered in the cities controlling the federation. Crudely, if *polis* autonomy is lost, the local elites are somewhat smaller frogs in a bigger pond.

Since they commonly stress their ancient lineage, their connections with local gods, their large holdings, and their longer residence in the local area, the upper class have strong motives for adopting a localistic outlook. Yet such a localistic orientation is not always compatible with their class position, and their continued commitment to localism depends upon the security of their class pre-eminence. If and when the latter is threatened by class conflicts and by the ambitions of the many, a local elite will often—as the history of the Peloponnesian War testifies time and again—feel closer to the upper class in enemy cities than to the lower class in their own. Not infrequently, when their class position is imperiled, they will invite in enemy foreigners to whom they surrender the autonomy of their city. For example, speaking of the oligarchy of the Four Hundred, Thucydides notes that "Their first wish was to have the oligarchy without giving up the empire; failing this to keep their ships and walls and be independent; while, if this also were denied them, sooner than be the first victims of the restored democracy, they were resolved to call in the enemy and make peace." [40]

In short, upper-class membership and localistic loyalties may conflict. Sections of the upper class are prepared to sacrifice the autonomy of their own community, along with their localistic loyalties and patriotic sensibilities, in order to safeguard their privileged class position. Yet this is a forced choice, not one which they most prefer. For while surrender of civic autonomy can strengthen the few against the many and can protect their position from internal threat—as happens after Chaeronea, when Philip declares a moratorium on basic stratificational changes in the *polis*—it also humbles the elites of the Greek cities. In consequence, many of the upper classes (especially those in a democracy) are deeply concerned to safeguard both their class position and their local privileges. They want to protect these both from the many who tax them with growing intensity and also from the hegemony of a foreign elite. They seek to safeguard their positions from enemies both foreign and domestic, so that they may remain foremost in honor, unhampered in their prerogatives, and protected in the enjoyment of their property.

After Philip's victory at Chaeronea, the autonomy of the *polis* is in fact dead, and in the long run the local elites will accommodate themselves to a place in a larger state system, preferring this restricted place to the threat of internal enemies and civil war. But at the time Plato is writing, the ideal aspirations of the elite *kaloi k'agathoi*—who feel themselves the community's natural leaders—aim at the control of class conflict in the *polis* and at the maintenance of local autonomy, both of which preserve their pre-eminent positions from enemies internal and external. It is to these objectives that Plato's *Laws* addresses itself, seeking a social order that will, through its concentrated military preparations and totalitarian arrangements, both guard the city's autonomy and stabilize its class system.

Certainly the relation between Plato and his reference group must be conceived as a reciprocal one. I can in no way imagine him planning his cities as he did *because* he thought to please them. Each is drawn to the other because of an experienced mutual compatibility rather than an intended accommodation; he to them, because his native sentiments are often akin to theirs and because they manifest a gratifying appreciation and a spontaneous understanding of what he is saying; and they to him, because he expresses in pointed ways congenial views of society which they have only vaguely formulated and felt. Like Antisthenes and Diogenes, Plato is doubtless drawn to his distinctive audience because of what he is and what he believes. He is, in turn, confirmed in his beliefs and has them somewhat reshaped by the audience within which he allows them to be expressed and dialectically tested: the bell's tone depends on both its cup and its tongue.

CONTEMPORARY POSTSCRIPT

Far from being peculiar to ancient Greece, the tensions between universalistic achievement values and established systems of property and authority are foreshadowings, on the small but intense stage of the *polis,* of tensions that long continue to permeate Western societies. In any society where men's communal prestige is based on universalistic achievement standards, those judged reputable and worthy may come to regard correspondingly high wealth and power as their due, and they may come to denigrate those whose wealth and power are individually unearned.

There are several common solutions toward which this problem drifts. In one of these, the society may surrender universalistic achievement values as a basis for awarding communal prestige—or give them only lip service —falling back on more particularistic standards. Or the society may, by an oligarchical interpretation of universalism, limit those to whom common universalistic achievement values can be applied. This is conducive to a closed community that will include only certain of the population and exclude others, blocking them from full participation and membership. But insofar as those excluded are part of the community's division of labor, producing desired objects and services, second-class membership is an unstable solution, for the excluded cannot be brought to a fully motivated and reliable performance of their tasks. They must be governed by the costly and tension-inducing methods of close supervision and coercion which, even if sanctioned by law, do not win their consent. Another familiar solution to which this dilemma leads is that of rejecting all preferential claims to power and authority that may be made on the basis of wealth or birth as such. Nor is this easily accomplished, for it disposes to a radical transformation of certain institutions, particularly those of private property and kinship, which alienate powerful sectors of the community.

The conservative solution to this problem in the West traditionally opts for a delimited and circumscribed community, often entailing an essentially oligarchical interpretation of legal universalism. Conservatism is sensitive to the disorganizing potential of universalistic achievement standards, and tends to view social problems as solvable by establishing and protecting an insulated elite who are defined as the bearers of higher values. Conversely, the progressive solution aims at an expanding and open community through the extension of universalistic achievement values, particularly by a democratic interpretation of legal universalism. The progressive solution is vulnerable to the disruptive resistance from the traditional kinship and property institutions, and progressives tend to resent these as barriers to the unrestricted sway of universalism.

Conservatism often calls for the strengthening of moral values and for the establishment of a shared belief system that will unify the community. Looked at closely, however, it usually regards only a section of the populace as members of the community. Moreover, conservatism never fully acknowledges the way in which its commitment to established property and kinship institutions, and its oligarchical legalism, require it to hedge on and indeed to betray its own moral avowals. Rather than appointing itself the protector of morality, progressivism for its part orients itself to standards of gratification and to the rational enhancement of gratification for as many as possible. Progressivism, however, often fails to acknowledge that some standards of propriety, as distinct from expedience, are necessary to govern the methods through which gratification is sought. It does not frankly admit that full gratification is impossible for human beings. Nor does it always recognize that gratification is possible only if the kinds and levels of gratification sought are limited in some manner by moral norms.

Conservatism prematurely and smugly accommodates itself to a tragic view of life; progressivism naïvely ignores it altogether. Conservatism tends to settle for less improvement than it needs to in the gratifications available to men. It is far too ready to resign itself to what is and to believe that this is the best that can be gotten. It seeks to bring contentment to men by inducing them to limit their wants rather than by using technology to realize them. Progressivism, however, seeks happiness rather than contentment. It commits itself to increasing gratifications through the development of science and technology. Indeed, the progressive's alliance with a dynamic technology has been one of his basic sources of strength. In some cases, progressivism has been able to mitigate the tensions between universalistic achievement standards and established systems of property and power by enabling all to have more than they had in the past. In this way, by enabling men to get more than they have had, the affluent and technologically advanced society diverts hostilities from those who have more or who have not earned what they have, and is thereby enabled to control the tensions between the ideals of spiritual, universalistic values and the reality of class privileges.

NOTES

[1] *Laws.* 859B.

[2] *Laws.* 762E.

[3] *Laws.* 762E.

[4] *Laws.* 951B.

[5] *Laws.* 890C.

[6] *Laws.* 720.

[7] *Laws.* 875A.

[8] *Laws.* 875C.

[9] *Laws.* 958E.

[10] *Laws.* 891A.

[11] *Laws.* 690 ff.

[12] *Laws.* 716A.

[13] *Laws.* 730D, 913D, 930D.

[14] *Laws.* 730D.

[15] *Hippolytus* iii. 216. 1234

[16] *Protagoras.* 323E.

[17] *Laws.* 854D.

[18] *Laws.* 863C.

[19] *Laws.* 864B.

[20] *Laws.* 861B.

[21] *Laws.* 863DE.

[22] *Laws.* 861C.

[23] *Laws.* 735D.

[24] *Laws.* 762E, 634E.

[25] *Laws.* 774, 775, 784, 785, 789, 753, 936, 745.

[26] *Laws.* 709 ff.

[27] B. Malinowski, *Magic, Science and Religion.* (Glencoe: Free Press, 1948), p. 67.

[28] *Laws.* p. 631.

[29] *Laws.* 760A.

[30] Gregory Vlastos, *"Isonomia,"* American Journal of Philology, 74 (1953), 355.
   If this is so, then it may well be that Vlastos has overdrawn his polemic against Ehrenberg, who had stressed the use of *isonomia* to refer to equality among nobles. As Vlastos sees it, *isonomia* becomes a compromise providing a middle ground between the most reactionary rich and the radical poor and is therefore by no means uncongenial to all the rich or noble. It is likely that it is precisely because it serves as a tool of political compromise that *isonomia* has this ambiguity in it.

[31] *Isocrates* i. 85.

[32] The translation is that of John Gould and is used here because it points up the issue under discussion.

[33] *Iphigenia in Aulis* iii. 322. 367.

[34] Isocrates i. 71.

[35] Isocrates i. 7–9.

[36] Ion iii. 45. 854.

[37] Isocrates i. 47.

[38] *Laws.* 890C.

[39] *Memorabilia* i. 6–13.

[40] Thucydides. 545.

10 The Fatigue of Reason and the Metaphysics of Authoritarianism

"Fatigue" is the antithesis of Reason. The operations of Fatigue constitute the defeat of Reason in its primitive character of reaching after the upward trend. Fatigue means the operation of excluding the impulse toward novelty. . . . The power of going for the penetrating idea, even if it has not yet been worked into any methodology, is what constitutes the progressive force of Reason. The great Greeks had this knack to an uncanny degree.
—Alfred North Whitehead [1]

THE dialectic and the Model-Guided Strategy of social change both rest on a conception of reason. They are the tactics and strategy of reason. On the one hand, they derive from and embody the concept of reason; on the other, they aim to build reason into law, institutions, and culture. Dialectic and the Model-Guided Strategy are the specialized extrusions of a protean notion of reason.

It is, however, no easier to say what Plato's "reason" is than to characterize that concept as it is used today in contemporary philosophical discourse; then as now reason is not a single but a multidimensional thing. It is clear, however, from the way that Plato alludes to it, that reason is an elemental and approbative state of mind. It is a complex way of thinking, the full resources of which cannot be seen at a glance but have to be explored patiently and revealed piecemeal as each different context allows.

On the level of casual allusion, Plato refers to reason in many ways: as the foil and counterpart of the passions or desires, as a nay-saying thing: "the forbidding principle is derived from reason, and that which bids and attracts proceeds from passion." [2] Or, more eloquently, he speaks of the "voice of the shepherd, that is, reason, bidding his dog bark no more." [3] Reason is the principle with which a man learns,[4] as distinct from the expressive or appetitive functions. It is distinct, certainly, from the senses or from mere experience, and it surely seeks a wisdom that is something more than information.[5] Again, it is that which is akin to law and order, for is "not that farthest from reason which is at the greatest distance from law and order?" [6]

REASON AND TRADITION

Many of the characterizations that Plato gives of reason are obviously negative and polemical; he clarifies it by indicating the various things that it is not; he defines it by setting it off from and contrasting it with diverse things —the senses, experience, the passions, the anomic or anarchical. Among the crucial things that reason is not, for Plato, and, indeed, to which it is opposed, is traditionalism as a mode of validating beliefs. Reason is a way of thought that does not regard beliefs as correct simply because they are old or, for that matter, because they are widely held. In this way—austere ruler though it must be—reason is also a rebel concept.

For Plato reason is centrally a way of justifying actions and of legitimating decisions without invoking tradition or common practice. Reason comes to be invoked under certain conditions, either because of a general waning of tradition or because of the growth of conflicting traditions or values, so that decisions can no longer be made routinely or be routinely legitimated by invoking shared values. Substituting for a declining consensus in communally held values, reason serves to facilitate and legitimate decisions that might otherwise be blocked by conflicting interpretations and diverging evaluations. It is a method that is likely to have more scope when traditional values either provide no routine basis for decision or else give conflicting indications for it. Reason, however, not only provides a way of legitimating decisions, it provides a mode of legitimating decisions that may run counter to remnant traditions still held by various groups. Reason is a force used to overcome the resistance of tradition.

For Plato reason is also a special mode of explanation, distinguishable from causes or material conditions of action, the different mode of explanation used by the nature philosophers whom he opposes. The rhetoric of cause is an explanatory mode of discourse in which men are seen as essentially no different from the rest of the universe. Reason, however, is an explanatory mode in which man takes himself, his interests, and his character as the base point; man accounts for things, especially his own behavior, in terms of what *he* intended, expected, sought, or hoped.

The use of reason as a mode of explanation implies that the men who employ it have a certain image of self. It suggests in particular that they conceive themselves as beings who are not coerced but consenting, as influencing as well as influenced, and that they regard themselves as centers from which power radiates out into their surroundings. It implies that men see themselves as potencies. Reason is a rhetoric of explanation consonant with a view of self as relatively autonomous. Such a self-image is likely to be more prevalent in places and periods where traditional values are fading and no longer so widely shared, and where the individual no longer feels these values to be part of an ordained and irresistible order of things from which there is no escape.

REASON AND CONTROL

From this standpoint it must be expected that reason will be allied with sentiments of control and mastery by men. It will be infused with impulses to dominate objects and to make them obedient. The knowledge, or *epistēmē,* toward which Platonic reason is oriented is not only a knowing about but also a knowing how. Platonic reason seeks to change as well as to be informed about the world. While Plato views reason as the universal essence of man, he also expressly counterposes it to other aspects of man's intrinsic nature which reason must strive to master. For Plato reason is not simply a logic or a purely cognitive interest but is inextricably intertwined with certain transcendental feelings: reason is a sentiment no less than a rhetoric of explanation.

One of the characteristic points at which the control and cognitive interests involved in reason are joined is the process of "classification." Like *nomos* and *mōira,* reason is a divider and allocator. Reason is an Apollonian impulse that introduces order by making divisions or by dividing things. It puts and seeks to hold things in their place. As Socrates says, "I am myself a great lover of these processes of division and generalisation; they help me to speak and to think. And if I find any man who is able to see 'a One and Many' in nature, him I follow, and 'walk in his footsteps as if he were a god.' " [7] Socrates views the dividing of objects into classes as an almost godlike process, giving order to the cosmos, controlling and binding down the slippery flux of events.

An interest in classification is an interest in dividing things into classes of like and unlike. From its earliest beginnings this process is associated with the most practical efforts at controlling the human environment. Clearly, if men behave in the same manner toward unlike things or in different ways toward like things, their actions will be more ineffectual and costly than they have to be. Anything that has been conceptually located in a logical class can be better controlled, for this permits us to mobilize pre-

vious practical experience with other objects like it. An interest in likenesses or differences, a concern with primitive classification, derives in part,
then, from an interest in controlling things.

The interests in classification and in practical control are linked together
in sympathetic magic, a technique of controlling the universe common to
many peoples. Sympathetic magic involves the assumption that like can
influence like—for example, to make a doll in the likeness of one's enemy
is to gain some control over him. A concern with likeness involves an
interest in the kinship or continuity between two or more particulars and,
in sympathetic magic, it entails the assumption that because of this kinship
one thing can be influenced by acting upon its like.

Certainly many Greeks of the fourth century B.C. still practice forms of
sympathetic magic and believe that a kind of "sympathy" exists between a
man and a part of him, such as his name, his fingernail paring, or a model
of him such as a doll. The practice of writing one's enemy's name on a plate
and burying it is believed to be able to affect him and is still common
around Athens at this time.[8] Indeed, Plato's Cratylus remarks that the man
who knows the name knows the thing.

In suggesting this, I am certainly not implying that Plato's stress on
classification derives from his belief in sympathetic magic. I am suggesting,
however, that underlying his classificatory drive—a core tactic of reason
as he conceives it—is an assumption that classification facilitates control
over the world. Yet there is something more involved in Plato's classificatory impulse than a bland cerebral judgment that a correct perception
of likenesses and differences will be instrumentally useful. There seems,
in addition, to be a strong background feeling that there is an intrinsic
potency in right classification. There is a feeling that proper classification
comes close to the essence of knowledge and almost provides the high
road to wisdom and the good life. There seems to be an intimation that
classification is a mode of attaining communion with sacred things, for it
provides the lens through which a glimpse may be had of the light of the
eternal Forms.

As reason emerges in Greece and is crystallized in Plato's philosophy,
it is associated with a syndrome of sentiments and values centering on
mastery and control that are especially powerful in Western civilization.
This sort of reason is an active rather than a passive process. It involves a
deliberate pursuit of truth in which initiative is seen to be within the self
of the knower instead of coming from the unpredictable and spontaneous
stirring of extrinsic "muses." It entails a mobilization of the energies of
the self in the search for truth rather than a relaxed opening of the self to
insight. It is a work process rather than a play process. In this conception

of reason truth is to be pursued with zealous striving rather than in brooding or serene meditation. In this view truth is the product of labor or struggle and is never a free gift. It demands discipline in the sense of self-control and in the use of a difficult method, the mastery of which entails effort and practice.

Intrinsic to this activistic posture is an expectancy that there are elements within the knowing self that can lead intellectual effort astray. There are sentiments of suspicion, distrust, and hostility to the passions and to the senses, both of which are regarded as subversive of the knower's proper intent. The dialectical reason of the Platonist is thus clearly distinguishable from the early views of the Ionian nature philosophers. The latter at least valued the senses and often sought to submit reasoning to the test of observation. They regarded the senses as necessary if not sufficient tools for knowing. Platonic reason, however, suspects the senses and regards them as corruptive of mind or logic.

Platonic reason is not only on guard against the self, but is also distrustful of received beliefs deriving from the social surround. Platonic reason is concerned not simply that beliefs may be wrong, but that even right views may be held for the wrong reasons. It thus tends to be flaw-finding, negative, skeptical, questioning. Its bent is critical rather than appreciative.

Intrinsic to this concept of reason is a judgment on and a view of the self. It premises that the highest and most valuable parts of the self are its cognitive faculties, the possession and display of which are the basis for making the most crucial claims for the self. To have failed in the successful employment of reason is not simply to have muffed a problem or to be lacking in a useful solution. It is also to raise doubts about whether the self possesses what is regarded as the most desirable, indeed the highest, human quality. Reason thus becomes the basis of a morality. It becomes a standard in terms of which the crucial evaluations of people will be made and the vehicle through which the good will be apprehended. Reason is a means through which the good will be known, and in itself it is an aspect of the good.

In this view, to know or to strive to know is to be good. Wisdom is the keystone of virtue while, conversely, evil is based on and derives from ignorance. Morality then comes to depend on the possession of knowledge, and the stupid man cannot lead the good life. In due course this leads in the Aristotelian development of Platonism to the view that the contemplative life is the morally highest form of existence. The equation of cognitive faculties and morality in this way serves to give morality a monolithic structure. In this view, there are not many good lives, each potentially worthy in its own way and each having its own kind of authenticity (as the Romanticists will much later hold). There is only one good life, and all others are merely more or less approximations or copies.

REASON AS RHETORIC

Closely related to the element of control and mastery in reason is, as I have suggested, the conception of reason as a rhetoric, as a way of persuading men toward certain forms of belief and behavior. Reason is therefore something with, and to which, one appeals. It is the presentation of certain kinds of grounds or arguments for requesting or giving consent to certain beliefs.

The truth reason seeks is sought, in part, because its possession is expected to have certain desired consequences. In particular, the use of reason is expected to provide a basis for social consensus. Platonic reason is a method by which a diversity of beliefs will be overcome and brought to unity. It is a strategy for overcoming conflicts within the individual and within the society by establishing a method to which all must consent, and must thus consent to the conclusions. Because it is suprapolitical, nonpartisan, and impersonal, reason will constrain men to adopt common beliefs. Reason is a way of producing a consensus of beliefs on which the state can rest securely.

Reason is thus two-faced. It entails a combination of cognitive elements and a syndrome of sentiment-infused values—particularly concerning control and consensus—and because of this it possesses certain inherent tensions. These become especially clear if we ask if such a concept of reason requires all persons always to tell the truth. In the Platonic case the answer clearly seems to be negative. Plato makes it plain that those who establish or who rule in the ideal city will deliberately lie, at least to certain people within it.

DILEMMAS OF REASON

Although in the *Republic* and elsewhere Homer is condemned for lying,[9] especially about the gods, Plato says there are nonetheless certain stories which should not be told—for example, the emasculation of Ouranos by Kronos—"even if they were true." [10] The rulers of the city, he holds, will have to use frequent lying and deception for the benefit of the ruled.[11] In particular, the citizens of the ideal Republic will need to be told a "noble lie." This is the myth of the earthborn and the metals, in which the new class system is to be legitimated by holding that it corresponds to inborn differences in aptitude which are symbolized by the different metals, gold, silver, bronze, and iron.

The intention of such a myth, says Plato, is to foster beliefs that contribute to the cohesion of the city. It therefore seems that there is some tension between the need to achieve this extra-cognitive end, civic cohesion, and the value placed upon knowing the truth. Those concerned with the good cannot, as Socrates had admonished, simply "follow the argument wherever it leads." It is evident that Plato justifies the noble lie in terms of what he takes to be higher moral ends, namely, the good of the city or the benefit of the ruled. Like many who came after, Plato is grappling with an existential problem of scholarship, with the relationship of truth to other values, and in particular to "goodness."

The key question, of course, is *why* does one want to know the truth? Does the scholar seek it for its own sake alone and without regard to its ramifying cultural consequences? Or does he also seek it, at least in some part, because he believes that its attainment will further other ends which he also views as desirable? Does the scholar value truth and the pursuit of truth only? Or does he also have other values with which his ambition for the truth must somehow be integrated?

Even if the scholar is concerned with truth alone, it is conceivable that its pursuit at any one time can impair its continued pursuit at later times. To take a contemporary example, the physicist's search for knowledge may, precisely insofar as it is successful, result in the development of weapons that threaten to destroy his own society and, with this, his science. If, however, he accepts other values as transcending the truth, such as human survival or social cohesion, then is he not under pressure, as Plato is, to conceal truths that are at variance with these other values, and perhaps even to assert things untrue because they foster such values? Insofar as the scholar takes responsibility for maintaining or furthering any kind of social system, be it one already in existence or one contemplated, his commitment to the truth must be limited and conditional. Truth cannot then be an absolute value. Insofar as the scholar makes an unconditional commitment to truth, however, he must be prepared to loosen or surrender his attachment to any given society, to limit or reject his responsibility for its welfare, and to reduce or liquidate his investment in his other social roles.

TRUTH VERSUS OTHER VALUES

The dilemma here is not simply a logical one, it entails a real tension; it involves a conflict of forces on the personal and cultural levels. It is notable, however, that whichever side of the dilemma he grasps, the scholar is making a morally consequential choice; he is usually choosing either to accept some abridgement or qualification of the truth or some impairment of the welfare of some group. It is well for a scholar to recognize that he lives inescapably within the gridwork of such a moral tension. Only the naïve are willing to assume that the pursuit of truth will always be beneficial to any given social system or will fail to recognize that the assumption, however common, that this is so "in the long run" is an undemonstrable item of faith.

While truth or knowledge is a crucial value for Plato and a basic factor in his matrix of the good, the two are nonetheless not identical. If truth is first extracted from the matrix of the good, there is a substantial residue, however uncertain its character may be. Certainly one important element within this residue is a concern with social cohesion. But it needs to be remembered that, unless we accept Platonic assumptions, there are various social forms in which cohesion and consensus can be organized. It seems unmistakable, however, that Plato is focusing on and prescribing only one specific kind of cohesion, the one built around an authoritarian relationship of the parts, a relationship in which some dominate and others are subordinate.

AUTHORITARIAN REASON

This authoritarian dimension is not, however, simply manifested extrinsically, by the nature of the ideal social system that Plato projects; authoritarianism is intrinsic to the very notion of reason with which he works. It is not simply the sociological conclusions to which Platonic reason comes on being applied to social problems that are authoritarian. The very method of reason itself, as Plato construes it, has an authoritarian component.

On the face of it this may seem strange, considering the fact that Platonic reason develops in polemic against conventionally authoritative bases of belief. Certainly Plato is at pains to indicate that he is not a "respecter of persons" and that his conception of reason requires a judgment about the validity of a belief apart from its source. Yet it must also be noted that for Plato reason is not just one among a number of valuable human faculties. Above all, reason is defined and located in terms of its stratificational relation to the other human faculties. It is said to be at the pinnacle of the system of stratification according to which individual faculties are to be ordered. It is held to be the master of the psyche or at least to have the only legitimate claim to command.

In this sense, then, there is an implicit and unlabeled analogy between the attributes or faculties of individuals and a system of social stratification. What seems to happen is that reason as an internal faculty comes to be viewed on the model of an external person or group, whose rulings are definitive and authoritative. Since there are various kinds of authority systems, it does not suffice, however, to say that reason is modeled after an external authority system. We also need to ask what kind of an authority system is used as a model. The historically concrete system of stratification which Plato knew from experience was the slave system. Whether a timocracy or oligarchy or democracy, the social systems which he knew were, in this respect, all radically authoritarian. In modeling reason after external systems of authority and in taking their most authoritarian aspect as given, Plato infuses reason itself with an authoritarian bent. Plato, in short, does not simply conceive of reason as an authority but as an authoritarian authority, particularly in its relations to the person's other impulses, interests, and faculties. He makes it clear that reason shall be the absolute authority in the personality. He conceives of it as a master in relation to the other impulses and faculties, which are viewed essentially as slaves or retainers. However concerned about their welfare, reason is still the unmistakable lord of the inner *ōikos*.

If we say that Plato's concept of reason is authoritarian, in what ways may we distinguish between an authoritarian and a nonauthoritarian reason? Platonic reason is authoritarian in at least one sense that this term is commonly employed in contemporary social psychology in that its most salient characteristic is made to be its stratificational position. Platonic reason is not simply interested in ordering things but particularly in arranging them hierarchically. What is problematic to Plato is whether reason rules the appetites or is ruled and corrupted by them. Reason can only be master or slave. Such a view of the elements of personality minimizes the significance of their mutual interdependence, of the value derived from the "lower" faculties, and of the need and dependence of even the highest upon the very lowest faculty.

Complementary to his view of the exalted nobility of reason is the frank disgust with which he views the bodily pleasures. There is a curious thing about pleasures, he says: "When we see some one indulging in pleasures, perhaps in the greatest of pleasures, the ridiculous or disgraceful nature of the action makes us ashamed; and so we put them out of sight, and consign them to darkness, under the idea that they ought not to meet the eye of day." [12] Of course if pleasure and joy are so ridiculous, it would seem that from an Olympian view so, too, are pain and suffering. To deny the importance of either pain or pleasure is to deny significance to human experience. And Plato's various metaphors of humans as puppets of the gods or as pieces in a divine chess game do indeed threaten to dwindle the entire significance of human life and of all earthly existence. In the end Plato's ultimate fantasy is to be rid of the appetites, and he savors death, seeing it as a deliverance of reason from the corruptions and distractions of the body.

Short of annihilating the other base impulses and faculties, Plato views them as things to be severely controlled. They are to be used primarily in the interests of their ruler, reason. They are to be trained and employed like horses, or to be allowed gratification as a way of rewarding and reinforcing their submission and proper performance. There is indeed a deliberate manipulation of the appetites as a way of ensuring obedience. The most notable instance of this is in the *Republic,* where Plato suggests that the most valorous of the Guardian elite are to be rewarded by allowing them sexual license, a completely free pick of sexual partners, whether male or female.

While authoritarian reason recognizes that reason itself matures and indeed requires deliberate cultivation and development, the other faculties are not viewed as capable of a comparable maturation. Nor does authoritarian reason regard these other faculties as having a value in their own right or as having legitimate claims of their own; it sees them as valuable primarily insofar as they contribute to the reign of reason.

IMPERATIVE VERSUS ADVISORY REASON

A nonauthoritarian concept of reason does not, however, deny or depose reason as authority. It is aware, however, that there are different ways in which reason can be an authority. With respect to knowing processes, for example, a nonauthoritarian reason grants the crucial importance of other attributes such as intuition, imagination, and insight. Nonauthoritarian reason can open itself to their creative stimulation, but authoritarian, Platonic reason is suspicious and distrustful of these. While Platonic reason does not involve an arbitrary domination—for it is ready to give such reasons as it has for the course it dictates—there remains the vital question of what happens after reason has stated her position and still meets opposition. Suppose, for example, a judgment has been made on the basis of reason, or on the basis of some method defined as reasonable, which stipulates that a certain course of action is preferable. How much authority shall be invested in it? How absolute shall its judgment be? Shall the reasonable judgment be imperatively commanding or merely advisory? Insofar as the reasonable judgment is defined as, among other things, a decision made in terms of a concern for the good or welfare of others, then, when faced with their resistance to the decision, those making the judgment may feel justified in imposing it.

A conception of reason oriented to the good of others disposes those who employ it to act with a paternalistic authority, to feel themselves like parents who must control their child, preventing it from crossing the street "for its own good," and, if necessary, to act with authoritarian severity if the child balks. The problem is a real one and is certainly familiar enough, even if the solution Plato adopts is rejected. In brief, the authoritarian bent in Plato's conception of reason is not an autistic intrusion or an accidental irrelevancy of his purely personal bias. It is one logically possible response to problems inherent in the rhetoric functions assigned to reason and reflects problems requiring some sort of solution, even if not that given by Plato.

Nonauthoritarian reason does not view itself either as God or as a prison warden; neither does it view the other attributes of personality as unregenerate sinners or as a pack of murderous inmates who must be kept under high security. In this connection, it is noteworthy that for the greatest part of his life, Plato—who first began his intellectual career as a poet—views poets and dramatists with deep suspicion. "In our State such as [they] are not permitted to exist," he remarks in the *Republic;* "the law will not allow them." They are to be exiled, abolished, and censored because they are perceived as impious, as picturing the gods as wicked, adulterous, as dispensing evil as well as good, as having a chameleon character and being elusive in form. Worse than that, they portray people in the grip of strong emotions.

It is curious, however, that the persistent animosity that Socrates has toward poets suddenly changes toward the end of his life. In his speech of defense in the *Apology,* Socrates observes that he is not afraid to die. After all, he notes, death is either a long sleep—and who could fear that—or it is really the gateway to an afterlife in which he can converse with the great men of Greece who have been long dead. Yet who are the great with whom he looks forward to conversing? The very first mentioned is Homer the poet.

Again, in the *Phaedo,* Socrates is asked whether the strange things heard about his activities in prison are true? Is he really composing verses? Yes, replies Socrates. While no Pindar, he is "turning Aesop's fables into verse, and also composing [a] hymn in honor of Apollo." During his life he has had a repeated dream, he says, which in more or less the same words tells him the same thing: "Cultivate and make music." Usually he has interpreted "music" in the broader or liberal arts sense, as an encouragement to a continued study of philosophy. Uncertain, however, that "music" was not intended in the popular sense, and now having time to pursue the matter, he thinks it better to satisfy the scruple by composing verse. Lacking in invention, as he admits, he takes Aesop's stories to versify.

Here at the end of his life, then, Socrates is portrayed as launching a more expressive and aesthetic work. He comes to have an intimation, it would seem, that he has been too unrelenting in his intellectualism and, in a halting way, to express doubts about an authoritarian reason which takes a hostile and repressive view of the intuitive and imaginative leaps of the expressive aspects of mind. It would be erroneous, however, to portray Socrates even before this episode as a narrow rationalist. His respect for his daemon suggests otherwise. It implies much more openness to certain of the irrational emotions and of the imagination than a conception of him as a rigid rationalist would allow. It is crucial to remember, however, that when Socrates' daemon speaks, it is always to tell him not to do something. It always speaks as a taboo, forbidding a planned course of action. But it never, as he himself makes explicit, tells him to undertake something in a positive way.

In short, there are moments when Socrates seems to respect the irrational side of himself. To do this, however, he uses a component—his daemon—which he externalizes and treats as a kind of divine force. He does not acknowledge it to be a true part of his own self. This force is not creative, constructive, and goal-directed but avoidant, inhibiting, and nay-saying. Socrates never brings himself to the point of accepting men's passions as a source of creative energy. Viewing man as a "copier" of an existent and unvarying perfection, he set small store by individual creativity (for it can only open the Pandora's box to a disorganizing diversity) and on the inner forces upon which it depends.

METHOD VERSUS METHODOLATRY

Here again one can see Plato as revealing and grappling with a basic dilemma of reason, the dilemma between openness to intuitive insight with enriching novelty and reliance upon a disciplined method with controllable and reliable results. In one of its important aspects, reason, as Plato saw, is a way of testing hypotheses and appraising the truth of belief. Without method there is no reliable way of resolving competing claims to truth or of distinguishing between the well-founded and the merely suppositious. Without method men are thrust back on the uncontrollable emergence of genius, and there can be no cumulative development of reliable information. Yet with method alone reason easily sinks into ritualism. It sacrifices the venturesome but chancy insight for the security of controllable routine, the penetrating novelty for the shallow familiarity, the broad for the narrow circumference.

Reason as method is fundamentally a mechanism of reliable demonstration and proof, critically inspecting the claims of discovery. It patrols the beach, surveying, appraising, picking up, working on, and reshaping the clutter of experience, the driftwood washed up by other elemental forces of the mind. Frightened off or disgusted by these forces, the mind will insulate and seal itself off against the threat of their disorder. Sealed too completely, however, the mind is cut off from immense powers and resources in the world and in the self. It seeks to live in the secure isolation of its own completely controllable resources, becoming an interminable dweller upon method. Reason then becomes "methodolatrous," compulsively preoccupied with a method of knowing which it exalts ritualistically and quite apart from a serious appraisal of its success in producing knowledge. Methodolatry is the anxiety of reason. It is the scholarly style of those who fear, and thus cannot come to terms with, themselves.

Yet methodolatry is only the pathology of method; it is not its necessary and inevitable character. Indeed a legitimate concern with method is one of the most important innovations of Platonic reason, for the functions of a methodology are as valuable as the dysfunctions of methodolatry are costly. Reason as method is much like the image of *mōīra;* setting limits on men's actions, it does not permit them to do whatever they wish. Reason as method provides a framework for analysis and investigation in which data must be examined independently of their source, either in tradition or in religious or civic authorities. Reason is impersonal, also, in the sense that it inhibits or forbids willful capriciousness or arbitrariness. It erects a barrier against the flux of mood.

Reason as method disestablishes inner conviction, or strength of feeling, as the basis of a claim to knowledge. The truth of reason is no longer held to be vouched for by a sense of intuitive certainty. This further implies that "common sense"—common in being widely held and settled opinion—is no longer perforce correct. To secure consensus concerning a view, therefore, is not to prove it correct. Reason as method says that people are not right because born to high station, and, further, neither does majority agreement among the many make something right. In this way, reason is both antiaristocratic and antidemocratic, and it has begun to become depoliticized in principle.

Above all, reason as method is a constraining force, leading men to conclusions that they did not know or believe in the beginning and, sometimes, to views opposed to those they held initially. Socrates is recurrently shown to be caught in the coils of his own logic, being led to conclusions that he does not like or which are manifestly uncongenial to him. When, for example, Socrates says, let us inquire into the nature of virtue so that we know of what it consists, he is taken somewhat aback when Meno replies, with a show of logic, "And how Socrates will you inquire into that which you know not? What will you put forth as the subject of the inquiry? And if you find what you want to know how will you ever know that this is what you did not know?"

That Socrates often extricates himself from a logical difficulty in ways that reveal he is all too human is beside the mark. Socrates sometimes gives more scope to unfounded assumption, to myth, and to imagination than he allows in principle, and this is neither new nor surprising. What is important is his commitment to a method by which his own biases and preconceptions can be confounded. What is important is that he demands and lays out the elements of an intellectual discipline to which men must conform, even at the cost of personal embarrassment and frustration. If methodolatry compulsively constricts intelligence, method may, however serendipitiously, generate novelty by requiring conformity to disciplined routines.

To sum up some of the differences between authoritarian and nonauthoritarian reason or, more accurately, between an authoritarian and a nonauthoritarian view of the role of reason in individual and social life: in the authoritarian view, reason is regarded as a method of mastering all other elements of nature, which are felt to possess inherently undesirable tendencies. Nonauthoritarian reason seeks, however, to cooperate with rather than to dominate the lawful dispositions in phenomena, whether human or otherwise. In the authoritarian view, truth is to be obtained primarily in the controlled use of an intellectual discipline. The nonauthoritarian view, however, while by no means opposing this, also sees truth as enhanced in less disciplined and less strenuously active ways by opening the self to insight, by passive waiting as well as by active initiating. Authoritarian reason regards other elements within the knowing self as suspect, as subverting the pursuit of truth. Nonauthoritarian reason sees these other elements as potential aids, no less than hindrances, and requires that inferences be subjected to the test of the senses. Nonauthoritarian reason regards intuition, imagination, and the passions themselves not only as distorting but also as creative forces, enlivening, energizing, sensitizing men in the pursuit of truth. Authoritarian reason tends toward a unidimensional view of reason and the good life, toward a belief that there is only one kind of good life, primarily that of the mind and contemplation, while nonauthoritarian reason regards a variety of life styles as imbued with value. Authoritarian reason aims at enhancing social consensus and sees reason as a rhetoric for yielding agreement; nonauthoritarian reason is as much concerned to place reason at the service of individual fulfillment as of social consensus and group integration.

What is the root of authoritarianism in Platonic reason? Essentially the fact that reason is not intended to be used by and for all men. The tacit social boundaries within which Plato expects the rhetoric of reason to be effective correspond, at their farthest reach, to those of the city's citizens who have full legal rights. It is not, however, expected that those outside this charmed circle will be similarly open to reason. For example, the possibilities of coercion with regard to other cities are assumed almost as a matter of course.

It is also clear that the rhetoric of reason is expected to be particularly ineffectual with one specific status group within the city, the slaves. Plato concerns himself hardly at all with winning the consent of slaves to slavery through reason. Like other Greeks he regards the slave status as so lowly and abominable that it is only natural for people to resist it and, indeed, to do so to the death. He cannot, therefore, realistically assume that any appeal to reason will persuade slaves to accept their position in society. On the other hand, an appeal to the reason of the slave is also senseless from Plato's standpoint so long as he believes, as he says, that those enslaved lose half their reason.

One of the basic considerations disposing Platonic reason to authoritarianism, then, is its assumption that certain elements in the system to be organized will resist persuasion. Plato never seems to see, however, that a major source of resistance to reason derives from the inherent authoritarianism of the social system which he knows or plans. The social role assigned to reason and to reasonable persuasion must be limited to the extent that the society will contain certain groups which are seen as necessary to its maintenance and conversely as unwilling to perform their menial tasks. Under these conditions, some kind of constraining mechanism, whether naked force or the invisible threat of starvation, will tend to be regarded as required.

Although Plato seeks to enhance the role of reason in society, he never acknowledges that it is contradictory to support social arrangements such as slavery which, by his own admission, impair reason. This discrepancy is in part due to his tendency to view society as a kind of organism. From this standpoint the important thing is that the organism as a whole be directed by reason, not that reason be permeative and manifested by all the system elements. In part, also, Plato's position rests on an assumption that reason is enhanced by withdrawal from work, that reason does not require or is not enriched by experience, that it is primarily an activity of mind alone and not of the total organism, including its senses and affect structures. The sociological premise of Plato's reason is a leisure class, which in turn implies the existence of a complementary class of slaves that will permit the others to have leisure.

Reason, then, in the Platonic system, is tinged with authoritarianism because it premises a slave system. That Plato does not see the way in which slavery is implicated in the basic tensions of Hellenic civilization, or that it embroils him in a contradiction by debilitating the very reason that he wishes to fortify—that Plato could not, in fine, systematically take slavery as problematic and see beyond it—is a phenomenon that must make all social theorists deeply uneasy. That a man of his puissant and original intelligence is so mired in the presuppositions of his own culture remains, for all its familiarity, a telling lesson in intellectual history, dramatically exemplifying the tangible limits within which even the best of human reason operates.

TYPES OF SOCIAL ACTION

Plato's authoritarian conception of reason expresses itself in his analysis of the various types of social action and of their interrelations. There appear to be three main types of social action considered in Plato's analysis; the rational, which is central and problematic, and two other residual types, the natural and the divine. As forms of social action, these last are residual in that they are taken as given and tend to be only weakly conceptualized. To Plato, the natural is intrinsically lower in value than the rational, while the rational is what distinguishes men and raises them above other animals. The natural has to do with the realm of constraint—of necessity or *ananke*—involving such things as the desire for food, drink, and sex; the rational involves mastery, choice, free deliberation, and effective selection among possible alternatives.

Divinely inspired forms of social action are those in which the gods act or speak through men. They include, for example, the actions of great statesmen who successfully benefit their community although lacking in art and knowledge and who, it seems, must be divinely inspired to have done such good in ignorance. So, too, is it with poets who, when asked to explain their own lines, are unable to do so, and whose efforts must therefore be understood as a divine seizure: "For all good poets, epic as well as lyric, compose their beautiful poems not by art, but because they are inspired and possessed; . . . the lyric poets are not in their right mind when they are composing their beautiful strains." [13] While Plato acknowledges that "love is the greatest of heaven's blessings," he also characterizes it as a form of "madness," [14] a divine madness which places the lovers "under compulsion." In short, blessing that it is, love often involves no rational choice and is thus a form of divinely imposed slavery in which men are ruled by their passions, rather than by reason as befits a man.

From a value standpoint such as Plato's, there is an edge of irony in characterizing something that departs from rationality as divine. This is exemplified in the dialogue *Ion* when, in attempting to account for the rhapsodist Ion's strange ability to recite Homer only, Socrates confronts Ion with the choice: either his interpretations of Homer are personally irrational and capriciously individual, almost a kind of humbug, or they are a gift of the god; for if Ion's talents involved rational skills he would not be confined to Homer. Ion, of course, quickly enough agrees to characterize his work as divinely inspired, given the other possible alternative. To characterize the poet and the lover as controlled by a divine compulsion is to employ a rhetoric that must resonate dissonantly with the ingrained and invidious Greek conception of slavery as the paradigm of constraint.

Plato's first aim is to appraise whether a given course of action is rational or not; it is this that is problematic for him. If he finds that it is not, he accounts for it by locating it either in the sphere of the natural, such as the passions or appetites, or in that nobler realm of constraint, the divinely inspired. It is clear, however, that Plato is not concerned to explore systematically the character of divinely inspired social action. That he tends to take it as given may imply that he cannot take the conventional view of the divine seriously. Or it may be that, taking it seriously in his own way, he feels that not much can be done about it. He may consequently devote himself more fully to the other category of action, the natural, which differs from divinely inspired action in that it *is* conceived of as subject to the mastery of the rational part of man and as needing control because it is subversive of the rational.

THE RATIONAL AND THE DIVINE

As a result, the basic polarity in Plato's analysis of types of social action is between natural and rational social behavior. Plato seeks to fuse the rational and the divine, to assimilate them one to another, thereby opposing the rational all the more strongly to the natural. He allies the rational with the divine by stressing the power it has over material things and by associating it with the soul, which, like the gods, has immortality. Like *moïra*, which, indeed, is above the gods, the rational arranges things into departments or provinces, bringing order by dividing up the world conceptually. In its use of the dialectic, the rational engages in an ascending quest for first principles, soaring upward to catch a glimpse of the eternal Ideas and the perfect Form of things. Like the divine, the rational is associated with mastery, control, and ordering.

Plato's conception of the divine is, however, transformed in the very process of wedding it with rationality. Plato's divinity no longer has the arbitrariness or the moral ambivalence of the Homeric gods. It does no evil and arranges things in a manner that is always for the best. The fusion of the divine with the rational disembodies the divine. The new divine is pure mind. The gods are stripped of their anthropomorphic character and, with this, their sexual proclivities: the liaison between the rational and the divine is Platonic. Above all, with the Platonic doctrine of the immortality of the soul, the radical Olympian distinction between mortal men and immortal gods is broken down. There is now a part of man which is immortal, a part of him which, therefore, partakes of or is in communion with the divine. The former hiatus between the divine and man is removed, and the two are now linked through reason. Plato, however, exacts his price: with his devaluation of the senses and the passions, man, too, has been disembodied.

The traditional relation between men and the gods was one of sympathy as well as fear of their powers, for the gods had many obviously earthly shortcomings, such as lust and deceitfulness. This relation is now to be supplanted by a fear of God's power and by a respect for God's moral perfection. I think it is mistaken to state, as is sometimes suggested, that the traditional Greek view of the Olympians provided men no inner psychological bond with them, that they could only admire the gods' power or envy their pleasures but could not be in communion with them. It would seem, rather, that there is indeed a bond, but that its nature now changes. It changes from an ambivalent empathy or sympathy to a severe respect which, precisely because it is based on a belief in God's complete perfection, makes it difficult for men to feel love for or empathy with God or to expect love or sympathy from him. (It may be that it is this dilemma—the difficulty of feeling both great respect and love for the divine—that will be resolved by the Christian conception of a God, who because of his suffering can be both respected and loved.)

Another basic power that Plato's God lacks is a capacity to make men happy. He brings no glad tidings, and his coming is not intended to spread joy in Greece. That there is this singular omission is not surprising. For, as has often been said, it is Plato's overriding intent not to make men happy but good. Plato, of course, is aware that the mass of men want happiness; indeed, he says that goodness will bring them happiness, adding, however, that even if this were not the case, he would pretend that it was, for this would be "the most salutary lie ever told." [15] Given Plato's image of God, and given his growingly pessimistic view of man, I would not be surprised if this is what he did.

Several things of consequence for Plato's social diagnosis flow from his polarization of the rational-divine, on the one side, and the natural—which is lowly, base, an ugly thing of mean necessity—on the other, and which must be kept under constant control. As mentioned, one consequence is that social actions and institutions associated with the rational tend to be regarded as more estimable than those associated with the natural. Those social relations which are under greater rational control, or which have developed in accordance with more deliberation and reflection, are most highly regarded and preferred. It is also partly because of his association of these institutions with the natural rather than the rational that Plato takes pains to protect the guardians of the ideal Republic from conventional marriage and family involvements.

In some part Plato is more favorably disposed toward friendship relations than kinship ties because they are relations into which men can enter voluntarily, and to which he enjoins them to apply rationally selected moral norms. Plato values friendship less because it entails a bond of deep sentiment than because it is susceptible to regulation by reason. In Plato's view, social relations regulated in accordance with universalistic rules, by reason rather than unexamined sentiment, are to be preferred. Men are categorized and evaluated in terms of whether they are good or bad. Their relation to one another is evaluated in terms of the degree to which they comply with certain general rules of morality. The absolute features of morality itself are stressed: things are to be judged impersonally depending on the extent to which they possess or participate in certain general attributes, rather than in terms of their uniquely individual relation to one another. There is, in short, a persistent preference for universalistic rather than particularistic social relationships.

For Plato the polity or the public arena of the city-state is the institutional center of attention, for governance is the realm par excellence of the rational rather than the natural. It is not that governance is in fact now properly guided by reason, but rather that it can and should be. The city is seen and evaluated in terms of its own compliance with the dictates of rationality. The public and political sector requires rational deliberation and choice and, corresponding to the highest controlling parts of the soul, is viewed as the proper communal locus of rationality.

For Plato the key social problems are those of the polity, and they center on the manner in which the state shall be ruled. If he sees social problems as lodged primarily in the political system, this is not to say that he sees them as political in the sense that their solution lies in a superior form of politics, for much of Plato's objective is to abolish politics. He views politics as an activity in which passion rather than reason customarily predominates, in which private and factional interests improperly supplant consideration of the public good, and as based commonly upon opinion rather than knowledge. The basic trouble is in the polity; but its solution requires that politics be transcended.

Plato does not use a concept of society or of the "social" as distinct from or inclusive of the political; nor does he systematically distinguish the public from the private arenas. In Plato's view of the ideal Republic, the whole of society is to be subordinated to the public polity. The latter's affairs should, he believes, come first and be most salient to its citizenry, just as concern for the state of their soul should come prior to that of their body. Plato's focus is on the public, political relations of men. He is primarily concerned with them in their roles as citizens rather than, say, in their roles as husbands, fathers, slave masters, or slaves. If only the polity is wisely administered, the whole and all its parts will be well and orderly.

Plato's orientation to occupational specialists is an ambivalent one. He esteems their operations within their area of competence. He respects them especially insofar as they bring knowledge and rational principles to the production of goods and services, and so long as they confine themselves to what they know rather than meddling in higher things of which they are ignorant. It is the ends, however, to which these technologies are put that disturb him, particularly insofar as they are pursued with a view to private gain. Those specializations which concentrate not on rationally guided production but on distributive processes pursued for a profit seem to him to be particularly dangerous to the public good. He is thus more favorably disposed to artisans and craftsmen than to merchants and retailers. He regards the private pursuit of wealth as incompatible with the maintenance of a virtuous state and tends to believe that cities cannot be both good and rich.

Kinship and economic interests tend to be viewed by Plato primarily in terms of their implications for political behavior and institutions. Both family life and economic pursuits consume men's time and energies, detracting from the leisure they require for the proper conduct of the city's affairs, which is the highest concern. The ideal Republic will carefully regulate marriages and births as well as mercantile activities. It will subordinate all other interests and roles to those bearing on the needs of the citizen role and of the state institutions. Kinship and economic activities largely have to do with necessity, with the satisfaction of private appetites and are in no way peculiar to men; they are necessary but not sufficient for the maintenance of the good state; they are natural and thus intrinsically of lesser merit.

PLATO'S METAPHYSICS: THE FLAW IN THE UNIVERSE

To grasp the fuller meaning of Plato's appraisal of the flaw in the nature of human beings, it must be seen for what it is, namely, as only one expression of a larger feeling—for Plato, as for the tragic dramatists and, indeed, for a pervasive stream in Greek culture—that the natural universe as a whole has an inherent flaw. Plato's most general hypotheses, his conception of the character of the *kosmos,* assume that there is a kind of evil in it. As he says in the *Philebus,* there is a "universal wantonness and wickedness of all things," especially in the sense that they inherently lack limits: "There was in them no limit to pleasures and self-indulgence." [16] Like other things, men too are intrinsically subject to lawlessness, or *anomia.*

Seeing this is the way of the world, says Plato, the goddess had to devise "the limit of law and order." That is, since things are not intrinsically orderly, they must have a law devised for and imposed on them. They must be regulated by a lawful order external to them, and Plato assumes that this regulation is never completely successful, although why this should be so is never directly analyzed.

This concept of the universe is clearly evidenced in the *Timaeus,* in which the three elemental categories of Plato's cosmology are discussed: God; the eternal, perfect Forms or Ideas; and a kind of pre-existing matter. Plato's God is *not* an absolute creator, for he works with pre-existent matter upon which he imposes the eternal ideas which serve to regulate the changes he has originated. The perfection of Plato's God is manifested by his complete communion with the perfect and eternal ideas which coexist with him. He never behaves arbitrarily or creates novelties, but always acts for the best; which is to say he acts through the same unchanging Ideas. God's power, manifesting itself through his employment of the Ideas, is thus lawful.

The question arises as to how this conception of God in Plato's system may be explained; for certainly, from a Christian viewpoint, he is a strange or at least a different God. It might be said that such a perspective on Plato's cosmology—seeing it from the standpoint of Christian beliefs—is precisely what makes it problematic and that, in actuality, from a Greek standpoint it is commonplace. Plato's God, it might be held, is like the Homeric gods; neither is an absolute or completely free creator. If the Homeric gods are subject to necessity and limited by *moīra,* Plato's God is similarly constrained by the eternal Ideas. Plato's God, however, is not viewed as subject to the Ideas but as freely desiring to act through them, since they are the embodiments of perfection. Moreover, in acting through the forms, Plato's God creates things for the "best," while *moīra* is the ordained, the way things are and must be, not necessarily for the best.

It has frequently been suggested, and I think with some force, that Plato is tacitly thinking about God on an analogy with artisans and craftsmen. He views God as if he were a craftsman who starts with certain raw materials on which he imposes a pre-existent design. Yet it is notable that

Plato's God differs from the ordinary craftsman in several important respects. Unlike the craftsman's, God's competence is not morally neutral. It is, rather, the power par excellence to produce the morally desirable, the good; Plato's God always acts for the best. He is, in fine, the craftsman whose product is goodness. Another, perhaps more vital difference: unlike the ordinary Greek potter, Plato's God does not experiment with, play with, or engage in trial-and-error activity on his materials, seeking to improve either his methods or his product. Knowing, intending, and capable of doing the best, he does that one thing which is always best. He knows and operates through the single, best design which is *unvarying*.

COEXISTENCE OF GOD AND THE FORMS

To understand the coexistence of God and the Ideas in Plato's cosmology, it may be helpful to note the consequences which follow if God is thus conceived, or conversely, if he were conceived as an absolutely free creator *without* coexistent Ideas through which he acts. Given the coagency of God and of Ideas which are eternal and unchangeable, then a diversity in the manners and morals of different societies is an indication of a corruption of God's work; diversity is then a manifestation of a departure from the Forms and a fall from perfection. The conception of unvarying and eternal Ideas, coexistent with God, serves precisely to prevent God from creating diversity and, in particular, to prevent social diversity from being attributed to him.

The God that can create freely can create diversity in human customs as elsewhere, and this diversity may then claim supernatural sanction. If this is possible, then the all too observable differences in human custom cannot, as Plato seeks, be repaired and transcended by the imposition of a single, unvarying standard or be evaluated in terms of it. Each varying social pattern or custom may then claim an authenticity and legitimacy of its own. Each may claim to be as morally good as some other, and there is then no single moral hierarchy in things. Such a God would be more congenial to those Sophists who emphasize the fulfillment of unique individuality than to a Plato who is seeking a basis of social unity and consensus.

It is also because Plato's God cannot be allowed to create diversity that he cannot be allowed to love men in their individual plight, for a God who loves is a God of mercy. Taking pity on men, he will be ready to act outside of the forms or law, or to suspend them miraculously in some manner, thus engendering variety rather than unity. The important problem for Plato, however, is and remains the need for social unity.

DRIFT TO DISORDER

The prime cause of things, then, is God: "God carrying into execution the idea of the best as far as possible." The prime cause is not natural process or matter, "for they are incapable of reason or intellect." [17] Nature being "deprived of intelligence . . . always produce[s] chance effects without order or design." [18] Creation, Plato says, is mixed, being composed of both necessity and mind. Mind, however, is the prime mover and persuades "necessity to bring the greater part of created things to perfection, and thus and after this manner in the beginning, when the influence of reason got the better of necessity, the universe was created." [19]

This, however, refers to the "time when God himself guides and helps to roll the world in its course." [20] But there is also another time "when he lets go," and then nature, by an inherent necessity, acts contrary to God. While the universe is endowed by God with "many glories," it also partakes of a bodily material nature "and therefore cannot be entirely free of perturbation." Released from divine guidance, and after an initial shock, the "universal creature" at first settles down into an orderly course,

> executing, as far as he remembered them, the instructions of his Father and Creator, more precisely, at first, but afterwards with less exactness. The reason of the falling off was the admixture of matter in him; this was inherent in the primal nature, which was full of disorder, until attaining to the present order. From God, the constructor, the world received all that is good in him, but from a previous state came elements of evil and unrighteousness, which, thence derived, first of all passed into the world, and were then transmitted to the animals. While the world was aided by the pilot in nurturing the animals, the evil was small and great the good which he produced, but after the separation, when the world was let go, at first all proceeded well enough; but, as time went, there was more and more forgetting, and the old discord again held sway and burst forth in full glory.[21]

God thereupon again intervenes to set things right.

There is, then, says Plato, an inherent tendency toward disorder in the world. This disorder is the essence of evil, as orderliness is the essence and paradigm of goodness: "Everything in society which is marked by order and is subject to law, has good as its outcome." Since this tendency toward disorder is in all worldly things, especially in their material or bodily manifestations, it is an aspect of nature. Thus the nondivine or nonminded aspect of the universe is given a twofold character; it is both disorderly and a thing of necessity. It is a subject thing which, when under the governance of mind or God, is orderly, persuaded to perfection, but, when left to its own devices, regresses entropically and drifts back into disorder.

The social world is not seen as having a natural tendency toward order any more than the larger universe of which it is a part. It does not manifest a self-regulation conducive to the maintenance of order. On the contrary, the social world is viewed as threatened continually on all sides: externally, by the ever-present danger of war and invasion, by foreign ideas brought by domestic travelers or aliens, by traders and merchants, by vulnerable geographical location; internally, it is threatened by disunity, by a diversity in ideas and dissensus in beliefs, by partisan and selfish ambitions—a concern for "mine" and "thine"—by individual differences, by the ignorance and evil in men and, especially, in their rulers, by injustice, by *anomia,* by a lack of values, and by a conflict in values. Even the best of cities is in constant peril. It is a city besieged and endangered; it is a Greek city. "Toil as it seems and danger is in every political construction." [22] Even a musical novelty may carry moral corruption. Ruin may come to the social order from anywhere and at any moment.

ON OPERATING METAPHYSICS

In noting Plato's most generalized image of nature we make contact with one of the most elemental orientations that any scholar-philosopher or social scientist can have, precisely because it transcends specialized scholarly roles. This is his metaphysics, his most primitive beliefs and feelings and most general hypotheses about the world. Developed early, during primary socialization, a man's operating metaphysics surrounds and permeates his critically inspected, later developed metaphysical *theories.* It is as difficult for a man to escape or become aware of his operating metaphysics as it is for a fish to escape or become aware of the water in which he swims. Since metaphysics is a hypothesis about the universe as a whole, it is not *derived* from a systematic sampling of the total universe to which it refers. Men commit themselves to their operating metaphysics and have internalized them long before the age of intellectual consent; long before they have seen the need for or had the opportunity of making a broad, systematic sampling. Metaphysical beliefs are ineluctably colored by a personal and limited experience with only a segment of the world.

Early operating metaphysics especially, and to a lesser extent, later critically refined metaphysics, tend to be projectively infused. An operating metaphysics comprises an effort to make orderly that which, prior to the institution of its own premises, is highly unstructured experience. It is therefore particularly susceptible to autistic influences and expressive of personal need. Early operating metaphysics develops out of varying individual needs and affect structures which are fused with culturally standardized and socially received modes of cognition. A man's early operating metaphysics comprises the unavoidable cognitive tools with which he must in some part seek a more sophisticated, deliberately wrought metaphysics. It therefore seems likely that a critically refined metaphysics will, in some part, accommodate to the earlier operating metaphysics and that there will be significant continuities between the two.

Because metaphysics are world hypotheses, they are all-purpose cognitive tools with which a scholar selects from and creates the particular tools of his specialized craft. Their consequences thus permeate his work. Plato's metaphysics of nature, as inherently subject to necessity and as possessing tendencies toward disorder, is not equally conducive to any and all proposals for remedying social tensions, but is particularly consonant with authoritarian and totalitarian solutions.

SOME SOCIAL ORIGINS OF PLATONIC METAPHYSICS

Putting aside its therapeutic and diagnostic consequences, which have been discussed earlier, I want to explore here the sources of Plato's metaphysics. In particular I want to focus not on the logical or theoretical inducements that dispose Plato to think of nature as both disorderly and subject to necessity, but on some of the social, cultural, and sociopsychological factors conducive to such a view of nature. In short, I want to examine some of the historical origins of Plato's metaphysics.

To gain leverage on this problem we may begin by noting that not one but two kinds of analogies underlie Plato's work. Only one of these is manifest and explicit, while the other is latent and implicit. As mentioned earlier, the manifest analogy that Plato commonly uses is the analogy to the craftsman. In particular, he compares politics or rulership and the making of moral decisions with the behavior of craftsmen. Callicles is surely correct in observing that Socrates frequently alludes to them: "[B]y the Gods, you are literally always talking of cobblers and fullers and cooks and doctors." [23] In using analogies from the artisan, Plato and Socrates know very well what they are doing, and they are concerned with the points at which the analogy is sound and where it is limping. The analogy with the craftsmen is a method deliberately aimed at exploring the characteristics of moral and political decision-making.

The second analogy at work is different in substance. This is the analogy with slavery or, more generally, with the existent system of social stratification. The slave and the slave system are used by Plato as a model for the exploration of many other phenomena. Here the content of the analogy differs, and it is different also in its methodological self-consciousness. Unlike the craftsman analogy, this is more often an unlabeled analogy. As Gregory Vlastos remarks, in a brilliant analysis that I frequently use below:

> [t]here is no difference in Plato's political theory between the relation of a master to his slave and of a sovereign to his subjects. . . . His conception of all government . . . is of a piece with his conception of the government of slaves. . . . Plato uses one and the same principle to interpret (and justify) authority in the case of both master and statesman and obedience in the case of both slave and subject.[24]

Vlastos then shows that Plato frequently refers to the body as the "slave" of the soul, that "the relation of mind to body has already been conceived as analogous to that of master to slave," [25] and that, in Plato's cosmology, mind and primary causes stand in a master–slave relation to mechanical and necessary, material causes.

Vlastos suggests that it is because Plato is using an implicit analogy with slavery that he has a twofold conception of the material order as being both disorderly and subject to necessity. It is because Plato implicitly likens nature to a slave that he thinks of nature both as subject to necessity and as inherently disposed to disorder. Plato's "views about slavery, state, man, and the world all illustrate a single hierarchic pattern; . . . the key to the pattern is in his idea of *logos* [rational understanding]. . . . The slave lacks *logos;* so does the multitude in the state, the body in man, and material necessity in the universe. Left to itself each of these would be disorderly and vicious." [26] Vlastos also mentions Plato's contrast between the free physician who treats freemen and the slave physician who treats slaves. In Plato's words: "The slave doctor prescribes what mere experience suggests. But the other doctor, who is a freeman, . . . carries his inquiries far back, and goes into the nature of the disorder." [27]

In brief, the slave is lacking in *logos,* being unable to give any rational account of illness; he operates merely on the basis of *doxa,* practical generalizations or experience. The slave, like nature, is basically devoid of reason. The slave must, therefore, be subject to the governance of some rational master *because* he himself is lacking in rational understanding. And nature, like the slave, is mindless and must also be subject to mind or God.

SLAVERY AND THE METAPHYSICS OF DISORDER

Plato's conception of nature as a realm of necessity, however, is not the most distinctive facet of his metaphysics. The Ionian nature philosophers had maintained this long before Plato. Indeed the essential idea is at least as ancient as the concept of *mōira* itself. That slaves also are subject to necessity is, as previously mentioned, commonly regarded by Greeks as their most obvious and distinguishing characteristic.

Far more distinctive of Plato's metaphysics of nature is his insistence that it is simultaneously a realm of inherent disorder. What is peculiar to Plato's view of nature is the view that it is inherently disorderly. And this characteristic also he attributes to the slave: "[T]he soul of the slave is utterly corrupt and . . . no man of sense ought to trust them." Man, Plato says, is in general a "troublesome animal and therefore he is not very manageable, nor likely to become so, when you attempt to introduce the necessary division of slave, and freeman, and master." [28] Plato is saying that it must be expected that slaves will not be readily amenable to management; that it is in the nature of the case that slaves will be refractory and disorderly—for who willingly becomes a slave? Slaves are a "troublesome piece of goods, as has often been shown by the frequent revolts of the Messenians, and the great mischiefs which happen in states having many slaves who speak the same language, and the numerous robberies and lawless life of the Italian banditte, as they are called." Slaves, like nature then, are inherently disorderly.

The suggestion is strong, then, that a closer look at the relationship between slavery and the metaphysics of disorder may prove fruitful. Here I must depart from Vlastos' important work to pursue the earlier line of analysis in which I stressed that the Greeks often defined slaves as living tools, tending to view them as "nonpersons." This means, among other things, that the slave's own goals, what *he* wants to do, are not regarded by the master as important or problematic.

When a man is viewed as a nonperson, those seeing him this way need not, and commonly will not, be alert to *his* definition of the situation, to his evaluations, beliefs, or feelings concerning the things and persons around him. In any hierarchical system, it may be expected that men are less likely to take heed of or to "take the role" of persons subordinate to them. This tendency is amplified to the extent that there is, as in Greek slavery, a culturally standardized definition of the subordinate as a mere tool, who exists mainly for the satisfaction of his superior's wants.

Those viewing the slave as a tool are less disposed to see the world through his eyes before they behave toward him in some way. They need not anticipate the slave's reactions to their intentions because, no matter what these are, the great power differential between the two enables the master to compel the slave to submit. The slave, after all, is a slave. As a result, the slave's behavior will seem—and will be—unpredictable to the master. It will appear, and it will be, disorderly.

To actors in a situation, "disorderliness" is always experienced in relation to their ends. Things can be disorderly and unpredictable only in relation to someone's standard. The slave's behavior appears disorderly to the master insofar as it departs from or is random relative to the master's wishes. The slave's behavior might not, however, appear disorderly or unpredictable if it were seen in relation to his own ends. It is because the master views the slave primarily in relation to his, the master's, ends—and because these differ from the slave's own ends—that the slave's behavior seems unpredictable and disorderly to the master.

It may be expected, then, that if a social theorist looks at society in terms of moral values, ends, or laws which are somehow external to it, rather than in terms of its immanent laws or ends actually held by men in it, the society will seem to be disorderly. Nature and society will seem more disorderly to those who believe God is the measure than to those who think nature and man are their own measure.

Insofar as masters view slaves as tools and ignore the slaves' own ends, they will indeed be relatively unsuccessful in predicting their behavior, and this makes slaves' behavior less controllable. Insofar as a master does not take account of his slave's feelings and beliefs, his chances of winning the slave's consent are diminished, and by the same token, his chances of increasing the slave's recalcitrance, evasiveness, and duplicity are increased.

The master's failure to take the role of the slave is not, however, simply a motivated response deriving from his definition of the slave as a tool. It is, doubtless, often a constraint imposed by circumstances upon the master, for people in vulnerable positions, such as slaves, will dissemble and conceal their dissident feelings from those powerful enough to punish them. Further, since many slaves come from barbarian countries, they frequently speak different languages and have customs unfamiliar to their masters. Having been subject to child-rearing patterns that differ from their masters, slaves probably also often have character structures, needs, and feelings which are not quite understandable to their masters. Thus, even if he wishes to understand or take account of his slaves' beliefs and feelings, the master may be unable to do so.

These conjectured effects of the slave system premise a relatively depersonalized relation between slaves and masters which, in the above, has been deliberately stated in somewhat extreme form. Depersonalization may, however, be mitigated, but not eliminated, by at least two circumstances: (1) There is good reason to expect more personalized relationships insofar as the slave lives and works in the same household as his master. Such personalized relations, however, wane with the decline of the earlier, more paternalistic slave relations and are probably less frequent in classical times with the growth of large-scale commercialized slavery. (2) The litigious zest of classical Greece sometimes leads slaves to inform on their masters. Masters do, therefore, have to take notice of their slaves and be careful to avoid impious or other legally actionable remarks in their presence. This, however, would seem only to reinforce from still another direction a feeling that the slave is untrustworthy.

It would be well to bear in mind that there are probably more slaves than free Greeks. In an urban context, especially such as Athens, freemen live in a social milieu permeated by slaves. Slaves operate in all manner of occupational specializations, and a freeman continually comes into contact not only with his own slaves but with slaves owned by others; slaves commonly play a part in the freeman's life from birth onward, helping to educate and rear him. Under these conditions, the freeman's feelings about the social world are diffusely but powerfully shaped from birth to death by his daily experience with slaves.

Since the freeman's interpersonal world is intimately interwoven with slaves and since his whole existence is interdependent with these nonpersons whom he feels to be a natural yet recalcitrant part of things, then he is likely to develop a diffuse feeling that his total social surround is somehow unreliable and possesses a pervading disorderliness. Freemen may feel that the very things closest to them—things in their everyday life to which they give only loose attention—have a kind of slippage, and they may develop a vague sense of the disorderliness of their immediate interpersonal surround. This latent sense of disorderliness resonates with and is validated and brought to a focus by the manifest and dramatic disorderliness in the public arena of Hellenic life: by the vicissitudes of the many wars, "For you have been with those who ran and with the pursuers"; by the inevitable failure of the perpetual contestant, "It is no easy thing to engage again and again and never be the loser"; and by the instability of even high position, "Being no more than a man, you cannot tell what will happen tomorrow, nor, when you see one walk in prosperity, know for how much time it will be." [29] Amplified by public experience, the vague sense of the inherent disorderliness of things is likely to be projected into the universe as a whole.

Both John Dewey and Benjamin Farrington have stressed that the Platonic view of the world is shaped by the freeman's prejudice toward manual labor. They view it as a philosophy which, not having been developed by those with a direct involvement in the artisan's productive practice, treats things only from the outside, as it were; as a philosophy that views things in the manner of spectators, of consumers rather than producers, who see and are concerned only with the external performance or finished product and who are, therefore, oriented primarily to its external *form*. In contrast to this, says Farrington, is the older Ionian view of "nature as infinitely various and ingenious but inexorable in its laws, [which] is the conception of technicians who attempt to exercise over matter an operational control. The new conception of Nature, as a power with ends in view, which enforces its will on a subordinate but refractory matter, is the conception of a master who governs slaves." [30]

Much of what I have suggested above relates to the intervening socio-psychological mechanisms by means of which such a metaphysics may come to be congenial to a master stratum. This does not, however, even remotely imply a view of Plato's metaphysics as a deliberate effort to formulate an ideology serviceable to a slave-owning group. My focus has been rather on the nature of the experiences common to freemen living in a traditionally slave-owning society and, especially, on the manner in which such experiences produce expressive dispositions consonant with the Platonic metaphysics. The experience of owning and directing slaves makes the Platonic metaphysics affectively congenial, as well as personally intelligible, thus generating a social audience for it, rather than necessarily explaining how or why it is produced in the first place.

A CONJECTURE ON SOCIALIZATION AND METAPHYSICS

Platonic metaphysics, I have suggested, is usefully seen in relation to the patterned social interaction existing between freemen and slaves, not merely in connection with the latter's economic or technological roles. It is well to emphasize that this relationship begins early in the freeman's life. The child of a free family is often nursed, educated, or chaperoned by his father's slaves who, together with his mother, are involved in rearing him. In brief, the free child is in great part prepared for his role as a master by slaves and women, particularly insofar as his father is away at war or performing his many public duties and who, like Plato's God, is not in constant attendance. It would seem that this has implications of such ramifying consequences that they deserve more attention than they have usually received or, for that matter, than they can be given here.

Here I can essay only a few speculative considerations. For one, it is notable that children of slave-owning families encounter and relate to slaves—with all the slaves' recalcitrance and latent hostilities—long before the children are able to understand this intellectually. The child is experiencing the slave's "disorderliness" well before he has conceptual tools for dealing with it and at an early period in his life when slaves will all the more be seen as a part of his natural surroundings.

For simplicity's sake, we may assume that a child's relation with the slave is either mutually friendly or unfriendly. In the latter case it does not seem farfetched to wonder about the extent to which the slaves' more general hostilities are displaced upon and directed toward the child himself. Where the relation between child and slave involves mutual liking and affection, however, the slave is more likely to reveal to the child his own various evasive strategies of adaptation to his slave role. Indeed, both may enter into a tacit alliance. They may mutually exchange tact and discretion with a view to their common interest in softening parental discipline or evading parental instructions.

As a child grows older he will increasingly adopt his parents' conception of the slave as a living tool to be used and commanded. He begins to behave toward the slave as he will when an adult. The slave who has been hostile to the child will be doubly motivated to resist the child's preliminary efforts at controlling him. The slave who has been friendly may view the change in the child's behavior toward him as improper and ungrateful, and the child's effort at control can also be made all the more difficult by the slave's claim for leniency held to be due him because of their former closeness. In any case, the child is still a child; he is likely to experience special difficulty in having his efforts at control obeyed. In his first efforts to control slaves, then, the child is likely to experience them as particularly recalcitrant.

Moreover, as he gets older the child becomes increasingly aware that he is being supervised by someone who, in the larger cultural scheme of things, is actually something less than himself. The child is subject to the authority of someone whom he is simultaneously learning to devalue and, ultimately, to control. Consequently, when the slave inhibits the free child's impulses, the child is not likely to regard this as unambivalently legitimate; it is dissonant with the role for which the child is being prepared.

For his part, the slave may also feel uneasy about exercising authority over someone who is culturally defined as higher than himself. Furthermore, the child's inevitable and sporadic resistance to adult control is more threatening to slaves than to parents who rear them, for if the slave severely and firmly disciplines the child, the latter may appeal to the authority of the parent. The slave is thus caught in the divergence between the child's impulses and the parents' expectations. In such situations, it may be expected that the slave's disciplinary behavior is more vacillating than that exercised by parents, and this, once again, induces the child to view the slave as unpredictable.

Placed in this precarious situation, one of the more obvious defenses of the slave—or, for that matter, of a mother—is to stress that the discipline imposed is paternally authorized. The child thereby begins to experience the difference between the slave's (or the mother's) own preferences and the constraints to which the latter is subject. The child learns that even powerful adults, who can act on him in such forceful ways, are themselves subject to something else, to the expectations of the father as these are reified in communication to the child. The child learns that the person immediately in charge of him is subject to another, coexistent regulator. In this way the child may come to make a distinction between power and the pattern through which power is exercised. Children in various cultures, of course, commonly develop such a distinction. But children reared by slaves would seem particularly likely to do so; for it is soon manifest that slaves, though having power over their charges, do not exert it willingly on their own behalf or in accordance with their own dispositions but, rather, in furtherance of another's goals.

Experiences conducive to distinguishing between power and pattern can be seen from still another, complementary viewpoint. In a patriarchical kinship system such as the Greek, the father's power is very great. Yet he is also comparatively remote, involved as he often is in public duties or distant wars. The child is therefore left to the governance of slaves or to a mother who must act in strict accordance with the expectations, rather than the direct supervision, of the male head of the household. The latter's presence is as much felt by allusion to his general regulations as by his direct intervention and personal contact. The child, particularly the upper-class boy, thus becomes a man by having the model of a man presented to him. That is, the process of socialization in the upper-class Greek family is constrained to place greater reliance on the verbal communication of an appropriate model and less on direct and close interaction with the person of whom it was a model. With such an emphasis, a verbal and conceptual model comes to assume an autonomy and reality of its own; and all the more so as this model is rigidly insisted on because of the authoritarian character of the family and because it is communicated by women and slaves who cannot claim to embody or exemplify it.

Relative to such an external and rigid model, the child's behavior will tend to be perceived as comparatively disorderly, and essentially for the same reasons that the slave's behavior is viewed as disorderly by the master. Indeed, Plato associates the male child with the slave and views both in much the same way: "nor can children be left without tutors, or slaves without masters. And of all animals the boy is the most unmanageable. . . . Wherefore he must be bound with many bridles." [31]

Assuming that children begin to see themselves as their significant others define them, the child is learning—because he is being taught—that there is something disorderly within him. He is learning to define his own spontaneous impulses as evil and unruly; in fine, he is learning to equate the natural with the disorderly.

INCREASED TENSIONS IN THE SLAVE SYSTEM

Many of the considerations sketched above, seeking to account for the growth of an outlook congenial to Plato's view of the material universe as a disorderly subject, deal with the basic structure of slavery which existed well before Plato's time. Are there, however, any circumstances involving the slave system which are newly pronounced in Plato's view and which could have been conducive to the same outlook?

One such developing circumstance is that, in the period prior to Plato's time, slave ownership tended to grow in scale. With the development of large-scale slavery and, especially so, the more they outnumber their masters, slaves become particularly threatening and are increasingly felt to be such. In a revealing fantasy, Plato has Socrates say, "[I]magine one of those owners, the master say of some fifty slaves, together with his family and property, and slaves, carried off by a god into the wilderness, where there are no freemen to help him—will he not be in agony of fear lest he and his wife and children should be put to death by his slaves?" [32]

After the tremendous tensions to which Hellenic society is subjected by the Peloponnesian War, with its incitations to and opportunities for slave insurrection, slavery becomes more institutionally precarious and more intellectually perplexing: "There is no difficulty either in understanding or acquiring most kinds of property, but there is great difficulty in what relates to slaves." [33] The entire slave system manifests disorderliness, both in the diverging conceptions of slavery held by the masters themselves and in the relations between the masters and their slaves:

> [W]e speak about them [i.e., slaves] in a way which is right and which is not right; for what we say about our slaves is consistent and also inconsistent with our practice. . . . Different persons have got . . .

two different notions of slaves in their minds—some of them utterly distrust their servants, and, as if they were wild beasts, chastize them with goads and whips, and make their souls three times, or rather many times, as slavish as they were before;—and others do just the opposite.[34]

That is, rather than punishing their slaves, some masters are admonishing them as if they are freemen, jesting with them rather than commanding them, thus inducing their slaves to become conceited and self-willed, says Plato.

It is thus not only that Greek slavery is intrinsically conducive to a view of the material universe as a disorderly subject, but that the slave system is then becoming increasingly disorderly. The institution itself—which Greeks long took for granted and which indeed had scarcely been questioned—is now surfacing into public consciousness. The latent social problems implicit in slavery are slowly becoming manifest social problems; there is an intensification of the crisis in the slave system and in the society at large. For Greeks, to observe disorder in the slave system is to observe it in one of the core areas of social life which they traditionally regard as natural.

Without in the least intending to reduce Plato's philosophy to a defense of the slave system, or for that matter without holding him specially culpable for doing so—for his basic attitudes toward slavery are scarcely unique—I may nonetheless suggest that in some respects it constitutes a complex intellectual response to the crisis of the Hellenic system of social stratification in general and to slavery in particular. There is in Plato's work a double legitimation of slavery which will later be elaborated systematically by Aristotle: first, slavery is suggested to be legitimate because the slave is diminished in the highest human quality, reason; second, slavery is held legitimate because it is ordained and natural, being an expression within the society of the hierarchal relationships said to be characteristic of the universe as a whole. Plato's metaphysics is, in part, a projection of the slave relationship and of experience within it onto the universe as a whole. Once projected there, it may then be brought back to earth where it serves in effect to legitimate slavery itself.

NOTES

[1] *The Function of Reason,* pp. 23, 45.

[2] *Republic.* 439C.

[3] *Republic.* 440C.

[4] *Republic.* 580E.

[5] *Republic.* 532C.

[6] *Republic.* 587B.

[7] *Phaedrus.* 266B.

[8] W. K. C. Guthrie, *The Greek Philosophers* (New York: Harper, 1960), p. 13.

[9] *Republic.* 377D.

[10] *Republic.* 378A.

[11] *Republic.* 459CD.

[12] *Philebus.* 66A.

[13] *Ion,* 533E, 534A.

[14] *Phaedrus.* 245C.

[15] *Laws.* 663D.

[16] *Philebus.* 26C.

[17] *Timaeus.* 46C.

[18] *Timaeus.* 46D.

[19] *Timaeus.* 48A.

[20] *Statesman.* 269C.

[21] *Statesman.* 273C.

[22] *Laws.* 736B.

[23] *Gorgias.* 491A.

[24] G. Vlastos, "Slavery in Plato's Thought," *Philosophical Review,* 1. n. 3, 293. Cf. Vlastos' qualifying remarks in his addendum in Finley, *Slavery in Classical Antiquity, op. cit.,* pp. 148–149.

[25] *Ibid.,* p. 295.

[26] *Ibid.,* p. 303.

[27] *Laws.* 720C.

[28] *Laws.* 776E, 777B.

[29] Lattimore, *Greek Lyrics, op. cit.,* pp. 15, 65, 48, 54.

[30] B. Farrington, *Greek Science,* Vol. 1 (Hammondsworth: Penguin Books, 1949), pp. 146–147.

[31] *Laws.* 808D.

[32] *Republic.* 578E.

[33] *Laws.* 776C.

[34] *Laws.* 777A.

11   *Death and the Tragic Outlook*

Heracles   Ah, do not mourn for her before she
dies. Wait for the time.

Admetus   The point of death is death, and the
dead are lost and gone.

Heracles   Being and nonbeing are considered different things.

Admetus   That is your opinion, Heracles. It is
not mine.

—Euripides [1]

"At this point I lay aside my pen: the sequel of the
story may haply commend itself to another."

—Xenophon [2]

IT MIGHT seem that headlong flight from reality would be the easiest and
most obvious solution to a theorist such as Plato who feels the human condition to be a tragic one. Yet the matter is more complex because the tragic
outlook is a perspective developed only by those who are deeply concerned
with the world of men and who are open to its suffering. The tragic outlook
is born of a disparity between great hopes for man and a high conception
of his estate, on the one side, and the belief that human beings labor under
inescapable limitations, on the other. In the tragic view, man is seen as being
less than God—rather than viewed as more than ape—and as a lower rather
than a higher being. Man is seen as a noble, heart-breaking failure.

For all its heady utopianism, Plato's social theory is suffused with a tragic
vision of life. It emphasizes that the coherence of things is precarious, that
the world tends to drift naturally toward disorder, that it is riven with contests and conflicts within the psyche, within the city, and between cities. To
this extent, Plato's theory reflects a tense liveliness. But Plato sublimates the
contest, making it a struggle for the prize of virtue which is to be awarded
in an afterlife; and he aims to supplant conflict with social unity. Plato's
utopias are an attempt to transcend tension and flux. There is something
strangely suspended about Plato's cities; they are rather like the paintings

of two Greek warriors on a vase, spear eternally poised against spear, forever locked in frozen strife.

There is no real history in Plato's social theory, no real development, no evolution, no determinate phase sequences, no laws of change. Indeed, there is no true change at all, for all change is in the mere appearance of things. It is the Ideas or Forms alone which are real, and these remain eternally the same. The gap between the reality of these perfect Ideas and the manifest imperfection of nature is enormous. From Plato's standpoint even the most perfect state is transient; even the ideal Republic. "Hard it may be for a society so constituted to be shaken; yet decay is the universal fate of all things in this world of change, nor will even a framework such as we have built last for all time: it must suffer dissolution."

The Platonic universe runs in an eternal cycle of forgetting and remembrance in which nothing new is ever learned. It has no real creation or creativity, no true novelty and growth. There is only the endless pouring of materials into the ageless mold of the Forms and the endless corruption of the casting. In its pessimism Plato's philosophy is at one with the deepest currents of Hellenic culture: we are "for the most part puppets, but having some little share of reality"; [3] "No human thing is of serious importance." [4]

It is because the theorist with a tragic view sees man as in part noble that he cannot let go and disengage himself altogether from the human scene. But since he sees man, too, as a failure who will never overcome his vital weaknesses, such a theorist must also find ways in which to detach himself. Thus the dilemmas of detachment and involvement present themselves in Plato in acute form. It is in this connection, as strategies of ambivalent involvement and detachment, that I will examine the question of Plato's aesthetic orientation and a specific expression of it, his use of the dialogue.

THE TRANSCENDENCE OF DEATH

I have earlier suggested a variety of historical developments conducive to the heightening of pessimism among Athenians in general and especially among those of Plato's aristocratic and conservative tradition. Born only three years after the plague had killed about a fourth of Athens, he writes after the exhaustion of the Peloponnesian War, at a time when there is a declining faith that happiness and success can be wrested, even temporarily, from this world. Yet Platonic pessimism, like Greek pessimism more generally, derives not only from the political and military calamities of the time—not only, in short, from the period's manifest problems—but also from the way in which these exacerbate the deeper, more latent currents of Hellenic pessimism, confirming them in their blackest anticipations. Platonic pessimism rests on something more lasting and more disturbing than the manifest social problems of the time.

No stranger to Hellenic pessimism, Plato has in fact plumbed its darkest corners. He has seen that it rests finally on a great and abiding fear, the fear of death. One of Plato's basic defenses against pessimism has always been a belief in reason and a confidence in its potency. The problem he confronts, however, is whether reason can suffice to still the fear of death. Plato's pessimism deepens when there is within him a confrontation between the characteristically Greek abomination of death and his confidence in reason. At this juncture Platonic reason falters. Not because it sets itself against men's deepest ambitions—as well it might if it had sought to persuade slaves to accept slavery—but because it accepts certain ambitions whose fulfillment are beyond its resources. And when reason falls too far short of men's dreams, they will turn elsewhere, to ritual and faith and art, for help. Platonic reason exhausts itself in confronting the problem of the nonexistence of the person, death. Whatever one may think of his solution, Plato sees that death is not simply a medical terminus but is overwhelmingly and uniquely important throughout the entire life of men, which, it must be said, is still something that few social scientists as yet grasp. Plato sees that death is not the end of life but its underside.

Tendencies to ritualization, we suggested earlier, are more likely to arise when men lack technologically adequate means for attaining their goals and controlling their environment. The next problem then becomes a search for the aim that the Greeks want to realize, and that Plato shares with them, for which technologically adequate instruments were not available and which presses for the relief of ritual. Certainly there are malign aspects of the Greek natural environment, such as plagues or earthquakes, in the face of which the Greeks feel hopeless and which they cannot realistically expect to control. Moreover, there are many aspects in the affairs of men themselves, as the events during and after the Peloponnesian War amply evidence, in which the neatest plans and the highest hopes are crushed time and again, and men come to feel that their social world is careening out of control.

The Greeks recognize that war in particular is intrinsically fraught with deep uncertainties and that even the highest military "science" can scarcely control all its contingencies, even though so much depends on it. A society in which war is a frequent if not continuous activity seems especially likely to be experienced as one in which men have relatively less control over the events crucial to their lives. The men in it will be motivated to seek supernatural assurances to augment their own practical preparations.

Certainly the conventional Greek view of the Olympian gods sees them as having the power to affect military events. Indeed, in Homer and the dramatists it is one of the chief functions of the gods to decide the outcome of battles. Zeus is the "turner of battle." The gods are continually invoked in the face of uncertain outcomes. There are, however, several crucial difficulties in using the Olympians to reduce the endemic anxieties evoked by the military and other uncertainties of Hellenic existence. First, tradition allows different gods to ally themselves with different sides in a controversy; the supernatural power of one side may meet countervailing power on the other. If, however, Zeus is won to one's own side, his supreme power can decide the issue favorably. But even here there is uncertainty, for the affairs of men are not all that fascinating to the gods, and Zeus might become preoccupied with his own intrigues and gratifications. Further, since the Homeric gods are capable of trickery, envy, and malice toward men, there is uncertainty concerning their benign feelings, and there is doubt about their readiness to aid even deserving men in their time of need. Even a pious believer in the Olympians may thus have difficulty in relying on them to control an uncertain environment. In Plato's time there is increasing skepticism and doubt about the existence of the gods, at the very time that heightened anxieties increase the need for supernatural protection. The gap between the supply and demand for supernatural protection is growing, and with this there is growing pessimism.

Pessimism, of course, is scarcely novel to the Greeks and long permeates their culture. This pessimism centers on at least two recurrent themes, one of which is the instability of life and the vicissitudes of fortune. There is, however, another focus of Greek pessimism that centers not on men's changing fortunes but on their unvaryingly bad ending and, in particular, on the fact that death is inevitable. The Greeks (and Plato not least among them) are obsessed with the problem of death—they really cannot reconcile themselves to it—and it is this that is at the core of the tragic outlook.

From the Homeric image of Achilles onward, the Greeks view man as struggling to surmount the finality of death. For all his stiff aristocratic pride, even Achilles acknowledges that he would sooner be a live serf than king of the dead. To the Greeks this life is all that counts; such existence as Hades is thought to provide their wraiths hardly seems worthwhile. Though this is an enduring theme in Greek culture, their melancholy about death grows more brooding and bitter from Homer onward. As W. C. Greene remarks,

> there is a difference between the melancholy of Homer at the spectacle of high hopes and powers ultimately cut short and the cynical, middle-

aged sort of pessimism that a later age was to experience. Indeed, Homer's age feels the death in battle of a young warrior like Achilles to be glorious as well as pathetic. Still less does any Homeric character suggest, as will come later to Greeks, that life is not good in itself, and that it were better never to have been born, or, having been born, to die as soon as possible.[5]

With Hesiod, however, Greek gloom takes on almost morbid colors: "The earth is full of evils," injustice prevails, and disease is abroad. In the middle or late seventh century, Simonides of Amorgos sings, sadly, "The time of afterdeath for us is very long / We live a wretched sum of years, and badly, too." About a century later his lament is echoed by Anacreon of Teos: "For the house of death is deep down / underneath; the downward journey / to be feared, for once I go there; I know well there's no returning." The so-called mystery religions or cults around the sixth century commonly stress the significance of the soul and the possibility of its happiness in another life, if it has been properly prepared and initiated in this one. While not rationally supported, the Eleusinian rites gave symbolic expression to men's desire for immortality through ritual enactments of the myth of Persephone, celebrating her descent into Hades and her return to the world and to her mother, Demeter.

In this connection, the myth of Orpheus' own descent into Hades and the historical changes it undergoes are of some interest. In its sixth-century form, Orpheus was said to have been the greatest of musicians, who ventured into Hades and who returned to tell of what he saw among the dead. At this period, the myth remarks somewhat incidentally that he was able, through his exceptional powers, to bring his wife, Eurydice, back from the dead with him. By the fifth century, however, this wish fulfillment takes on heightened pathos, and it is held, in some accounts, that Orpheus could not keep Eurydice with him for very long but soon had to return her to Hades. It is apparently only later, as evidenced in Virgil's account, that her return will be held to be Orpheus' fault, his punishment for having disobeyed the command that he must not look at Eurydice until they reached the upper world. For the Greeks, however, the dominant sense of the myth seems to have been that only a demigod of remarkable powers could hope to return someone from Hades, and even he, it came to be believed, could not do so permanently.

The continuing concern and the increasingly bitter feeling about death during the classical period are reflected in Sophocles' and Euripides' treatments of it. In his *Antigone,* Sophocles eulogizes and recites the virtuosity of man: "Many the wonders but nothing walks stranger than man," paeans the chorus; he is the creature that crosses the sea despite winter's storm; he snares birds, beasts, and fish, he has domesticated the horse and the bull, and he has even taught himself language, feeling, and thought. The Odyssean image is also invoked. Man, we are told, "can always help himself. He faces no future helpless." [6] Yet wondrous though he is and clever beyond all dreams, "There's . . . death that he cannot find an escape from." The greater the Greek triumph, the keener the resentment at the remaining barrier.

For Euripides this limitation is also a limitation within man's character. He recognizes a profound ambivalence in man's orientation to death, as shown in his *Alcestis*. On the one side there is Alcestis, who does accept death, who for the love of her husband, Admetus, dies willingly. There is also Heracles, who in his heroically traditional way surmounts mortality and returns Alcestis from the gate of death. There is, in short, hope for a kind of transcendence of death, through man's own character and through the intervention of a demigod. But all this is only the foil, the invidious contrast that sets off and magnifies Admetus' own egoistic clutching at life, his willingness to let his loved ones die for him, his readiness to do anything rather than die.

Alcestis' sacrifice, however, is just that. It is a sacrifice precisely because her attitudes toward death remain characteristically Greek, viewing it as an abysmal finality. Comforting her lord's grief with pathetic irony, she reminds him, "Time will soften it. The dead count for nothing." [7] Admetus knows it, too, echoing her: "The point of death is death, and the dead are lost and gone." [8] Admetus' father shrugs off his son's complaint that "you at your age . . . would not, dared not, die for your own child," replying, "Do not die for me, I will not die for you. You like the sunlight. Don't you think your father does?" [9]

Sophocles' grandeur has become Euripides' savage irony. Yet both know that it is death that is man's immortal enemy, spearing him not only through the sturdiest armor, but mouldering him, body and soul, from within. The Greek obsession with death persists. It seems noteworthy that Diogenes' famous sleeping tub apparently still had, for his contemporaries, certain associations as a coffin. And later Epicurus takes up the struggle, teaching that death is not to be feared.

It is, then, in the Greek resentment at death that we glimpse a frustrated aim of major magnitude—the desire for immortality—for which there is no technologically realistic solution at all. Indeed the Greeks believe that human death is a matter that even the Olympian gods themselves may not alter or basically control, but is in the hands of destiny. The traditional gods thus could not aid men in relieving their anxieties in this most crucial of contingencies. "It seems clear," says Richmond Lattimore, "that in Plato's time and immediately before it any strong and clear belief in immortality was rare," although most acknowledge death to be "the bitterest of evils." [10] The theological core of Plato's philosophy may be understood as a response to this basic insufficiency of the Olympians. It seeks a solution, first, by advancing a conception of a god who, far from having any traces of envy or hostility toward men, is uniformly benign toward them and to whom no evil at all can be attributed; and, second, by seeking to provide men with a rational basis for relieving anxieties about death.

There are some respects in which Plato's philosophy departs markedly from traditional Greek views on these matters: in the directness of its expression of a desire for a kind of immortality and in the rationally justified claim that it exists for men. The autistic impulse behind this claim is suggested by Plato's insistent efforts to demonstrate the immortality of the soul by logical means and, especially, by his repeated search for new lines of demonstration when earlier strategies fail. Plato differs from Greek tradition, not in expressing the fantasy wish for immortality but in the relatively open, forceful, and rational framework in which he voices it. From Greek culture onward, human immortality has been the highest item on Western men's not so "secret agenda."

The Greek desire for immortality had commonly to be repressed, for insofar as they traditionally associated immortality with the gods and insofar as they feared that those seeking to emulate the gods will be punished for their *hybris*, the wish to be immortal could hardly be given open expression. It had to be masked, even from the self, for thoughts were known to the gods. Commonly the wish for immortality could be given only symbolic expression, as in the Eleusinian rites. Plato, however, at last says openly what Greeks had long wanted but feared to acknowledge—that men wish to be immortal. And Plato promises them immortality. He believes that this is one of their most devout hopes. As he states in the *Symposium,* men's creative activities, both biological and intellectual, are born of a desire for immortality.

There are at least two curious things about the desire for immortality that Plato imputes to men. The first is that it has an obscure relation to men's other desires and to the threefold anatomy of the psyche that Plato employs. It is not at all clear from which of these three parts of the psyche that the desire for immortality derives or, indeed, whether it springs from any of them. Given the universality and the importance that he attributes to this desire, it is difficult to understand his failure to have confronted the question directly. He takes it as given that men want to be immortal. A second notable aspect of the desire for immortality is Plato's own attitude toward it.

Unlike the other appetites or drives of men, he does not approach this one with caution, suspicion, or distaste. He manifests no inclination to warn men of the dangers involved in pursuing it insatiably, or of the need for this pursuit to be engaged in temperately. In this respect the desire for immortality seems to be something like reason and wisdom, of which men cannot want or have too much. Plato, in short, approves men's quest for immortality. He believes that the greatest of poets, artists, lawgivers, the wisest and best of men, are inspired by a hope for immortality.

Regarding the desire for immortality as a noble one, Plato strives strenuously to permit men to believe in it. Yet however imperious, he will not allow them to surrender to their need to believe without the sanction of reason, and so he seeks to provide a logical demonstration of the immortality of the soul—which is such immortality as men may have.

When, in the *Phaedo,* Socrates' first proof of this is shown to fail, he is described as having a "quick sense of the wound which had been inflicted by the argument" [11] and a keen desire to heal it. Using still another contest metaphor, we are told, "He might be compared to a general rallying his defeated and broken army, urging them to accompany him and return to the field of argument." [12] Plato has a vivid sense of how strongly men wanted to believe in the immortality of the soul and a keen awareness that most men have an insatiable desire for life and will never be fully reconciled to anything less than immortality, at least of the soul.

As he has Cebes put it, if one cannot prove the soul imperishable, then "he who is confident about death had but a foolish confidence . . . [I]f he cannot prove the soul's immortality, he who is about to die will always have reason to fear that when the body is disunited, the soul also may utterly perish." [13] And Echecrates, who is hearing this story of Socrates' last hours recounted by Phaedo, echoes Cebes' dismay: "What argument can I ever trust again. For what could be more convincing than the argument of Socrates, which has now fallen into discredit? And now I must begin again and find another argument which will assure me that when the man is dead the soul survives." Then Socrates sets forth once more to find a proof for the immortality of the soul. It is clear that this search for a proof by a man who is perhaps an hour from his execution is not entirely of academic significance. The explicit statements of the onlookers and the foreseeable dramatic denouement of the dialogue make it manifest that the search is infused with a deep personal need.

What does Plato intend in portraying Socrates as seeking a proof of immortality into his very last moments? A picture of a good and brave man, pursuing his life's mission selflessly and without concern for himself? Does he mean to heighten Socrates' triumph by revealing his greatest success to have come at the last moment? Is the anticipated climax to lend credence to Socrates' assertion of belief in his second proof of the soul's immortality, on the assumption that a doomed man's word may be given a deeper reliance? Or does the very dramatic situation surrounding the second proof instead undermine the credence with which it may be viewed by heightening awareness of the manner in which urgent need may corrupt reason?

Without doubt, Plato felt that a logical proof of the soul's immortality is of the greatest moment to men, particularly to reasonable men. The immortality of the soul is of vital importance to his philosophy, for, if there is no such thing then the deepest, legitimate desire of good men will be broken; if there is no such thing, then the ultimate fate of all men, good or bad alike, is the same; if there is no immortality in which to reward good men then there is considerably less gratification for them to anticipate as compensation for the life of self-control and denial that they are enjoined to live on earth. In assuring men that their soul's fate after death depends on how they have lived, Plato is again giving men a way in which they can, through their own actions, control their own destinies. He is enhancing their sense of control over this most vital interest and providing them a way of accomplishing what piety toward the Olympians could not.

Yet I cannot help but wonder whether Plato himself was convinced even by the second proof of the immortality of the soul, and whether he expected others to find it convincing. Both Cebes and Socrates are shown as claiming, after Socrates' second proof, that they are convinced of the immortality of the soul. Indeed, Socrates says at one point that he is convinced "beyond question." Yet it does not seem unreasonable to wonder about Plato's own judgment, considering that he juxtaposes the second proof to the defeat of the first, concerning which he has had Echecrates say that none could have been more convincing. If the first, most convincing of proofs was wrong, why not the second?

Plato, in fact, presents Simmias as not fully sharing Cebes' certainty concerning even the second proof and has him remark, "But I still feel and cannot help feeling uncertain in my own mind, when I think of the greatness of the subject and the feebleness of man." [14] Indeed Plato has Socrates himself concur in this sentiment, adding that first principles should be carefully considered, and even when satisfactorily ascertained, one should then proceed only with "a sort of hesitating confidence in human reason." [15] Socrates' conclusion, then, is that the very nature of the question and the means through which an answer to it must be sought, human reason, can permit no more than a reasonable confidence in the solution.

But is this enough to quiet anxieties centering on this most vital issue? Is it enough even though it is the most that can be won by reason? Or will rational men still wonder and doubt, and does Plato? Does Plato feel that on this most ultimate of issues the resources of reason are commensurate with the intensity of men's needs? We are dealing, it must be remembered, with a man who is a proponent of the "noble lie" and who thinks it more important to do good than to tell the truth.

Whether Plato believes in the immortality of the soul as much as he hopes for it, I suspect that his faith in reason's potency is strained as it comes aground on this hard problem. On the record, it is perfectly clear that Plato finds nothing more difficult than to provide rational grounds for men's desire to believe in their own immortality, for he has seen how the wisest of Athenians was admittedly wrong on the question, at least once.

We will remember Plato saying in the *Laws* that men must believe that the gods are such as the laws ordain. This implies that men might well not be convinced by rational persuasion, and they must therefore believe that things are as the law describes. Plato's installation of the law as the surrogate of reason and his emphasis that the best men are those who obey the law reflect a more than remnant uncertainty about the potency of reason. Plato's own "tragic vision" derives not so much from a despair of death but from a failure of reason to prove, with the kind of certainty that the issue requires, that the despair is needless.

Faced with men's dismay of death, Plato seeks to abate anxieties with the use of reason. He seeks to make reason do what no technology then or now can hope to do, give men a purchase on immortality. He attempts to prove that men have immortal souls and thus give them a rationally supported confidence that this life is not all. In arguing that the fate of men's immortal souls in the afterlife depends on how they behave in this life, he gives men grounds for feeling that their afterlife depends upon their own actions and decisions and is thus subject to their control. It is in this perhaps supreme effort that Platonic reason strains its resources to the uttermost and falls back shaken. Undermined by the very boldness of its ambitions, it needs increasing support from faith and ritualization. It is thus, even as he wages his struggle against Greek pessimism and obsession with death, that Plato succumbs to them.

In the end, Plato seems less convinced by the elaborate arguments in favor of the immortality of the soul than by the simple affirmation that death is not to be feared. "Those of us who think that death is an evil," says Socrates, "are in error." [16] For Plato, however, death, unlike love, must not be allowed to remain beyond good and evil, and he adds that death is a good thing. The soul's quest for truth is encumbered and deceived by the body and thus "any man who has the spirit of philosophy will be willing to die. . . ."[17] [T]he real philosopher has reason to be of good cheer when he is about to die, . . . he is always pursuing death and dying. . . . [T]he true philosophers, and they only, are ever seeking to release the soul." [18] The capstone is set by the rhetorical question: "For is not philosophy the study of death." [19]

While all this is in no literal sense a death wish, it does seem to embody a death fantasy which transvalues the Greek dismay of death. Death is now transformed from the worst evil to the greatest good that can befall a man who has lived life properly. Death is no longer the end of things but a beginning. By the same process, however, life changes from the highest arena of consummation to a subordinate prelude and preparation for death. In the end, the argument in favor of immortality becomes not so much a consolation and promise that a life well spent may be left without fear or sorrow but an intimation that life—as even the best live it—is a crippled thing and that death will release and fully heal it.

THE ETERNAL FORMS

The Platonic concern with death is, I believe, deeply linked to his orientation to aesthetics, and, in a way, art too is made to serve as a defense against death. The deepest expression of Plato's aesthetic impulse is given in his theory of the eternal Ideas or Forms, and a brief discussion of this theory is in order before considering the problem of aesthetics more directly.

Plato postulates that the Good toward which men can strive through the use of the dialectic exists eternally in some hyperspatial realm where it has a perfect and immutable Form. It is this pure Idea or Form which is mirrored or realized, but only imperfectly, in the concrete particulars visible to the senses. On occasion, Plato speaks of the Forms as a model to be imitated by the concrete particulars, the latter being like an actor in a play who interprets a part written by the playwright. Closely related to this dramatic metaphor is his use of the artisan and his work as a model of the relationship between the particular and the Form. That is, the artisan, perhaps a shoemaker, has a model or norm of what a pair of shoes looks like and in some measure embodies this in a particular pair of shoes he makes. Since any pair of shoes never completely embodies the shoemaker's conception, each pair varies somewhat from the others as well as having certain similarities to them.

The nature of the model is therefore not revealed by examining any one pair of shoes, and its character is, in some way, to be gleaned by searching for the features common to shoes. Plato may thus begin an analysis of justice or virtue with certain varying common-sense notions or particular expressions of them, but the aim is to discern the characteristics common to these particulars. The Forms must be apprehended, in consequence, not merely by the senses or by observation which, at most, provide the raw materials of dialectical exploration, the starting point of analysis, but they must be seen by and indeed can be seen only by the mind. The dialectic quest for the Form then entails a kind of ascent from experience and a reliance on purely mental or symbolic manipulations rather than a material manipulation of the concrete particulars.

Plato clearly sees that the facts do not speak for themselves; they cannot be taken as they are given to sensory observation but must, somehow, be cross-examined. The assumption is that the particulars would be known or explained when the Form or class in which they "participated" was seen in its purity. The differences or relations between the Form and the particulars are not regarded as explainable by stipulated laws; they are rather seen as something in the nature of a random fault, or a "forgetting." Patterning in nature or human behavior is thus accounted for in terms of a striving of the particular to embody or participate in the perfect Form, while variations around the pattern are essentially regarded as due to ignorance or miscalculation concerning the perfect Form, or as a kind of loss or inadequate understanding of it.

The Forms or Ideas are, however, more than simply logical classes. They are norms in the sense that they are akin to plans, exerting a kind of regulative influence on particulars. The Ideas are not merely stipulations of boundaries indicating which particulars are within and which are outside of a given area. They are more nearly like centers of power or like genes, which reproduce themselves and exert a shaping force. The Forms are thus not simply logically inclusive of the particulars or the examples but are something real apart from them.

Plato's effort to find transcendental universal Ideas which he postulates to be real is probably related to the very practical problem confronting the Greek morality of his time: finding a common ground among diverse beliefs and establishing a basis for unifying them, of composing competing claims and values so that all need not be treated relativistically, as if they were of equal value. The development of universal definitions may, then, not only have emerged from the disinterested stirring of an idle curiosity anxious to think more clearly for its own sake, but also as a response to the crisis of Greek moral and belief systems. On a sociological level, it is in effect an effort to identify a hidden, common ground among warring views and a rhetoric serving to win consent to a method aimed at producing consensus.

In the Platonic view, the quest for truth about human behavior, as anything else, is in the nature of a disciplined mental effort to search out and discover the hidden realities, the Forms, lying behind the distorting mask presented by sensory appearance. There is an assumption that there is a difference between reality and appearance, with a corresponding ennobling of the hidden reality and a devaluing of the manifest appearance of things. The major point is that the Form is real, existing apart from the formulation of any particular observer; it needs to be unveiled by an effort of mind. The approach to truth is regarded as a search process, a looking for with the mind's eye. It is not a creation or a construction, it is akin to the restoration of a painting which lies beneath the patina awaiting application of the cleansing dialectic to reveal it in its full beauty.

From this standpoint, of course, not all beliefs can claim equal virtue or validity; those that more nearly embody the hidden eternal Ideas are the superior. For example, not all Forms of slavery are equally valid; those most embodying the ideal type of slavery are the best. Yet the question arises as to why *any* form of slavery must be ideal. How can one be sure that there is a perfect Form of slavery? How can one know whether slavery is an accidental or an essential characteristic of a system of production?

Here we may note some difficulties in working with a theory of Forms or Ideas, and, in particular, some of the problems to which it may lead on the level of social analysis. Essentially what the theorist working with the Platonic theory of Forms does, in practice if not in principle, is to commit himself to a certain level of abstraction, to express an interest in an entity which he simply takes as given. The problem, however, is on which level of abstraction is he to work? Why not simply search for the Ideal Forms of production or economy, rather than for ideal modes of slavery? Why must there be a perfect and eternal Form corresponding to any entity that can be imagined or conceptualized? And what of the relations between one entity and another, as well as the relations among their corresponding eternal Forms? What, for example, are the relations between the eternal Idea of the *polis* (or group) and that of the individual? (Much the same kind of problem will later be faced by Max Weber, whose theory of "ideal types" has many similarities to the Platonic theory of Forms.)

With the Platonic theory of Ideas, it may be assumed that any given social structure or arrangement is necessary and desirable in its "essential" respects, and that only its existent, historically limited expression is imperfect. On the one hand, the Platonic theory premises an eternal form from whose standpoint the historically concrete social structure may be criticized. On the other hand, it also tacitly premises that the concrete structures can only be reformed, but not eliminated in essentials. Indeed, far from eliminating it, one should attempt ever more diligently to enact its ideal, basic characteristics. Since the ideal form is timeless, the social structure which corresponds to it, however imperfectly, is functionally indispensable and unchangeable in essentials. In its sociological usage, the Platonic theory of Forms is therefore capable of providing an ideological legitimation for any concrete social pattern by claiming that it reflects, and may be made to attain, an ideal and perfect form. The theory implies that the concrete social structure cannot be changed in its essentials, and this, indeed, may be precisely why Plato's social theory is utopian. For the theory of Forms incites a radical criticism of society which, at the same time, it assumes to be unchangeable in essentials. The resultant dilemma can never be resolved in practice and politics, but only in utopia and art.

THE AESTHETIC ORIENTATION: DETACHMENT AND INVOLVEMENT

For all Plato's suspicion and hostility toward poets, when he holds that the essence of existence is to be found in the eternal Forms, this implies that he feels that an aesthetic dimension is at the very core of reality, for the aesthetic is centrally, though not exclusively, concerned with form and style. Indeed it is not farfetched to say that Plato views God as the master artist. Our suggestion that an aesthetic orientation is particularly important to Plato is certainly consistent with his mythopoeic inclinations, with the artistry that he invests in his dialogues, with his use of dramatistic metaphors, as well as with the biographical fact that he began as a poet.

That Plato's own specific conceptions of good art typically express an emphasis upon simplicity and harmony, and are at variance with many modern emphases, ought not to be taken as evidence that he was not aesthetically oriented; they imply only that the content of his aesthetic orientation differs from ours. That Plato wishes to control and censor various forms of art in his ideal cities testifies to the practical importance he attributes to art, not to his disinterest in it. Plato says:

> [T]here is no difficulty in seeing that grace or the absence of grace is an effect of good or bad rhythm . . . good and bad rhythm naturally assimilate to a good and bad style; and that harmony and discord in like manner follow style. . . . And will not the words and the character of the style depend on the temper of the soul . . . and everything else on style? . . . grace and harmony are the twin sisters of goodness and virtue and bear their likeness.

The artist, he holds, must insensibly "draw the soul from earliest years into likeness and sympathy with the beauty of reason." [20]

In broaching questions of aesthetics, I am particularly mindful of my own lack of credentials in such matters. Social scientists have scarcely studied, indeed, have said next to nothing about the nature of aesthetic orientations and experience. Since, however, I do intend to have my say about some of these questions, the reader will soon be able to judge for himself that this prefatory comment has not been unduly modest.

Perhaps the most difficult question is that of the character of the aesthetic orientation: How are people relating to things when they are relating to them aesthetically? What kind of experience is the aesthetic experience? Under what conditions is it possible to have one?

I might begin by observing that, particularly for Plato, the aesthetic orientation is an orientation to the style or form of things, over and above their other values and services. In this view, "beauty" is the value dimension of style; it is the perfection of a style or form. In order for persons to have aesthetic experiences in this sense—in order to be oriented to the appreciation or, more generally, to the evaluation of the formal or stylistic aspects of things—they must, at least momentarily, surrender or relax other kinds of orientations to objects. And the more salient or intense the aesthetic orientation, the less can they relate to objects in other ways. They must not, for example, ask themselves, in any conventional sense of the term, of what use are they, are they true or false in some purely intellectual sense, or are they good or bad morally.

It is precisely because Plato's moral orientation is so salient that it is possible to underestimate his aesthetic orientation; and there is indeed a tension between his aesthetic and his moralizing orientations. Nonetheless, Plato recognizes that there is a distinction as well as a connection between the aesthetic and the moral, grace and harmony being the twin sisters of goodness and virtue, and that even reason has the special attribute of beauty. An aesthetic orientation is one that treats the form or style of objects as a distinct, and in its extremity as an autonomous, consideration. A judgment concerning style is not reducible to judgments made in terms of other conventional orientations to objects: the beauty of a boy (such as Charmides) to Socrates is quite distinguishable from his goodness, while Socrates' ugliness is distinguishable from his wisdom.

The aesthetic orientation can develop to the extent that the observer can detach himself from thinking about objects in terms of their conventionally defined multiple functions. It occurs when, for example, we do not think of a building as spacious or comfortable. The aesthetic orientation is, therefore, more likely to be directed toward objects which do not have manifest culturally prescribed and multiple uses, such as a flower garden, a twilight, or works of fine art. The existence of an aesthetic orientation as such premises the development of a distinction between the uses and the sensuous character of things; between, say, the magical, religious, or sacred function and significance of a drawing and the enjoyment of it as a sheer composition of lines, masses, and colors.

The aesthetic orientation is one in which objects are not appraised in terms of the instrumental value they may have in facilitating the pursuit of our aims, solving our problems, or resolving our moral quandaries, but develops in contrast to such practical interests. An aesthetic experience may be had even if one has not been deliberately seeking or expecting it. Aesthetic development constitutes a readiness to be gratified by the form or style of things: one can accidentally glance up at an evening sky and be overwhelmed by its colors.

The aesthetic experience and orientation is not a "natural," inborn one. Different kinds of style will, of course, be valued by different groups, and what seems beautiful will vary from culture to culture; the aesthetic orientation is learned in cultural settings and refined by individual experience. Yet specific aesthetic gratifications do not depend solely on the viewer but vary greatly with the objects to which the actor is aesthetically oriented. The same viewer, however cultivated his aesthetic tastes, will somehow derive much pleasure from the work of one artist and perhaps none at all from the work of another. Indeed, aesthetic gratification may derive from the work of no one at all but simply from the sight of some natural phenomenon such as an ocean. And it may be greatly dependent on differences in the natural talent of the creating craftsman or artist, as well as that of the viewer. In brief, there is considerable slippage between the human energies put into objects and the degree to which they afford aesthetic gratification. There is, in this sense, an element of "unearned gratification" in the aesthetic experience.

In order for the person to have a readiness for aesthetic gratification, it would seem that he must not then be under the press of other urgent impulses, interests, or needs. Which is to say that he must not, at the moment, be interested in the other gratifications that objects may normally provide. The aesthetic orientation is one in which the style of objects is problematic and which is able to focus on this, screening out at least momentarily other properties and uses of objects.

There seem to be at least two main conditions conducive to the development of such an orientation. One is where the person has a surfeiture of other gratifications, perhaps because he owns many things or has wide access to the conventional uses of many objects—where, for example, he is very rich; a second is where he is alienated from those values of his society that would dispose him to seek gratification from objects in conventional ways.

The aesthetic orientation, in short, is likely to be intensified and most salient among those who already have a sufficient supply of worldly goods and honors, and/or those who have turned from or do not care for them.

Plato, it would seem, qualifies on both counts. Two auxiliary points need to be made here: first, that this is a far cry from saying that only when men's material needs have first been satisfied can they develop an aesthetic orientation. I am not saying that only the rich can develop an interest in art, for obviously an aesthetic orientation can also be developed by those who reject worldly goods and honors and who may be destitute by conventional standards. Yet while by no means confining the aesthetic orientation to the rich, our formulation does take account of what seems to be their distinctive proclivity in that direction. It will also be noticed that having an ample and unthreatened supply of worldly goods and caring little for them are not mutually exclusive conditions. Indeed, not only may they coincide but, in fact, the former may be conducive to the latter.

Ennui, or boredom, may be conceived of as the sentiment of those who are characterized by both conditions: it is a blunting of the ability to derive gratifications from conventional worldly goods by those who possess them in ample supply. In brief, though they need not coincide, these two characteristics may be combined in persons or groups, such as an aristocracy— as seem to be found among some of the *kaloi k'agathoi* who were concerned with maintaining a proper style of life—who take their property and privileges for granted. *Ennui* may, in fine, be the sentiment distinctive of an alienated elite who are not so much hostile but disgusted and estranged from the main drift of their society.

Though a seemingly trivial sentiment, *ennui* is important because it is dangerous to life. It undermines the desire to continue living, for men are kept alive by what they want, by the experience and by the expectation of gratification. Persons who are wantless, who neither experience nor expect gratification, have a slender hold on life. More likely to be vulnerable to depressive moods and suicidal impulses, they are all too ready to die. A heightened and intense development of the aesthetic orientation, at least on one of its sides, serves as a form of defense against wantlessness, for it provides a way of deriving gratification, through the experience of desirable styles and by the appreciation of the form of things. Heightened development of the aesthetic orientation is, in one part, the way in which the "man who has everything" or the man who rejects "everything"—the surfeited and the alienated—holds onto life.

There are several distinctive characteristics of the aesthetic orientation that permit it to serve in this way, staving off wantlessness and providing life-binding gratifications. For one, the strongly developed aesthetic orientation may be exercised in any kind of a situation. There is no one specific setting to which it is necessarily tied and no one kind of object by which alone it must be gratified. Anything may be seen and appraised in its stylistic character, from the beauty of "natural childbirth" and mother-love, to the beauty of "death in the afternoon." The intense aesthetic orientation is situation-free, and those who have it highly developed may at any instant find gratification in almost anything.

Moreover, the highly developed aesthetic orientation may provide a claim for a certain kind of superiority of the self, a claim as a person of refined taste and sensibility. The aesthetic experience is a dimension in terms of which even the very lowly may, indeed, feel superior to those who in other respects tower over them. It is also a way in which men who are wealthy and powerful may legitimate their superiority and assert themselves as worthy, marking themselves off as a deserving elite from those who are merely wealthy and powerful.

A claim for the superiority of the self on the basis of a capacity for culti-vated aesthetic experience or "good taste" is, at one and the same time, a particularly precarious and an especially safe claim. It is a precarious claim because no reliable or official credentials are available to certify the claim, as there are, for example, for anyone who claims to be a doctor or a lawyer. It is also a relatively safe claim, for almost anyone can claim good taste for himself, and it is rather difficult to reject this claim on firm grounds. Since it cannot be measured, weighed, or counted, it is difficult to validate or in-validate a claim to good taste. Essentially, the validation of such a claim depends on its acceptance by others. To feel secure in one's taste—to believe oneself a person of good taste—it is necessary to receive consensual valida-tion, to be a member of a group who commonly acknowledge and validate one another as people of good taste. Consequently, for an intense develop-ment of the aesthetic orientation, and for its secure placement in the indi-vidual's self-image, there need to develop groups either of alienated "bo-hemians" or of upper-class artistic coteries such as the *kaloi k'agathoi.*

I have said that the aesthetic orientation enlarges the situational arena in which gratification is possible; it thereby staves off *ennui,* attaching men to things and tightening their hold on life. Yet there is another and contrary side to the intense aesthetic orientation. It is also a form of detachment from the culturally prevailing use and meaning of objects and, therefore, a form of detachment from other people who relate to objects in conventional ways. Those with highly developed aesthetic orientations are likely to focus on aspects of situations at variance with those that are culturally prescribed or preferred and in ways divergent from people who adopt the culturally pre-vailing outlooks.

If, on the one hand, those with highly developed aesthetic orientations may thus extract gratification from situations that might otherwise be boring or painful to them, thus reducing the costs of involvement, they do so at the price of surrendering or relaxing attachments to objects that are shared by others. To that extent they cut themselves off from culturally shared meanings, from the men who share them, and from the objects themselves. In this way the aesthetic orientation is a manifestation of low object attachment. For "one" object—as culturally defined—may be rendered in many styles and many different objects in one. The focus on style, when intensified, diverts the observer from the other meanings of the object and therefore from other attachments to it.

The highly developed aesthetic orientation, then, entails a tense ambivalence; it is a way of holding onto objects while keeping them at a distance, particularly from the basic affects. It is a way of being in contact with the world without being open to disturbance from it. There is, then, in the heightened aesthetic orientation the ambivalence of attachment to style but detachment from other aspects of the object.

Plato's basic orientations manifest a similarly profound ambivalence to the world of objects. On the one hand, it conceives of "wanting" as deficiency, as a state of tension manifesting a lack of perfection of some sort. To want is to lack something and to be incomplete. The realm of the eternal Forms, of true being or valid existence, for Plato, is wantlessness; it is to possess all that one wants and to want nothing that is not already possessed. It is a kind of Apollonian self-sufficiency which neither reaches out to another nor allows others to intrude upon the boundaried enclave of the perfect thing. From Plato's viewpoint wanting is a kind of pain and evil, the locus of whose contamination is in the natural body and from which, therefore, one should look forward to release in death. That one should relish death and despise wanting is consistent; for wantlessness is akin to death.

Yet this is only one side of Plato. The other is a clinging to a kind of life, to a desire for the soul's immortality and a fantasy wish to live forever. From Plato's standpoint knowledge and truth must be wanted, if they are to be obtained, and men are enjoined to want the goods of the soul.

Plato's aestheticism, we suggest, is a compromise between these two opposing impulses. His conception of the eternal Forms as the truest existence or life is, on the one side, a resistance to the natural corruption that overtakes the things of this world—it is a fight against death. On the other side, it is a denial of the value of existence and of life as humans ordinarily experience it—it is a surrender to death.

DIALOGUE AND DRAMATURGY

The dilemmas of involvement and detachment in Plato's orientation are implicit not only in the content of his theory but also in the style and in the very way in which the theory is *written*. For this reason, and also because it may give us a better grasp of the way in which his metaphysical pathos is woven into his theory, it is useful to consider certain broad characteristics of the style in which he writes. Style, after all, is one of the gross features not only of art but of scholarship; a theorist's thoughts are expressible only in some manner that is formulated stylistically. He is never just stringing words together solely with a view to communicating information; wittingly or not, there is always some expressive surplus. To ignore a theorist's style is to ignore one of the most evident pieces of information we have about him and his theory. To ignore the aesthetics of scholarship is to neglect some of the most accessible materials we have for approaching its latent content.

Although style is not the man, it is surely revealing of him and his intentions. This is obviously so when, as in Plato's case, we are dealing with a man who is aesthetically sensitive and deliberate. But it is no less the case even when, as for most modern social scientists, the scholar is attending primarily to intellectual content and when his only conscious criterion of style is, presumably, exactness of expression. It is doubtful if this is ever the sole criterion of style that consciously shapes his work; but even if it is, a sensible awareness of style may then be all the more illuminating because it alerts us to inadvertencies in his expression which may be especially revealing of his permeative interests and inclinations.

From the standpoint of contemporary scholarship, the most distinctive feature of Plato's style is its use of the dialogue—a form which he shares with such contemporaries as Euclid and Antisthenes—in which all ideas are presented through the speeches of participant characters. From the modern social scientist's viewpoint, the salient features of a dialogue are those that are likely to be visible when it is contrasted with the usual style of contemporary social science discussion, the impersonal treatise, or article. While the treatise affords a sharp contrast with the dialogue, it can, however, dispose us to a perspective on Plato's style that may be rather different from his own conception of it. This, of course, is not to imply that a treatise form, more or less like our own, was unknown before or during Plato's time. It is simply to suggest that Plato's aim in using the dialogue may not have been to set his work off from the treatise. He may, instead, have aimed at demarcating it from, or associating it with, literary forms other than the treatise.

One especially limited conclusion is likely to be derived from an analysis of the dialogue which is based solely on a comparison with the treatise. This is a conclusion that emphasizes the informal character of Plato's discussion. In brief it may be said that the dialogue affords a stylistic framework in which it is relatively easy to conceal the formal inadequacies of Plato's logic. For with immersal in the dialogue, one comes to expect and accept a level of rigor that more nearly approximates spontaneous, everyday conversation rather than carefully prepared, systematic analysis. In brief, the allegation may be made, with considerable justice, that the dialogue form may make Plato's argument appear more convincing than closer inspection would warrant because it invites the reader to utilize less exacting standards.

From the standpoint of contemporary scholarship this appears to be a deficiency of the dialogue style justifying its obsolescence. Yet such comparisons of the dialogue and the treatise are somewhat smug. It seems evident to the modern scholar that the dialogue is a style, that it is a kind of literary embellishment having rhetoric functions. Unfortunately it is not equally clear to the modern scholar that the treatise form that *he* employs is also a style and that it, too, has its own rhetoric appeal. The modern treatise is imbued with its own stylistically insinuated claims. Its form is the form of impersonal, dispassionate scholarship. It is infused with a rhetoric that implies that it is above the dialectical confrontations of everyday scholarly life, and it tacitly presents an image of a detached scholar who, like a solitary spider, spins his materials from an entirely inward substance. If the dialogue invites us to lower our standards and to accept what is unproved, the treatise often promises speciously to abide by the most careful and impersonal standards and thus, by its form, applies for a loan of credibility that its substance may never repay. The dialogue may win its way by pretending to be less than it is; the treatise may win its way by pretending to be more.

Comparisons between the dialogue and the treatise have the unfortunate tendency of focusing on the relative merits of the two as ways of transmitting information, and they disparage the dialogue solely from the standpoint of its cognitive dysfunctions. Yet this omits analysis of the rhetoric advantages and uses of the dialogue which, even if not intended to do so, may nonetheless be revealing of certain of Plato's dispositions.

Whether intended or not, the dialogue may serve as a way of changing people's everyday behavior; it is a stylistic form of a therapeutically ambitious social theory. It permits the reader an involvement with persons, through identification with whom he can come to feel the predicament and the power of various intellectual standpoints and the manner in which they are embedded in and consequential for social interaction. The dialogue's very conversational character is a way of communicating that reason can be made a part of everyday life and of inducing an awareness that there is a need for it there.

Rather than contrasting the dialogue solely with the treatise, it may be helpful to see it in relation to the theater, the drama, and particularly the tragedy. That such a perspective is appropriate is suggested by Plato's use of dramatistic metaphors, as for example in his discussion of the Forms or

Ideas. Similarly, in the *Philebus,* Socrates remarks, "and the argument implies that there are combinations of pleasure and pain in lamentations, and in tragedy and comedy, not only on the stage, but on the greater stage of human life." And again in the *Republic,* when the figure of the cave is introduced, we are told that "you will see, if you look, a low wall built along the way, like the screen which marionette players have in front of them, over which they show the puppets." [21]

It is notable that Greek tragedy evolved from earlier forms in which, like the dialogue, the question and answer form was employed, with the chorus questioning the dramatic protagonist. The dialogue form is obviously akin to a play, being written as a play would be. Indeed Plato expressly likens the characters in his *Laws,* who are designing the new city of Magnetes, to playwrights. The creation of such a city as an ongoing community is, he says, the acting out of a tragedy, "the noblest of dramas." In this vein, the Athenian remarks that if a dramatist should ask for permission to present his work in their new city, they shall reply: "Best of strangers, . . . we also according to our ability are tragic poets, and our tragedy is the best and noblest; for our whole state is an imitation of the best and noblest life, which we affirm to be indeed the very truth of tragedy." [22]

Aside from the *Republic* and the *Laws,* where the drafting of the script-plans for new communities are a central part of the action, many of the other dialogues may also be thought of as a deployment of the characters to write an "act" or to prepare materials for a play. The plans for the new cities that Plato presents are, in effect, plot outlines or scripts for plays. The city is a tableau of characters and choruses. Seen from this perspective, the dialogues do have a plot: they are plays within which the dramatic task of the characters is to write a play; the utopian communities are plays written within plays.

To note that Plato uses a dramatistic metaphor is not to suggest, however, that he employs the theater, as, say, Erving Goffman does, as a model (ostensibly) to help him explore and to understand social life. Plato is not simply a researcher mindful of the heuristic value of metaphor. He is in one part a social planner who thinks of the social planner as a kind of dramatist and who aims to create a community that will have the fixed, invariable sequence of a play. It is not simply that Plato thinks that social life may in part be understood as a play, but rather that it should, as far as it can, be made into a play.

The use of the dialogue form by Plato in part suggests that he is taking the role of a dramatist. To an important extent it is from a dramatist's standpoint that he chooses to comment on human life. It is in part because Plato feels tragically about the human condition that he writes dialogues, for these enable him to take the role of the tragedian. That Plato adopts such a view of himself and his work is not, however, entirely a matter of choice; he is limited in the available supply of roles that would be suitable for his enterprise. When the secular social theorist first emerges and seeks to differentiate himself from the shaman and other men of sacred knowledge, he has at first no culturally standardized social role to play. He must either begin to create a new role or to adopt one already existent, bending it to his purposes. Plato, in effect, does the latter, borrowing the familiar role of the dramatist, who was both the popular commentator and the moral teacher of Athens.

In suggesting this, however, we are far indeed from believing that Plato's was not a serious purpose, or that his social planning is to be thought of as a charade or entertainment. It is precisely by his use of a stylistic form akin to the theater's that Plato signals the special gravity of his intention. It will be remembered that the ancient Greek theater, unlike our own, is imbued with religious significance and is intimately connected with religious occasion; it has a context of quasi-ritual solemnity. In being associated with the theater, the dialogue form is associated with sacred things. Its use implies that questions of the utmost gravity and paramount importance are at issue. The Platonic dialogue implies that the search for knowledge about man is not just another experiment on nature.

Certainly the dialogue form is especially well suited for conveying the contest of minds inherent in the dialectic. It is a vehicle particularly appropriate for communicating the Socratic interest in the dialectic as a method rather than in a positive doctrine. The dialogue not only talks about the method but in its very form displays the method of question and answer that Socrates believes so crucial to the dialectic. Yet for all of its seeming dynamism, little of its interest derives from the actions of people, from the vicissitudes of fortune, from failure or success in war or love. In the Platonic dialogue the protagonist is an elegantly disembodied self. It shows that what matters is not what happens to people as embodied beings. What matters primarily is what they say, their ideas, and their character.

In this the Platonic dialogue is manifestly different from the standard literary fare of the Hellenes, the Homeric epic, in which action in the forms of battles, adventures, and travels is central. It is set off also from the dramatic tragedy in which people are shown to feel passionately about what happens to them, as well as from the lusty comedy and its often bawdy satire on current events. Although it conveys an intellectual excitement, the Platonic dialogues are drama, philosophical drama, largely stripped of emotions. They are the stylistic exemplification of what Plato feels is the philosopher's deepest ambition, the extrusion of bodily impingement and the pure expression of mind.

From a purely aesthetic standpoint, perhaps the basic problem of the Platonic dialogue as a literary style is that of doing justice to the complexity and force of intellectual standpoints with which the author disagrees and of preventing the adversary from degenerating into an empty foil for the hero, Socrates. Often enough Plato fails in this way, but these failures are more than compensated by the many occasions when his dialogues do attain a genuine dramatic force. The essential condition for successful use of the dialogue in this way, like that of tragedy more generally, is a peculiar state or skill of mind. The author must be able to take the role of, or empathize with, persons and ideas with whom he disagrees, indeed strongly disagrees, otherwise the issue between the protagonists will seem contrived and lacking in suspenseful outcome. The author must be so skillful at taking the role of his opponents that he is able to recognize their strongest arguments and can put forth the best possible case for viewpoints to which he is opposed. The very development and pervasiveness of an artistically effective dialogue is thus indicative of the development of a self with powerful role-taking talents.

For the Greek dialogue to have emerged it was necessary for diverse and competing views to have been present simultaneously in the same mind, for their force, cogency, and appeal to have made themselves felt and not to be viewed as entirely alien, outside things. The ability of the dialogist to take the role of others with whom he disagrees—to see the world from the standpoint of his enemies—implies that Socrates probably had some inner affinity with the Sophists he so vehemently condemns, as well as with the nature philosophers in whose work, as Plato tells us, he had an early interest. Of similar import it is notable that Plato on occasion represents Socrates not simply as describing what some opponent, such as Protagoras, believes, but as acting out a playlet in which Socrates himself actually takes both contending parts with great skill. The dialogist, I believe, senses that there is something of himself in many others and of them in him. He uses the dialogue as a way of exploring and separating various sides of his own tense identity. Yet he uses a stylistic technique that casts a thick shadow over his own identity and viewpoint, effectively guarding it from clear view.

Note that the dialogist does not directly present his own point of view. Indeed, had he wished to do so he need only have given one of the characters his own name. The dialogist deliberately presents himself and his standpoint in a manner that is radically ambiguous and for which therefore it is difficult to hold him strictly accountable. It is by no means always certain through which of his characters he speaks, whether he always speaks through the same character, or whether he speaks through one or several of them. Even where it is plain that his sympathies lie with one character, there is always a reasonable doubt whether this protagonist's speeches are in all respects an expression of the dialogist's own views, especially where, as in Plato, they are often attributed to historically real persons. Shortcomings in the sympathetic character's speech cannot always be discreditably attributed to the dialogist. They may, rather, testify creditably to his accuracy as a reporter or to his talent as a dramatist.

The dialogist is a hovering presence who pulls the strings invisibly. He is the puppeteer whose intentions have to be inferred complexly from the movements of his marionettes. He is much like the God to whom, as Plato mentions, men are puppets and playthings; but he is a God who loses himself in his play. Plato conceives of the social planner in a similar manner as a kind of dramatist-God immersed in staging a social world; in plotting, casting, and rehearsing it; and as mildly amused or annoyed by the pretentious temperamentality of his actors, who, forgetting that the whole thing is a show, persist in seeking to have their own ways.

The dialogist, like the dramatist, wants to have everyone's say. Like the dramatist, he wants to create the illusion of life's spontaneity, diversity, and intrigue, yet all the while retaining complete control over it. As a dramatist, the dialogist does not say all that he believes through a single character, however clearly one of them is his favorite. He speaks and lives through them all, through the orchestration of his entire cast. His aim is not merely the exposition of an idea for which he willingly takes responsibility; nor is it enough for him that he somehow expresses his own viewpoint. The dialogist seeks to be able to tell himself that he is right, through the intelligent or wooden assent, the tactful silence or agreeable concurrence, of some of the play's characters.

The dialogist thus creates a symbolic world in which he vicariously gives himself both consensual validation and dialectical friction. He creates a dramatic world over which his control is all the more complete because the dialogue is a play that is not produced. He avoids the inherent uncertainties of social interaction by substituting aesthetic control for social control, the inner for the outer confrontation. For Plato the dialogue is in part a way of avoiding the dilemmas of his own utopianism, for none of his characters will ever be allowed to present a compelling critique, not so much of his logic, but of his practical therapeutics and social planning. Indeed the problem of his utopianism will be solved dramatically. Social power will be assumed vicariously by tacitly premising that certain of the actors will themselves stage the impending performance. Or they will be presented as prospective role takers with whom the reader may identify, and where it is imagined that they are already men of power: "You and I, Adeimantus, at this moment are not poets, but founders of a State." [23]

The Platonic dialogue, then, embodies in one of its aspects a compensatory fantasy of social control. The theorist as dramatist enacts through the dialogue what he cannot, as planner and citizen, do in life.

Whatever else it is, then, the dialogue is a literary form in which the writer treats his friends and his enemies as characters in a play, and he must, therefore, view himself also as involved in a play. He has chosen not to write an autobiography, a history, or an analytic treatise, but a kind of drama. In using the dialogue, the author is telling us that, for whatever reason, he thinks dramaturgically of himself and his world. For a professional dramatist the stage is always a world; for the dramaturgist, however, the world has become a stage. In the Platonic social circle, as in Plato's own work, there seems to be a growing sense that all of life is a play—much as we find it among increasing numbers of social theorists today. The line between the theater and life outside is growing dim. One interesting expression of this is formulated in the dramatic theory of the tragedian Agathon, who is a friend of Plato and Euripides. Indeed, it is Agathon's banquet, in honor of his dramatic victory of 417, that is the setting of Plato's *Symposium*. Among his several dramatic innovations, Agathon proposes that poets live like the characters in their plays, even to the point of reproducing the details of their appearance. The realism of Euripides also serves to pull down the barriers between the stage and the *polis,* showing Athenians as they are and at the same time drawing back from both. As H. O. F. Kitto remarks, "For all the sympathy and the tragic power with which Euripides draws his characters, . . . it seems clear that he is fundamentally detached from them." [24]

When is this dramaturgic view of life likely to develop? It seems to be born when men lack or lose their historical moorings. As they lose a sense of their place in history, they come to feel themselves moving through a mere succession of situations, each linked to the other by sheer propinquity or by a surface symbolic consistency, rather than inwardly as cause and effect. The dramaturgic perspective on life sees it as lived in a narrow, interpersonal focus—as ahistorical and noninstitutional—as an existence beyond history and beyond society, as coming truly alive only in transient moments of face-to-face encounter.

The dramaturgic view of life arises when experience is losing its continuity and is dissolving into episodic shreds, when the larger architecture of experience is crumbling, when the rhythm and movement of life sprawls and lacks organizing centers or familiar punctuations and accents. The dramaturgic view arises when living leaves no sense of residual accomplishment, where each moment is much like the other (for there are no culminations in prospect), and when men are becoming dangerously bored. It is when social theorists do not believe that "the best is yet to come," when they lose a sustaining sense of the upward trend, that they devise dramaturgic perspectives on human life and groups. A Plato enters, then, when social theorists come to feel that history has no exit.

Such dramaturgy has its inner dialectic. On the one side, it insists on the importance of appearances, for it says that appearances are normally all we have and may therefore constrain us to take them seriously. On the other side, the dramaturgic view devalues realms of life that men ordinarily imbue with special value, for it tells us that, like the others, they, too, are no more than appearances. In saying that appearances count and that how things look is important, the dramaturgic view says that life is serious. Yet it *is* appearance—a flickering shadow on the wall of the cave—and should not be taken too seriously. This ambivalence about the seriousness with which life may be viewed is expressed quite clearly in Plato: "[H]uman affairs are hardly worth considering in earnest and yet we must be in earnest about them—a sad necessity constrains us." [25]

The dramaturgic view heightens an appreciation of things conventionally slighted and slights things conventionally exalted. Plato, for example, insists on the importance of children's games for the welfare of the state, yet he ignores work and devalues human love. If dramaturgy ignores history and society, it does so in a skeptical search for sources of human hope and vitality within something eternal. If it puts men outside of history, it also frees them from the hold of empty solemnities; it seeks to have men find a new depth for themselves in an abiding life force. Yet in subordinating history to some essence that stands beyond, dramaturgy does so at the cost of casting doubt upon the importance of human experience. A world without history is one where men are losing their hold on posterity and their hope for honored remembrance. As men are stripped of the armor of heroism, their fear of death is laid bare. Death then threatens to signify a lonely terminus of only personal proportions, a flat finality that betrays all of life's promises.

There is, of course, one way in which Plato seems to have set himself apart from and against a dramaturgic view of life, for the latter implies that there is no significant difference between the world and the stage, or between visible, mere appearances and a hidden, truer reality, while Plato's theory of the Forms asserts the very opposite. But in the end the two converge, for Plato's insistence on the reality of the Forms maintains the distinction between appearance and reality only by removing reality from life as men experience it. It thus leaves the world—as the dramaturgists did and do—as a sphere where the distinction fades and all is now appearances.

NOTES

[1] *Alcestis.* 526 ff.

[2] *Hellenica.*

[3] *Laws.* 804B.

[4] *Republic.* 604C.

[5] Greene, *op. cit.,* p. 25.

[6] ii. 337 ff.

[7] i. 381.

[8] i. 527.

[9] ii. 690–91.

[10] Richmond Lattimore, *Themes in Greek and Latin Epitaphs* (Urbana: University of Illinois Press, 1962), pp. 47, 215.

[11] *Phaedo.* 89A.

[12] *Phaedo.* 89A.

[13] *Phaedo.* 88B.

[14] *Phaedo.* 107A.

[15] *Phaedo.* 107B.

[16] *Apology.* 40C.

[17] *Phaedo.* 61C.

[18] *Phaedo.* 67D.

[19] *Phaedo.* 81A.

[20] *Republic.* 400, 401.

[21] *Republic.* 514E.

[22] *Laws.* 817B.

[23] *Republic.* 379A.

[24] H. D. F. Kitto, *Greek Tragedy, op. cit.,* p. 201.

[25] *Laws.* 803A.

Glossary of Greek Terms

This glossary uses the conventional translation of Greek terms employed in the text. The controlling or more limited meaning of the terms, however, is that of the context in which the terms are presented and discussed.

agathos, agathoi: good, brave, gentle, skillfull
agōn, agōnes: gathering, assembly met to see games, struggle, contest
aischron, aischra: lowly, shameful, despicable
alētheia: truth, reality; also according to truth and nature; true event, realization; sincerity
anankē, anankai: necessity, force, constraint
andrapodon, andrapoda: one taken in war and sold as slave, a captive
anomos, anomoi, anomia: lawless, impious, lawlessness; the negation of law
antidosis: a form by which a citizen charged with a tax might call upon any other citizen, either to exchange properties or to submit to the charge himself; repayment, requital, exchange
archōn, archontes: chief magistrate, city official
aretē, aretai: goodness, excellence, distinction
aristeiā: excellence, prowess
aristos, aristoi: noblest, best in birth and rank
atē: divine temptation
banausia: handicraft; the habits of a mere artisan, vulgarity, bad taste; quackery, charlatanism
boulē: a decree; council of elders, senate
chorēgos, chorēgoi: the wealthy citizen who defrayed the cost of bringing out a chorus
dēmos, dēmoi: the sovereign people, the free citizens, district, a deme
dēmotikos, dēmotikoi: for the people, common, one of the people
dikē, dikai: custom, usage; right, just, judgment
doxa: expectation; notion, opinion, judgment; the opinion which others have of one, estimation, repute; mostly good repute, honor, glory
drachmē, drachmai: as much as one can hold in one hand, standard monetary measure
drēstēr, drēstēres: laborer, worker
eidōlon: phantom, any unsubstantial form, image

389

eisphorā, eisphorai: at Athens, property tax levied for purposes of war

ekklēsia: assembly duly summoned

elenchus: refutation; argument of disproof; generally cross-examining, testing; scrutiny

epigonos, epigonoi: offspring, posterity, breed; the Epigonoi were the sons of the chiefs who fell in the first war against Thebes; commonly in English, disciples, or intellectual followers

epistatēs, epistatai: at Athens to be presiding over the boulē; overseer

epistēmē, epistēmai: acquaintance with a matter; understanding, skill; professional skill, hence profession; scientific knowledge, science

eranos, eranoi: loan raised by contribution for the benefit of an individual

eris: strife, quarrel

eristikon: eager for strife, fond of wrangling, captious

eupatridēs, eupatridai: well-born, the old aristocracy at Athens

gennētai: members of genē at Athens

genos, genē: race, stock, kin

geras: gift of honor, present, reward

hektēmoros, hektēmoroi: those who paid a part of the produce as rent, like "sharecroppers."

hēliastēs, hēliastai: member of the heliaia court of justice at Athens; a juror

Hermāī: sacred pillars surmounted by busts with two faces

hetaira, hetairai: a female companion, prostitute

hoplitēs, hoplitāī: heavy armored foot soldier

horos, horoi: boundary stone, pillar set up on mortgaged property

hybris or hubris: insolence, wanton violence, outrage

isomoiria: equal share, equal fate; equivalence of degree

isonomia: equal distribution, equilibrium, balance; equality of political rights

kakos, kakoi: bad, lowly, ill-born

kalon, kala; kalos, kaloi: good, most creditable, beautiful

keimēlion, keimēlia: treasure, heirloom

kosmopolitēs, kosmopolitai: a citizen of the world

kosmos: world, earth; order

Lakōnizon, Lakōnizontes: affecting or sympathizing with Spartan manners

leitourgia, leitourgiai: at Athens, public service performed by private citizens at their own expense

logos, logoi: computation, reckoning, account; measure, tale; esteem, consideration; statement, narrative, right of speech or discussion; rational understanding

metoikos, metoikoi: alien resident in a foreign state, denizen

misthos, misthoi: payment, salary, hire, fixed wages, allowance at Athens for public service

mōïra: portion; lot, share; destiny, fate

nemesis: distribution of what is due; retribution

nomos, nomoi: law; that which is in habitual practice; usage, custom; statute, ordinance made by authority

ōïkos, ōïkoi: house, household, dwelling

oimōgē: wailing, lamentation

ostrakon, ostraka: potsherd, fragment of pottery used in voting

phratria, phratriai: political subdivision of the phyle, political brotherhood

phye, phylai: race, tribe

polis, poleis: city-state, community, body of citizens

prytanis, prytaneis: ruler; at Athens, member of the tribe presiding in boulē or ekklēsia

rhyppapāï: a cry of the Athenian rowers, "yoho!" hence the crew, one's messmates

stratēgia: leaderships, generalships

stratēgos, stratēgoi: leader, commander of the army, general

synarchia: joint administration or government, or concerning military expenses

technē, technai: art, skill, cunning of hand; craft, way, manner, a set of rules, system or method of making or doing

themistes: decrees of the gods, oracles

therapōn, therapontes: attendant, companion in arms, squire

thēs, thētes: servant, propertyless worker

thiasos, thiasoi: religious guilt, confraternity

thymos: soul, spirit as the principle of life, feeling and thought especially of strong feeling and passion

triēres, triēreis: trireme, a galley

Major Dates in Greek History

B.C.

2000–1500 The Hellenes occupy the eastern Mediterranean.

1500–1100 Mycenaen civilization centered in Argolis.

1400 Burning of the palace of Knossos (Crete).

1000–900 Dorian invasion of Peloponnesus.

about 900–700 Composition of Homeric poems.

820 Lycurgus at Sparta (aristocratic constitution).

776 First Olympic Games.

750 Beginnings of Greek colonization. Hesiod's work done around this time.

743–724 First war of the Messenians against the Spartans.

704 Birth of the poet Archilochus at Paros.

about 640 Birth of Thales, first Greek philosopher-scientist.

621 Legislation of Dracon in Athens.

594 Solon's reforms in Athens. Suppression of debt slavery.

580 Birth of Pythagoras in Samos.

561 Pisistratus, tyrant of Athens. Standardization of Homeric poems.

507 In Athens, the reforms of Cleisthenes.

506 Athens repels an expedition of Spartans, Thebans, and Chalcidians.

499 Revolt of the Ionians against the Persians.

495 Birth of Sophocles. Victory of the Greeks under Miltiades at Marathon.

490 Darius leads a first expedition against the Greeks.

480 Second Median War (Xerxes). The Persians in Athens. Victory of the Greeks, under Themistocles, at Salamis. Birth of Herodotus.

479 League of Delos headed by Athens (Confederation of Cities) against the Persians.

478 Athens reconstructed and equipped with a port.

470 Birth of Socrates.

462 Abolition of the Areopagus, which had limited popular sovereignty.

461 Pericles comes to power.

about 460 Birth of Democritus.

about 455 Antisthenes born at Athens.

454–438 Building of the Parthenon.

about 450 *Prometheus Bound,* by Aeschylus.

450 Phidias directs work on the Acropolis.

449 Under Cimon, the Athenians win victory over Persians. End of the median wars.

446 Peace of Thirty Years between Athens and Sparta.

440 Youth of Hippocrates, father of medicine.

431–404 Peloponnesian War.

431 First invasion of Attica by the Spartans

430 Death of Pericles. Plague in Athens.

427 Birth of Plato.

421 Peace of Nicias between Spartans and Athenians. Comedies of Aristophanes.

420 *Oedipus Rex,* by Sophocles.

415–413 Sicilian expedition. Destruction of Athenian army.

413 Spartans occupy Deceleum, in Attica.

411 Oligarchical government of the Four Hundred, then of the Five Thousand.

406 Death of Euripides in Macedonia.

405 Death of Sophocles.

404 Lysander (Sparta) captures Athens. End of Peloponnesian War. Government of the Thirty Tyrants. Death of Alcibiades.

403 Restoration of democracy.

400–394 Spartan victories in Asia Minor against the Persians. Diogenes born in Asia Minor (dies 325).

399 Death of Socrates.

395–387 Athens, Corinth, Thebes and Argos unite against Sparta.

395 Spartans under Lysander are defeated at Haliartus, in Boeotia.

387–386 Persian "King's Peace."

384 Birth of Aristotle at Stagira.

379 War of Thebes against Sparta.

375 Death of Hippocrates.

370 Thebes invades Peloponnesus. Messenia regains independence.

362 Epaminondas invades the Peloponnesus. His victory and death at Mantinea.

360 Philip II accedes to the Macedonian throne. Antisthenes dies at Athens.

357 Philip seizes the Aegean coast.

355–346 Third sacred war against the Phocians. Philip conquers Thessaly but fails at Thermopylae.

348 Philip conquers Thrace.

347 Death of Plato.

346 Peace between Philip and the Athenians.

about 342 Epicurus born at Samos (dies about 270)

339–338 Defeat of the Athenians at Chaeronea. Philip proclaimed general of the confederated Greeks.

338–326 Government of Lycurgus in Athens.

336 Assassination of Philip. Alexander succeeds him.

335 Thebes destroyed by Alexander. Zeno, founder of Stoicism, born at Cyprus (dies 263).

334 Alexander conquers Asia Minor.

333 Victory of Alexander at Issus. He takes possession of Phoenicia, Palestine, Egypt. Founding of Alexandria.

332 Fall of Tyre.

330 Assassination of King Darius. Uprising of the Spartans.

327–325 Expedition of Alexander to the frontiers of India. Diogenes dies at Corinth.

323 Death of Alexander in Babylon. Perdiccas becomes regent. Antipater commands in Macedonia and in Greece. Ptolemy governs Egypt.

INDEX

Absolutes, theory of, 183, 192; *see also* Ideas or Forms
Achaeans, 5
achievement, Apollonian and Dionysian, 122–123; class structure and, 12–13; fame and, 97; group tensions and, 13–17; social orientation toward, 101; universalistic norms of, 308–309
Achilles, 14, 45, 54, 60, 79, 104, 109, 112, 115
action, as Greek ideal, 69
"action morality," 82
actor, self-consciousness and, 114
Adkins, Arthur W., 13, 15, 81, 142
Admetus, 116, 366
Aegean Sea, seafaring on, 7
Aeschines, 138
Aeschylus, 25, 43–44, 47, 56–57, 60, 88, 107–108, 114, 133–134
Aesop, 336–337
aesthetic orientation, 374–378
Agamemnon, 14, 26, 54, 71, 79, 88, 104, 107, 114
Agamemnon (Aeschylus), 108
agathos, 12–13, 16–17, 48, 215
ages of man, Pythagorean conception of, 116
aggression, homosexuality and, 60; killing and, 109
agōn, 47
agriculture, of Homeric age, 17
"*aischron,*" 82
Ajax, 98, 104, 109
Ajax (Sophocles), 58, 111
Alcestis (Euripides), 112, 366
Alcibiades, 50–51, 54–55, 57, 68, 94, 96–97, 147
Alcmaeonidae, 20
alcohol, 245

alētheia, 261
Alexander, 51, 314
"Alexander problem," 95–96
Anacreon of Teos, 365
analogy, in dialectic, 265
anankē, 341
anarchy, 221
Anaxagoras, 57, 183–184
andrapodon, 31
anomia, 214–215, 221, 225, 279, 297, 346, 349
antidosis, 140–141
Antigone (Sophocles), 58, 226, 365
Antilochus, 14
Antiphon, 31
Antisthenes, 314, 319–320, 323, 380
anxiety, guilt as, 84
Aphrodite, 245
Apollo, 117
Apollonian and Dionysian characteristics or outlooks, 116–123, 221, 287–288, 309, 379
Apology (Plato), 178, 280, 336
Archalus, 158
Archetypes, theory of, 183
Archilochus, 59, 115
archōn, 46
aretē, 139, 194, 240, 301
Arginusae, battle of, 152
Aristides, 57–58
Aristogiton, 64
aristoi, 9, 11, 13–14, 16
Aristophanes, 246, 293
Aristotle, 7, 24, 32–33, 60, 124, 167, 180, 330, 359
Arrowsmith, William, 119
Arthur, King, 14
Asch, Solomon, 105
Asia Minor, trade with, 9

atē, 79
Athena, 117
Athens, class structure in, 148–151; democracy in, 19, 135, 138; drive toward empire of, 150; financing in, 140; individuality in, 102–103; in Peloponnesian War, 141–158; plague in, 313; population and size of, 6; rationality in, 66; self-image in, 107; slavery in, 24–34; social and generational changes in, 73–74; vulnerabilities of, 151–154
athletic competitions, 13; *see also* contest; contest system
Attica, 18
authoritarianism, 289, 326–359
authority, gods and, 27; law and, 298–299
awareness, versus knowing or information, 267–272

Bacchae, The (Euripides), 99, 113, 118
banausia, 203, 240, 250
barbarians, 6; as slaves, 28–29, 34; threat of, 147
blood feuds, 14
body, as integrated organism, 79; value placed on, 69
Boeotian federation, 154–155
boredom, or *ennui,* 377
boulē, 135
Briseis, 26
bureaucracy, 135

Callicles, 201, 291, 350
Callipus, 158
Cassandra, 26
catharsis, 110
Catholic Church, 231
cavalry, 7
cave, image of, 387
Cebes, 368
Chaeronea, battle of, 153, 322
change, all-at-once, 284; generational, 73; "Model-Guided Strategy of," 260, 280–282, 285, 304, 326
character, temperament and, 228–229
Charmides (Plato), 195, 205, 254
child, relation of to slave, 356–357
child-raising, 87, 230
Chion, 158
chorēgoi, 47
chorus, in Greek drama, 110–111
Christian Science, 126

Cimon, 57, 146
citizen, relationship of to city-state, 137–139
citizenship, Greek concept of, 138
city-state, as autonomous unit, 236; citizen in, 137–139; financing in, 139–142; ideal, 235; Plato on, 344; warlike activities of, 15–16; *see also polis*
civil war, conduct during, 234; in *polis,* 3–34; *see also* Peloponnesian War
class conflict, 17–21, 135
class influences, 97–98
class structure, achievement system and, 12–13; Athens and, 148–151; economic opportunity and, 21–24; in Hellenic age, 21–24; development of, 9; in Peloponnesian War, 142–146; *see also* class system
class system, contest and, 51–55; and Platonic value system, 311
Cleinias, 144
Cleisthenes, 72, 88, 152, 308
colonization, beginnings of, 6
comedy, 46–47; *see also* drama; theater
commitment, in contest system, 51
communication, 6
communism, 289
community, changing concept of, 19; as organism, 260
competition, in Greek culture system, 43; zest for, 46
conformity, shame and, 83
connectedness, functional, 253
conscience, 85
consensus, 252–255
consent, imposition and, 285–286
conservatism, versus progressivism, 323–333
contest, as game, 47–49; objective of, 48; as zero-sum game, 49
contest system, 45–55; characteristics of, 47–50; commitment in, 51; division of labor and, 92; dysfunctions of, 52; envy and, 56; excess and, 58–60; homosexuality and, 60; *polis* and, 54, 60; shame and, 96; values and, 315; zest for, 46
control, reason and, 328–331; total, 288–289
"convention," versus "nature," 190–193
conversation, dialectic and, 273
Copreus, 102
Corinth, 6

Corinthians, 73–74
Cornford, F. M., 116, 119–121, 274
"Cosmopolitans," 188–189
Cratinus, 293
creation, God and, 347
creativity, intellectual, 276–278; theoretical, 177–180
Creon, 71
crime, ignorance and, 302
criticism, social, 169–171
Crito, 276–277
Croton, 68
cultural patterns, envy and, 55–58; excess in, 58–60; pessimism in, 58; rationalism and, 64–74
cultural revitalization, 124
cultural system, 69–72
cultural themes, 42–45
Cyclops, 100
Cyclops, The (Euripides), 118
Cynic school, 314

death, cultural revitalization and, 124; as evil, 370; fear of, 115–116; life's processes and, 387; as release from appetites, 335; of Socrates, 336; and tragic outlook, 361–387; transcendence of, 362–371; war and, 363
decision-making, 81; legitimatizing of, 327
defeat, acceptance of, 50
Deianira, 25–26
Delian League, 140, 142
Delphic oracle, 45, 66, 79, 104, 178
Demeter, 117, 365
democracy, character of, 135; foundation of, 19; *see also dēmos*
democratic universalism, 309–310
Democritus, 220
demographic factors, 211
Demonicus, 81
dēmos, 16, 19, 54, 88, 98, 101, 137, 143, 320
Demosthenes, 23, 57, 138
dependency feelings, 108
detachment, involvement and, 379–387
deviance, concept of, 122–123, 298–302; coping with, 82–85; defined, 298; theory of, 204
Dewey, John, 354
diagnosis, individual, 199–200; social, *see* social diagnosis
dialectic, alternation of, 254; conversation and, 273; dialogue and, 383; as impersonal method, 264–266; pathologies of, 278–280; as repossession, 266–267; as small-group theory of knowledge and change, 273–276; structure of, 263–264; as therapy, 260–263
dialogue, dialectic and, 383; Plato's use of, 380–386
dikē, 80–81, 219
Diogenes, 20, 314, 319–323
Dion, 157
Dionysianism, 116–123, 221, 309
Dionysius, 21, 46, 99, 117
Dionysius I, 156
Dionysius II, 157
Diotima of Manintineia, 246
disaster, belief in, 44; self-blame in, 133
discipline, 108–109
disorder, drift toward, 254, 348–349; slavery and, 352–355
dissensus, 209, 216, 255
"divine," versus "rational," 342–345
division of labor, 87, 90–94, 218–219, 222; as abstraction, 254; flaws in, 234; integrity and, 248; slavery and, 241
Dodds, E. R., 45, 81
"dole," 138
Doric invasions, 6, 8
doxa, 351
drama, competition in, 46–47; dialogue and, 383–385; *see also* theater
dramaturgy, life and, 386–387
drēstēr, 9–10
drinking songs, 41, 68–69
Durkheim, Émile, 92, 215

Echecrates, 368
ecology, 7–8
economic opportunity, 21–24
Eddy, Mary Baker, 126
education, socialization and, 228–230
egalitarians, 90
egoism, 201
Ehrenberg, Victor, 52
eidōlon, or "soul," 69
Einstein, Albert, 126
eisphora, 140
ekklēsia, 135
Electra, 107, 118
elenchus, 278
Eleusinian rites, 365
empathy, 34
Empedocles, 3, 116

ends, Socrates' emphasis on, 184
ennui, 377–378
entropy, 254, 348–349
envy, 43, 55–58
Epaminondas, 154, 157
Epicharmus, 43
Epicureans, versus Stoics, 314
epigonoi, 179
epistatai, 135
epistēmē, 267–268, 271, 328
Epistles (Plato), 173, 285
equality, law and, 301
eranoi, 33
Erechtheum, 22
eris, 59
"eristic," 65, 187, 261, 278
Eryximachus, 245
Eteocles, 112
eternal forms, 371–374; *see also* Ideas or
    Forms
Euclid, 380
Eumaeus, 220
Eumelus, 14
Eumenides, 33
eupatridai, 17, 19, 284
Euripides, 12, 15, 47, 52, 56–57, 60, 69,
    88–90, 96, 99, 109, 111–113, 116–118,
    133–134, 146, 190, 301, 316, 361,
    365–366, 386
Eurydice, 365
evil, death as, 370; hereditary, 100–101;
    pessimism and, 365; Plato's concept
    of, 227; power and, 291
excess, Greek idea of, 27, 58–60
exile, political, 15

fame, contest and, 48; in Greek culture
    system, 42–43, 213; posthumous, 96–
    97; Pythagoreanism and, 125
family, as institution, 230–232; nuclear,
    110; rule of, 226; slavery and, 356–357
farmers, independent, 9
farmholdings, size of, 11
Farrington, Benjamin, 354
Fascism, 290
father–son relationship, 211
federations, rise of, 154
feudalism, slavery and, 24
Field, G. C., 57, 173
financing, in city-state, 139–142
Finley, Moses I., 25
flaw, in *kosmos,* or universe, 134, 253–
    254, 345–347

Forms, 290, 329, 342, 382; Platonic the-
    ory of, 371–374; *see also* Ideas or
    Forms
Four Hundred, conspiracy of, 149, 322
freedom, versus authority, 299
freeman, interpersonal world of, 354
French, A., 17, 117
Freudianism, culture change and, 287
Friedl, Ernestine, 47, 91
friendship, versus kinship, 344; need for,
    60–61
Frogs, The (Aristophanes), 47
frustration, in Greek civilization, 134
functional connectedness, 253
funeral oration, Pericles', 74, 110

genē, 5, 15, 226, 308
genealogies, 41
generational turnover, 73
gennētai, 5
gestalt, 250
gift-exchange, 11
Glotz, G., 29, 137, 149
God, coexistence of with Ideas or Forms,
    347; creation and, 347–348; dialogue
    and, 385; as measure of society, 192;
    Plato's concept of, 343–347, 374–375;
    as prime cause, 348
gods, belief in, 227; blame of ills on,
    133; envy or jealousy of, 27–30; in-
    tentions of, 104–105; men and, 343;
    moīra and, 121–122; self-image and,
    103
Goffman, Erving, 382
Golden Rule, 114–115
"gold" talents, versus "bronze," 317
Gomme, A. W., 151
Good, ideal, 371; Plato's idea of, 212
good taste, 378
Gorgias, 263
Gould, John, 176
Graeci, 5
grain, importing of, 17–18
gratification, moral standards and, 287–
    288
greatness, doom and, 27
Greek civilization, dynamics of, 134
Greek philosophy, 134
Greeks, colonization of, 6; slavery
    among, 24–34; *see also* Hellenic world
    or age
Greek state, 135–142; *see also* city-state;
    polis

Greek unity, 147–154
Grene, W. C., 43
group opinion, 96–98
groups, wholistic view of, 252
group tensions, 13–17, 106
Guardians, Plato's concept of, 208, 215, 217, 228, 230–231, 235, 279, 317, 335
guest-friendship, 11
guilt culture, 82–85

Hadas, Moses, 133
Harmodius, 64
Hasebroek, J., 137
hatred, in Hellenic age, 21
Hector, 12, 60
Hecuba (Euripides), 114
hektēmoroi, 18
Helen, 60, 89, 100
Helen (Euripides), 99, 112
hēliastai, 137
Hellenes, 5
Hellenic League, 146
Hellenic world or age, achievement values and group tensions in, 13–17; agriculture in, 17–19; class conflicts in, 17–21; cultural system in, 69–72; division of labor in, 87, 90–94, 218–219, 222–225; economic opportunity and class structure in, 21–24; hatred in, 21; pessimism in, 362–363; power in, 290; power vacuum in, 154–158, 314; slavery in, 24–34; social change in, 19–20; world "flaw" of, 134, 253–254, 345–347
Helots, 32, 143, 146, 149
Hera, 117
Heracleidae, The (Euripides), 102
Heracles, 112
Heracles (Euripides), 112
Heraclides, 157
Heraclitus, 42, 79, 234
Hermai, 55
Hermes, 21
Herodotus, 12, 221
heroic tradition, 49, 112
Hesiod, 17, 22, 44, 78, 81, 220, 365
hetairai, 62–63
hierarchy, in social diagnosis, 247–252
Hipparchus, 64
Hippias, 64, 191
Hippodamus of Miletus, 293
Hippolytus, 98, 134
Hippolytus (Euripides), 85, 88–90, 113

Homer, 9, 22, 44, 79, 90, 104–105, 133, 342, 364
Homeric literature, 8
Homeric poems, 12
Homeric society, 9
homosexuality, ideal of, 63, 68; and interpersonal strain, 60–64; knowledge and, 205; origins of, 45; *polis* and, 64
honor, in Greek value system, 42–43
honorific expenditures, 51–52
hoplitai, 7, 16, 21, 53
horoi, 18
human condition, diagnosis of, 198–199, 206
humanism, 269–270
human nature, evil in, 227; *see also* evil
human relations, social science and, 295
hybris, 28, 33, 53, 89, 95–96, 100, 105, 116, 301, 367
Hyperides, 153

id, Freudian, 202
Ideas or Forms, 183, 191, 290, 329, 342, 362, 371–374, 382; God's coexistence with, 347–348
identity, search for, 99
ignorance, deviance and, 298–300; versus knowledge, 200–201; punishment and, 301
Iliad (Homer), 10, 12, 14, 44, 60; *see also* Homer
immortality, Greek desire for, 367; *see also* death
individual, diagnosis of, 199–200; power or influence of, 101–102; state and, 79–80, 251
individuality, in Greek cultural system, 70–72, 78; social conflict and, 105–106; tensions of, 106–127; theater and, 113–114
information, versus awareness, 270–271
injustice, 223
inner-directedness, 193
inner flaw, concept of, 134, 253–254, 345–347
integration, reason and, 260
intellectual creativity, 276–278
intellectual novelty, 274
"intention morality," 82
interdependence, consensus and, 252
interpersonal dependence, 315
interpersonal strain, homosexuality and, 60–64

intimacy, homosexuality and, 61; self-image and, 167
intuition, 268
involvement, 374–387
Ion (Euripides), 99, 118–119, 316, 342
Ionian "enlightenment," 180
Ionian school, 330
Iphigenia, 71, 99, 102
Iphigenia in Aulis (Euripides), 112–113
irrigation, 8
Ismene, 71
Isocrates, 12, 43, 58, 73, 156, 187, 316
isomoiria, 310
isonomia, 310

James, William, 97
Jason of Pherae, 156
Judaeo-Christian tradition, 41
judgment, reason and, 335–336
justice, of *aristoi*, 14–15; *anomia* and, 221; and division of labor, 222–223; Greek concept of, 219–221

kakoi, 17
kaloi k'agathoi, 320, 322, 377
keimēlion, 11
kidnaping, 29
killing, rage and, 108–109
kingship, hereditary, 135
kinship system, 19; friendship and, 61, 344; group opinion and, 97–98; individuality and, 79–80; land and, 10–11
Kitto, H. O. F., 24, 386
Kleon (Cleon), 52
klērouchiai, 145
Knidos, battle of, 154, 157
knowing, awareness and, 267–272
knowledge, *epistēmē* as, 267; freedom and, 175; homosexuality and, 205; versus ignorance, 200–201; in Pythagoreanism, 125; quest for, 274; self-mastery and, 203; small-group theory of, 273–276; as social therapeutic, 175; sociology of, 5
kosmopolitēs, Diogenes as, 20, 321
kosmos, 253, 346
Koyré, Alexandre, 173
Kronos, 331
Kynoskephalai, disaster at, 30

labor, division of, *see* division of labor
Laches (Plato), 182
Lakōnizontes, 62

Lancelot, 14
land, cultivation of, 10; shortage of, 17
Lattimore, Richmond, 118, 367
law, *anomia* and, 214–215; authority and, 297–298; equality and, 301; formal, 226–228; functions of, 226–228; sacralization of, 303; universalism and, 297–324; urban, 225–226
Laws (Plato), 24, 144, 176, 189, 208, 211, 217, 227–228, 235–237, 248, 281, 288–289, 297, 302, 317, 370, 382
leadership, competition for, 94; fame and, 97; military prowess and, 93
learning, Plato's theory of, 266
leitourgiai, 140
Libation Bearers, The (Aeschylus), 107–108
life, dramaturgic view of, 386–387
limits, excess and, 59
"Locals," versus "Cosmopolitans," 188–190
logos, idea of, 351
loneliness, 122
love, as "divine madness," 341; Plato on, 244–246; Socrates on, 246
loyalty, 69–70
luxury, versus simplicity, 125
Lysias, 140, 155

Macaria, 102
magic, sympathetic, 329
Malinowski, Bronislaw, 304
man, two natures in, 205–206, 227, 343
manual work, in Hellenic age, 22
Marathon, battle of, 152
Marx, Karl, 193, 206, 256
Marxism, culture change and, 287
master–slave relationships, 9, 241–243
Medea (Euripides), 96, 109, 111
melancholy, 43, 93
Menelaus, 89, 99–100
Meno (Plato), 205
"meritocracy," 316
Messenia, 149
metaphysics, authority and, 298; operating, 349–350; Plato's, 198–199, 247, 298, 305, 345, 349–353, 358; slavery and, 356–359; socialization and, 355–358; social origins of, 350–351; social planning and, 305–307; wholism in, 253
method, versus methodolatry, 337–341
metic, 216

metoikoi, 6, 22, 24–25, 29, 33, 139, 240, 242
Michell, H., 139
military exploits or virtue, 12–16, 93, 109–110
mind, individuality and, 79; supremacy of, 183–184
mind–body dualism, 125
Minoan culture, 5
misthoi, 137
Model-Guided Strategy of Change, 260, 280–282, 285, 304, 326
mōıra, 91, 121–122, 328, 342
money, love of, 235
morality, law and, 225; reason and, 330
moral law, 204
moral standards, 287–288
Morrow, G. R., 100
Murray, Gilbert, 117, 275
Myrdal, Gunnar, 270
mystery religions, 365

nature, versus convention, 190–193; imperfections of, 362; as realm of necessity, 350–352
nature philosophers, 180–182, 327, 330
Nazism, 290
nemesis, concept of, 121
Neoptolemus, 98
Nietzsche, Friedrich, 13, 116–117, 119–120, 178, 257, 259
"noble" character, 43
Noble Lie, 193, 332
nomos, 221, 328
nonconformity, 83–84
nonpersons, 32, 352
"nothing in excess" philosophy, 59
nouveaux riches, 141
nuclear family, 110
number, in Pythagoreanism, 126

obedience, 136
object attachment, 69–74
object cathexis, 71
Odysseus, 44, 71, 74, 93, 100
Odyssey (Homer), 9–10, 44, 220
Oedipus, 82, 99, 121
Oedipus at Colonus (Sophocles), 82, 197
Oedipus Rex (Sophocles), 99
ōıkos, 9–10, 15, 21, 136, 334
oimōgē, 30
Old Oligarch, 152

oligarchy, universalism and, 309
Olympian religion, 19, 27–28, 44, 88, 103, 117, 121–122, 343, 367
Olympic games, 46, 155–156
one–many relationship, 328
open system, 253
opinion, sensitivity to, 90, 94–98
Orestes, 60
Orestes (Sophocles), 15, 115
Orpheus, 365
Orphism, 119, 123
ostracism, 57–58, 96
other-directedness, 81–90, 315; Plato and, 193
Ouranos, 331

Panegyricus (Isocrates), 156
Panhellenic festivals, 46
Panhellenism, 155–156
Pantheon, 88
Park, Robert E., 269–270
Parmenides, 183
Parsons, Talcott, 97
party strife, Hellenic age, 21
passions, ignorance and, 201
Patroclus, 54
Pausanias, 245
peasants, in Hellenic age, 23
pederasty, 62
Peloponnesian League, 154
Peloponnesian War, 16, 20, 66, 109 110, 133–158, 313, 321, 358, 362
Penelope, 44, 220
Pentheus, 99
Perdiccas II, 158
Pericles, 20, 22, 43, 50, 52, 57, 67, 107, 137; funeral oration, 74, 110
Persephone, 365
Persia, war with, 65–67, 154–156
personal autonomy, 91
personality, Plato's concept of, 249
pessimism, 43, 307, 363–364; in cultural pattern, 58; Plato's, 235; rationality and, 74; social diagnosis and, 256–257
Phaedo (Plato), 195, 254, 336, 368
Phaedra, 113
Phaedrus, 245
Phaedrus (Plato), 64
Phaelus of Chalcedon, 293
phalanx, 7
Phidias, 57
Philebus (Plato), 262
Philip of Macedonia, 156, 322

Philoctetes, 71
Philoctetes (Sophocles), 107, 111
philosopher kings, 252, 291
philosophers, nature, *see* nature philosophers
Phoenician alphabet, 8
Phoenician Women (Euripides), 69
phratriai, 5, 226
phylai, 5
Pindar, 58–59, 90, 122, 336
Pisistratus, 19, 64, 72, 152
pity, 34
plague, in Athens, 313
Plato, 24–25, 30–31, 64, 74, 78, 81, 90, 94, 97, 109, 114, 127, 134, 144, 150, 183; Academy founded by, 187; a historical diagnosis of, 256–257, 362; cave image of, 387; concern with values, 267–268; on death, 363–371; defense of slave system by, 241–244, 319, 359; diagnostic assumptions of, 247–249; dialectic of, 261–267, 277; dialogue in, 381–386; on division of labor, 222–225; enemies of, 195; God of, 343, 346–347, 374; Ideas or Forms in, 183, 191, 362; informal norms in, 225–226; knowledge theory of, 203–206; lacunae in social diagnosis of, 235–258; on love, 244–246; metaphysics of, 198–199, 298, 305, 345, 349–353, 358; as pacifist or warmonger, 236–237; personality concept of, 249; pessimism of, 235, 362–363; planned social change in, 259–296; on population and ethnic factors, 211; on poverty, 238–241; on property and family, 230–232; rationalism of, 192; reference group of, 319–323; role analysis in, 218–219; in Sicily, 156–158; on slavery, 241–244, 319; social action in, 342–343; social diagnosis of, 318, 343–345; social disunity and, 207–208; social theory of, 3–4, 166–172; Socrates and, 178; Sophists and, 190–192; spiritual values in, 312–315; spiritual values "therapy" of, 259–296; traditionalism of, 193–195, 201; tragic outlook of, 361–387; two sides of, 194; universalistic achievement values in, 311–312; utopianism of, 289–293; value system in, 212–214, 319–323; wholistic view of groups by, 252
Platonic reason, 331–343

Platonism, Aristotelian development of, 330–331
Plato's Academy, 156–157, 187
Plutarch, 51–52, 58, 69–70
poetry, Plato's betrayal of, 134
polis, autonomy of, 321; civil war in, 3–34; contest system in, 47–50, 54, 60; death and, 115; defined, 5; Form and, 250; homosexuality and, 64; other-directedness in, 87–90; as private corporation, 138; slavery and, 24–34; theater and, 386; tribal structure and, 19–20, 44; war and, 15; welfare state and, 138; and "world flaw," 134
political role, value of, 109–110
political struggle, in *polis*, 15
politics, individualism and, 106
poll tax, 23
Polus, 277
Polyxema, 102
posterity, uses of, 96–97
posthumous fame, 97
Poulydamas, 90
poverty, Plato on, 238–241
power, 123; arbitrary, 300–301; evil and, 291; self and, 112; wealth and, 315, 323
power hierarchy, 216–218
power vacuum, 154–158
prestige hierarchy, 216–218
Priam, 60
primary group, 97–98
progressiveness, versus conservatism, 324
property, institution of, 230–232
Protagoras, 203
Protagoras (Plato), 114, 264
Protestant conscience, 85
prytaneis, 135
psyche, Plato's concept of, 202–203; reason and, 333
punishment, ignorance and, 301
purification, Dionysian, 123
Pythagoras, 124, 126, 195, 220
Pythagoreanism, 119, 123–127; asceticism of, 68; as social movement, 124; versus Socratism, 175–176
Pythagorean theorem, 126–127

rage, killing and, 108–109
rank, wealth and, 14
rational, divine and, 342–344
rationalism, 44; cultural pattern and, 64–74

rationality, in Athens, 66, 110; individuality and, 70–72; pessimism and, 74; total-commitment, 66–70

reason, authoritarian, 333–335, 341; control and, 328–331; dilemmas of, 331–332, 337; as explanation, 327; fatigue of, 326–359; imperative versus advisory, 335–337; morality and, 330; nonauthoritarian, 335, 339; Platonic, 259; proof and, 338; as rhetoric, 331, 340; tradition and, 327–328

relativism, Sophistic, 203

religion, Apollonian and Dionysian aspects of, 116–121; mystery and, 365; Olympian, 19, 27–28, 44, 88, 103, 117, 121–122, 343, 367

remembrance, learning as, 266

Republic, The (Plato), 166, 176, 208, 215–216, 222, 231, 235, 237, 250, 277–278, 281, 285, 317, 319, 331, 335, 345, 382

reputation, guarding of, 81–82

revenge, 15

revolutions, in Hellenic age, 21

Rhesus (Euripides), 99, 111

rhetoric, reason as, 331, 340

ritualization, death and, 363

ritual state, 303–305

role analysis, Plato's, 218

role reversal, 114, 149

role specialization, 218–219

role systems, 207

Roman Empire, slavery in, 145

Roman sculpture, 79

"rule tropism," 189

ruling class, as Republic's Guardians, 80, 208, 215, 217, 228, 230–231

Russell, Bertrand, 126, 193

sacrilization, 303–305

Salamis, battle of, 65–66

Sappho, 78

Sargent, Rachel L., 152

Sarpedon, 13

scholarship, aesthetics of, 380

sculpture, individuality and, 79

seafaring, physical features and, 7

self, defined, 108; as master, 203; as object, 99; sacred mystery of, 99–100; society and, 78–127; theater and, 110–115

self-conception, dialectic and, 278

self-consciousness, death and, 115–116

self-control, 108–109

self-image, freedom and, 297; modal elements in, 98–106; shame and, 95; sources of, 103–105; theater and, 110; underside of, 107–110

self-interest, 72

self-mastery, knowledge and, 203

self-sufficiency, 379

self-transformation, dialectic and, 282

sensitivity, to others, 97–98

Seven against Thebes (Aeschylus), 111

sexual license, 335

shame, defined, 84; failure of, 94–98; fear of, 81–82; and social control, 85–86

shame culture, 81–90, 134

sharecroppers, 18

Simmias, 369

Simonides of Amorgos, 365

Simonides of Ceos, 136, 220

slave–master relations, 9, 241–243

slave–nurse relations, 86

slavery, Athenian democracy and, 136; authority system and, 334; brotherhood and, 191; disorder metaphysics and, 352–355; functions and dysfunctions of, 24–34; in Hellenic age, 24–34; versus hired workers, 9; homosexuality and, 62–63; implications of, 319; increased tensions in, 358–359; as institution, 241; mitigations of, 33–34; "naturalness" of, 307; Plato on, 241–244, 319; psychic cost of, 25; in Roman Empire, 145; war and, 145–146

slaves, child's concept of, 356–357; citizens as, 22; contempt for, 34; disorderliness of, 356; killing of, 34; logos and, 351; number of, 25; other-directedness and, 86–87; recruitment of, 28–30; women as, 10, 62–63

small-group theory, dialectic as, 273–276

Snell, Bruno, 79

social change, in Hellenic age, 19–20; planned, 259–296

social conflict, individuality and, 105–106

social control, shame and, 85–86

social critic, 169–171

social diagnosis, 197–232; lacunae and assumptions in, 234–258; pessimism and, 256–257

social diffusion, 209

social disunity, 206–208; hierarchies and, 216; Plato's analysis of, 197–232
social influence, 89
socialism, 290
socialization, education and, 229–230; metaphysics and, 355–358
social mobility, in Hellenic age, 19
social movement, Pythagoreanism as, 124
social planning, 236, 305–307
social problems, 254–255
social science, knowledge theory and, 203–206
social scientist, pessimism and, 257–258; two conditions for, 295–296; value-free actions of, 294
social stratification, 216–218
social-system analysis, 254–255
social theory, as alternative to politics, 173–175; changes in, 177; dialogue and, 381; formative factors in, 4–5; history of, 167–168; intellectual complexity of, 169; large-scale, 243; legitimizations of, 180–182; social action and, 251–254; "technicians" and "utopians" in, 184–185
social unity, size and, 235
society, individual and, 78–127; pattern-oriented versus person-oriented, 304
sociology, as natural science, 268
Socrates, 3–4, 9, 21, 45, 64–65, 78–79, 81, 85, 136, 199, 220, 250, 291, 320, 328, 332, 342, 350, 370, 382; analogies of, 265; central aims of, 175–176; character and appearance of, 165–166; charisma of, 178–179; conflict with Sophists, 185–188; on death, 336–337, 368–369; dialectic of, 276–279; emphasis on ends, 184; legitimization of, 181; logical difficulties of, 339; on love, 246; Plato's representation of, 172–173, 178; supremacy of mind in, 183–184; "useful" conception of, 182–183
Socratic method, 264–266, 276, 380–381
Socratism, Platonism and, 176–177; versus Pythagoreanism, 175–176
Solon, 13, 29, 42, 44, 51, 70, 72, 115, 152; reforms of, 18–19, 135
Sophism and Sophists, 31, 65, 179–180; Cosmopolitans and, 188; Plato's polemics against, 184–185; relativism of, 190–193, 203

Sophocles, 12, 25–26, 58, 69, 82, 98, 104, 107, 109, 134, 197, 365
Sorokin, P. A., 144
soul, immortality of, 368, 370; Plato's concept of, 194, 202–203, 249, 318; salvation of, 119; value system and, 213
Soviet socialism, 290
Sparta, characteristics of, 67–68; class structure and, 148; decline of, 314; in Peloponnesian War, 141–156; self-image in, 107; size and population of, 6; slavery and, 32
specialization, 91
spiritual values, 312–315
state, individual and, 79–80, 251
Statesman, The (Plato), 216
status, competition for, 15
status incongruence, 17
Stoics, versus Epicureans, 314–315
stratēgoi, 52
strife, 59
striving, in Greek culture system, 43
submission, to authority, 299
success, disaster and, 44; Greek idea of, 27
suffering, dismemberment and, 120
Suppliant Maidens, The (Aeschylus), 44, 111
Sybarites, 68
sympathetic magic, 329
Symposium, The (Plato), 245, 367, 386
synarchia, 142
Syracuse, Plato's intervention in, 156–157
system isolation, 286–287
system-starting, Plato's theories of, 283–284

taxation, 139
technē, 268
technology, contempt for, 68; tribalism and, 106
temperament, character and, 228–229
Thales, 70, 180
theater, flexibility of, 65; religious significance in, 383; self in, 110–115
Theban League, 154
themistes, 5, 226
Themistocles, 57, 65–66
Theognid literature, 16
theoretical creativity, 177–180

theorists, Socrates' conception of, 185–188

therapontes, 9

therapy and therapeutics, 297–324; as dialectic, 260–263; Plato's concept of, 259–296

Theseus, 47

thiasoi, 5

Thomson, G., 117

Thrasybulus, 139

Thucydides, 12, 34, 51, 54, 58, 64, 68, 134, 148–149

thymos, 109, 202, 205, 224, 249, 263, 304

Timaeus (Plato), 229, 253, 290, 346

traders, class structure and, 9, 21

traditionalism, Plato's, 201; reason and, 327–328

tragedy and tragic outlook, catharsis of, 110; death and, 361–387; knowledge and, 45–47; self-blame and, 133; sense of, 43–44; shame culture and, 134

tribalism and tribal structure, beliefs in, 105–106; kinship and, 80; *polis* and, 19–20, 44

trières, 140

truth, dialectic and, 261; knowledge and, 332–333; reason and, 329–331

Tumin, Melvin, 270

two-generation cycle, 73

universal, Plato's analysis of, 199–200

universalism, dysfunction of, 316–319; oligarchical and democratic, 309–310

universe, flaw in, 134, 253–254, 345–347

"upside-down" existence, ignorance and, 200–201

urban environment, slavery and, 33

urban law, 225–226

"useful," Socrates' concept of, 182–183

utopianism, Plato's, 289–293

utopian socialists, 193

value-integrating mechanisms, 215–216

values, consensus versus diversity in, 254; Plato's concern with, 267–268; role of, 199–200; universalistic achievement and, 311–312

value system, 41–42, 313; citizenship in, 139; integration of, 212–214; Platonic,

311; reference group for, 319–323

Vasilika, 47, 91

vendettas, 21

Vermeule, Emily, 119

vices, private, 230

violence, self and, 108

virtue, communality of, 215–216; as own reward, 318; poverty and, 240; spiritual values and, 312–313; war and, 15–16; wisdom and, 330; *see also aretē*

Vlastos, Gregory, 310, 351–352

volitional theory, 203

Walbank, F. W., 139

war, class culture and, 142–146; classic conception of, 144; death and, 363; fame and, 48; intercity versus civil, 234–235; love of, 235; as normal condition, 144; *polis* and, 15; preparation for, 237; slavery and, 145–146; social theory of, 234; virtue and, 15–16

Warner, W. L., 269

warrior code, 17

Ways and Means (Xenophon), 140

wealth, and military skills, 14; versus poverty, 240; power and, 315, 323

wealth hierarchy, 216–218

Weber, Max, 178, 269, 373

welfare state, *polis* and, 138

Whitehead, Alfred North, 172, 326

wholism, in social diagnosis, 247

Williams, Robin, 269–270

wisdom, versus military achievement, 93; virtue and, 330

women, as slaves, 10, 62–63

Women of Trachis, The (Sophocles), 25–26

world, defect or flaw in, 134, 253–254, 345–347

worldly values, retreat from, 314–316

Xanthippus, 20

Xenophon, 30, 57, 140, 145–146, 165, 181, 320, 361

Xerxes, 65, 67

Zeno, 314

zero-sum game, 49–50

Zeus, 44, 79, 105, 117, 133, 246, 319, 364